A Romantic Friendship

CYRIL CONNOLLY

NOEL BLAKISTON

A Romantic Friendship

THE LETTERS OF CYRIL CONNOLLY
TO NOEL BLAKISTON

CONSTABLE
LONDON

First published in Great Britain 1975
by Constable and Company Ltd
10 Orange Street London WC2H 7EG
Copyright © 1975 Mrs Cyril Connolly

ISBN 0 09 460890 3

Set in Monotype Fournier
Printed in Great Britain by The Anchor Press Ltd
and bound by Wm Brendon & Son Ltd
both of Tiptree, Essex

PREFACE

At the time of the earliest surviving letters of this correspondence –
January 1923 – Cyril was 19 years old, I was 17 and still at Eton. Cyril
had already passed on to Balliol College, Oxford. But our friendship
had had quite a history before these letters begin. One of the more
visible evidences of Cyril's influence had been a cooling of my enthusiasm for cricket. A good wicket-keeper, I was in the running for playing
in the school eleven. Yet, though I never received a satisfactory answer
to the question how he reconciled his admiration of the Greeks with
his dislike of athletics, I was already in retreat from the character of
'hearty' before I left Eton.

What emboldens me now to publish these letters? Shortly before
Boswell set out on a continental journey, he records that 'Johnson said
he would go to the Hebrides with me when I returned from my travels,
unless some very good companion should offer when I was absent,
which he did not think probable: adding, "There are few people whom
I take so much to as to you." And when I talked of leaving England,
he said with a very affectionate air, "My dear Boswell, I should be very
unhappy at parting, did I think we were not to meet again." I cannot
too often remind my readers that although such instances of his kindness are doubtless very flattering to me, yet I hope my recording them
will be ascribed to a better motive than to vanity; for they afford unquestionable evidence of his tenderness and complacency, which some,
while they were forced to acknowledge his great powers, have been so
strenuous to deny.'

The readers of the following letters will agree that Cyril speaks of
their recipient with hardly less affection than Johnson did of Boswell.
Let me then at once echo Boswell's rejection of any charge of vanity
that might be made against me for allowing this publication. If there
has been vanity, it has pulled all the other way, against the embarrass-

ment, the vulgarity, the profanation of letting the laity in on such a privacy. Yet the forward pull has proved even stronger. For I desire to provide unquestionable evidence of Cyril's tenderness and complacency, and to express my gratitude, without measure, for the generosity with which he handed out the treasures of his teeming brain. Moreover, it is surely a pious duty to make public so much writing of Cyril's early period.

In these letters, on 21 April 1927, he was already saying: 'one's golden age seems to be in the past. . . . This sense of living in a sequel tends to be the canker gnawing at the heart of undergraduacy and to make one feel so old at times.' No Etonian can ever have looked back with such nostalgia on his schooldays as did Cyril Connolly. If the letters here published do not quite reach back to the golden age, they probably get as near as can now be got.

Travel occupies a good deal of the letters, and what a stimulating travelling companion Cyril was, from the moment a journey was being conceived. The romance of geography in the days before air travel is like song within these pages. Milton is one of the great figures that preside over the letters. Like the lists of place-names that appear in *Paradise Lost*, the lists of places Cyril wanted to go to tripped off his tongue, being like Milton's lists as much poetry as topographical information. Sagunto, Segesta, Selinunte, Corcubion, Seo de Urgel. . . . Then the planning of the trip, its approach, the excitement, the fever heat and we were off to adventures and discoveries and changes of plan, and important things being said in unforgettable places, and the fun and jokes. And perhaps there would be bad moments. *At tu, Catulle, destinatus obdura* was a quotation Cyril had made peculiarly his own. Scribbled on fly-leaf or hotel blotter or marble table top, *At tu, Cyrille, destinatus obdura* would record the dudgeon of Cyril Connolly.

With regard to the manner of editing, Cyril himself made a striking declaration in a review, written in 1966 and published in *The Evening Colonnade* (p. 300), of a volume of Gide-Valéry letters: 'Letters are most alive when freshly delivered in the sender's handwriting, something perishes when they are typed, more when they are printed, most of all when they are translated.' 'Freshly' is surely the operative word here; and if, from what I quoted above, the reader supposes that the letters of Cyril as an undergraduate are the deadbeat products of an exhausted talent, he will soon find that is not the case. It is their freshness that is their first quality. The editor would have them read as when the envelope was slit open fifty years ago. Let the reader make what he can, as I did, of untranslated Greek and Latin, French and Spanish.

He will need aids to the persons in the book, many of whom have been given a brief biographical footnote at their first mention. They appear in the index under the names by which they went at the date of their appearance in the letters. There are cross references from Christian names and nicknames. Several of the people named figured in Connolly's *Enemies of Promise*, either with their own names or with pseudonyms. I was Nigel, William Le Fanu was Walter le Strange, the diarist. The letters KS. after a name signify King's Scholar at Eton, and are given to all who were, or had been, King's Scholars.

With regard to the text, it has been the editor's aim to print the words as Cyril wrote them. In English, in living foreign languages, and in dead languages, the reader may spot oddities according to his erudition. The sources of quotations have in some cases been given, but not by any means always. This editor is well aware that a structure of scholarship could be built on these letters that he has not attempted. He is also aware that there are key words, allusions and private messages to which his memory has lost the clue.

The story is again and again interrupted when the letter-writers were together, at my home, or at Cyril's, or when we were travelling. The gaps are often accounted for to some extent in the letters that follow them.

Various excisions, not many, have been made from Cyril's text, for various reasons. Some readers, perhaps, who have only given a brief perusal to the book, may think that a great deal of trivial matter could be removed with advantage. I doubt it. This book is primarily concerned with a personal relationship. Who shall say what personal words are trivial? I wonder how many paragraphs, even the shortest ones, could be entirely discarded as trivial. How quickly, in the intimate flow of the words, the reader is suddenly in the centre of seriousness and intensity, joy and despair, fun and the black fear of loneliness that so disturbed this only child! *Est tibi frater sed mihi nemo.*

Noel Blakiston

2 Jan 1923. Postcard. Siracuse. View of the Anapus.

H. N. Blakiston, Esq.,*
Gautby Rectory,
Lincoln,
Inghilterra.

My dear Noel,
   This is the Anapus at Siracuse the only place where Papirus grows wild. I am having a superb time, having seen Rome, Naples, Amalfi, Palermo and most of the things in Sicily and Florence and Pisa on the way back – will you be in town in the teens of January? I still like you very much!

Cyril†

9 Oct 1923. Postcard. Campden, Glos. Photograph of the Noel Arms Hotel.

H. N. Blakiston, Esq., KS,
Eton College,
Windsor.

Greetings!

Cyril/Bobbie‡

*BLAKISTON, Hugh Noel (b. 8 December 1905). Second son of Rev. F. M. Blakiston, Rector of Gautby, and, from 1924, of Kirkby on Bain, Lincs. KS. Magdalene College, Camb. Public Record Office 1928–1970. O.B.E. Socio dell' Istituto per la Storia del Risorgimento Italiano. Hon Fellow of Eton College 1974. Married Georgiana Russell 10 October 1929. Two daughters, six grandchildren.

†CONNOLLY, Cyril Vernon (b. 10 September 1903, d. 26 November 1974). Only son of Major Matthew Connolly, an eminent conchologist, and Muriel Vernon. KS. Went to Balliol in 1922 with Brackenbury History Scholarship. Did little work for his History Schools and took a third class degree in Modern History 1925. Journalist, author, editor. Chevalier de la Legion d'Honneur. C.B.E. 1972. Married (1) 1930 Frances Jean Bakewell, of Baltimore, (2) 1950 Barbara Skelton, (3) 1959 Deirdre, daughter of Hon. P. W. D. Craig. One daughter Cressida, one son Matthew.

‡R. P. Longden. Bobbie (b. 15 October 1903, d. 8 October 1940). KS. Trinity, Oxford. In the autumn of 1926 he became a don at Magdalen, and then at Christ Church. Later he was Master of Wellington, where he was killed by a German bomb.

9

1924. Postcard, Athens. Picture of relief of warrior, Athens.

H. N. Blakiston, Esq.,
Kirkby on Bain,
Lincoln.
ΑΥΥΛΙΑ

Dear Noel,

Sorry for not writing – I will soon but I have such a lot to say and
pens and paper in this heat are so sticky – and anyhow it will keep
and is only about places – you may get this at camp, if so I hope you
are having a pleasant one. I heard from Sligger* and Bobbie that they
had seen you – I have had quite a good time except for having con-
tracted boredom in Constantinople, loneliness in Athens, fever in
Crete, a cure for them all at Delphi and now penury in the Cyclades –
so that I crawl slowly by steerage and 3rd class to the chalet des
Mélèzes St Gervais. I'll write again soon. I hope it is all right about
September first part of – a good warrior don't you think, *ὥς κάλος
ὤν ἔθ....*

$\qquad$ Cyril

August 1924.

Noel Blakiston, Esq. $\qquad$ Chalet des Mélèzes,
[Lincoln] $\qquad$ St. Gervais les Bains,
$\qquad$ Haute Savoie.

Dear Noel,

If you still want me to come to you which I would like to very much
will it be all right if I come on the 1st September? I am coming back
to England with Bobbie and get there that morning and could come
up by the train after lunch and it would suit me best though I could

*F. F. Urquhart. 'Sligger' (b. 1868, d. 18 September 1934). Fellow and Tutor
of Balliol 1896–1934. Dean 1916–33. Examiner in Modern History Schools,
Chairman of the Faculty of Modern History 1927–9. Sligger was a father figure
for generations of Balliol men. His hospitality extended in the vacations to
reading parties at Minehead and visits in the summer to his chalet on the Prarion
above St. Gervais, below Mont Blanc. Cyril Connolly visited the chalet every
year from 1923 to 1927. N.B. went there in 1925. Sligger was a person of great
benevolence and is the subject of a memoir: *Francis Fortescue Urquhart* by Cyril
Bailey (Macmillan 1936).

come later if you'd rather – I got here at last after a superb journey back with no money at all – steerage on a Greek ship from Athens to Brindisi with no food but what I could get at Corfu on the way and there they had plague very badly. In Brindisi I managed to unearth 2 bits of a red figure vase and a lovely goddess on a bit of a black one which I will give Beazley* – then I came to Ravenna and saw it all – the town is not impressive the mosaics are superb – so are the basilicas – the tomb of Theodoric not impressive – then I came on by Bologna and Milan to Courmayeur where I walked 2 days round Mt. Blanc to the chalet – 10 days and from Athens to here on seven pounds! I had a glorious time coming here 4 hours in the snow in a thunderstorm at 8000 feet! and knowing I would die of exposure if I did not get to the refuge before it got too dark to find the path in the clouds – I got there at 8 at night so ran it fairly close. I have learnt from my voyage that Greek art is the greatest thing in the world – almost – The Parthenon is so shattering that it made me [K† sends his love] weep which I don't usually do under those circumstances – also Greek sculpture up to 480 is simply shattering I've got some photos of the best things for you if you want them – I only like the rather archaic stuff – not Pheidias and certainly not Praxiteles. Also I think the Greek temple is far the most spiritual and perfect form of building – very moving and inspiring and making Gothic seem a prison though Romanesque is good – Santa Sofia is very fine indeed so are the Ravenna basilicas and the Byzantine monastery of Holy Luke where I spent a night in the mountains – I have seen a lot of Greek and a lot of Byzantine Gothic and Romanesque now and Roman; and Greece wins absolutely, Roman last I think, then Gothic – The best thing in Athens is Buschor, the head of the German school, to whom I had an introduction from Beazley – he is a wonderful man, ageless, attractive, frightfully brilliant, frightfully industrious, Spartan and always laughing like one of the first Franciscans, he spoke a little English but very attractively and made the sculpture, etc., wonderful – at present I am very influenced by him and my Spartan journey back – I am rather tiresomely hearty and youthful, I think a lot and am serious minded but fresh as well and am trying to become independent of material things like food and comfort etc. I don't mean not to like it

*J. D. Beazley (b. 1885, d. 1970). Don at Christ Church. Professor Classical Archaeology 1926. Knighted 1946.

†Kenneth Clark. 'K' (b. 13 July 1903). Winchester; Trinity, Oxford. Director of National Gallery 1934–45. 1969 Lord Clark of Saltwood.

but not to succumb to it. I am trying also . . .

> He who bends to himself a joy
> does the winged life destroy
> but he who kisses the joy as it flies
> lives in eternity's sunrise –

I try to enjoy a thing and then give it away before I have tired of it because then I am not bound by it and without feeling a qualm but hearing Buschor's merry laugh and 'better you have that my friend' – I find Bobbie rather tiresome – he is so very florid and worships his own comfort, arranging cushions for about 5 minutes before sitting down and always swinging golf clubs about and chortling and guffawing from his arm chair – he has very little idealism and is rather self satisfied and tepid. I miss your seriousness and way of moralising from things you see which he hasn't and I have – he is rather spoilt by social life of the naval regatta kind and very insular and critical of foreigners and travelling – he is bound to comfort and food and tennis and an intelligent interest in things – while I want fanaticism with good manners, seriousness, and the sacrifice of what one thinks good for what one thinks better. Still I am frightfully fond of him and he is very adequate – we will have a superb time don't you think if Sept. is all right? I may have some money – do you think we could go off to York on the bike and see it? I have never been there and want to badly – I am quite keen on Mediaevalism now.

Love from
Cyril

I find luxury amusing and I like Homeric comfort, pints in pubs, but not yawning complacency.
This is the earthly paradise – I wish you were coming.

Aug 1924. Postcard, St Gervais. Picture of Ravenna mosaic.

H. N. Blakiston, Esq.,
Kirkby on Bain.

Dear Noel,
    Thank you so much for your letter – it looks as if I shall come at the end of September – between 20th and 25th unless you get a frantic

wire in a day or two – it all sounds rather crowded but should be
fun – we must go to York if we can. Foul weather here.

Love
Cyril

13 Sept 1924. Postcard. View of the piazza at Siena.

H. N. Blakiston, Esq.,
Kirkby on Bain.

Dear Noel,

May I come Monday 22nd arriving by 4 o'clock train from Kings X?
If not let me know *at once* to Minerva Hotel Florence. I am sorry to
be a nuisance but I have had to send a box to you and some books
(industry, not art) too from France. I can't remember who your
house party is at present but I hope there will be a vacancy. I have
escaped from the chalet thank God – I had a wonderful time with
R.P.L. but poor since, what with work and weather. These places are
nice, melancholy and 'jolly' in the worst sense of the word and I fly
to Sardinia and back to Perugia and Florence. I may write to you again.
I am scheming a nice plan on which I will report progress when we
meet. I shall be pretty dead after 2 nights in the train.

Love
Cyril

21 Sept 1924. Postcard. Picture of a goat at Taormina, posted Rome.

Signor
Noel Blakiston,
Kirkby on Bain.

Dear Noel,

This is only to warn you that I may get held up on the way as I have
run out of money and have to spend three nights Third in the train
so I will be very limp and dirty I fear also I have a boil on my face –
how much nicer is this goat.

Yours ever
Cyril

I shall be at Florence to-morrow night and try and cope with any alterations if you have made them. It is Woodhall station isn't it? I shall ponder long on food and security these next 3 days so it will be nice to see you.

[?15] *Oct 1924.*

H. N. Blakiston, Esq.,   Naval and Military Hotel,
Kirkby on Bain.   Harrington Road,
                                          South Kensington.

Dear Noel,

It is very sad without you. I cannot return to hedonism for the seed you have sown is bearing fruit and I am veering again to my old idealism that you have kindled anew – it is curious that the only other person who has lately restored me to a proper contempt of the world, Buschor, should have killed my Platonism with it and it is still so dead that I maintain that all your ideal world is but the same world either informed by your imagination or observed in those regions where spirit is the finer form of matter. I used to think the finest phrase in the prayer book was 'Through the dimness of this visible world' – 'dimness' is superb – but here again one must differentiate between the visible world of nature who if nothing better, is never dim, and the other world of good and evil, fame and money, and all our artificial values. I don't believe there is any dualism in nature really, we have given up calling her good and evil, true or false, mother and foe, but can she be classified under beautiful and ugly either? Has she any attributes at all do you think – heartless when she 'tempers the wind to the shorn lamb' witless when she frames the chameleon?

We differ rather about nature for you admire it and I imitate it. The latter is nearly always the result of the former but no better for that – and I expect our next meeting will have brought one of us into line. I saw Shelley described as the 'poet of motion & Keats of quietness' which would perhaps explain our difference there – similarly Shakespeare could never have written

from morn he fell, from noon to dewie Eve
a summer's day –

Though I don't know; for the lines following

if music be the food of love; play on

are just as wonderful.

I saw Charles* last night and took him to supper at a cabaret – he had been racing all day at a suburban meeting so much is he prey to it now and came round after dinner in evening dress and a top-hat – he has been shooting capercailzie and other lovely birds except for a riotous week in Paris. I think he will succumb entirely to these delights in the end – for it *does* matter what you do, once a lily is not always a lily and they are killed easily by environment. We sat and supped and drank the rich wine and saw the dancing girls but I was very listless and could only think of you and me and Sebastian† preparing for his long journey and that generous view of children.

I hope you realise I think you are entirely right in your contempt of food and raiment and sport and golf, bridge and tennis and learning that masquerades as thought and habit and confidence and all that cause them and I am with you in all of it. I do not suppose a corroborator can give authority but I would otherwise. You see I am a Sir Guyon who has not passed unscathed through the palace of delights so hence my preference for the cloistered vertue. You see in all renunciation and difficult choice the worst pain is that rending 'why' that undoes in a moment's common sense the fruit of days of uncommon spirit and when the questioning is purely a rational '*cui bono*' it is not so bad but when it comes with an appeal of sensuous beauty it is almost irresistible, compare 'alas what boots it' and the great doubt of Lycidas. Moreover the dimness of this visible world is no proof of any other and I am not greatly thrilled by the possibilities of fame or family as instruments of my immortality.

My mother says she thinks Reproduction to be the sole purpose of nature but what the type she eventually desires to reproduce is it is quite impossible to discover – an unhappy marriage for instance being due to two people who were merely required to produce an offspring, trying to make some thing more out of their union though again it is quite impossible to tell what sort of human type she wants and she may not know herself.

I imitate your asceticism to some extent and neglect my food – the only thrill in those two hours with the pupils was saying to Prabaka‡

*W. C. A. Milligan. Charles (b. 27 October 1904). KS. Magdalene, Camb. Edinburgh University. Sorbonne. Writer to the Signet 1933–9. Army 1939–46. Whisky merchant. Farmer, Midlothian.

†See note at end of this letter.

‡An Indian boy who was a pupil of N.B.'s father.

'Food is a very unimportant thing you know' and seeing his blank face light up and his bag of sweets go down as he said 'Yes that is what Noel said, food is a very unimportant thing'.

The only thing we require to do, I think, in order to improve our worth as a unit in the search of truth and appreciation of beauty is to conquer a certain slovenliness of convention that makes me think to treat you as I treat Bobbie and you to treat me as you would treat anyone etc. who impinges on your egoism – that sounds as if you came off worst but I don't mean that – I think in any decision about what we are about to do – for I feel we are meant to do something together and such a slender intuition is good evidence when we are idealists without ideals so let us slowly discard in preparation for our long journey though we do not yet know where we are to be sent – did Sebastian know either? Anyhow you must take the lead, for I regard you as an end in yourself and I am less likely to mind where it leads to – besides

the dog will come when you may call, the cat will walk away.

Except for that evening with Charles I have made no attempt to see anyone – I prefer to talk to my mother, cope with my father, and think about things you said and conclusions we came to – do read those two poets, I think they are both frightfully good though Housman is very difficult – Hodgson you will find gives authority for ours (and my mother's) views of bird and animal. Stupidity Street, Eve, The Bull, The Song of Honour, and Reason hath Moons are all superb and I should think the Journeyman wins if you could understand it – but if I said any more you will never read them! I hope Jack* wasn't bored with *Picturesque Greece*† – I thought we had looked at it and enjoyed it and it was time someone else did and I wanted to give him something – that epigram was much more trouble and even if bad poetry, is a very sincere compliment. Mackail 6.12‡ seems to indicate that the first a of ἄεναος can be long though it seems improbable. δία would mean 'across the cares' rather than through them which is not quite the same thing is it because there is no φῶς in washing up but remote from it in your mind – that is what is so good

*J. M. G. Blakiston. Jack (b. 2 May 1904). Elder brother of N.B. Aldenham. Magdalene, Camb., where he shared rooms with N.B. Schoolmaster at Lancing, Marlborough, Winchester. Librarian at Winchester College.

†A picture book.

‡*Select Epigrams from the Greek Anthology* ed. J. W. Mackail.

about you that you never enjoy your duties but forget them, much finer – I can see R.P.L and O'Connor* washing up with enthusiasm and would dislike it rather but you wash up with your hands only and so quietly and well too – it is partly your incuriosity, partly your fine ability to go on doing a thing without getting to like it and largely because it is part of the dimness I suppose – but I think that finally turned the scale with me about 'ideas' – Alfred burnt the cakes, O'Connor would have got excited over them, but you would have cooked them adequately thinking of something else – it is the difference between you and Jack rather for he was very conscious of driving the car for instance but you can do those things without having to give them an interest they do not deserve or without taking vain delight in the work of your hands. Goodnight.

Of course one must take some and I mean comparatively.
Monday.

I have been walking in the Park with Charles all the morning; he was very nice and asked about you – I told (him) we disapproved of his slaughter of capercailzie but he only gives you 3 weeks at Cambridge to retain your idealism (we didn't 'discuss' you) of course it is tiresome again to be the enthusiastic O'Connor type about food and smoking for instance one must refuse a cigarette with no righteous show but practice quiet and unobtrusive abstinence like Sebastian's discarding. I may be maligning H. M. O'C. – but it is useful to have certain people to stand for certain things – O'Connor for crazes – Jacky† for genial intolerance – R.E.S.T.‡ for spots – coping with my father is become rather a strain. I inadvertently said I thought conscientious objectors brave men and provoked an outburst. My mother however is superb and there is one small boy in the hotel who is quite nice of the B.O.P.§ type – which, as you say, is not a good one. I wish we were going to our cottage or to beg our bread abroad. I don't want Oxford a bit – ἡ μαθε παῖϛειν τήν σπουδην μετάθεις ἡ φέρε τάς 'οδυνας. The Syrian's remark about the house of Rimmon is very searching – one must choose absolutely – but what is worth choosing – come here whatever you do if you are up for the day. I can't tell

*H. M. O'Connor. Timothy, Tim (b. 26 July 1905). KS. Trinity, Oxford. Chairman of a discount company. British Joint Staff Mission in Washington in war. US Legion of Merit.

†John O'Dwyer. Jackie, Jacky (b. 13 January 1905). KS. R.M.A. Woolwich. Joined RE 1925. OBE.

‡R. E. S. Turner. Ronnie (b. 26 June 1905). KS. New College, Barts.
§*Boy's Own Paper.*

you how I enjoyed myself [at Kirkby] – it was the best bit of the vac except the gr. St. Bernard. I think better than Gautby too which was rather baccalaurian. You were very patient with me too.

I am writing to thank your father, tell him, but been delayed by the Latin epigram.

We will have a fine quiet week end and some cathedrals so you must come when Charles's 3 weeks are up!

My love to Jack.

Cyril

My mother loved the apples and grapes – ich auch.

χαίρε Νόελ φιλερήμος, ὅς ἄγλαος ἔσσεται ᾄει
φῶς ὁρόων διὰ τὰς φρόντιδας ἄεναον

[Farewell solitary Noel, who always will be very fine, beholding the ever-flowing light through many cares].

SEBASTIAN VAN STORCK

[It is unlikely, I suppose, that Walter Pater's Imaginary Portrait, *Sebastian van Storck*, is the favourite reading of any undergraduates in any University at the present time. For two or three years Sebastian was one of our inspirations. The Portrait begins as follows: 'It was a winter scene, by Adrian van de Velde, or by Isaac van Ostade. All the delicate poetry together with all the delicate comfort of the frosty season was in the leafless branches turned to silver, the furred dresses of the skaters, the warmth of the red-brick housefronts under the gauze of white fog, the gleams of pale sunlight on the cuirasses of the mounted soldiers as they receded into the distance. Sebastian van Storck, confessedly the most graceful performer in all that skating multitude, moving in endless maze over the vast surface of the frozen water-meadow, liked best this season of the year for its expression of a perfect impassivity, or at least of a perfect repose. The earth was, or seemed to be, at rest, with a breathlessness of slumber which suited the young man's peculiar temper.'

Sebastian lived in the great age of Dutch painting, yet 'the arts were a matter he could but just tolerate. Why add, by a forced and artificial production, to the monotonous tide of competing, floating existence?' He preferred in the matter of art 'those prospects *à vol d'oiseau* – of the caged bird on the wing at last – of which Rubens had the secret, and still more Philip de Koninck, four of whose choicest works occupied the four walls of his chamber; visionary escapes, north, south, east and west, into a wide-open, though it must be confessed, a somewhat sullen land.' 'They were the sole ornaments he permitted himself. From the midst of the busy and busy-looking house, crowded with the furniture and the pretty toys of many generations, a long passage led the rare visitor up a winding staircase, and (again at the end of a long passage) he found himself as if shut off from the whole talkative Dutch world, and in the embrace of that wonderful quiet which is also possible in Holland all around him. It was here that Sebastian could yield himself to the supremacy of his difficult thoughts. A kind of *empty* place! Here, you felt, all had been mentally put to rights by the working out of a long equation, which had zero is equal to zero for its result. Here one did, and perhaps felt, nothing; one only thought.' In Spinoza he recognised a kindred spirit.

'His mother thought him like one disembarrassing himself carefully, and little by little, of all impediments, habituating himself gradually to make shift with as little as possible, in preparation for a long journey.' 'His dispassionate detachment from all that is most attractive to ordinary minds came to have the impressiveness of a great passion.' He at length committed himself to the 'renunciation of all finite objects, the fastidious refusal to be or do any limited thing.'

Such was the exquisite, if bleak, companion with whom we set ourselves to outstare the infinite flatness of eternity. Those who only knew a later Epicurean Cyril may be astonished to find him in such company.   N.B.]

18 Oct 1924.

H. N. Blakiston, Esq.,   Balliol College,
Magdalene College,   Oxford.
Cambridge.

Dear Noel,

Thank you very much indeed for Boston Stump* which looks very fine and much admired by me and Roger† – also for your nice letter. I think you are right about ethics being an unprogressive form of

*The tower of the fenland church of Boston, Lincs., is known as the Stump.
†R. A. B. Mynors. Roger (b. 28 August 1903). KS. Balliol. Fellow and Classical Tutor Balliol 1926–44. Professor of Latin at Cambridge and then at Oxford. Knighted 1963.

domestic politics – it was what I was trying to say in the vinery about sacrificing truth to goodness by making allowances i.e. letting one's grandmother think one is Church of England and the like. I am very glad you are doing ancient history too. I have been rather in the academic lime-light owing to my neglect of the English constitution, but nothing has been decided. Sligger could not let me go and my tutor* was very nice so now I do 1688 onwards which is dull but not so antagonistic to classical ideals as the Middle Ages.

I am being extremely quiet this term. I meditate on the vita Sebastiana and on many other things we discussed – the last two or three days I have had a stye in my eye and spent most of the time mopping it in my room reading poetry and the *Inscriptiones Insularum Graecarum* – the first Thera inscription in incredibly archaic characters is 'Εὐπυλος τάδε-πόρνος' the latter in another hand and it amused me to think of Eupulus coming to contemplate the pride of his eye and finding 'bitch' added one fine morning in the 8th century.

I had lunch with Beazley to-day who was quite superb and he has told me to come and look in his books, photoes and the like whenever I want which will provide a haven – Oxford is very limiting and there are so few escapes – of people Roger is adequate in Balliol and we have long discussions about art etc and what the Greeks really were like. Bobbie is rather florid and bustling and rather brusque in his judgements but superb when calmer and we find daylight intercourse rather an ordeal for he fusses and I chafe. I think I am very trying too. However we refrain from bickering or getting bitter over differences of taste. John Brooks† is superb at present nice outside and in and that is about all I see. I think Peter‡ quite nice and subdued – though he has plastered his room with quantities of pop photoes each more waxen and lifeless than the last – he will probably be all right till he finds his feet. I feel I am fighting a losing battle with autumn who has already driven me into lines of quietness and sober thinking and soon will drive me into listlessness and scepticism and general depression and futility. Damp afternoons of endlessly chiming bells are very wearing I find.

*Kenneth Bell (b. 1884, d. 1951). Balliol. Historian. Tutorian Fellow of Balliol while Connolly was there. Fellow of All Souls.

†John Brooks. Corpus Christi, Oxford.

‡P. N. Loxley. Peter (b. 27 March 1905, d. 9 February 1945.) KS. Trinity, Oxford. Entered Diplomatic Service October 1929. Killed while employed on a special mission on way to Yalta.

When have I last looked on
The round green eyes and the long wavering bodies
Of the dark leopards of the moon?

(surely romantic enough for you, though Yeats!) and rather an echo
of hide and seek in the dark – I found one Shelley poem I quite liked,
it is called Evening and begins

'the sun is set, the swallows are asleep'.

It is amusing to think that though all the greatest masterpieces of
Greek sculpture, nearly, were done by 480 B.C. everyone is taught to
admire Pheidias and the Apollo Belvedere; Laocoon; the Venus of
Milo and the Hermes of Praxiteles as its highest products – still that
leaves the good stuff for the few instead of the many which you know
I have no fondness for. Your epigram about the sepulchre is becoming
rather vital for me as every poem at sometime should – my present
doctrine, composed 20 minutes ago, is

πρᾴως ὦ κυρίλλε βιῶν, το παρὸς μελετῶνδε
εὑρήσεις τὸ μονὸν καλλος ἐν ἠσύχιᾳ

(Living gently, O Cyril, and considering the past, you will find the
only beauty in quietness.) Without you I have no crusading vitality
and so just exist σπέρμα πυρός σώζων – we have not really arrived
you see at any more conclusion than that we want an ideal and so
have nothing much to put into practice – except to dis-embarrass
ourselves little by little for our long journey – so I stick to that and
try to eliminate society to some extent – but every step that sounds
on my stair and turns away rouses a hope and a disappointment – still
I can be more humble out of society and people seem to like me like
this. Can you tear yourself away for to-day week end? The light will
still be good for churches and K will take us to some though not too
far away and we can have our wintry dinner in the country inn that
he is so looking forward to – I know it is rather early in the term but
the weather is passable and to-morrow week further than it seems.
Sligger will be away so only Bobbie, Roger, and K to cope with – do
try and come as I shall probably be too depressed by the week after
to be a host of any merit and K and Roger are hoping to see you. I
feel pretty sure you won't come; but hope is not dead.

Love to Jack and Charles
Cyril

P.S.

ΔΙΟΝΥΣΙΕ
ΧΡΗΣΤΕΚΑΙΑΩΡΕ
ΧΑΙΡΕ

is rather a good epitaph don't you think?

χρῆστε καὶ ἀώρε – good and dying – too – soon.

P.S.S.

Bobbie sends his love and hopes to see you soon.

I would meet you Sat. say for tea and dinner and K's gramophone. Churches and Thame for Sunday. And talk and nice photoes *χαιρε*.

22 Oct 1924. Postcard of carving of horseman from Cordes.

H. N. Blakiston, Esq.,
Magdalene College,

Dear Noel,

Καλῶs – I have got a room Saturday night and will meet you for tea. The only drawback is that K. has got a man for the week end too owing to a muddle but we dine at Thame all right without him and he is probably coming churching on Sunday so all is well. Looking forward to seeing you.

Cyril

The horseman is rather nice don't you think.
Love to Jack and Charles.

26 Oct 1924. Postcard, of Zaragoza.

H. N. Blakiston, Esq.,
Magdalene College.

Dear Noel,

Of course give *Byz. and Rom. A.** to some one else if you want to

*Byzantine and Romanesque Architecture, a book he had given to N.B.

or when you have enjoyed it if you write in it under where I have it will look pleasingly symmetrical. Remember to tell your mother that. Only keep the photoes.

[A Greek couplet follows, not easy to read.]

31 Oct 1924.
H. N. Blakiston, Esq.,
Magdalene College.

from Balliol College,
(writing paper of
Hotel Simon, Almeria)

Dear Noel,

Thank you so much for your letter. You are fairly accurate about Sligger – by the way what did you say to him for he seems very angry with me and very impressed with you as a wit – had the reign of slander quite ended? Also I never held that because a thing was archaic it was good, I am not a die-hard – but I think there is more to learn and more to appreciate in Greek archaic art than in later art. I will not quote authorities because it tends to become mere bandying of names though you have Bobbie on your side about thinking the slim idol from the Archipelago bosh – and I have Roger on mine. Bobbie's taste is good but never enterprising, K. Clark's very good indeed, it is all he is fit for – Roger's and mine wayward but in the case of this sculpture we have seen the originals – Maurice Bowra* is full of appreciation and nearly always right, the superb amateur; Beazley, and his friend Gow† unassailable though whimsical and austere – Lobel's‡ and Sligger's for instance non-existent. I cannot see the harm in good taste if it is bold and natural – it is only when people allow it to influence action and make a critical power creative that they become K. Clark's – and to some extent Charles's – trying to live by taste alone – this is only a tentative view which I will withdraw if you convince me. I agree with you about no slander but I think one must be fairly fugitive and cloistered to avoid it – some people, Charles and M. Bowra in my case, make me nearly always succumb – God's behaviour last week end was unpardonable I think – I had done

*Maurice Bowra (b. 8 April 1898, d. 1971). Cheltenham, New College. Fellow and Tutor, Wadham 1922–38, Warden, 1938–70. Professor of Poetry 1946–51. Knighted 1951. For Connolly, as for many others, the most powerful educational force in Oxford.

†Andrew Gow, Master at Eton, don at Trinity, Camb.

‡Edgar Lobel (b. 1888). Balliol. Fellow of Queens' Greek scholar, papyrologist.

my best and was not prepared to have this new Trinity enforced of Rum, Rain, and ball bearings – (what *did* you tell Sligger at breakfast!)

Later you must have made a good story out of Thame for Sligger's coolness to me and appreciation of you as a wit have been traced to that by Bobbie – Roger by the way enjoyed it more than any evening he had spent and thought Fothergill superb – after all he is an inn-keeper not a don – and Sligger is quite capable of having him put out of bounds which would be sad for him. Here is a photo of A.M. (?) which explains the name – I am sorry if I have sounded bitter but it is a tendency of both of us to try and be all things to all men and nothing therefore to anyone and I think one ought to get rid of it absolutely beyond the minimum due to good manners – seeing you has done me a lot of good and both of us – for I think we feel much stronger for knowing that in an environment so different from Kirkby we can still go on in the same principles and though squalor makes one noble comfort is apt to make one comfortable – the great thing is that every time I let myself down over some limitation I let you down too and vice versa which makes it (for if one of us gets lazy about casting off the other has committed himself alone) easier to resist temptations to comfort and complacency. But you must stand by me as I have let myself in for much trouble with Bobbie for the sake of your ideal for he is not only unmoved but definitely against it and yet I could not trust you not to corroborate everything he says against it if he asks you.

It will be fun don't you think to see the loneliness gathering round us and I am often thrilled now to wander down what bleak road our principles will lead us φεῦ γαίης ὁδον ἀφ ἡμετέρης – it will be a long way from the anaesthetic of knowledge and the pleasant pastures of the mind. Mackail 9.18 has some bearing don't you think and of course 35. I think one must take a strong line about property – at any rate one's own and decrease what one has, let alone not get any more. You will give that book away won't you if you want to – buying a thing is rather like picking a flower from its proper life in the fields and putting it in one's room where it quickens the life of the spirit and then fades – but it can bloom again for someone else – most of one's books and pictures are the dead husks of a spiritual joy – yet though they are dead husks one belongs to them which is so absurd and so should promptly give them away – much of matter is for a moment the window of reality and therefore good but soon the blinds are drawn and we are left treasuring the dark pane which might be light for someone else – enter Sligger and the coolness ended. I think one must take up a strong line about animals too but we rather settled that – and also we should be grateful for all we possess that is lost or broken by us or by others and see in it the kindly hand of circumstance helping us to cast away what we are too weak to cast away ourselves for when we renounce things ourselves we repent afterwards but when they are renounced for us we should feel no regret for we merit no reaction and if we feel regret we charm it away by saying 'better we lose that' or 'better it be broken'.

I go on fretting, bored with work and people and interested chiefly in castings off though on these wild windy nights when rain obscures the stars I have a terrific desire to pack a little luggage and rattle off to Dover. Bobbie is very ineffectual and bustling and terribly limited by property and conventions – habeor non habeo in almost everything to my despair for I would like his company and I am fonder of him than any one because he is warm and affectionate and loyal. Roger is the best substitute for you and we see eye to eye on almost everything, he liked you very much indeed by the way and would be the closest companion we could find – and I think has gone further than us already – but he wants some scholarship at present and makes a fetish of knowledge.

Did I show you this on knowledge?

Embittered academics
Gray, Callimachus, Housman,
With scholarly polemics
Enlarged the mind of man
But now that they are gone away
We weep for bones in Africa
And for the death of Richard West
And games that Cretins used to play.

O'Connor tells me Maud* is converting him to religion. I wish him all joy of the worm. Maurice Bowra and John Brooks are as nice as they can be. Roger and I are probably going to Cambridge together towards the end of the term – I am becoming rather a strong Platonist in the matter of ideals and the real and visible worlds – it would be fun to make a pilgrimage somewhere abroad and earn our food and keep as we went along – it would teach us the nature of people and

*J. P. R. Maud. John (b. 3 February 1906). KS. New College, Fellow and Dean of University College 1932–9. Permanent Sec., Ministry of Education 1945–52. Master of University College since 1963. Lord Redcliffe-Maud 1967.

to travel light and quicken the life of the spirit by feeling – I am rather moved by the parable of the talents and the disciples sent out two by two – Roger and Bobbie and Sligger send love and mine to you.

Cyril

Who said sepulchre of etc. ?

24 Nov 1924.

Noel Blakiston, Esq.,   Balliol College,
Magdalene College.   Oxford.

Dear Noel,

I am sorry I have not written for so long. I have had nothing worth saying. The spirit we serve has retreated a little leaving me rather a husk. The sixth week of term deals a hard blow to the Theory of Ideas and everywhere malice reigns. Slander seems the keynote of existence, and only in absolute seclusion, fugitive and cloistered, does salvation lie. Maurice Bowra, Roger and I present a front of untroubled loyalty but rejoicing in our unity we slander everyone else so little good is gained. Mrs. Beazley makes intercourse with Beazley hardly worth it: Sligger's catholic susceptibilities have been outraged by criticisms of the deity. Away from the arena where reputations crumble and bad blood is made is Bobbie, superbly loyal and affectionate, and John Brooks in the school boy world of Corpus with a log fire and the César Franck symphony on his gramophone. These two alone provide Romance and Milton above all. By reading his life and his prose works and all his poetry something of his greatness has permeated and disclosed an intimacy and a wistfulness that makes any statement of an inhuman quality in his work impossible to believe – things like

the pledge
Of dalliance had with thee in heaven, and joyes
Then sweet, now sad to mention, through dire
change
befallen us unforeseen

or

Yet beauty, though injurious, hath strange power
After offence returning, to regain

26

Love once possest – nor can be easily
Repulsed, without much inward passion felt
And secret sting of amorous remorse –

if you know he could feel like that it gives extraordinary force to his
purely classical allusion
like

> not that faire field
> Of Enna where Proserpine gathering flowrs
> Her self a fairer Flowre by gloomie Dis
> Was gatherd, which cost Ceres all that pain
> To seek her through the world

But it is unbearable to go on quoting: above all I am haunted through
Milton by Orpheus – not the jolly Orpheus of L'Allegro and Penseroso,
twice coupled with Eurydice, but the solitary figure among the
Thracians, the man who had descended into hell playing his sad tunes
to the barbarians till the rejected maenads tore him to pieces, (the two
sides of Greek religion) nor could the muse defend her son – Milton
was obsessed by the lyrical pathos of this in Lycidas but in Paradise
Lost (Bk. 7 beginning) it had taken on a less melodious, and more
tragic note – he was Orpheus, the sons of Belial flown with insolence
and wine become Bacchus and his revellers and then the young
Royalists tearing through Bread Street, the puzzled Thracians of the
Restoration while Milton sings of his lost Eurydice of Liberty – or
possibly Mary Powell – he actually was in danger of death and could
not be sure of the protection of the thankless muse – There seems a
strange comparison between Orpheus' last days among the Thracians,
Milton's own later sublimity, our dubious future in spiritual loneliness
and possibly Lycaon's body drifting down the eddies of the Scamander
into the sea

> O little did my mother ken
> The day she cradled me
> The lands I was to travel in
> Or the death I was to die

I think you know now all I can offer towards the life of the spirit
at least all I have been really feeling. If there was more it would only
be more Milton – the transition in blindness from Bk. III (1–55)

> but not to me returns
> Day, or the sweet approach of even or morn

Or sight of vernal bloom or summer's rose
Or flocks or herds or human face divine

which is Sophoclean, to the blindness of Samson – Isaiah or Aeschylus

O dark, dark, dark, amid the blaze of noon
Irrecoverably dark, total eclipse
Without all hope of day.
The sun to me is dark
And silent as the moon
When she deserts the night
Hid in her vacant interlunar cave. . . .

it is really our ethics and metaphysics turned to mysticism – Orpheus,
Milton, and Lycaon – you and me – expression to restraint. No, not
altogether, more

but love toward the mountains bent his feet
And hid his face amid a cloud of stars.*

Do excuse all this but a mystical emotion, however earthy, is harder
to explain than other sensations.

Do you know this of C. Rossetti

The wind has such a rainy sound
   Moaning through the town
The sea has such a windy sound
   And will the ships go down?

The apples in the orchard
   Tumble from their tree
O will the ships go down, go down
   In the windy sea?

It is, as you said, a nice time of year quando ignis murmurat, et
marcescat frons – nice to retire from the world to quiet teas, firelight
on people's hair, music at times or walking through the streets on a
windy evening and seeing the first Christmas presents in the lighted
shops, then turning out of the cold into the warm darkness of a cinema
or back again to Milton and

*The last verse of Yeats's 'When you are old . . .' reads:

And bending down beside the glowing bars,
Murmurs, a little sadly, how Love fled
And paced upon the mountains overhead
And hid his face amid a crowd of stars.

. . . all that bowery loneliness
And brooks of Eden mazily murmuring
And bloom profuse and cedar arches. . . .

I have thought a lot about you and you have taken such root in my imagination that no amount of absence or occupation can drive you from first place there. I am coming over next week end and hope we can be together much of it, alone, if possible, as nothing much happens otherwise – do read Iliad 21 105–135 for the superbest extant paganism and the knell of all the world in κατθανε και πατροκλος.

Much love till Saturday
Cyril

3 Dec 1924.

<table>
<tr><td>Noel Blakiston, Esq.,
Magdalene College,
Cambridge.</td><td>Balliol College,
Oxford.</td></tr>
</table>

Dear Noel,

Thank you for your letter. Bobbie and I hereby declare that Charles is a doddering old muddler though do not tell him so. Can you give me dinner on Saturday, Bobbie must dine with his hosts. We might go to the play if you like – I don't mind a bit but Roger instructed someone to approach Charles with tickets. If I am not staying in Magdalene, as Charles seems to think, it might be more fun to talk. If you can't give me dinner can you ask Freddie* or William† or Freddie and William if they would – can Charles give you and me and Bobbie dinner on Sunday? Bobbie and I are having tea with Steven Runciman‡ on Sunday. Otherwise I don't know his plans. There is no way we could go to Ely for lunch on Sunday is there? I would like to see Freddie and William some time if possible and would

---

*F. E. Farmer, Freddie (b. 3 November 1905.) KS. King's. Deputy Chairman, P&O.S.N. Co. 1957–70. Knighted 1968.

†William Le Fanu (b. 9 July 1904). KS. King's. For a short time master at Eton. Librarian, College of Surgeons.

‡Steven Runciman (b. 7 July 1903). KS. Trinity, Camb. Fellow of Trinity 1927–38. Historian. Knighted 1958.

be curious to inspect the ménage of Ronnie* and Jake.† If you can't give me dinner Saturday perhaps we can have tea together. Forgive me for being so explicit but it seems hopeless to expect anything from Charles. I will let him know later when we arrive.

I sublimate you, if I do not idealise you – what is wrong in that, we all have kernels as well as husks – Though I should crash if you acted against your sublimation i.e. were a charlatan or a worldling or disloyal but not if you were stale and unprofitable – it will be nice seeing you.

Cyril

Bobbie as he will be staying with the Corpus people may be rather inaccessible.

[? 11] Dec 1924.

H. N. Blakiston, Esq.,   The Lock House,
Kirkby on Bain.   Deepcut,
                                                      Surrey.

Dear Noel,

Out of the depths have I called unto you! My father came here on Saturday and I yesterday. I refused 3 invitations for this week in order to get down at once to solitary coping so will you please give me a good mark for that. It was very ghostly coming back here after 3 years – the taxi creeping through thick white fog, bumping over holes in the neglected road and crashing against overhanging branches in the unkempt avenue. My father hobbled out to argue with the taxi-driver whose face was bleeding from branches and we sat down to dinner together. We have no servants but a soldier and his wife rent our cottage and the wife comes in and cooks and makes beds. There is absolute silence but for my father who has a typewriter in the drawing room and clears his throat and makes body noises and swears at intervals. He gets rather drunk and fuddled when he becomes maudlin or

*A. R. D. Watkins. Ronnie (b. 20 August 1904). KS. King's. Master at Harrow. Theatrical producer.
†John Carter. 'Jake' (b. 10 May 1905, d. 18 March 1975). KS. King's. Bibliographical Consultant. CBE 1956. Watkins and Carter shared rooms in Gibbs Building at King's.

irritable and says the same thing several times with long pauses between each word, his speech grows thick and laboured and he failed dismally to say 'a new species from Mauritius' last night. Nearly all his remarks shock and nauseate me and the drawing room is not improved by a typewriter and growing collection of empty bottles. Outside this room desolation reigns. Wall papers strip and peel, damp splodges appear in the ceilings, plaster falls down, mist condenses on the window panes and the only literary parallels are Mariana and the story at the beginning of *Come Hither, Fortitude*, by Hugh Walpole (last part) and the descriptions of forgotten cities in Isaiah 13, 33 and I think Nahum. Outside leaves die everywhere and the mist hides everything but the ragged outlines of untrimmed yew hedges. We have no neighbours, are 3 miles from a station and two miles from a shop and do not possess even a bicycle.

> With blackest moss the flower plots
> Were thickly crusted one and all
> The rusted nails fell from the knots
> That held the pear to the gable wall.

I don't think your case can be worse than mine for you have a brother at any rate and I must function alone having written to tell my mother not to come as she couldn't stand it. I was rather worried about your flippant refusal to come and stay here. I suppose one has really to do the drabbest things by oneself but I would like to feel that we could count on each other to share them. Personal relations are the most important thing and if two people are in harmony they can tolerate almost any conditions which other people regard as unbearable. I think we have proved that, so it does not need explaining, our worst moments at Kirkby and elsewhere have always been when our foundations of good will collapse and consequently whatever we are doing becomes hateful. You don't consider personal relations very much – but I think you will find that they are the most vital means, if you don't accept them as an end – you couldn't do much coping at home if you did not get on with Jack. I could do none here if I did not think that I was acquiring merit with you and having sympathy from Bobbie.

The chief snag in our relations seems not to be that I find you boring or you me humourless (my God that rankles) but that you object to me taking your arm etc which makes me think you don't like me – especially as you seem only to do it to annoy – I am not promiscuous but I can't be loyal to an icicle and so I stick to Bobbie who is very affectionate and very constant – it is silly of me to think you don't like me for that reason but it rankles a lot – I don't think I underrate you – you are less striking with William, Freddie & Co because they have not the admiration for you that Roger and people have but I know we are right. I think you are right about taking myself too seriously but you see my friends at Oxford do too and I them; I grant I have a photo of you and Charles laughing at me together which makes me embarrassed. Do try Paradise Lost. You see I regard you as an end in yourself as much as a means for creation and causes – I think you regard me only as a means and so the machinery gets out of order. Shoes are a means of walking but they last much longer if they are polished and cleaned – also I am all for seriousness and I think our seriousness together is rather admirable. On the other hand I am not a normal person, I can be normal at a pinch but have always been accepted as rather a phenomenon and you often affect a rather brutal common sense in the hope of refusing to observe that I have a temperament.

This is all very inelegant. I am sorry. I am looking forward awfully to Minehead* it would be hard not to in this house and Sligger and Maurice are very pleased you are coming. John Brooks and Piers Synnott† are both nice and in no way terrifying. We ought to be able to take our time to corroborate, synchronise, and create. I have got quite a lot of Plato to read here, and Milton and Yeats and Proust. Minehead begins on the 27th, I think – Sligger and Maurice have to go away on the 10th of Jan. but Sligger says we can stay on if we want to or you might like to come here with me for a day or two. My mother will be here then and will have got servants and made this place presentable. You see it is not the discomfort I mind but my squalid father and the strain on my imagination – the empty house and the fog and damp and lonely evenings and my father's limping step fitfully going up stairs or his silhouette alone in the dining room after dinner or grumbling or fussing or being maudlin or worldly (he is a very mean snob) or any of his unbearable mannerisms or his forthcoming paper on snails as carriers of disease. I did enjoy lunching with you on Sunday, Noel, and I wish we had been alone more and

---

*Sligger was holding a reading party at Minehead.

†P. N. N. Synnott. Pierce, Piers (b. 6 September 1904). Oratory School, Balliol. Assistant Principal Admiralty, 1928. Deputy Secretary 1958. CB 1952.

that I had not had persecution mania. Write to me and tell me how you are coping – will you have Prabaka with you? Love to Jack, and to your mother and father. We must try and get abroad with Mrs. Connolly at Easter. I am glad we had the same views about reality – we have much the same sense of values too which is important don't you think. I think too we are getting to rely on each other in practical things – i.e. we keep engagements which is essential. Think of me. Much love.

Cyril

Thank you very much for all the meals you gave me – the spell of your birthday breakfast made leaving very hard – If you like we might meet in London and travel down together the next day. I can pay for things.

[? *15 Dec*] *1924 Friday night.*

Noel Blakiston, Esq.,   The Lock House,
Kirkby on Bain.   Deepcut,
                                           Surrey.

Dear Noel,
Thank you so much for your letter. Minehead ends probably on the 10th so you could go then to Rye.* I should not scratch Minehead if I was you. I think you would enjoy it more. Sligger might be tiresome but Maurice would be very good for you (what a bloody thing to say) and the others are nice.

You know I would love to see you here, I had to go and get some meat this afternoon and imagined the difference some conversation with you would have made, also I used to picture you here when I came over on 4th of June – but you resent that?

My father would be delighted if you came, he says, any time next week or after. My mother may come soon, then the servant trouble will be acute. We can afford servants you know but we have not got any and my father is too inefficient or frightens them away and I am not supposed to be able to do anything like engaging servants and

*A. C. Benson, Master of Magdalene College, Camb., had invited N.B. to stay with him at Lamb House, Rye.

quite resigned not to. I can offer you freedom from ἀσχολιας and good country for walks and we can get a bus and go to cinemas but food is poor owing to no cook and we have no car or bicycle and very few books. We could see a good deal of each other at Minehead but it might be hard to be alone and nothing very vital happens when we aren't – you know I would love to have you here – and it is nice of you to think of coming – wait and see what Benson says and then let me know – before Christmas would be best and the sooner the better. I could meet you in town. I read nothing but books about animals all my childhood and there is nothing here but Ernest Thomson Seton, and a few books I have brought from Oxford, my father only likes magazines and books on shells and wishes there were more girls for me in the neighbourhood – we could probably have a sitting room to ourselves if you came – this page is written last of this letter and the part which follows first – it is an attempt to explain some of my values more intelligibly so that you can corroborate or dismiss or discuss, as you feel – my friends not my sensations are the only thing to me – I mean I would like to help you to get what you want as much as to pretend you are what I would like you to be – anyhow see if this conveys anything to you – Good night.

realities etc.

Ethics.

Chief virtues.

Courage.

a. Courage with oneself, self-humiliation, seeing one's faults, how one has deteriorated, facing facts and crises of aesthetic, intellectual or erotic nature – being sincere and without illusions or strong to bear burdens etc. γνῶθι σεάντον.

b. The courage of one's own and one's friends convictions (eating birds etc.)

c. Physical courage.

Charm.

Intellectual or physical, enough to give spirit to the flesh or enable the mind to be perceptible through the senses.

Sensibility –

Aesthetic, intellectual and physical – a hard thing to explain but you must know what I mean. The opposite of 'missing so much and so much' a sensitive person is also touchy, it can't be helped, he suffers more, feels more, and understands more. More creative than good taste.

Loyalty.
>probably least real to you – preference and circumstance have set you with me but you are fond of affirming 'you never were attached to that great sect' etc. which makes my tenure seem rather precarious.

Kinds of loyalty
>*physical* loyalty – sleeping with one person only and not getting tired of them.

>*dependability* – keeping engagements, being trusted always to come at a pinch and usually without one and to come because you want to as much as because you are wanted. 'Coping' for a friend.

>*verbal loyalty* – not being malicious before or behind a friend but making good blood.

>*ultimate loyalty* – thinking no principle to stand before a friendship – i.e. if you became a militant Jesuit you would not be justified in giving me up.

Also necessary intolerance and incuriosity, the refusal to put up with the 2nd best, to be limited, to be fussy, to love comfort or power or to be wrapped up in one's own sensations, and the capacity to choose rather than accept, to be good at games and not to play them, to possess and yet refrain (see the bit from Areopagitica).

Vices
>Worldliness – to prefer things which do not matter to that which does, to like the right things for the wrong reasons, intellectual snobbery, and the lower forms of ambition – 'social' success.

>Meanness – over money and property generally and in all things.

>Insincerity – to one's self or to other people which matters less – the other is disloyal to the intellect – hypocrisy, self-deception, injustice, etc.

>Womanising – women are less beautiful and less intelligent than men ∴ they destroy sensibility, they destroy sincerity by flattery and loyalty by love, nor can courage long withstand them, also they are more worldly than men and far less sincere.

There are 4 virtues and 4 vices which seem fairly fundamental – Thus – courage and sensibility encourage truth, worldliness and insincerity defame it, charm also is a tribute to beauty and meanness

35

a foe to goodness, loyalty its friend; women are a root of all evil. (I mean taken seriously, all right at dances).

Metaphysics

The best grouping of things is into real and unreal – this is not entirely the same as subjective and objective nor does it preclude the existence of Reality in the platonic sense existing outside ourselves. It is our aim to get into touch with that Reality by quickening the life of the spirit. Thus you are real to me and Burtenshaw is not – that does not mean that you are only real in so far as you are so to me or to anyone else but that by you being real to me I am enabled to get into touch with Reality for a moment, when something is real to me then I am real myself – the sensation of being real we call a thrill; there are gradations of thrills but the mind is not usually sensitive enough to grasp them. It is my belief that personal relations provide the best medium for getting thrills and $\therefore$ being real-friends are not only the ends but the means also. You and I moved by a sunset or some emotion such as love for each other are the most real thing I know. Feeling, then, rather than thought or knowledge is the test of reality, thoughts are real when we feel them and knowledge the same.

Truth is not always real – it is true that 2 and 2 make 4 but it is unreal – at dinner on Sunday it was real as well as true – no, then they did not make 4 – a point you must decide is if $2+2=4$ is not real to me, is it real to anyone? – if truth is not always real, is that which is real always true – $2+2=5$ is not more unreal than $2+2=4$ is it then more false? The explanation seems to be that truth is of the intellect, reality of the emotions – we cannot *feel* deeply about $2+2$ being 4 or being 5 though we can *know* definitely. Also we are becoming too subjective, again $2+2=4$ has no power to make us real for we become real by apprehension as much as things become real by being apprehended.

Soul and body are best understood by the metaphor of the electric light, the body is the glass and the wires and the current, reality. If ever the silver cord be loosed, or the golden bowl be broken, break the glass and the light goes out, the body and the soul dies, but the light is not the glass, the filaments are the five senses, through which the light shines, break one and the others shine brighter. Milton and Homer were blind, Beethoven deaf and Belisarius a eunuch. Break too many and the light goes out – Oh heavens, my father is drunk again and practically incapable of succinct speech – what line would you take if yours had these Noah-like propensities? If he was no relation one would not mind but I feel at all costs I must not show I notice or hurt his feelings and if I must not laugh, I must take it seriously and then it is absolutely ghastly – though it is all right at present because I can write to you – I think treating one's father as an equal will sometimes make them play up, i.e. voicing one's liberal views as moderately and candidly as possible so that they cannot legitimately explode into meaningless prejudice and rage. You may ask how Sebastian comes into those theories, I think he found reality in thought and neglected everything else – (my father has repeated after an interval of 2 minutes 'I expect you sometimes get a tune running in your head that blocks out everything else, like this one' (sings) – me, hopefully, 'it's called "What'll I do!"' my father, 'Thank you'. If he makes the remark and sings the tune a third time and asks me the name, I think I shall collapse – (he has gone to pick it out on the piano) – it is so awful Noel, to see one's flesh and blood behave like this and wonder if I shall get drunk and incoherent and permanently lame and noisy in my digestion in 20 years time. (My father thinks he has invented that tune, and is writing it down) – on the whole he is very well meaning and would not sink as low as this if you or my mother were here but it is a little grim seeing no one but him all day and the house being quite empty – and he provides me with a test for coping on – I might be in Scotland with Patrick* or in Ireland with Piers but I think I have chosen best if only you approve and understand – I am afraid I can cope no more with 'reality' this evening – I hope I don't bore you – I remember saying to Maurice Bowra that somebody bored me and he said nobody can be boring who is essentially serious, only flippant people are boring and Harrod† is serious, which I thought rather an enterprising outlook don't you think!

τέρπνον ἐσθ' ὑπὸ στέγαις
πυκνῆς ἀκούειν ψακάδος εὐδούσῃ φρένι

'it is sweet under the roof to hear the drip of rain, with sleepy mind' – (A Sophocles fragment)
likewise

Ὄλβιος ὅστις ἐρῶν γυμνάζεται, οἴκαδε δ'ἐλθὼν
εὔδει σὺν καλῷ πάιδι πανημέριος

*Hon. Patrick Balfour (b. 25 June 1904). Winchester, Balliol. Writer. Succeeded father as Lord Kinross 1939.
†Roy Harrod (b. 13 February 1900). Westminster, New College, Lecturer, Student at Christ Church 1922–67. University Lecturer in Economics. Knighted 1959.

and

χαίρε καὶ εἰν ἀΐδεο δ ὤμασι καλλίμαχε

I really must go to bed. This will cross one of yours too, probably.
Much love

Cyril

If you really don't want to go to Minehead, do come if you can face
this. A lot of rubbish in this letter.

My love to Jack.

22 Dec 1924.

H. N. Blakiston, Esq.,   The Lock House,
The Rectory,   Deepcut,
Kirkby on Bain,   Surrey.
Lincolnshire.

Dear Noel,
     Thank you so much for your letter and your card. You eluded the
latter's point. You simply must come here on the 10th if you can. My
mother will be here and wants to see you we shall have servants etc and the
pick of K. Clark's records for my gramophone and peace and security and
fires. I really think you would enjoy it and I would love to have you;
please don't let any views about unworthiness stand in the way. My
father would be delighted too and is already sounding me as to
whether you despise wine and if not what kind you like. We could
have my sitting room to be unmolested in and the country is lovely
while we can take a bus, if you do not scorn them and go as far as
Winchester or Chichester, Hindhead or Petersfield. Also you would
be giving me great pleasure and I would like to know how you like
this house because if you like it you must come and live here with
me when it is mine. I find it incredibly quiet and lovely and very
understanding. I am rather gone on it and prowl round the empty
rooms or turn on one light or all the lights when my father has gone
to bed and go out to the end of the garden to see the golden shafts

shining through latticed windows and stretching over the grass to where I stand by the dark yew hedge listening to the soft splashing of our stream, my feet in the dead leaves. I do not know if it is really lovely or if I love it because I have been a child here or because I must love something or because one day it will be mine. It is not a 'place' but rather a large small house, mostly 18th century but skilfully added on to and with a lovely garden now rather run to seed, abiding in a hollow by still water and encircled by protecting trees. My father does not like it because it is damp and because it is out of the way, but my mother loves it more than me. It is full of nice creatures, birds that my mother knows all about, squirrels and rabbits and even foxes and very kindly trees. Not as admirable as yours of course, nor have we a vine. We have a stream that is a trickle beside the Bain* but more enterprising as it goes over several waterfalls and bog and ravines and impenetrable scrub. Lovelier than it or the Bain is the 'Oxus', the chief stream of the châlet, which is incomparably beautiful rising in grassy mountain solitude and leaping down a flowery ravine to end in waterfalls and almost impenetrable undergrowth while Sligger leads his troop far away from such meaner beauties because further away means more up-hill. Water is very thrilling don't you think? Air and Fire are elements one hears a lot about, but if one starts moralising about fresh water it seems to promise certain of the finer aspects of truth – our canal I think is really better than the Bain and very different from what it is at Mytchett – praise God for the César Franck Symphony, a parting gift from John Brooks and now pealing joy loudly enough to drown my father's digestion. As to him, I am nearing the limit of my endurance. Besides minor faults (objecting to classical music on the gramophone because it is 'a beastly noise' though he continues to typewrite during it) – he has 4 major ones, he fusses, is vain and hypocritical, eats and digests terribly audibly and 4, is greedy and drunken. These may not be deadly sins but they are too much for me and my temper the last two days has gone up completely – I continue to cope admirably because I have set out to do so and to fail now when it gets so hard would shake my faith in being able to do anything, also in my eagerness to keep my real life of thought and feeling from my father's soiling eyes, I am scrupulous to hide even my detached hate from him and when I am most furious or most disgusted I appear most obliging and thoughtful. One can only make every conceivable allowance when one has failed to reach any con-

*The little river that runs through the parish of Kirkby.

ceivable understanding – at the same time even to leave the room when I can stand him no longer seems to me a confession of failure, to be granting him a reality that he does not deserve. But now he has gone to bed – Do you mind if I leave the points in your letter till to-morrow and go rambling on for the present? You have no idea what a comfort it is to write to you, if you can really bear to read it. I am glad you have Pat* and Prabahka back, they ought to be very cheering. It is nice to have people fond of you who do not know what they are giving you; do not know really what you are giving them, but go on quite unselfconsciously being extraordinarily helpful – I read nothing but Proust because he gives me the escape into another world in detailed volumes of extraordinary truth and distinction. I recommended you *Thais*† a long time ago, do you remember? It is so fine and sympathetic don't you think as well as the exquisite irony 'quand le Seigneur créait le monde, certes, ce fût une grande crise dans son existence?'

I have also read the Phaedrus and my Chinese poems. I know you know the Phaedrus but do read Socrates' long speech in honour of Love again, it is quite inspired on the subject of Reality, with which it deals at some length and also rather thrilling about love and friendship and reciprocity. It is the very long speech, the one with the charioteer simile. Do tell me what you think of Paradise Lost – especially if you think it bloody. My father gets up at 12, goes to bed at 9, so my office hours are short, my first duty as it were being not to be late for luncheon. Much of my time is taken in purely physical exercise, running and throwing assegais mainly through fear of becoming like my father who is fat from over eating, lame from drinking, flatulent from want of exercise, and pimpled from God knows what – in the afternoon I go for a long run with an assegai which I send vainly after rabbits or whistling through the air to embed the poisoned blade and the quivering shaft in the bark of a pine. The country is lovely and wild and deserted though I know it well it is full of variety, sometimes I go for my run at night if my temper has broken up, at night it is very thrilling. We might go out sometimes when you come. If I am tired I go quietly along the canal which is wonderful in the evening.

*Patrick Blakiston. Pat (b. 2 December 1914). Younger brother of N.B. Lancing, Magdalene. Clergyman, at present vicar of Whittingham, Northumberland.

†By Anatole France.

but that is only because I think you are not used to expressing abstract thought and find the longer words more potted and subtle. Anyhow the point behind all those brackets was that it is a kind of loyalty not to mind being beholden to one's friends, because it is false pride that would not take a service from a friend as if the friend were seeking an advantage by conferring a favour κοίνα γὰρ τά τῶν φιλῶν, ὦ Σώκρατες (is not the ending of the Phaedrus almost perfect, with that proverb and that prayer) – if it can be managed we will go either to Rome, Sicily and Tripoli or to Andalusia and Tangier (we could probably fit in Avignon, which ever we did) – Italy is so trippery in Spring and Spain thrills me more but I think Paestum and Segesta will prevail but I may not be allowed to sell capital, if not we must go somewhere in June. One thing I have to thank you for which is very vital, is the proof that it is possible to cope without being fussy, to be efficient without being interested. The difference your example of detached coping has made to me who was always afraid to be competent because it seemed to involve being bloody is very real indeed, and now good night.

Saturday night.

A bleak day. My best assegai is stuck in a pool till I can get a boat and get it out. I sprained my knee in a sand pit and listened to a lecture from my father on the value of fox hunting (good training for the cavalry and the fox likes it) – since dinner he has found speech difficult but requested me to take Boris Godunov off the gramophone and play 'When Irish Eyes are Smiling' – but these things are immaterial – here are some reflections on your *confessio fidei* – not denials but different aspects –

As to your dualism of home and Xty, home has never meant much to me, owing to military migrations though I have a feline passion for houses. Xty I do not like much in so far as it means 'the Church' or 'the Catholic Church' but I approve strongly of Christ as a man and as a disturbing thought and of his ethics and sense of values. I retain a certain religious childishness, a tendency to pray, to make compacts with my maker (i.e. I will clean my teeth if I am not 'wanted'* to night, O God) but it has passed into more pagan tendencies to

*An Eton expression for being summoned for chastisement.

animism, pantheism, τὸ φθόνερον etc. Your antithesis of appearance and reality has always attracted me.

You say reality was fulfilment and achievement for me, I think it was, certainly is, an emotional state, nearer thus to your 'intangible perfection' – I find achievement more an effect than a cause of reality – almost a gesture, let us set up three tabernacles (because in that place they had been real). Thus you and I 'realise' each other and then feel the desire to do something about it. Make beds for night-up people or lay breakfast. Though inversely those actions make us more real. Xty for you has meant a kind of universality of outlook which my more pagan view lacks, I should have been a Pharisee probably like Nicodemus, but I will come back to this. My conscience has always seemed to be someone else's. That everyone is *capax dei* I think you have almost converted me to, though formerly I had great contempt for the *profanum vulgus* but I think I really agree with you now, though Bobbie is more conservative. As to the importance of ethics I know what you mean – they have always been very real to me, almost increasing aptitude for envisaging abstractions makes me find them rather flat after the wings of 'Plato or his airie burgomasters'. Still I have an intense desire to practice what I preach (like Sebastian's report) and to find others doing so and also I hate people who will not think ("of course I hate to think of the poor birds being killed but they taste very good" etc.) also I would like Platonists and Aristotelians to be recognisable by their walk. What you meant about an ideal permeating. I agree absolutely there – [most ethics on the other hand, do seem to approximate very closely which seems to show that they are a world to themselves in which adepts find the same precepts valid without any relation to their philosophy or metaphysics or to accepted social traditions]. A point for discussion whether ethics are parallel or derived from less earthy thought. I think derived and ∴ less important but no thought is any good that is not translatable to ethics; and sound ethics at that – very close to the part played by ethics is that played by action to me. I always feel the desire for action so as to balance my individualism, but I find something very one sided about a life devoted purely to creative thought or emotional appreciation, I want to do things as well as to be them, perhaps even in order to be them – but being matters most. Ethics are so much concerned with appearances. 'The self is realised by effort' yes I agree there but I think even more, effort is an extension of one's reality, the 3 tabernacles again – 'No individual possesses objective reality in sufficient ultimateness to be worth particular study' – hence frigidity and meanness.

(I) 'No, no, no'. II. Yes.

The individual is *capax dei*. Some, Christ, Plato. M. Angelo, L. Vinci, very much indeed, would they not have been worth particular study? And was not Sebastian worth it or the study of him would not have had such an effect on us – moreover the best way to make people 'ultimately real' is by particular study – your point is "the vine is not healthy enough to be worth watering though every vine is capable of health' – This is my experience, that if you take trouble about a person, they become worth taking trouble about – if I idealise you according to the general tendency of your character (according to your own ideal, if you like) it does help you to become it just as I am able to cope with my father because I am acting up to your ideal of me. "Of course it's no good thinking one has no limits only one can go a long way before you find them" said Kenneth Bell to me (a propos of the fact that he could not get down to 5 hours sleep instead of six) and I think everyone has a kind of trend which they can so control, but not profitably – I can enjoy a dance or a rugger match but they are pleasures by the way side and though I enjoy them I know it is not really what I ought to be doing and if I idealised you contrary to the trend of your development it would not do you much good (hence parents, the blindest idealisers, fail). Thus with a false ideal one says 'I will not undeceive the poor old thing, if she thought I did not believe in the ark it would kill her' with a true one 'I must try and be like that if they think I am so' – I find Bobbie or Roger's ideal of me for instance most inspiring and it fills me with

holy hope and high humility

but you may have meant that ultimate reality cannot be contained in the shell of a human body,

Sunday night.

that the vine, for all its watering can only be a vine, if you think that, I think you may be right, on all sides one sees nothing but the presumption of human beings i.e. in considering all the works of nature made for their use; the stars then being a typical example of waste. Also you may find reality more perfect in abstraction, as an idea or aspect of truth and beauty or an ethical state rather than penned up in a person. You may be right there, it was rather Sebastian's line

43

but more or less leads one to find mathematics more beautiful than art because it has less appeal to the senses. As for us, I hold absolutely to the absolute dependence of spirit on sense and vice versa,

> till the divine
> Idaea take a shrine
> of chrystall flesh through which to shine

With me senses and intellect (and the proportions are five to one) are irretrievably fused, thus for some one whose mind I admire, like Roger, I naturally feel physical affections as a consequence, also for someone who is externally attractive I desire to find a mind to match and if it is not there I leave them – but it matters little if I take some one's arm because they are nice or because it is a nice arm. I cannot pigeon hole sense and spirit, the most abstruse shared thought produces quite natural demonstration and I would rather not go to one person for intellectual and the other for sensual enjoyments. I do not feel that the body is the soul's prison, the soul may exist apart from the body but in no personal or perceptible form, we know what a drop of water looks like but we cannot say it goes on being visible as such when it is put into a pond. Thus I do not believe in any personal immortality, you do, don't you? I have sometimes wondered if your desire for children and the immortality of the soul is not an expression of your egoism – wanting for yourself two kinds of survival or is it Jewish upbringing? I do not think I understand what you mean by the feelings of oneness or atonement. Oneness with someone else, yes – but I don't think I know atonement by that name. Can you explain it some time.

About being a novice in amicitiology it is a difficult point – perhaps the thing in which you are most removed from Bobbie and people (the Mimnermi in Church) is in your ability to find the masse real, it comes as you say from a unifying Xty but the fact remains that you would like to feed five thousand; to benefact people you do not know, to educate children not your own as J.C. was able to love people with out being exclusive – This may be your best point, the one way you may escape from being limited or mediocre – and therefore if you became like me who thinks friendship 'the only thing' (and would therefore probably follow you to slums or lepers, for Jesus had a disciple whom he loved) you might be stunting yourself – you see I have lost nearly all ambition because of loving friends in stead of finding them useful – in fact I am a typical 'chained friend' who

44

abandoned Sebastian rather than fight with Bobbie (for I could not serve two masters) still I chose my bondage and rejoice in it and also it provides many short cuts to reality and a pleasant feeling of renunciation and what is better still, security – *suave mari magno* – also literature means a lot to me. I appreciate poetry (Narcissus at the pool?) more than any other art and can write it enough almost to excuse myself from taking part in much ethical action, σιγχάινω πάντα τα δημόσια*, better sonnets than slums. Anyhow I find literature the best form for feeling and adding to beauty and truth (after friendship). (I am not as truthful as I would wish, but I do think Truth very real and admirable, this makes me hate to deceive myself rather than Pride or hatred of one's vanity by which one is deceived. I feel disloyal to Truth when I am deceived – consequently I like frankness and sincerity (you do not excel in these vices I put up) – you have cast out worldliness, and almost insincerity (you were very insincere at Eton and now are never so, excepting a mild superficial duplicity (Minehead e.g.). You were never mean. I think you have won a great victory over yourself and passed from phases of expression to phases of restraint but I think you cast away, with worldliness and insincerity and other faults, much of your fondness for me (I don't think I was wholly responsible for them). By the way our qualities good & bad were really only the virtues & defects of a friend of being necessary & of insuring [?] friendship – you see how it has [? permeated]. Environment has made me more individualised than you, being an only child and in a dud election and usually treated as an exception to many rules (especially at Oxford) – being an only child has given me a lot of ego centricity, years of 'playing by myself' etc but that solitude inculcated an even stronger ideal of the pair system (chained friends) which has finally predominated – thus while I travel much alone as a result of my old conception of myself as a solitary creator of romance (you may laugh!) as a rather predestined person like the Messiah, or the muses enchanting son (you know the feeling) – all the time I would rather travel with Bobbie or you, and find when I am with you and Bobbie I am happier and feel more allotted – but I would rather travel alone than with anyone else [you have much *a priori* precedence over Bobbie but at present I put him first from gratitude – though I think much more of you here and it is almost entirely due to you that I bear it – and am bearable –] Listlessness and irritability come closer now, like wolves in a hard winter

*'I loathe everything popular', Callimachus (Mackail 4.31)

45

and I shall only just get through without collapsing into apathy and bad temper.

I would like to travel with you, materially and metaphorically, and climb mountains, explore countries and sleep out under unfamiliar stars. Do you feel that kind of heartiness at all? I have been much influenced by Africa where I spent four years and acquired a very strong love of animals and scenery and stalking and assegais and exploring and camping out and redskin adventures. Since rather obscured by Irish melancholy and Greek intellectualism, though I like best the archaic ripeness of Greece, not ripeness but 'the woods of Athens before the middle summer's spring' – all that remains of Telesilla is one fragment 'γλύκυ δε τις'αείδων' which has rather the spirit. Sorry for writing all this but it has cheered me up. I will write to your πυτνια μητηρ for Christmas. Let me know about Jan. I have quite a week more here 'αλλ ἔκας ὀυκ ἔκας ἔστι.

Much love
Cyril

κυρίλλος Νοήλι μεγὰ χάιρε ἀθύρ

on the envelope
 rura quae Liris quieta mordet acqua taciturnus amnis
 suits the Bain, don't you think?

23 Dec 1924. Postcard of train leaving Algeciras. Deepcut.

H. N. Blakiston, Esq.,
Kirkby on Bain.

Tues. ἐν μεταιχ μι ω σκοτοῦ
 The rock of Gibraltar, the Roman aqueduct and the aloes by the rail side are delectable don't you think? To-night has been one of the worst so thank you for your card. 'On the borderland of darkness' partly because the lighting has just failed.

Love to Jack.

24 Dec 1924.

H. N. Blakiston, Esq.,   [The Lock House,
Kirkby on Bain.   Deepcut.]
                                                        Surrey.

Dear Noel,

Thank you so much for your letter. I have not run away but am near to it. Major C. has taken to talking to himself in a very unlovely manner which was very unnerving last night when the lights failed and I sat there in the dark and my father with his port in the dining room having a vulgar soliloquy – oaths coming out of the darkness. I find if you are in the same room with someone you can't bear, sitting absolutely still and not moving or fidgetting is a kind of comfort, it emphasises my remoteness from my windy parent who swears and fusses with his typewriter. As you guessed, he grows festive and is worried because he could not go to church last Sunday. I nearly had to walk four miles to carry him back a turkey and I was afraid he would want crackers. He is really very well meaning you know but has terrible vanity and a mania that he is being persecuted by everyone though he does all the persecuting; he is capable of much static affection but very easily dissipated – I don't like to leave my mother with him alone. The trouble is that he will probably go worse and may quite likely go mad, probably in some sordid way or become unable to move as he is now almost unable to walk. Tragedy in life seems always squalid and farce to have its roots in pain – I don't know if he knows about it himself and he brought on his arthritis through his own incompetent drinking but it means one has rather a grim future to look forward to, looking after him. Especially as he would rather be alone in London or in Paris or Marseilles and begins to hate me now because he cannot be what he is in front of me. He likes us better when we are not with him and his self-pity has more play. He is not an ogre really so don't let nausea prevent you coming to stay, as it well might – it is partly because my mother and I are both very sensitive people and are perhaps rather easily appalled, but he has got so much worse lately. My mother is coming down tomorrow so the worst will be over but she and I do not really trust each other as she is convinced I do not love her, though I do – and she has a good many prejudices contrary to mine which clash as the more I love people the less I make allowances for them (part of my desire for equality I suppose), making allowances involving a superiority, not really now I come to think of it as humility can permeate anything, but the way I do, does. Point to alter. Please don't stop comforting, it is nothing like Job's and each of your notes, even the coloured card with nothing on works wonders and leaves me fresh and gay. I can't thank you enough. If I see anything nice I will send it you if you don't mind as we have been very close this time and I would like to give you a token but only if I come across one –

> Oh how comely it is and how reviving
> To the spirits of just men long oppressed
> When God into the hands of their deliverer
> Puts invincible might

not that you or I are Samson but that is how I feel. I think you would love my mother and she is anxious to meet you –

I expect Christmas must be very tiring for you and the offices must be wearisome but I will think of you perhaps playing hide and seek in the dark or reading or thinking of me. I will drink your health at a quarter to eight on Christmas night (in champagne!). Much love and write to me ὥς σέο νῦν.

Cyril

This is chiefly to wish you a merry Christmas

> 'The time draws near the birth of Christ'
> 'Everywhere the feast of the babe'
> 'The rain set early in to-night'
> 'And sadly feel our Christmas eve.'

Tell me some bits you like of *Paradise Lost*.

27 Dec 1924.

H. N. Blakiston, Esq.,   [*Posted in Reading.*]
Kirkby on Bain.

In the train Saturday.

Dear Noel,

Thank you for your letter – your distinction of mystic and humanist is a good one – they war in myself and each finding satiety in expression is weakened and yields to the other – isn't this our old trouble of being different at day and at night? in maturer form. II. If reality is a perpetual postponement our thrills for instance would be in the nature of acutely shared longings, the ἵμερος of the soul in the Phaedrus – or they would be moments of intense hope but never moments of satisfaction for that would mean we had achieved reality which you say is impossible but I think myself that some thrills are of fulfilment though open to conviction – imitation is the best way to taste, if you want it, which I do – meanwhile can't we imitate each other till we find someone better I do not mind if you are not the Messiah, being perfectly willing to seek a reed broken in the wind. Tell me more of the man in the house. I had a dismal Christmas and am glad to leave – my mother has shipped Major C. off to London so is not alone with him. He is trying to conceal his joy under an air of martyrdom. ½ an hour would not be worth it but go to the Master* the 10th and meet me in town on the 9th and we can go and see some thing and talk and have a good dinner and stay the night. I will come up on the 8th if necessary and we can do the same – we will have more time then and be less retrogressive – only be willing to abandon yourself to the joys of food and wine and light and colour – I have plenty of money and if this suits you I will book a room only I would rather 9th than 8th – bring tails if you have them – as Minehead and Lock House have failed may I count on you for this? York House Minehead – I will think of you as before.

I hope you enjoy your dances – Roger asks to be remembered to you and has sent me a lovely Augustine. Rain is driven by the gale which shrieks outside Reading waiting room like the Mistral in wayside stations of Languedoc but I am free!

Much love.
Cyril

30 Dec 1924.

H. N. Blakiston, Esq.,   York House,
Kirkby on Bain.   Minehead.

Dear Noel,

Thank you for your letter. Well, can you manage some arrangement on your way back? it would suit me much better and gives you a last

*A. C. Benson.

chance to compensate for this and the Lock House – the 19th or 15th or 16th which ever you like. We can meet as before and talk and dine and go to the B.M. or something, it would suit me best to meet you for tea, say at Jules Hotel in Jermyn Street but I will have to get a room in advance so let me know. A.C.B. does not know when you leave him I suppose so you can easily take a day off at that end. We would feel less hurried if we met only for the afternoon and besides dinner can be rather nice – so do come – Maurice and Piers came last night, J.B. is doubtful as Sligger has been writing to the wrong address. It is very nice here though pouring with rain. One can see the coast of Wales and the hills of Exmoor and there are quite nice shops and old houses and churches with v. lovely rood screens and this is a comfortable house with excellent food. Sligger is being very nice indeed and Maurice is very happy and witty in proximity to Piers who is lovely and pleasant though humanism entirely prevails and German and Greek are almost the only tongues spoken – we have the pleasant private school feeling which is the best atmosphere for Sligger's parties and Maurice is really incredibly witty though in no way a strain. I hope John turns up as I shall be rather aimless otherwise. I shall probably stay on here alone with Piers after the 10th rather than go home again as I doubt if I shall have anywhere to go – it is after lunch, the rain is beating on the window, the fire blazes and we sit in armchairs talking and reading, if only you were here it would be perfect

ὃν μὲν γὰρ ζωόι γε φίλων ἀπανεύθεν ἑτάιρων
βουλὰς ἐζάμενοι βουλεύσαμεν

Piers' soft Irish voice quoting the Iliad, the roar of wind and rain, the crackling fire and we could have gone out and had tea together. I think I shall have to work all next vac. for schools, would you be able to come to some little place on the coast of Provence, in the Montagnes des Maures, near Garde Frainet with me and Sligger. I would try and get Roger too, or one other person and we could see Avignon etc on the way and then rest quietly by the sea φιλεοντέ τε τερπομένωτε enjoying the mountains and the sea and the spring sunshine and working and talking. Don't refuse yet anyhow, though it may not come to anything; if we did that I could take you any where you want to go in the summer probably – still Easter on that unspoilt coast of the Riviera would be very lovely though I pine for the asphodel on the ναος of Segesta, the orange blossom rising up to the walls of

Monreale, and most of all for the little boat from Syracuse crossing the glassy jade green waters of the Syrtes to the white curving beaches, the palms and white houses of Tripoli in Barbary, Tarábulus el Gharb – go on sending lines when you feel like it till you feel equal to writing a long letter as it is very nice getting them and try and manage Town at the end of the vac. I wish you were here though. Sligger sends his love and will write, Maurice ἀγγέλιαν ἱκάνην – I can only think of you as being abroad with me at present. This party is joyful but unreal and I suppose you are in the midst of those dances – your proximity has increased if anything since I left home.

Cyril

1 Jan 1925.

H. N. Blakiston, Esq.,   York House,
Kirkby on Bain.   Minehead.

Dear Noel,

Thank you for your letter. Of course I don't loathe you, it was a forlorn hope wiring only I would not like to miss you on your way back from Rye. This conspiracy to make you think you are ordinary seems to me deplorable. Of course you can be ordinary if you choose and sometimes it is best but I do not think you for instance can ever overdo Sebastianism (except in so far as you exclude me!) – if you go on saying that you are ordinary you will certainly become so but aloofness suits you far better than anything else and it seems to me a pity that you should submerge such a fine individuality and become affable and curious rather than serious and remote. You often adopt Sebastian's trick of not signing letters for instance which I don't think deliberate but a pure coincidence as you have probably forgotten that point of his yet it shows that in the qualities that produced it you must be similar. I grant a prophet is without honour in his own country and one cannot do much with home as a setting – I don't think I deceive you about not being ordinary nor do I urge you to pose, only to be enterprising and brave, to choose and reject rather than take things as they come – when you have been at Oxford you have not behaved at all unusually yet you overwhelmed Roger and Kenneth Clark, as also Sligger and Maurice Bowra who thinks you are an 'astoundingly great man' though he is hard to please. All these

I grant had been prepared by me to some extent but they would not be so impressed if there was not truth in it and they would notice a false note at once – they are better judges than Freddy and the King's crew who have grown so used to you that they do not realise what you are or how you have changed or than the people of Magdalene or Lindsay and Kesteven and Holland whom you wish to convince that you are nice at the cost of ceasing to be fine. I do not urge you to be affected or to cause pain but I think you have genius and it must naturally isolate you (cf. 'what was he doing the Great God Pan') and genius is the blessing of Reality and to be disloyal to it is almost the unforgivable sin, it is not by your doing that you have genius and it needs all humility to try to serve it and obey it and follow the rough and lonely journey far from lights and comfort and culture and home after wishing you had not gone and often thinking you have gone wrong but knowing that you have realised yourself and have given yourself for the talent entrusted you, as the soil gives its strength and fertility to the plant it has to nourish and if you know that, though you are hated or forgotten, what else is fame? I do not know any one else who I think has genius but I think I have some myself (it sounds complacent but no one has denied it and it is a terrifying rather than a comfortable thought) and though we both have very little indeed it is enough to be rather overwhelming when combined, as I think it is meant to be – you remember the contrast between Shakespeare and Bunyan in Pearsall Smith's* prose book? Apart from you I am a Shakespeare individualist, with you we are Christian and Faithful, but though we are only the gloves which great light is wearing but not of our giving we are far removed from others by it be we never so humble or careless of ourselves – but I think at present aloofness and quietness and seriousness and no little incuriosity and intolerance are the best and most progressive things in you but the fonder you are of me the better as it makes us a better unit for whatever we have to do. I don't think either of us can really stand alone, we are both rather doubters and humanism would prevail. Is this all rubbish? Of course by imitating each other we get nearer to the compound character of you and I which is the really progressive thing, don't you think,

*Logan Pearsall Smith (b. Millville, N.J. USA, 18 October 1865, d. 2 March 1946). Educated Harvard University and Balliol. Man of Letters. Naturalised as British subject 1913. Had two houses, 11 St. Leonard's Terrace, London SW3, and Big Chilling, Warsash, Hants. Brother of Mrs. Berenson and Alys Russell (q.v.).

and the point is to include as much of ourselves as possible in that character – it is like the shadow of a thing that two candles throw, there are two shadows but there is a darker, intenser patch where they overlap, and as they move closer (imitation) this patch grows and finally becomes almost all embracing, each candle retains a little faint and individual shade but they have produced a deep and black impression on the wall they could never do alone. I am afraid that is tortuous, but you see what I mean. I do not think we need rush the process but we must improve our personal relations as much as we can because if either of us rattles the other, he naturally retreats to the fastnesses where he is alone and in cricket or modern French prose for instance, increases the area of his individual shade – but I think we are doing admirably at present and have rather put absence in its place – the secret lies I think in exploiting the postal services, a scrawl that is the result of a minute's thought is more binding than an hour of sterile longing; at least there is a cumulative force in your p.c.'s etc. which proves ἀλλ ἔκας ουκ ἐκας 'εστι more than any amount of picturing you coping at home or travelling abroad, but everything helps. I must stop now to have a bath for water is failing but I will go on to-morrow and pour out my more personal woes.

Friday. Of course I disagree with the parable of the talents in that I think everyone has perfect free will to neglect the talent like the man *che fece il gran rifiuto*, and there is no retribution for people who do – only one's own conscience can punish one and one is at perfect liberty to dispense with that. I am beginning to find though that there do seem some curious laws of cause and effect, crime and suggestions, and a very real irony of fate by which certain deliberate acts of selfishness or cruelty do seem to bring about pain to me or a certain blight on action or a very ludicrously appropriate rebuff, however much I may think I have avoided any remorse. This is partly because I tend to connect things to myself by suggestion – if I find I am hurt by Bobbie I think it is because I have not written to my grandmother and if I hurt Bobbie I at once expect nothing I do to prosper till I have been forgiven, and it usually doesn't, partly also because I have a strong though superstitious conception of ὕβρις and το φθόνερον, which corresponds to the influence of your 'Jewish upbringing' in you – both these ideas are very Herodotean and I think suggestion was at the back of the efficacy of the oracles though the 'jealous God' is essentially Jewish but I hope he doesn't visit the sins of the fathers upon the children! Irony works in the way that the selfish man is never punished till the influence of love or vanity makes him desire to be unselfish when follows pain and failure. Deliberate cruelty I think must inevitably react in an indirect rather unfathomable way on the person who inflicts it.

But how awful for you to wade through these cautious and qualified meanderings when you are not feeling serious. I understand perfectly the staleness that seizes one and please don't feel you ought to be doing anything about this sort of rubbish only write to me or send me postcards and make allowances for me feeling rather thoughtful at present. I find myself I have hardly any control over sudden failure of reality etc. and being busy very easily accomplishes it but it is all right as long as we understand each other and do not expect *confessiones fidei* or try to screw ourselves up to make them when the rocks of conviction are submerged by the high tides of ἀσχυλιαι – wait for the ebb. As you say the defection of Brook largely through Sligger muddling, partly through panic at the intellectual level of the rest of us, has left me rather stranded. We are all very fond of each other but I retire a lot by myself and think about you, φιλοσοφοῦμεν ἀνευ μαλάκιας – I wish I had your power of self examination, the best kind of courage, and still have your capacity to act on the conclusions you draw. Sligger is admirable, very witty at times and very perspicacious beneath his mask of insensitive benevolence. He holds strong views about you and thinks you have a very good effect on me 'I am so glad Cyril is making a new friend' which shews rather an ignorance of our intimacy now nearly 5 years old. He told Maurice that he thought I was too good for this world; which shows I must have changed – he would do a lot to bring us together and is the sort of security that parents like. I can't help feeling a little resentful of A.C.B. the friend of Rylands* and the author of *The Reed of Pan* whose clever manipulation of dates has robbed me of 3 chances of your company. Do not fail for the 13th or whenever suits you.

> 'As thou from year to year hast sung too late
> for my relief; yet hadst no reason why,
> whether the muse or love call thee his mate
> Both them I serve and of their train am I.

(don't take that seriously but it has been on my brain). Maurice is

*George Rylands. 'Dadie' (b. 23 October 1902). KS. King's. Fellow of King's. University Lecturer in English Literature. CBE 1961.

very fine and has to bear many slights which make me sad though I am looking forward to being here alone with Piers which will probably happen while you enjoy your deserved freedom at Rye. Meanwhile the wind howls and the rain falls and you are very real, the companion of solitary walks and the associate of thoughts that are often wistful but never painful because our relations are so adequate now and it makes it a pleasure to be alone, to linger in my bath or in my bed room and pursue undisturbed quiet dialectic with you – this does not mean you are only real when no one else is in the room. The Lock House will probably be sold as my mother cannot face home life with Major C. I expect you must have a lot of floods round you.

Much love. Cyril.

Maurice sends love – Piers is very curious about you. Maurice goes on the 8th. and Sligger on the 10th and Piers and I will stay on or go off to Dartmoor together till it is time to see you. My mother and father are in London. You must be very patient to have read all this.

8 Jan [?] *1925.*

N. Blakiston, Esq.,   York House,
Kirkby on Bain.   Minehead.

Dear Noel,

I am so glad you like Milton. Once you have grasped his icy convention one finds it packed with real feeling, don't you think, nothing of the Augustan unreality of Pope and Co, though I am afraid he is not much of a mystic, but perhaps he was for he pleased Blake. I haven't read either of those Plato dialogues. Maurice speaks very highly of the *Timaeus* but says it is mannered and incredibly difficult. I only like the early ones and *Symposium* really. The most appalling realistic touch in Plato, I think, is the way his young men flag and lose their touch as the argument goes on and on. Phaedrus is the only one that I can really visualise and Alcibiades and Lysis. I feel stimulated by all the topics of conversation you proposed but would like to have devoted a long time to yourself.

We went a very nice trip over Exmoor on Monday, it is rather good country with excellent churches. I sat in front and thought of you and the car stopping in the lanes by Waynfleet. I go for runs by myself in the afternoon, which is intolerably hearty, 6 or 7 miles over the hills or along the shore in shorts and sweater and sandals from Naxos. I am really getting rather good at the endurance side as well as mere sprinting, at which I am so far undefeated. We have had no visitors except some people called Orwin, a son at Eton. Maurice goes tomorrow which cheers me as when he is here though he is witty and helpful and fine and inspiring and indeed almost faultless he makes the atmosphere of intrigue and intensity overpowering.

Much love
Cyril

25 Jan 1925.

H. N. Blakiston, Esq.,   Balliol College,
Magdalene College,   Oxford.
Cambridge.

Dear Noel,
    Thank you so much for your letter and the remarks about egoists and God the metaphysician. I like your emendation very much – do you know the story of the Jews coming to Alexandria and being questioned about their philosophy and finding that 'I am that I am' though good enough for Palestine was there criticised 'this statement predicates existence merely', – or 'this statement, while merely predicating existence, assumes the attribute of speech' which drove them to translate the O.T. into Greek, hence the Septuagint. The best picture of God (humanist is speaking) is the scene in heaven fairly early on in Anatole France's *Ile des Pingouins* – God makes some very good remarks especially 'though immutable in essence age has softened me a little as is apparent to anyone who has read my two testaments' – the mystic has little chance here, I expect you find the same – the intensity of the earlier Minehead has put everyone into the 8th week of term feeling – social life has almost ceased – the last week of Minehead, all too short, left me with an intense reclusiveness which I try to continue here – I see mainly Bobbie and Piers with a good deal of Roger and Maurice and a bit of K. Clark – who is usually bearable for the first three weeks. Also something of Loxley and O'Connor – Loxley is definitely nice but dull and O'Connor though a vain little egoist carries it off with some sincerity and charm.

Bobbie is lovelier than ever but more complacent and insular and self indulgent than before – he is superb to me but there is a summary and tacit intolerance in his views on people and things that is very distressing and comfort seems always to come first – his best point I think is the utter absence of vanity which makes him distinguished and refined and his infinite warmth with me – he is very just and ethically one of the finest people I know, again because he is proud but never vain – Maurice is quite admirable and devoted to Roger and K, and I never see a soul beside them and Bobbie which may be narrowing but I find not so as all the spade-work is done and one can carry on a conversation from day to day finding it always easier to get straight to realities and we pass from masterpiece to masterpiece with the united appreciation of several minds – we are not heartless about each other but very considerate and though we laugh a lot, almost excessively serious in our attention to values. Egoism is very disastrous I think – I am pretty bad that way – I am very obsessed at present not so much with the egoism of the type of William for instance but the tacit implied Narcissus complex (excuse the jargon) of Bobbie and Piers – both lacking most of the vanity of the ordinary egoist just as one imagines Narcissus looking into the pool, not with vanity but with troubled curiosity or flower-like absorption. Bobbie and Piers are both gentle and considerate, never go to see anyone, never talk about themselves (the vain egoist on the other hand must have an audience) but spend hours stroking themselves, having baths, and carry self indulgence to excess, both seem remote when in the room and seem to ooze οὐκέτι ἥζω πρός σέ, πρός σέ οὐκέτι ἥζω. They correspond closely to Albertine if ever you read any Proust, their egoism lies in their reserve not in their loquacity, it is fugitive and cloistered, often wayward and listless, their consideration and niceness is usually that of a mother to her child when she is going out for the evening, remorse for leaving it for pleasure it cannot understand, they are bad people to love.

furitis procaces Naiades
amore sacro et irrito
Ephebus iste flos erit

Sorry for all this – I saw Ronnie Watkins for a little the other day and thought him rather nice. I wish he wouldn't smoke a pipe. He seemed a good deal more serious and less selfish than the William-Freddy-type.

I find Sebastianism working rather in spite of myself – would you like a small owl made of Copenhagen china, very good modelling and glaze, as a token of last vac? It is a good bird as it looks both mystical and humanist, the emblem of wisdom and Athens and of mystery and night – tell me if you would like it and I will send it you. Tell me also if there is any hope of you being able to come abroad next vac – we could probably spend a week in Provence or the Midi while Sligger goes to Rome and then subside and work at some village on the Provençal coast between Hyères and Cannes where there would be no distraction beside sun and scenery – I would enjoy it enormously, I must work though, unfortunately – anyone else you wanted could probably be got. Finances would not be much, you could be Sligger's guest you see but if you could raise about £10 for your journey there and back it would be rather helpful. I would probably have money if we want to go sightseeing in Provence at all – try and view this project with some warmth, can you? The rather odd locality has been carefully chosen so that I cannot start from there and go somewhere else by any logical process. Italy means Sicily, Sicily means Tripoli and the Pyrenees mean Seville with me as a rule but if the weather is good the *Côte des Maures* would be lovely and we could almost certainly take a week for Provence or Carcassonne. I have πόθος for a place called Seo de Urgel near Andorra which we might manage too. I have never been there. Write to me when you feel like it and don't mind what sort of letter – let me know about the owl. Jack's Christmas card of Angers came yesterday, can you thank him very much.

Much love
Cyril

Sorry if I seem to gossip.

10 Feb 1925.

H. N. Blakiston, Esq., Balliol College,
Magdalene College. Oxford.

Dear Noel,
  Χαῖρε – Thank you for your nice letter. I will send you the [owl] but I have been idle about doing it up in string – though I packed it myself in a box. I am so glad you think Provence feasible, let me know how it is received at home. There is a nice – Tuesday. I can't remember

what that remark was going to be. I am fairly happy and the even tenor of the term is well under way – oh yes – there is a nice 'way of all flesh' flavour about the man who felt the need for religion and liked social work. I made good blood to O'Connor about you – it seemed quite unnecessary, though he was very pleased to be given your love. I see a lot of him now, practically every day, he and I and Bobbie and Piers dine or lunch or breakfast together quite a lot – I doubt if he has such real qualities as Loxley, his ideal is a kind of self-development on lines of capacity and restraint till he considers himself sufficiently a 'man' to present himself to his lady as fit to be her friend – like the knight doing deeds for his mistress. Loxley on the other hand cares for nothing but his friends but he is rather awkward and a little boastful (golf etc.), as Bobbie says O'Connor though not as good looking has twice as much charm and considerably better taste in the company he keeps. He is modest and thoughtful and humorous in a quiet way. Peter [romps?] rather or corroborates too much. Kenneth Clark likes him. He by the way is indignant about Louis Turner whom he says he has only met once, on a boat, and hated him – he came down to stay with some quiet and intellectual Trinity men whom he annoyed so much by his bad manners and vulgarity that they threw him in the river and tied him to a lamp post. I said you had not thought he could really be a friend of K's – he is very nice this term; much improved, though I only see him about once a week. Turner was not at Marlborough or any other public school. Rylands was here the week end. I did not see him hardly as I forgot about the meal I was supposed to have with him and had it with Bobbie. Bobbie and Roger and Maurice send their love, so does O'Connor and Loxley. Bobbie is being very nice indeed. I struggle with history but reality has fled. The nights are wet and stormy and engender restless desires to pack and start off in the wind and rain alone on a long journey. If you could raise £10 or a little more it would be all you would need next vac. for coming abroad. Sligger has just come in, sends love, and hopes you can come. I think it would be great fun if you can manage it. We should see something of Provence – probably alone and pick Sligger up later. Aigues Mortes, Avignon and the Pont du Gard are certainly desirable. After it would be a case of working, basking in the sun, and scrambling about the Montagnes des Maures or the Iles d'or. We could boat and bathe if necessary. Sligger has to go and see the Pope about something in which time we could make a little trip on our own. We might go down to Carcassonne or Albi or the

Cerdagne too. Sorry for not writing before. Let me know about your plans. If you can't come you won't be letting me down at all as I can get Piers so don't worry. Would you care to come over here at all? K's car is all right if you would like to risk another effort at sight-seeing when the weather is better. Roger is anxious to see you.

Much love
Cyril

28 Feb 1925.

Noel Blakiston, Esq.,   Balliol College,
Magdalene College.   Oxford.

Friday (in die ven.)

Dear Noel,

SUIT*

Thank you for your cards. I am glad you liked the owl. I planned

AWL

getting it for you when I was at home at Christmas but was not in London to choose it. I think it is an appropriate fusion of mystic and humanist don't you think? (THINK.) Let me know soon about the vac. The present state here seems to be that Sligger has found a v. small place called Pardigon (PARDIGON) with a hotel, 'quiet and healthy' and in the most unspoilt part of the riviera (RIVIERA), near St. Tropez (TROPEZ) he himself can't go there till the end of March but suggests I should go out first – in which case if your Tutorship begins in April (private schools break up then) you could come first especially if it takes place in the S. of France (FRANCE) – if you don't have this tutorship you could come any time for as long as you liked. I don't know about the YORK COCK Lock COOK COCHIN House at present – it would be very nice there in Spring and my mother has made it perfectly all right again with servants and warmth. If you could not come abroad with

ME

we could probably meet there but try and come to Pardigon

GAUDY

(PARDIGON) if you can – it sounds a lovely place with a sandy cove

STUMPS

and woods and hills and rocks and Mediterranean shrubs – and would

*A joke on the illegibility of a previous letter.

60

LIVELY
be lovely in the sunshine.
SHRIMPS   LONELY
STUBBS   WAIVE
The hotel is an old chateau I believe. You need only raise your journey
money (about £5 each way and we could go out together – and wait
for Sligger who has to see the Pope (POPE). It sounds ideal for us as
                                              COULD
Sligger lends security and sanity to the proceeding and it would be
very nice if we went out together. Let us know soon as things are
rather held up – it sounds a good place because that part of the
Riviera has a sort of Greek flavour because it was colonised by them
and also it is very unspoilt and lovely and we can run wild I should
think instead of tennis etc. – nor is there anywhere near to tempt one
to sightsee except Toulon (TOULON) which has battleships and old
streets by the harbour and a good bookshop. It would be nice to have
a day at Avignon on our way out if we could spare it – we needn't
bother about anywhere else. Sligger wants a fourth. I don't know who
it will be but no one very bloody as I have a veto. Everything is nice
here in a subdued way. I have read a lot lately. Propertius who is
good, Ovid's metamorphoses some of which, Narcissus for instance,
are admirable and a certain amount of the bloodiest kind of constitu-
tional history. I have little time or interest for people but see a lot
of Bobbie – who is superb – and O'Connor whom I find very adequate.
Sensible – sensitive and restrained – we went a 10 mile walk on Sunday
– Piers is immersed in work and Maurice rather tiresomely emotional
with several people who being always out, cause him pain. I never
go and see anyone except Bobbie. Loxley is rather tiresome and
cultivates Trinity men, all and sundry. He was described by one of
Bobbie's friends as 'rather a stiff' which is true at present. Sebastianism
is on the rise with me. How wise of you to go away for the last week
of term. I find people on the whole not to justify the trouble of talking
to them at present if you know the feeling. Bobbie is not like that
and Timothy nice because he does not talk at all, but K. Clark and
Sligger and Co leave me cold. The unending wind has come to obsess
me a lot – I do hope it will be all right about next vac. It seems a
marvellous opportunity. Write to me sometime.
                    Much love
                      Cyril
                    [CYRIL]

9 March 1925.

Noel Blakiston, Esq.,   Balliol College,
Magdalene College.   Oxford.

Dear Noel,

Thank you for your letter. It was lucky as a matter of fact as the day before I got it Sligger had to abandon Pardigon as (i) they had no rooms. (ii) he has to take a sister out to Italy and bring her back. He wants me to go to Florence with him in April and Piers may come too. Meanwhile could you come for a week to the Lock House if I am there? Any week in March but I am not sure yet if I will be there – with any luck my father won't, only my mother; in which case it would be quite fun – if you don't mind no entertainments much. I could probably get Roger or Timothy for a night while you were there – if you liked – I don't expect your tutorship will be till April. I could see you in France on my way to Sligger probably if you liked. There is nothing to dread at the Lock House much except Major C. you know. It was very wise of you to wonder if I saw no one without being morbid – when I wrote to you I wasn't but all this week I have been – very. But I can't feel fondness for people though I am unhappy by myself, or if I do feel fondness it is always undone by some discovery. K. undid P.N.L. by describing his golf team against Eton, in which K was playing and Peter was a model of academic heartiness and said 'Toot-toot' each time he addressed the ball which was too much for K! K. himself is rather an old sinner I feel and Maurice rather bloated – Roger leads a full college life and can drink half a gallon of beer in half an hour which he seems to regard as an accomplishment also he dines with dons he despises because they have votes at All Souls. Luckily Bobbie shares my aversions at present so all is well. Also Timothy is very nice indeed and Piers in his lucid intervals from an exam. I am sorry to sound so uncharitable, I feel very lonely. My fire burns and the wind moans in my window, withered Narcissus droop over the mantelpiece and the Lincoln Imp has never been cleaned

Lod . . .   What dost think on?
Flam . . .   Nothing; of nothing: leave thy idle questions
               I am in the way to study a long silence:
               To prate were idle. I remember nothing.
               There's nothing of so infinite vexation
               As man's own thoughts.
Lod.   O thou glorious strumpet!

Why does one read, think, and feel so much more in the vac. than here? It is really rather creditable that we have kept up communications the way we have – I have not written to another soul and can only manage to write home once a fortnight and then have nothing to say, so forgive these drear effusions. They are all I can do. Think of the intensity of our confessions of faith – the time I took unravelling yours and our, mine at any rate, present sterility.

What is that noise?
    The wind under the door
What is that noise now? What is the wind doing?
    Nothing again nothing.
Do you know nothing? Do you see nothing
Do you remember
Nothing?
    I remember
        Those are pearls that were his eyes.

The bottom of the last page was my low-water mark. Maurice came in and cheered me up and then Sligger to say that his other sister also wanted him in April and would I be content to go a fortnight anywhere I liked by myself. Visions of a leisurely exodus in April gladdened me; of early morning in Aquitaine and the streams and fields and green trees and pussy willows from Poictiers to Bordeaux and Angoulême – then the gorse blooming on the Landes the snow on the Pyrenees, the Adour at Bayonne and crossing into Spain 'by Fontarabia'. Then I read some Dante and went to sleep. I have been through Beaulieu – it looked nice. I could come out part of the way with you and your boy if you liked and leave you at Avignon and go on down to Spain by Perpignan – I want to go to the extreme south and Tangier. I am sorry we can not go abroad together for your first time but it would be nice if we went as far as Avignon. I haven't heard from my mother yet about home but I presume you can come and stay if we are there – what is your *puer** like, have you seen him? I should think a good deal depends on it, whether he is like Prabahka or Ian.

I am slowly coming round to Vergil and Dante which I never thought I would do – but I read the Eclogues which I thought admirable, better often than Theocritus, at least more humorous and some lines

ite domum saturae, venit hesperus, ite capellae

*The pupil N.B. was going to tutor, Howard Hartog, at Beaulieu. From this time N.B. and J.B. tutored him in alternate holidays.

rather magical – and
Sunday night:

I am improving and read Spanish time-tables. I went a 13 mile walk with H.M. O'C. I hope you enjoy Rye, it must be nice there now.

Much love
Cyril

6 April 1925.

Noel Blakiston, Esq.,   Hotel Simon,
at   Cordoba.
Villa Les Nénuphars,
Beaulieu,
Alpes Maritimes,
Francia.

Dear Noel,

This is only a scrawl as I am dead tired from having to stand 12 hours in a 3rd class carriage all to-day. I had a mediocre journey after I left you. I met quite a nice small boy who is at my private and a bearable mother and travelled as far as Biarritz with them. It was nice crossing the Gironde at night and seeing the lights of Bordeaux and there was a good sunrise over the Landes and I went all the way 1st on a 2nd class ticket. I reached Spain yesterday morning and went on to Segovia. Castile was looking rather superb, endless vistas of rolling hills with churches on the horizon and the green of young corn or the brown of fields changing with white ranges of mountains, dark green pine forests, magnificent combinations of sky and cloud and a yellow streak where the sun is shining 25 miles away. All very exhilarating. At Segovia I met Coghlan* and A. Goodden† in the hotel, I had felt rather apathetic till then but meeting them taking an intelligent interest and exuding a stream of filth soon restored my independence and I left there this morning rejoicing at being alone, '*colui che vince e non colui che perde*', like the green cloth at Verona. The Sierra de Guadarrama were bathed in mist but once through them the sun shone and I drove across Madrid and caught the Andalucia express.

*R. L. Coghlan (b. 1903 d. 1960(?)). KS. Went to India.
*A. Goodden (b. 7 December 1901). KS. King's. Diplomatic Service. Consul General. C.B.E. 1956.

S. of Madrid, 'La Mancha' is just like what I said of Castile but a bit bleaker but the Sierra Morena are a very good tangle of wild and wooded mountains with rocks and gorges and oleanders by the water and once through them there are men in enormous black sombreros and fields of asphodel and blind beggars go along the platform singing oriental folk songs to people in the train. The country up to here has been more rolling uplands of corn and olives but the air is very moist and warm and smells divine and the towns are rather good. It is not the real south yet but more enormous and thrilling open spaces and retreating ranges of hills and blue sky and spotless clouds and *ver novum, ver iam canorum, ver venatus orbus est, vere concordant amores, vere nubunt alites* –

I am rather getting over the apathy I was in when I left you and will be happy as soon as I can rest from nights in trains etc. I cannot believe it was only the day before yesterday we were together. I suppose one cannot travel over 1000 miles without it having some influence on the time. To-morrow I see the mosque here and go on to Xeres for the night, or Cadiz, then I rest at Cadiz for a bit and try Africa if I can afford it then to Gibraltar and Ronda from where I hope to walk 4 days through the coast mountains to Granada via Malaga. Pastoral, but hardly cold, that is what I shall be doing on Easter day I expect. Then I shall spend a couple of days at Granada and if you can manage it I will meet you in the evening of Saturday 18th at the Regina Hotel Avignon. We can stay the night there, see it the next morning, and if we are rich enough take a car in the afternoon to the Pont du Gard. If you don't want Avignon we could do Nîmes and Aigues Mortes but I am only writing now so that you will have time to let me know if you can manage Avignon on the 18th. I think it would compensate for the car falling through if we could manage that, so I hope you can. I loved being with you at Kirkby. I think I have never felt so effortlessly intimate with you before, it makes it incredibly hard to remember anyone else now, let alone write to them. We must certainly do a walking tour in the summer. I did enjoy sharing that room and realising that however listless I was I could not be so about you which is rather important, don't you think, when one considers how a slump in the imagination kills absent friends, Lysis or Sebastian. I think you are magnificent too at talking about things because I am interested in them and all sorts of sacrifices like that that you probably think I don't notice. This is a rotten letter but I am dead tired and rather feeble and frail. I think I am going to enjoy this trip, but we must meet at the end. I couldn't reach you before 18th I am afraid. I think of you a lot and the rest of the time am looking at time tables and working out expenditures. Spain is still rather unreal.

Much love
Cyril

8 April 1925.

Señor Don Noel Blakiston,   Hotel Reina Cristina,
Beaulieu.   Algeciras,
                                                      Spain.

My dear Noel,

I am sorry for not writing before but I have hardly had a moment to spare. This place is the complete earthly paradise, though I have only come here for lunch. It is an enormous hotel but beautiful to look at, long and low and rambling wings all covered with flowering wistaria and yellow roses on dark green shutters and a low dark roof, it is all cool and long somnolent rooms ranged round a courtyard full of flowers and a fountain playing. A clock ticks and there is a white bearded gentleman asleep in an arm chair, outside comes the noise of German and the murmur of the wind in the palms. There is a magnificent garden, roses and geraniums and orange blossom and every sort of palm and pine and below a sheet of waveless blue sea and the white cliffs of the rock of Gibraltar on the other side of the bay. No wonder Ulysses stayed 9 years on Calipso's island if it was really near here. The mosque of Cordova is very good indeed, I wish you had been with me, it is quite incredibly large being perfectly square and a forest of pillars and Arab arches and occasional superb doorways and mosaic chapels while it has superb Arab gateways on the outside and a sleepy courtyard to the mosque with oranges and urchins and a fountain playing. I saw a very good service there of the 'professional' kind – magnificent singing and gorgeous sombre vestments while the roof seemed to sway to the echoing organless gregorian chants – yet there was a congregation of two, and the bishop stopped in the lesson to spit, the priest gossiped loudly when the other side was singing, some of the older ones went fast asleep, choir boys left the stalls to talk to friends through the bars and were spanked by the canons when they came back, it was a triumph of

formalism – Seville cathedral is purely Gothic and dark and sombre aisles and magnificent stained glass, deep bells etc. the tower is very fine, it was the minaret of a mosque. Cadiz is an Ionian city of white houses and flowers in the balcony, narrow straight streets and flat roofs ending in every direction in blue sea. It is very like Valletta and Tarentum, all pale symphonies of blue and green and gold. I came back from there by bus along the coast to Algeciras, past some very good places, Tarifa, the most southerly place in Europe looked entirely African with narrow dirty streets, Arab doorways and walls all ruined and veiled women inside with a marvellous view of the mountains of Marocco all along the south and a little further on the lights of Gibraltar. I went from here to Ceuta and down to Tetuan which was superb. It is a completely unspoilt Moorish hill town separated from the sea by 10 miles of waving asphodel and dwarf palm and flowering gorse and broom with enormous crags and precipices behind it. It is full of narrow tunnels and white streets with eastern smells and Arabs and berbers and mosques and dervishes. I wandered about for a long time and saw some dervishes perform in the evening, grave and bearded Arabs sitting round with incredible small boys while they sang and beat a drum till someone had an ecstasy and danced till he fainted and another tore a live snake in pieces with his teeth and ate it raw, all this in a little square under the full moon with minarets and bazaars, lepers and stray cats all round. Here I suppose the spirit was all that mattered not the form, it was very disturbing listening to the throbbing drum and wondering who was going to spring up with closed eyes while someone tried to pull his coat off before he started dancing, completely mesmerised. I came back to-day and go up to Ronda in the mountains where I am going to walk to Granada, 4 days or more, by Malaga and Alhama where there are very good Moorish ruins. I avoid wine and tobacco and went for 2 days without food to discipline the flesh. No time now as my train is going.
continued in the evening.

I am writing in a superb café surrounded by sturdy men playing poker, in enormous black hats red silk jackets mauve knickerbockers and top boots. Someone is playing tangoes on a guitar – I feel as if I ought to fling down a purse of gold dust when I want to pay. Ronda seems rather a bleak town with enormous mountains on every side and cut in half by a gorge that drops down several hundred feet of sheer precipice to a stream below. It is very narrow and there is a Moorish, Roman and Spanish bridge across it. The journey up from

Algeciras is superb chiefly gorges, mountains etc. but quite close to Algeciras are the cork woods which we must certainly explore some time. They cover miles of rolling hills and are nice trees to look at with every sort of other tree growing among them and all the leaves out and white blossom on wild cherries or tangles of broom and vetch and asphodel or reeds and orchids and black pools covered with white water lilies, it looked very tropical and yet homely enough to begin on – We must certainly be explorers. It has always been my chief ambition only I could not face it alone it gives one enough physical activity to keep one happy and thin and one is nearly always in touch with reality through nature and the sense of worship not allowed to decay but gaining strength, like Antaeus from the earth – we could write rather well about it too – but I couldn't face theodolites – the cinema atmosphere in here thickens – enter a lady in riding breeches and scarlet boots who ogles the poker players – it is rather exciting being on the eve of my five days walk. I bought some thick socks in the market and have had my luggage sent on and had a look at the ranges of mountains fading away under the full moon to the Sierra de Tolox 8000 feet high where I must sleep to-morrow night 25 miles from here. Next day I go on 12 miles to Corin where there is a light railway to Malaga going down from the hills to the plain where sugar cane and bananas grow then up into the mountains again to Alhama and Granada on Easter day. I hope to see some good unspoilt villages and un-Americanised inhabitants if possible – it will be nice arriving at ventas, wayside inns with dark cool courtyards and men riding up and tethering their horses in them and talking round the fire in the middle after dinner. I wish to God you were coming too. I shall think of you and drink your health – we must certainly walk to Santiago in the summer it is only a question of whether to start from Ronces-valles or Fontarabia, Namancos, or Bayona's hold. Namancos about halves the distance from the other 3 – though I don't think it matters much where we walk. I hope it is all right about Avignon, if it is can you write and book a room for the 18th at the Regina Hotel and I'll try and meet you there about six o'clock. Don't visit anything if you arrive first but sit in a café – I'll do the same. I shall be pretty uncouth and dirty I expect after nights in the train but I can have a bath there. It is a moderately cheap hotel – a room would be about 20 francs. If you'd rather meet anywhere else – Narbonne, Nîmes, Arles, Toulouse, Carcassonne, Cette, Perpignan I can join you. I hope you are having a nice vac. at Beaulieu. I should think if the weather was nice and you were not required much socially you couldn't help it. I must stop as I must rise early to-morrow – to-day has been my best day so far – in Africa in the morning and 2 hours crossing the straits, a glimpse of the earthly paradise and then the cork woods and the mountains here – also a sense of returning vitality and with it reality returning too and the capacity to write you a better letter than the last one – Arab children are rather shattering and the men are either ridiculous Thief-of-Bagdad creatures or else have dark eyes, straight noses, white teeth and black beards and superb figures altogether e solo in parte vider il Saladino. Spanish children are B+, healthy and animal, and young men, but elderly and middle aged peasants very good indeed, the palm is carried off by the women of Castile and Aragon or occasional better class small boys or young gipsies.

A happy Easter etc. I get laughed at a good deal here you would be pleased to hear (trousers chiefly) Your reality is high.

Much love
Cyril

[? *April 1925*]

H. N. Blakiston, Esq.,
Magdalene College.

Naval & Military Hotel,
Harrington Road,
South Kensington.

Monday night
Sent with diffidence – Tuesday morning –

Dear Noel,

Out of the depths, my mother went to Paris on Thursday and is there now. My father is here and I dined with him, he was bitter and fuddled, full of creeping bitterness about the black box, old sores and modern instances. Hishwish, he said and tried again. He abused the food and the waitresses and martyred himself at intervals; I think he was angry because though I had left it to the last moment I had still been able to get a room here. I was just able to be polite but am haunted by his malignant leer and welcome home, his spotty face and huge wind blown stomach with heaven knows what unpleasant, mean, abuse intended in that meaningless 'Hishwish' like the abuse of tongueless beggars – and over all the enormity of the black box

hanging and hate for me because I never got his wire, *mea culpa,*
mea culpa, and because when I went to Waterloo the box was there
all the time, *mea culpa, mea maxima culpa,* then a vindictive tale of
accumulating tuppences that he must pay and not me or else my guilt
would be removed – then several bills which I have not opened and
a nice letter from Maurice. You must be greeting people you like now,
I envy you. To-morrow I shall be doing the same, but not liking them.
You know there is no longer any question of me liking Bobbie more
than you, this has nothing to do with his behaviour but was the
natural consequence of your letters at Christmas. Also you have the
qualities that I try to attribute to Bobbie, freshness, cold pastoral,
exploring. I thought this was because I saw you less than him, but it
is not so, they remain – at Avignon there began to dawn that feeling
of existing alone with you in the world which made London so awful.

Also you liked the Lock House – Excuse all this you must be very
angry indeed by the time you have got as far but I don't want you to
think I would criticise you to Bobbie in the same way and it cheers me
to know now for certain even if it only embarrasses you. I have always
wanted to like you best but it seemed unfair to Bobbie when I saw you
so little. Not that it matters much only know where you stand. Also
remember that we create the atmosphere in which we live and don't
think chalets etc. will be cess pits of intensity – also that one can say
absolutely anything in a railway carriage if you assume an ordinary
enough voice and in a ship cabin if you turn the fan on. Please don't
think I dither about you but you are very like Tessa* – especially
eating dry bread and Perrier for dinner.

Goodnight

Cyril

Remember to write, and to keep an eye on next vac. I will try and
arrange about our excursion in K's car. Also send you some money
when it comes back to Oxford. I think you are very good about it
and part with it to me with more indifference than I do to you. Also I
can trust you to conceal things from me absolutely, a very useful
quality – though don't think I expect you not to want to know people
when in your first year. My love to Jack. I will ring you up when I
feel desperate – I think you have done a very good Sir Guion about

*Heroine of *The Constant Nymph* by Margaret Kennedy, published a few
months before. Many references to the characters in that book, Tessa, Florence
and Lewis Dodd, and others, appear in these letters.

Monte Carlo, amused or unscathed – I should have probably succumbed and emerged hard and crashing. Also you know I feel nothing but wonder for small boys and am not a vile old man, though besides wonder they are good travelling companions – but that porter at Avignon!

Cyril

23 April 1925.

Oxford.
(writing paper of
Royal Hotel Washington
Irving, Alhambra-Granada,
España.)

Noel Blakiston, Esq.,
Magdalene College.

Dear Noel,

How are you? This place is empty as the grave. I came up yesterday and dined on a rumbling train that seemed to ebb through the green fields as noiselessly as a stream. Then I went and saw the Arab on the cinema and was taken back to Tunis and saw my friend Tayeb in a close-up for a moment in his black burnous. Then I coped with Sligger who was affectionate and kind. No one is up but him and Maurice whom I saw today. He was very refreshing indeed and was facing the term as unwillingly as me. He only wanted to see me and Piers and Yorke* he said. He had seen a lot of Yorke in Paris, also *Henry IV* which he thought superb. Piers got a first in Mods which is rather good as he is a commoner. Maurice told me a nice romantic story of how an incredibly lovely young Prussian nobleman fell from an aeroplane into his battery in the war and for 2 hours Maurice gave him drinks and stroked his hair and the airman was touched and gave him his boots. I have been alone the rest of the day and at last managed to get on with my book. I wrote a whole chapter to-day by my fire and still feel fresh from Naucratis and happy at something done. I began after tea and stopped to go to dinner and found it was half past ten! Sligger and Maurice asked a great deal about you and were very nice. Both are going to Cambridge, and want to see you – Sligger you won't be

*Henry Yorke (b. 1905, d. 1974). Oppidan at Eton. Magdalen, Oxford. Novelist. Pen name, Henry Green.

able to avoid, Maurice is very diffident about whether you would receive him but I would like you to be kind to him as he has a very large capacity for awe indeed and is not such an egoist as he seems and hates Florences* more than anything in the world. Also he is extremely presentable in any society. Do read some Chinese poems. Charles has a copy, the best are some of the '17 old poems' and the ones on pages 90–100. I like best Tchirek river which must be the words of the Tristan piping and also plucking the rushes on p. 84. They are very short but you are probably put off by them now.

I heard from Bobbie at last. Your money is on its way back from Avignon. Excuse my last letter. I have a boy like Jackie in my book but no one else is anyone we know – It is fun doing parents. My love to you.

Cyril

[?1925]   [Oxford]

Dear Noel,

Thank you for your letter. Yesterday was a bloody day. I went without all meals and sulked. To-day was saved by Timothy who came early and with whom I lunched and dined – He wants to learn Spanish for commercial purposes and also to sing and play the mandoline for social ones but was very disarming and attributed his refinement to his brother and me, which was polite but not true.

Here we rebel against Trinity, Maurice and me chiefly, well backed up by Roger, Piers and K. Clark to some extent – it gives one something to rebel against, as you say, and is rather an invincible institution full of budding Florences. Cowardice, complacency and self-deception – we are chaps but we do not say so and that perpetual mutual admiration which is the price they pay to their neighbour not to find them out. I am probably going to run with Timothy this term – I bought Forest Murmurs but part I is not a patch on part II. I miss you rather a lot. To-morrow I dine with Beazley.

Of course I would show you my book first but I think it is rather bad and self-conscious and it gets on very slowly.

*Florence Dodd, of the *Constant Nymph*.

27 April 1925.

H. N. Blakiston, Esq.,   Balliol College,
Magdalene College.   Oxford.

Dear Noel,
    Thank you for your 2 nice letters. I am sorry about the glasses.
They must be rather a nuisance. Bobbie is supposed to wear them. I
don't expect you will have to wear them for long but they seem to
oppose one's Sebastianism like gloves, vests, and walking-sticks. Here
it pours with rain outside and I am writing in Piers' room on his paper
while he reads Proust. Bobbie wrote to say he would send me a long
letter on Friday and come back to-night. Neither have materialised
and dejection, disappointment and a kind of disdain for him make
me in poor form to write to you. Oxford is just bloody, work is
intolerable, there only remains to waste time – one's parents' money,
one's own time. Romance is dead in this self-conscious city and I do
not want experience of which I have had enough or knowledge which
puffs me up, but only romance, I mean the knowledge that one is
using mind, heart and body worthily enough to satisfy one's conscience of what is beautiful and true. The one quotation it is impossible
to corroborate here 'for this is our portion and our lot is this' though
I felt it often at Kirkby, Minehead, The Lock House or watching the
morning in some sunny café watching the passers by. The only
consolations are that Bobbie will probably come tomorrow and my
conscience is regrettably tolerant of time wasted in sweet delight – also
I have three friends who compensate for the total lack of anybody
else whom I want to see. Timothy is incredibly bracing and one
listens gravely to him like a small boy who is trying to interest one
in his latest craze – and one feels it is after all about as valuable as
anything one's parents are interested in and considerably more real
to him than their interests to them so one goes to see the model farm,
the toy theatre, the Indian fire – and so why not commercial Spanish
and the mandoline? Also he is sympathetic and understanding besides
being so refreshing, rather pleasantly exclusive, and it so happens I
can see him every day without losing one vestige of my independence
which usually goes wholesale into the hands of the type he represents.
Piers asks a lot of questions about you, his soft Irish voice is very
soothing, he pulls the blind and turns the light on at 3 o'clock because
he is in no mood for summer and sits indoors reading Proust – you

73

would like him a lot I think – he is modest (aware, loyal, etc!) serious, amusing, exclusive, enormously appreciative and so sympathetic that I never dare pour out my woes to him because he would weep and I should feel a brute. Also he is incredibly lovely, and Timothy tries to copy his clothes! Talking to him or Maurice is like getting into one's bath. I had a letter from William yesterday, rather a bad one. This is a tiresome letter I am afraid but I am in a poor way. I meet Yorke at lunch with Maurice on Tuesday and the latter hopes to call on you next Sunday morning. I can't cash the cheque for you to-day but will write again to-morrow sending money. I wish to God you were here nobody is very real despite my apparent enthusiasm for them which is only because they are fellow sufferers – how nasty undergraduates are, I feel like the Labour Party. Sligger's being quite nice but will urge me to eat more and get to know more people.

Much love

Cyril   and to Jack

I think the ugliest vice one is prone to is that brutal cowardice one learns at school where one is meanly embarrassed by people through snobbery and then is bloody to them – especially one's parents, it takes one so long to eradicate and also fails for no one is going to like one for looking as if one did not belong to one's father. I suppose it is not wholly cowardice but partly the acute sensitiveness of scholboys.

I wish it was this time last week.

[? *29 April 1925.*]

N. Blakiston, Esq.,   Balliol College
Magdalene College.   Oxford.

Dear Noel,
    Thank you for your letters. Maurice would love to lunch on Sunday. This is not really all I owe you I don't think. I should cash it quickly! We are settling down. Bobbie is back and I have something to worship and no one else matters much, though they are all nice, and send their love to you. About Sligger's chalet, would August suit you and the party to consist of F.F.U., ἱέρευς τις, you, me, Piers, Roger, Henry

Yorke, Tony Powell* and probably someone else harmless. Piers and I settled this this evening but if you can think of any changes let me know. I doubt if Timothy could get away but I could ask him – I am as it were forming the cabinet which will then be submitted to Sligger, who however has already put forward you, Piers, and Roger and would certainly approve of the other two. We can leave questions of time and money, the point is if you would like those people, granted we create the atmosphere etc and that everyone wants peace. It is extremely nice getting letters from you, and makes the mornings bearable. Everyone sends you their love. I don't like this term. Piers and I still keep up the pretence of winter but soon we must yield. I pass the time with Bobbie, kill it without him – much love.

Cyril

It sounded a nasty dream – my father wants to come down here but is torn with indecision because he wants to eat lobster Newburg which the chef will only make for four ∴ either I must invite two friends (natural conclusion) or (preferable) I must say it is for four and he will eat their shares. I dread his coming but it will be good for my natural cowardice and with luck indecision about the lobster and dislike of travelling till it is hot will keep him away, especially if dreams go by contraries – but perhaps I *have* got some brothers. It is nice to lie in bed trying to think of a reason for getting up and be given it by hearing the messenger leave a letter from you.

Love is sent by Timothy, Piers, Bobbie, Maurice – I am tired of people in my sitting room.

7 May 1925. Telegram.

Noel Blakiston,
Magdalene.

Isn't life awful what do you recommend.

Cyril

*Anthony Dymoke Powell. Tony (b. 21 December 1905). Eton, Oppidan. Balliol. Novelist. CBE 1956.

8 May 1925.

Noel Blakiston, Balliol College,
Magdalene College. Oxford.

Dear Noel,

I am sorry for not writing before. I began a letter to you but it was so lugubrious that I thought I'd wait till I was more cheerful which doesn't however seem likely to arise. Maurice enjoyed his week end very much and most of all lunching with you. He appreciated Jack and William very much indeed and was able to transmit a good deal of his enjoyment of the party to me when he came back. I hope you liked him.

Don't say anything to Sligger that may make him think I am extravagant, not that you would, only he has rather the parent complex – but can be very witty. I have just asked Yorke to lunch, with Maurice and Timothy. Roger is better a little this term though the day Maurice came back from Cambridge he and Dannreuther* rolled a beer barrel across the lawn amid applause and Maurice and Bobbie and I had to pull the blinds down. Gordon Maxwell† is coming here this week end. I can't get K's car as he is using it which is a bore. Sligger is going next week I believe. He wants to see you about the chalet – it would have to be August or not at all I think he has gone and asked another awful man in spite of warnings so it is not worth moving heaven and earth to go there as it might be bloody. Especially as I have an almost permanent dislike for the Alps – though the country just around the chalet itself is magnificent – turf and stream and forest – but we might go off and climb something or walk into Italy or travel out.

I am in a very low state – finding it almost impossible to work, at the same time being actually guilty of wasting time. There is no romance in this city: only experience (γ) and learning (δ), there are not even any walks and I don't like the buildings. Only a devastating sense of lacking an object, of acquiring pernicious habits, of loneliness and humiliation. Bobbie is more social than ever and now has taken to cricket. Timothy and Piers are nice and Maurice indispensable. I mope and read guidebooks chiefly of Turkey from wanting to visit

*Denis S. Dannreuther (b. 16 February 1904, d. 17 July 1939). KS. Balliol. Fellow of All Souls 1927. Barrister-at-law.

†Gordon Maxwell (b. 2 May 1905). KS. Operating Manager (Railways) London Transport 1947–70. CBE 1967.

Constantinople and Asia Minor. There is a very good place called
Amasia. Have you tried the Chinese poems? Honestly they are good,
though slight. Forest Murmurs too I find a cure. I think a pilgrimage
is indicated. Much love. Forgive telegrams, not wholly serious. *Vox
quoque Moerim deest.*

Cyril

May 1925.

Noel Blakiston, Esq.,	Balliol College,
Magdalene College.	Oxford.

Dear Noel,

How are you? I am sinking. I feel dissatisfied with everyone and
study time tables and guide books. July will be no good for the chalet
as I have to be in Oxford in the middle of it for a viva and Sligger has
asked a lot of New College people then. I shan't go to the chalet at
all I don't think if you don't come, so we might meet somewhere else.

I hope Maurice behaved himself. I don't think he would bring back
bad blood as did Sligger (about Thame) — did Jack have a nice 21-ster?

I see a good deal of Bobbie, we are in difficulties — (Trinity etc) —
I would rather quarrel with him than talk to anyone else but neverthe-
less am miserable. Damn Oxford.

late

boat from England
to Gibraltar
Marseilles
from France
to Gibraltar
Marseilles
from Marseilles
to Italy.
Seo. scheme

not late

staying in England
going to Holland
to France — Normandy, Central France,
Southern France
to the Rhine

there must be a pilgrimage.

14 May 1925.

H. N. Blakiston, Esq.,   Balliol College,
Magdalene College.   Oxford.

Dear Noel,

Thank you ever so much for your letter. The cowslips recovered beautifully and scent the room – it was very nice to hear about your difficulties. Newton sounds nice, especially reading Sebastian with him, I haven't read any Pater either since last autumn – I have nothing to advise about your planning except that I entirely approve of any plans to quicken Jack's spiritual life – whether the

    divine
Idaea take a shrine
of Chrystall flesh through which to shine

or not – also it is nice to think of you benefacting and being appreciated. Nothing so thrilling happens here – we are all so experienced and consequently so unromantic but your flowers and letter have made spring rather a reality at last and I walked along the river fields with Piers yesterday and to night after dining with him took him out to Dorchester in a car while green hedges and alluring woods glided by in the setting sun and we saw the abbey and returned, δύσετο τ'ἠέλιος etc but Piers and I cannot get beyond an elderly and genial comradeship now – we eat meals without talking; where there are others, our eyes rove, and in the car we said little and I thought of the Wye with you and have no idea what he thought of at all. He is a companion in distress and no more. Timothy I have even less in common with and after Bobbie, I think I care more for Maurice than anyone else here – and the fact that such affection can be nothing but platonic enhances it, if anything. Sligger I find difficult. His appalling lack of frankness is very unpleasant after Maurice's ruthless sincerity. It is very aggravating to see Sligger roping in attractive young men on the wildest pretexts so that if he is sincere with himself he must be a colossal hypocrite while Maurice made all kinds of nice and true observations on you and Jack and thought he had never seen brothers so alike. Sligger can only repeat that you have a brother who is utterly different from you which, when one wants to know how you are, is not very satisfactory. It was Jack's seriousness chiefly that impressed Maurice by the way.

I would rather be somewhere else with you than the chalet if it could be managed . . . i.e. walking to Compostella or in the Pyrenees with my mother so don't accept altogether yet as
  (i) there are some pretty awful people coming to the chalet
  (ii) I shall probably be much too restless to settle down there, and don't want to be with any Oxford people when schools results come out (August).
  (iii) It is rather fraught with associations of Bobbie etc.

None of these points are vital but I think it would be more fun if we were with my mother or abroad together. (I may have some money) so leave a loop hole. Maurice wants to start a counter chalet in Italy – about the Wye I have secured a car etc so mind you can manage a week end in June – we could motor the first day by Gloucester and Tewkesbury to Symond's Yat and Monmouth then the next down the river to Tintern and Chepstow walking a good deal of it then back again by the Severn or Forest of Dean. Only you would have to get leave from Saturday morning to Monday night to make it feasible – if it didn't rain it would be heavenly and the thought of it is my chief solace here. I go long walks alone and alone to the cinema but am less unhappy thanks to your letter and advice about cowslips etc. – only you must come that week end – I could pick you up outside Oxford if you did not want to enter it though there are many who would be glad to see you, it is fear of being laughed at that keeps me from Cambridge. Is there anywhere you would rather go than the Wye? Write soon and tell me more of your campaign. Much love

Cyril

I am probably going to London Saturday to a party of Edith Sitwell's –

16 May 1925. Postcard.

H. N. Blakiston, Esq.,
Magdalene College.

Dear Noel,
  Blossom by blossom the spring begins thanks to you, not that I have found anyone to share it with but go for walks and bicycle rides

79

to the woods by myself. Though Bobbie is going to give it a trial
instead of tennis, one day.

Much love
Cyril

18 May 1925.

H. N. Blakiston, Esq.,   Balliol College,
Magdalene College.   Oxford.

Dear Noel,

Thank you for your card. I shan't have my fellowship in October
and probably not at all if I fail with my schools but if I can sell more
shares of mine which I hope to do to pay my debts with I can easily
support us from July 10–25 in France or Northern Spain. It would be
superb – and go on with you to the chalet from 25–11th August. I
should probably stay on at the chalet after that or join my mother.

September I think I am going somewhere with Bobbie. I think the
Wye would have to be before the 13th as I rather think my schools
begin then – if not it could be that week end we could go.

Later. Alas, schools begin on Thursday 11th and it would have
to be the week end of 6th–8th or if it would suit you better 8th–10th.
Let me know if you can manage either.

I am bearing up a bit better with this weather. Bobbie and I canoed
for 7 hours on Saturday up a side stream which was rather exciting
as we had to tow it some of the way and carry it across a field in
another.

I retract what I said about finding trees a consolation rather than
an inspiration by the way. It will be fun planning where to go from
July 10–25. I should think I could subscribe 40 or 50 pounds for us
if I can get my share certificates from my father. I must pay about £200
of bills and will have about £100 for the vac plus what my father gives
me. I must keep 50 for September but can do on what I get from him
for the time I am not with you or Bobbie. I want to go to Turkey
again very much. I might try and do that with Bobbie in September
or when you leave the chalet.

If we had £50 in August that would mean £10 journey each and
£1 a day expenses – we could usually manage on 10/– and so have

some cash for excursions from the chalet e.g. to Aosta or Geneva or the snow. About August I suggest somewhere not too far out of the way from the chalet.

We could go by boat to Galicia (Vigo or Corunna) and come back but I think better to go to the Catalan end of the Pyrenees and visit Andorra and the Greek ruins on the coast and Perpignan and Carcassonne – or we could go to the Balearic islands or Corsica. Cerdagne would be coolest but we may get our fill of mountains at the chalet. If my mother is still at Pau we might join her by wandering through S.W. France. It will be hot everywhere but on the Mediterranean it is rather Hellenic and the butterflies etc. are lovely also the bathing. Acquitaine rather more green and golden and less white and blue – anyhow let us deliberate.

Much love
Cyril

I am deep in the works of Li-Po
Why not Corsica?

May 1925.

H. N. Blakiston, Esq.,   Balliol College,
Magdalene College.   Oxford.

Dear Noel,

Thank you for your nice letter, bringing balm. I am not quite at the suicidal stage still being hopeful enough to think that one place is better than another. Running away was all I was contemplating and had got as far as sending my passport up for some transit visas. I was thinking of trying to collect my £300 from my father and disappearing when I get a week end off before schools vanishing on the orient express probably. The chief drawback is leaving one's debts behind and the consequent assumption that is why I had gone. Spring would be admirable, as you say, but there is no spring here, perhaps it came and we have missed it, perhaps it is still to come, perhaps there isn't one this year. Piers thinks it is still to come and waits patiently in his darkened room. I only see it ebbing as the surrounding greenness deepens and the rain drips more perpetually from the chestnut leaves

April is the cruellest month, breeding
Lilacs out of the dead land. . . .

Turned to jade are the boy's rosy cheeks,
to his sick temples the frost of winter clings
Do not wonder that my body sinks to decay
Though my limbs are old my heart is older yet –

As you say spring and us are a strong combination but where is spring and where are us? It is not fair to you to expect anything more than occasional sympathy with my senile ravings – you apparently have seen something of spring in Cambridge, you have better buildings, you do not waste time, and you have only been there two terms but I am glad you are cheered by my depression, it cheered me up more than anything as I was afraid of boring you with it or making you feel you ought to be depressed too, which was why I hadn't written. My chief recollection of spring and us ceases after Provence. Notre Dame was winter and us – but the gardens of the papal palace and its outlines and gray radiance across the islands of the Rhone and above all the hills and the willows by the bend of the Gard River make the beginning and end of my spring and somehow I think one has a right to expect more – Think of a nice A. C. Benson spring lasting and meandering through several chapters, half a volume, of collected thoughts. Slow and English and punctilious in all its nice gradations from snowdrops to catkins, daffodils, lambkins, the strange unrest and sense of impending adventure that was suddenly to be explained by the old college garden awaking to the note of the first cuckoo and, in French perhaps, *le temps des lilas* – and last of all the swallow and the nightingale, the death of an old colleague, who, scholar and gentleman as he was, could well have been spared, and that tremulous morning when Peter awoke with a new sound in his ears to find the tennis court marked and mown.

The post is going in a moment. Maurice was much impressed by Jack. I will let you know if I am going to do anything rash but I think it unlikely. Timothy is still nice. Piers finds life 'an aggressive vacuum' – Maurice *odis et amos* – Sligger can't understand what all these young men find to grumble about – K. writes in his engagement book 'golf with Eileen', has a letter from his father saying 'the new budget makes things easier 6d. off up to £30,000 and 1/– after' – to celebrate which he asks Roger and me to tea a week in advance. I am really very miserable indeed.

> We are the hollow men
> We are the stuffed men
> leaning together
> headpiece filled with straw alas!
>
> Tchirek river
> lies under the Dark Mountains
>
> La Rivière de Cassis roule ignorée
> dans ses vaux étranges.
>
> There the eyes are
> sunlight on a broken column.
> There, is a tree swinging
> and voices are
> in the winds singing
> more distant, and more solemn
> than a fading star.
>
> When days are long and sunny
> the flower of youth is blown
> we waste our parents' money
> and time that is our own.
>
> The days grow dark and colder
> beyond the summer's prime
> we, before time is older,
> are old before our time.
>
> (C.V.C. after A.E.H.)

By the way I never dared show you this, Housman at Kirkby, but if you forgive the circumstances it is rather good –

> By endless rooks in alien trees
>   the fenland river flows
> and once my heart knew how to please
>   and took delight in those.
>
> Now love is flown and friendship dead
>   and only I remain
> and fields I do not dare to tread
>   along the winding Bain.

other readings, could not bear to tread,
do not care to tread, a trembling Bain.

We must try and get those two days together whatever happens. Forest Murmurs makes one think of dewy hazel woods and one very nice faun leading one on without the sultry and troubling discontent of Debussy's faun who in any case could only make one lose one's way and then laugh. I play the herdsman in Tristan prelude Act III and then pt. II Forest Murmurs on K's gramophone when he is not there and recommend the 2 as a good method of expressing and then curing one's desolate and chafing moods.

'Plucking the rushes' in the Chinese poems (p. 84) is a good description of life at Kirkby or any cold pastoral, don't you think. Kirkby must be nice now. Love to Jack. We must get that week end whatever happens – Wye valley indicated don't you think. Woods.

Much love
Cyril

I certify that I have quoted freely only to express myself and not at all to make you familiar with things I think good. C.V.C.

26 May 1925.

H. N. Blakiston, Esq.,   Balliol College,
Magdalene College.   Oxford.

Dear Noel,
Thank you so much for your 3 letters. 8, 9, 10th settled then. If there is anywhere you would rather go to than the Wye let me know and we can go there but we can't manage much more than 75 miles from Oxford in any direction, and woods are rather essential don't you think? We might be able to fit the Black mountain in as well, but it would be nice to do a little walking the second day. If you leave Cambridge at 9 something you get here at half past twelve and we could start before or after lunch. If you would rather lunch here I can ask Maurice or Bobbie or Timothy or Piers or Henry Yorke or Sligger or anyone you want to see; if we lunch on the way we would have more chance of seeing the Black mountain via Tewkesbury, a minimum of fuss is necessary don't you think so let me know which you would like. It is quite a nice car and one can be comfortable in it

if it rains but the chauffeur is rather a rough diamond. I am rather in favour of an indolent opulent trip with such comfort that the hardy Borderers can afford etc.

Life here is still on the minus side. I have made it up with John Maud and Maurice interviewed him and discovered he lived in panic of me and also said very nice things about me so I wrote him a note explaining why I always cut him and he wrote back one of his typical grovel letters and then I dined with him and found he had really thought rather a lot though I could find nothing else to praise and shan't probably see him again. I gave your messages to Maurice and Co. I am very interested in China and Maurice is there very helpful with his description of the scenery, the culture, and the witty embittered over-civilised mandarins. By looking at maps the topography of the literature is getting clearer and the tropical horrors of Yunnan, the streams and forests of Szechuan and the cultured cities of the Yangtse materialise going north to the capitals of Lo Yang and Chang'an on the Yellow river and the exodus from the latter to the Jewel Gate pass and the Tartar wars beyond the great wall. Otherwise I feel like 'the Scholar in the Narrow Street' if you have that book of Charles – (honestly this is not proselytising but the simplest method of explaining an emotional state).

I went to a concert alone on Sunday night and heard the Mother Goose suite. The first, *belle au bois dormant* one, I found incredibly moving despite the hard seats and glare of the Town Hall, but it seemed to express all my mood complex, better even than Forest Murmurs; with its picture of the rainy leafy troubled woods and the tragedy known only to a few birds, of the still house among them –

Beneath those laden boughs the gardener sighs
Dreaming in endlessness forgotten beauty lies.

I haunt the Oxford canal where the squat tower of the castle looks more like Provence than anything else I have seen in England and where the water eddies beside old houses and flowers of chestnut and May and lilac hang over the dirty water and music comes from ancient inns.

I heard someone in the yellow crane house
playing on the sweet bamboo flute
the tune of the 'Falling Plum Flowers' . . .
It was May in the waterside city.

I go on reading Dante, I lounge in trim gardens with Bobbie, I
stare at people in the street and they stare back. I go canoeing. I see
Maurice and Piers and Timothy. I say good night to Sligger. I am
lunching on Thursday with Henry Yorke.
Shall we canoe down some river?

It is so far to the woods here without a car and one has to be content
with reading about woods, hearing music about them, and thinking

> Of all that bowery loneliness
> and brooks of Eden mazily murmuring
> by bloom profuse and cedar arches.

I wish you could come to the woods too, I do not go with anyone else,
but we can when you come in June

> *ambo florentes aetatibus, Arcades ambo*
> *et cantare pares et respondere parati*

Write when you feel inclined and let me know what you would rather
do about lunch. I hope you are coping well with Jack etc – June will
be good.

Much love
Cyril

Do not, if any of this is alien, feel you ought to understand it or that
it deserves censure!
Don't you think Georgic II 458–490 rather inspired.

30 May 1925.

H. N. Blakiston, Esq.,   Balliol College,
Magdalene College.   Oxford.

Dear Noel,
   Thank you for your letter and the epitaph which I liked very much
indeed. I am in very low spirits at present and the weather is foul. I
am longing to get away with you, we could go to the Dorsetshire
coast by the way if you would rather be by the sea. Lulworth Cove.
I don't mind. Let's leave it all fairly open. Very much love.

Cyril

4 June 1925.

Noel Blakiston, Esq.,   Balliol College
Magdalene College.   Oxford.

Dear Noel,

We are going to Dorset, do you mind? I think it will be nicer on
the whole, we shall see several cathedrals and the sea. You needn't
bring any luggage if you don't want to, as I can lend you everything
and take them back when we get back here on Wednesday. I can't
say how I am looking forward to seeing you. Won't it be marvellous
if this weather lasts. Can you get here by the train arriving 12.55?
Timothy wanted to ask Maurice and Bobbie as well and I said you
wouldn't mind, so he has asked them.

Much love. How time drags.
Cyril

God has got to behave himself this time.

[? June 1925]

Balliol College
Oxford.

Dear Noel,

Thank you very much for your letter. I liked your poem and have
learnt it by heart. I knew you could only manage 2 nights, but it will
be all right if you are back in Cambridge on Wednesday evening,
won't it? Timothy has asked you and me and Piers to lunch for
Monday which seems best as he wanted to ask you and at the same time
Sligger can be avoided that way and not feel he should have been
asked as if I had had you to lunch. I had lunch with Henry Yorke
to-day. If we leave about 3 we could still have plenty of time but we
could lunch at one and get away a little earlier. Piers is liable not to
utter and to wear slightly gaudy clothes but is looking forward to it.

I canoed all last night round the canals in the slums which were very
beautiful and Venetian with furnaces and railway engines and May
and Lilac and rickety over hanging houses and deserted gardens along
the narrow channels.

'May in the waterside city'

I went with Peter Quennell* who likes those sorts of adventures and

*Peter Quennell (b. 9 March 1905). Berkhamsted Grammar School, Balliol.
Poet, writer, editor. CBE 1973.

goes to Albania by himself. He writes the best poetry in Oxford and looks fair and ethereal.

Timothy is looking forward to seeing you and I find little else to think about, and the country too, I mean, if only it is fine –

Much love
Cyril

13 June 1925.

Noel Blakiston, Esq.,   [Balliol College,]
Magdalene College.   Oxford.

Dear Noel,

Thank you awfully for your p.c. We had quite a nice drive and heard nightingales and saw 4 counties from the top of the hill, but were rather depressed though the others enjoyed it. I think Piers liked you very much. I am frightfully busy with these foul exams about which I know nothing.

fear and the pit and the snare are upon thee,
O inhabitant of the earth.

I think of you most of my spare time and call people Noel by mistake and that tune is in my head. Still I shall see you on Thursday. For me our argosy was the revelation of England, a country hitherto that I have not fairly appreciated – and I can't say how I enjoyed being with you. Harry says you are a jolly decent chap. A great deal of love.

Cyril

after one paper.

Thank you for your letter. I haven't done very much. I dined in All Souls with the Professor of Byzantine Greek last night which was quite nice; and told my tutor about our trip. I am giving Bobbie dinner to-night. I have just faced a paper on Economic history completely unseen which was rather an ordeal and am having a tutorial with Kenneth Bell on the one I have to do tomorrow morning. I am sure education should teach one to do without books, to think and feel and seek romance and take exercise in the best tradition of cold pastoral. The uneducated person would be bored. At the same time one might be allowed such books as long since have ceased to convey any message but the fondness of familiarity and the beauty of lines known so well as to be quite unintelligible. We cannot be children, and hardly boys, so there is only boatmen.

I have had deep humiliation for my showmanship – I think both our evenings were very good, I still can't get over those lines of disappearing cliffs or those gaunt quiet tracery of the red arches.

Write to me again
Cyril

15 June 1925.

Noel Blakiston, Esq.,   Balliol College,
Magdalene College.   Oxford.

forwarded to
Kirkby on Bain.

Dear Noel,

Thank you for your letters. You help me in schools a lot which are very hot and tiresome and I find myself constantly hampered by ignorance of the set books. When not doing them I attempt feverish work or feverish dissipation. Bradfield also is being held up here. My Bobbie* is generally apathetic, Timothy has seen it already. I have quarrelled with Piers (hot weather). I will give him your message as soon as some change in the situation appears. I dined with John Brooks last night who was nice and had Tony Powell, Henry Yorke and Bobbie to breakfast, Eastwood† to lunch and Penderel Moon‡ coming to tea and Bobbie to dinner. I have just read J. A. Symonds book on Greek friendship (*A problem in Greek ethics*, privately printed in Holland for the Areopagitica Society) – it is extremely good and establishes fairly conclusively the general healthiness of their attitude. I have papers Monday, Tuesday and Wednesday morning, then Bobbie,

*Bobbie Longden. Bobbie Newton, 'my' Bobbie, was an undergraduate at Magdalene, Cambridge.

†Christopher Eastwood (b. 21 April 1905). KS. Trinity, Oxford. Colonial Office. Commissioner of Crown Lands. CMG 1947.

‡Penderel Moon (b. 13 November 1905). Winchester, New College. ICS 1929–44. Knighted 1962.

Kenneth Bell, and Humphrey Sumner* to lunch to celebrate my freedom.

(*fuor sei dell' este via, fuor sei dell'arte*)

Why not let's meet at Bradfield anyhow or are you too dependent on Your Bobbie's plans. I suppose you can't come if you are staying with him. I dreamt of William last night.

No more news but much love. It is very nice finding your letters when I come away from my morning paper.

Cyril

22 June 1925.

Noel Blakiston,   Balliol College
Kirkby on Bain.   Oxford.

Dear Noel,

Thank you most awfully for your letter Fowey Hotel, Fowey, Cornwall. I think of you a lot and will write very soon.

Much love
Cyril

Piers sends love.

22 June 1925. Postcard of the cathedral, Exeter.

H. N. Blakiston, Esq.,
Kirkby on Bain.

μνάσατο γαρ κατα θυμον
'αυιμονος Αυτιλοχοῖο

C.

---

*Humphrey Sumner (b. 8 August 1983, d. 1951). Winchester, Balliol. Fellow of All Souls 1919–25. Fellow and Tutor in Modern History at Balliol 1925–44. Warden of All Souls 1945–51.

[June ? 1925]. Postcard, Princetown, Devon.

H. N. Blakiston, Esq.,
Kirkby on Bain.

Dear Noel,
   How are you? We have had 2 very good days here having done an enormous walk to Tavy Cleare where we bathed. It is very high and open but rather unimpressive, too green, we go back to Oxford to-night. Freddie has asked me to go somewhere in July which is strange! The prison here is rather awful.

23 June 1925. Postcard, Fowey Harbour entrance.

H. N. Blakiston, Esq.,
Kirkby on Bain.

   Still evening and too dark to write.
                              C.

24 June 1925. Postcard. Fowey Harbour.

H. N. Blakiston, Esq.,
Kirkby on Bain.

   Greeting.
after breakfast.
   Wednesday.

24 June 1925. Postcard, Fowey Harbour.

H. N. Blakiston, Esq.,
Kirkby on Bain.

   This is written a bit later, before lunch.

26 June 1925.

H. N. Blakiston, Esq.,   The Fowey Hotel,
Kirkby on Bain.   Fowey,
                                                        Cornwall.

Dear Noel,

Thank you so much for your letter. How by the way is the fig and the vine? My letters went down well with Buchan and Newbolt and I have to set about writing 6 articles on Spain which J. Buchan will probably get published but I don't see myself doing them at present – it is frightfully hot and sunny here and very lowering – we watch the tide go in and out and occasionally row up a creek. I miss you a lot and long for Corsica. I hope you can face it. We are going up the Falmouth estuaries tomorrow in a launch and sleeping on board! There is a good church we went to see at St. Just in Roseland. Much love – no time for more – goodnight

                                        Cyril

The Greeks themselves muddled Harmodios and A[ristogeiton] with strokes & bows too so it was natural.

[?*27*] *June 1925.*

H. N. Blakiston, Esq.,   The Fowey Hotel,
Kirkby on Bain.   Fowey,
                                                        Cornwall.

Dear Noel,

How are you? This is a very lovely place and quite unspoilt being a port chiefly with Norwegian and Japanese tramps loading china clay and lots of little boats going out and coming in and nothing better to do than to sit and watch them, it is a nice hotel, not pretentious right up above the water with a good balcony at one mouth of the river and ferries go across to the village on the opposite side, it is all rather foreign and the white and green boats sometimes look like caiques on the Golden Horn especially as there are a lot of Turkish lascars there. I missed you a lot all the journey down and wrote you a poem which I will send sometime – it was nice getting your letter before starting. Charles stayed the week end with me and was very sweet, we motored to Henley with Harry on Saturday night and dined and went out in a launch and again on Sunday with Bobbie, Maurice, Patrick and Piers added – it was very nice and the launch on the darkening river was like my chinese poems. I thought of you a lot and the 6 of us drank your health, no-one else's – I breakfasted with Patrick and his mother before going away. Would you like to share a two roomed cottage with me for 2 weeks in September on the island of Iona – celtic and haunted and apparently very beautiful. Patrick and family will be at one end of the island with possibly one or two of his friends, our cottage 3 miles away at the other. We can get someone in to cook and wash up and otherwise lead a pastoral and monastic life. Patrick's mother is very nice. I had a strange interview with John Buchan and Sir Henry Newbolt about my future, I had to bring something I'd written and could only produce a couple of poems and 2 letters to Bobbie as I was in a great hurry but I believe there were some awful things in the letters of which I wish them joy. They enjoyed viva-ing me very much, both are better men than their books would lead one to expect. I enjoyed the end of term very much really, I saw a lot of Penderel Moon whom you would like very much I think sane and humorous and scholarly, like the [?] Hermes in Pater and extremely good on the country side and very lovely to look at but nothing more because he is so small. Bobbie is very nice here but Lulworth has taken the bloom off my enjoyment of anything like this and I feel I am only giving my 2nd best and get no thrills only content and quiet. I wish it was you, really. About our plans will you arrange the programme of the 15th–19th as you like and let me know where we are to go and where to meet, after that I want awfully badly to go to Corsica because it is an island and because I want to see a little of the Mediterranean summer and it would not be too hot up in the beech forests and a day or two idling by the sea. Does it rouse you at all? The point is will you stand by me in not coming to the chalet till August 1 or 2nd as it would be impossible to go to Corsica in less. This is rather vital so let me know if you will and we will let Sligger know at the beginning of July – he can't object really but he won't like us being too independent of him but we must go abroad then as you have to go home afterwards. This will probably upset your theories of politeness but it is rather essential, and Corsica might be very lovely. I will bear brunt with [Sligger]. It is impossible to consider watching things waste of time don't you find? Naturally it is nice for your father to enjoy wasting time because he has earned frailties it is always youth that has the duty of suffering, don't you think, incidentally.

No more now but I will write again. I think a lot of Kirkby. I
heard from Bobbie Newton it was nice of him to write. Quiller Couch
lives here. My mind is getting active again after schools and I enjoy
reading. Will you start a rapid fire of postcards etc. if I do, just for a
bit? Your reality is very strong at present. I am sorry about Jack but
I don't think examinations are much of a criterion do you? My love
to you – Cyril.

We covered a good deal of ground last week too don't you think?

29 June 1925.

H. N. Blakiston, Esq.,   The Fowey Hotel,
Kirkby on Bain.   Fowey,
                                                Cornwall.

Dear Noel,

   Thank you most awfully for your letters and postcards – I like the
white gate and also the drawing of Lincoln. Thank you for your
admission about the ginger beer. I quite agree, literally, and drink
it for breakfast here as well as at lunch but I like to have good wine
when in a place where they have it – restaurant or wine district etc.
but on the whole I agree with you though you must allow that most
luxuries become necessities during a heat wave. If we went to Corsica
it would have to be on the cheap but we might leave it for a little and
see how you feel. I can pay all expenses quite easily. If we don't go
anywhere before the chalet I shall probably go to Tripoli after you
leave. Piers may come as far as Sicily. I should love to come to Kirkby
on 15th if your mother would not mind but make quite sure about
that. Our trip to Helford and Fal estuaries was superb – Roseland was
very beautiful and we anchored miles up the Fal between wooded hills
and green water to the noise of owls and doves in the trees and slept
very well in the cabin and came back about dawn, 30 miles of extremely
rough open sea for a small launch. To-day we go to the Duchy Hotel
Princetown Devon to see Dartmoor whence we go back to Oxford
for a night on Thursday and then I go to stay with my grandmother
in Bath till I come to you. 18 Bennett Street is the address. What do
you really want to do about going any where before the chalet? Do
exactly what you like about it only finance doesn't matter much at
the same time I would be quite content not to go anywhere and go to

Tripoli later as I have always wanted to go there so I leave it entirely to you. We had better settle soon in case we have to arrange with Sligger. I will write from Princetown – my mind is fairly stagnant here.

Much love
Cyril

5 July 1925.

Noel Blakiston, Esq.,   18 Bennett Street,
Kirkby on Bain.   Bath.

Dear Noel,

Thank you so much for your letter which it was nice to find here. I have had measles all right; everything indeed except mumps and scarlet fever. It is fairly trying here, Bath proves astonishingly beautiful, very like Florence, with good hills and houses and redolent of the most somnolent side of the 18th century. It is also intolerably slack; speech, thought, and exercise are reduced to the search for somewhere to sit down. My grandmother and aunt spoil me the whole time and seem to think I am happy or not according as to whether I am eating something, whatever the time of day. I get nearly mad with perpetual fuss and being asked to decide on the merits of unessentials. It is going to be very nice seeing you. I miss Bobbie a good bit too which makes me bad company as he was extremely fine on our trip and after 10 days and nights alone with someone one feels very transplanted without them. Otherwise I resent Oxford and most of the people in it a good deal but it was better perhaps than perpetual feeding and being forced to simulate an appetite and choose whether I would rather have Stilton or Cheddar, disliking both and if I think such and such a girl is pretty and what kind of prettiness do I admire and do I like this new brown hat and I don't remember Miss So and So do I but she remembers you. Cary's Dante is rather depressing don't you find, Carlisle's translation is much better, it is the prose by the side of the Italian in those blue books I have. I was surprised at Freddie liking Dante. I feel I ought to work for my viva but hate the thought of history; at the same time I ought to do something about Spain of to-day for the Buchan-Newbolt combination who found my letters to Bobbie 'very vivid and interesting' – pause for an enormous and unwanted dinner.

Sunday.

We went to a rotten cinema last night which made me miss you and the Kirkby one, I am dragged round meeting old women, old servants and anyone who is sufficiently old and those awful cousins we avoided at Bibury are coming here tomorrow, I have been taken to the cemetery to see tombs and to the abbey to see the bits of my great grandfather restored and have to go to see more relations at East Harptree on Wednesday, it is all quite loathsome when not coping with elderly ladies without charm I am being stuffed perpetually with food, my grandmother is a very lively old lady of 80 with great dignity and knowledge but will spoil me. Still I glean a lot from her about my Connolly ancestors who seem to have sailed as near insanity as the law allows. There is one very good one who had a ship through the peninsula war and at Trafalgar who was called the 'King of Bath' and though always rude and disagreeable (I quote my grandmother) no party was complete without him. He had all the servants up once a month and rehearsed his funeral telling them where people were to sit and what wines were to be opened and whenever he passed a house with the blinds down he rang and asked if there was a corpse in it and if there was, if he could go in and shake his dear friend by the hand; which has a nice 18th century flavour. I shall probably go to Tripoli then after you leave the chalet via Naples, Taormina and Syracuse. We can settle if it is worth going anywhere from 20th–23rd at Kirkby. I think Lulworth is best as it is really. We might go to Chartres. personally I would rather like a day or two in Marseilles, I should think it would bear some exploring and I like the noise and heat and shipping and general mingling of races there. Tripoli thrills me a good deal. I should probably have disliked the Frenchness of Corsica and in any case have been there before and remember it quite well – Do write again and excuse my stagnation. You are probably right about classes but at present I can tolerate no one at all except possibly children – relations and parish seem equally fussy, sensual and muddle headed. We might do a long walk or so if it is cool at Kirkby.

Much love
Cyril

Incidentally an explorer can hardly be indifferent to geography can he? though it begins to appeal to me as an idea.

8 July 1925.

Noel Blakiston, Esq.,   18 Bennett Street,
Kirkby on Bain.   Bath.

Dear Noel,

   Thank you so much for your letter and the nice poem. I am looking
forward frightfully to seeing you – I am getting very fond of Bath
which I have sublimated into mediaeval Florence, it requires an
effort. I am sick of relations and old servants of which there seem
no end. As my grandmother kept 14 gardeners when she lived here
you can imagine the amount of surviving retainers. She says her father
restored the whole of the south transept of the abbey and put all the
glass in which is new and also the organ and spent £50000 on it so it
was not as venerable as we thought but that doesn't make it any less
moving – I am afraid I did not get up till 11 on Sunday so I missed
church at the abbey though the others went. I think of you nearly all
the time, it is force of habit now but I find it very mild and pleasant
and nicer than anything else. Of course a name like Noel it is possible
to go on thinking again and again without feeling anything except
what a nice name it is but I do manage on the whole to associate you
with it. I enjoy the evenings most when I go away after dinner and
listen to the band in the park. You would like it too. Marseilles has
palled – do you think you could face a scramble which would give us
time to see Carcassonne, the republic of Andorra, and the Spanish
cathedral town of Seo de Urgel (Cerdagne)? I have not seen any of
them properly though have been very close and I want frightfully
to see Seo and we could just do it in the time or by taking an extra
day and it could be inexpensive if we went 3rd and not too hot being
very high in the loveliest part of the Pyrenees (though 3 days would
be walking). I am very stagnant I am afraid at present and see no
chance of recovering till I meet you and leave this 'ασχολια of food
and relations.

                         Cyril

13 July 1925.

Noel Blakiston, Esq.,   18 Bennett Street,
Kirkby on Bain.   Bath.

Dear Noel,

I have just found a p.c. of yours which I never saw which is very
refreshing. I agree about good taste, it was perspicacious of you – I
think perspicacity is the highest intellectual quality, the fusion of
analysis and imagination in a bold guess at Truth, it requires the least
amount of tools, i.e. books etc. which commends it. I have been to
a rose show with a little girl, it is a nice pagan festival of flowers and
printed frocks and summer with plenty of children and an atmosphere
of Marius and Apuleius. Yesterday I was very limp so dashed off to
Bristol in the evening and dined there and took a bus to Avonmouth
and saw a watery sunset over the Severn estuary and a glamorous pale
Banana boat unloading and thought of you, dare I say? and found a
circus rather remote and lurid and won several packets of cigarettes at
shooting celluloid things on fountains and missed my train and spent
the night at Bristol, a loathsome place I think, though I like the wharves
and the Clifton Suspension Bridge and the new tower of the University
is amazingly beautiful – was it there when you stayed there? I have
got very fond of Bath, the Royal Crescent is the best row of houses
I have seen – we might live there in old age, all that is best in the 18th
century – and lovely views. I often go to our hotel and round the
abbey, I have found several family relics there, which have given me
a mild dose of ancestor worship, especially the morbid corpse loving
Connolly one who has an image of his wooden ship there and was
'a dutiful son, an affectionate father, and a strictly honest man' – also
a brother of my grandmother's who has a stained glass window and
was drowned off Carthage when he was a midshipman of 16 and whom
my grandmother says was very like me. This probably all annoys
you – I have a vague feeling of having annoyed you which may be
due to

     (i) appearance of boasting – I am sorry if you think this and you
          probably know better if I am than me.

or (ii) references to Bobbie – unlikely

or (iii) unwelcome suggestions of exploration. This I am fairly sure
          of; I have therefore cancelled the Iona cottage which seems
          to have fallen on stony ground, also Seo as well as Marseilles

and suggest either we stay at Kirkby till 24th or I meet you in London then if there is no room for me and stay somewhere else from 20th–24th which I could do fairly easily – naturally being independent of geography you probably don't want to explore so we had better leave it. I am more and more obsessed with Tripoli and quite content to save up for it as I should like to go there in comparative comfort because of the heat. Bobbie doesn't want me to go to Courmayeur with you because he and I were very happy there last year, which is rather a blow – I don't know where else there is and how much he would really mind. I went there twice before I went with him.

The chalet by the way is the nearest approach to Milton's Eden going, did you know that? I have just read *Wuthering Heights*. It is a most shattering book and upsets one's idea of Victorians very much as well as being superb in itself. I don't much mind if you read it or not but I cannot be silent how good it is.

I don't know how to palliate it but on Tuesday I am spending a day with Freddy and on Monday I am giving my Bibury cousin lunch at the Berkeley and taking her to a theatre because her red shingled hair and the shape of her head reminded me of Bobbie and also to see if I still can think of anything to say to a woman. I am going back to Cirencester for Monday night with her and her mother. This only in case you have fears of me being over fond and wanting long letters, which I don't as the real joy of you is the frequency with which you write and the sense (2), fondness (1), and humour therein. Naval and Military will find me.

Much love till Wednesday
Cyril

Aug 1925.

H. N. Blakiston, Esq.,   Chalet des Mélèzes,
Kirkby on Bain.   St. Gervais des Bains,
                                          Haute Savoie.

Dear Noel,

Thank you so much for your letter. I am still here but leaving about next Thursday I hope. For Venice I think. It has been bloody here and I am still plumped in apathy so I won't write much. I will write properly as soon as I get away. To-morrow we go to Lake of Geneva where I hope to see Timothy.

σιβύλλα, σιβύλλα, τί θελεῖς;
ἀποθνήσκειν θελῶ

I am glad you liked my mother. My best love to yours and your mother. I hope to spend a night at Le T. on my way back if I can't see more of Jack but I can't stay here till he is free – meanwhile 'it is not many miles to Mantua no further than the end of this mad world.'

I have got some nine photos of you ἄστηρ ἐμός. By the way it was very cowardly of you to answer 'I don't know' to that question I asked you – no would have been much more satisfactory than that.

Much love
Cyril

28 Aug 1925. Postcard.

H. N. Blakiston, Esq.,
Kirkby on Bain.

Dear Noel,
I am still at the chalet, dull and dead and woebegone. How are you.
Cyril

Love: Timothy

28 Aug 1925. Postcard, Geneva.

Love from
Cyril
Roger

7 Sept 1925.

Noel Blakiston, Esq.,
Kirkby on Bain.

Hotel du Chapon Fin,
Bordeaux,
France.

Dear Noel,
Thank you for your p.c. I hope you got some of mine. I left the chalet on Wednesday and spent a night at Limoges, then came here.

I stopped at Perigueux on the way, it has a queer cathedral which looks too new and like a school library. I am waiting for Jack here and find it hard to move. The weather is not very good, it is a pleasant, respectable town, the Garonne is magnificent, the sunsets very fine everything is flat and homely after the chalet, this is a quiet hotel next door to a *barber, **a book shop and a *** the fruit market where they have marvellous muscatel grapes, my favourite food – incidentally though a small hotel it has a very famous restaurant and incredibly good wine – both a great joy after the privations of the chalet. I made one excursion to Arcachon but the bleak, trippery sea side put me off and I came away at once. I am sorry you have been transplanted again. There are no English here which is pleasant. Occasional celebrities flit by. The Marchesa di Casati (of amazing portrait by John) who keeps tame leopards, girls dressed up as boys, drugs, crystal gazing etc. had to leave Italy for killing a page in gold leaf, has just passed by, but for the most part I see only claret kings and read French novels and go in steamers on the Garonne and feel every inch a citizen. Next week I may go and stay with my aunt near Pau or any rate go S. for a day or two. I meet Jack here on the 12th, we are thinking of going to Santiago and the far west of Spain which is green at this time of year when the rest of Spain is colourless. We may come back by boat or go there in one. I hope we shall get on. I have enough money for my share. I had planned a circular trip to Venice, Innsbruck (a night with William), Salzbourg (a night with Freddie) Munich (a night with Siegfried) Basle (a night with Timothy) – but I couldn't afford the journeys. I had a long letter from William did I tell you and have been exchanging telegrams with Freddie. Sligger took us to Lake of Geneva where I saw Timothy who was refreshing. The chalet dragged to its close. I was delayed by Sligger wanting me to go straight to England but finally all went well and Major C. sent me some money – the last, so I have freedom and a last glimpse of Spain then England about the 22nd *et dieu sait ce que sera*. I have read Lear which is magnificent and the *Purgatorio*. Lear is desolate in just the right way especially the scenes on the heath. Write to Hotel du Chapon Fin up to 12th and after that *Hotel du Panier Fleuri Bayonne*. We need to write rather often I think.

Much love
Cyril

point against the chalet

the murmuring surge
that on the unnumbered idle pebbles chafes
cannot be heard so high.

8 Sept 1925. Postcard, Bordeaux.

H. N. Blakiston, Esq.,
Kirkby on Bain.

This is the bridge at Bordeaux. I leave for St. Jean de Luz on the South express in 10 minutes. *Hotel du Panier Fleurì* will find me. I was last there on my way to you.
Much love
Cyril

22 Sept 1925.

<table>
<tr><td>Noel Blakiston, Esq.,
Kirkby on Bain.</td><td>80 St. Georges Sq.,
S.W.1.</td></tr>
</table>

Dear Noel,
   We have returned – Autumnal depression is settling down on me – write to me soon. I liked Jack awfully and we got on without a single incident to mar but the English boat was bloody.
Cyril

Kirkby must be nice now. Mummy sends her love. My love to your parents don't let them think I led Jack into extravagant ways.

[? Sept] 1925.
80 St. Georges Sq.,
S.W.1.

Dear Noel,
   Thank you so much for your letter to Bayonne, your p.c. here and your p.c. to Granada which I have just retrieved. I am in fairly low spirits at present. I don't like London and not a soul I know seems

to be in it. Sligger is destining me for journalism. I go unwillingly. One career seems very like another and this one seems the most precarious and possibly the most degrading. I shall try and get a tutorship or something to carry on with as I have not got enough written to show journalists or anyone. I feel a fairly strong determination to do whatever I have to do pretty thoroughly and to get something at once that will remove me from dependance on parents but I haven't the smallest hope of finding my life work in anything that turns up. My mother is doing rather well. I am meeting Jack to-day on his way to you and will give him this. I haven't read Othello yet. I have been reading French mostly at present. I shall try and get abroad as quickly as possible and may even go and learn a language ?Arabic if it seems advisable. I loathe this drifting here. 40 years time may still find me lingering here crabbing situations. Autumn depression is at hand. My mother talks often of you and makes good blood though soon she is certain to make you the mouthpiece for adverse criticism. It is a way parents have.

I see Sligger on and off and saw Timothy in Oxford on Friday where I went to bury the dead. I hope the Kirkby season is in full swing. Write again. I will.

Cyril

28 Oct 1925.

Noel Blakiston, Esq.,   Naval and Military Hotel,
Magdalene College.   Harrington Rd.,
             S. Kensington.

Dear Noel,

I have hardly written to anyone for ages and owe Roger, Piers, Patrick, Father David,* Jack, William, Bobbie all letters. I don't want to write to anyone till I know what I am doing. Also you know that we have both felt constrained since the chalet and my letters would only have been forced and self-conscious. My ideal of you has been a bit groggy since the chalet; probably also yours of me – that was what I meant when I wrote from Bordeaux that we needed to write to each other but it was too difficult and I was waiting till some

---

*Father David Knowles (b. 1896, d. 1974). Downside, Christ's, Camb. Fellow of Peterhouse. Mediaeval historian. A frequent visitor to Sligger's chalet.

conjunction of wind and rain restored your reality and my faith – I hope this is not hurting you – it is not a question of resentment or injury but only that there are some temples that can be destroyed but not re-erected in 3 days. As a matter of fact I am coming to Cambridge next week end. I expect Freddie has told you and I want to dine with you and Jack or you or Jack on Saturday night then what I hoped you would do, I was going to write to-night to you anyhow; is to come up to London either Sunday or Monday, get a hamper and go down to the Lock House for the night and next evening. I can probably pay all our fares etc – the house is empty – it would be Childe Roland to the Dark Tower came I don't think it is any good trying to impinge at Cambridge (do you?) and I had been hoping you would come away to the Lock House where we could talk and be alone in the world. I am very probably going to Jamaica next week possibly on Monday even in which case I would try and dine with Freddie on Sat. night and we could go home Sunday. Jamaica is five thousand miles and more away and I should be gone six months tutoring the world's bloodiest boy unless I have to take him abroad instead. It is all very uncertain but Jamaica next week seems likeliest. I shall probably spend most of my earnings exploring the Caribbean when I've finished and come home in the summer and live on shares when one could meet again – meanwhile the Lock House seems our last chance and I would like to say goodbye to it with you – if you can't come I should probably ask Jack or Freddie or Charles – and of course we could meet in the middle of the week if Sunday or Monday don't suit you and I was leaving later only for God's sake don't think it is a case of take him back to where he was happy and his memory will return etc. I have to go down there to get some riding breeches and I should like to see it before it is let again and given a light frost or a misty evening it would be a nice place to go together – ains ke ve oltre mar. There is no case of a quarrel or anything. I would love to have stayed with you at Christmas, perhaps I shall still – but wolves saw Moeris at the chalet and he has forgotten so many songs. Please don't feel I am thrusting an experiment on you or expect you to take up any line about it – we are too fond of each other and too alike to have anything to fear even if we go to the Lock House as the most desultory pair of old acquaintances – which is not likely to occur. All I ask is that you do not feel resentful because I have not written and that you come home if you can so that we may see each other in peace and quiet and so survive the separation which we aren't quite in training for now – you see I am afraid I might never come back from the West Indies after my tutorship expires because the lure of Spanish America, desert islands, tropical forests, Mayan temples may prove too strong, on the other hand I may not go to Jamaica at all. I should know to-morrow and I will send you a wire. I won't say any more because you would not like affection which you might feel to be only remorse and because I shall see you soon – only the fonder you feel of me the more I shall be happy; if you can come home with me all I ask is that we can be like that alone and that I know you would not mind me saying goodbye to my house as I have always wanted you to live there too. I shan't be going to Oxford before I go or making a round of these partings. Pascal says the end of love is respect and I think lack of that at present is our trouble. Give Jack my love and don't let anyone know about this letter. I will try and let you know for certain to-morrow when I go away.

Cyril

28 Oct 1925. Telegram.

Noel Blakiston,
Magdalene.

Sailing Monday can you manage Sunday
Cyril

2 Nov 1925. Avonmouth.

Noel Blakiston,   S.S. Patuca.
Magdalene College.

Dear Noel,

This is a very white boat but not very big. I have met the elegant cock-eyed lady. The boy has been rather trying but his mother has coped. Bath looked lovely and oppressive, thunder clouds etc. I thought of us there. I do hope you had a nice lunch. I am sorry if I was bloody last night but I was terribly overwrought and it has made me like you more than ever. Honour has come back again, as a King to earth – and our ideal selves have met again to the exclusion of this more material parting which doesn't seem to count. I daren't stay away writing any longer – I'll send you another letter if possible. Please trust me in future etc, it gives one a motive for behaving. I'm afraid this is a sentimental letter. I hope you had a nice lunch with my mother. I think she was appeased when I told her too about the Lock House. Thank you for coping so well through all this fuss.

My cable address is Connolly, Ethelcosta, Jamaica – it is inspiring and not desolating to have seen you. Give William my love and Jack, memories of the Almanzora, tell him, meet me all the time. Dear Noel.

Cyril

I thought we were fairly compatible yesterday.
I hope you won't mind being my best friend again. I know it's a strain. χαιρε.

29 Nov. Telegram. Kingston, Jamaica.

Noel Blakiston,
Magdalene.

Dear Noel,
    There are no salt marshes in Eden. Otherwise happy. Lovely letters. Send more. Writing.

30 Nov 1925.

H. N. Blakiston, Esq.,
The Rectory,
Kirkby on Bain,
Lincolnshire,
England.

Auburn,
    Half Way Tree PO,
    Jamaica,
    B.W.I.

Dear Noel,
    You must have got my cable to-day which cheers me up. It is lovely getting your letters – they always seem to come when I want one most and never arrive in batches. I am very happy here. The voyage was awful at first but it grew calm with the Azores – which

seemed green and soft like Ireland and after them the sun shone, the sea grew bluer and the nights hotter till we got really into the tropics with all the crew in white, flying fishes, phosphorus, blazing sun and calm seas and new and brighter stars. I used to sleep on deck, all our party did and one dark night there came a lovely smell of wild jasmine and I knew we were near land. The next day we passed Hayti and Tortuga and saw Cuba in the distance and then we arrived on a rainy morning. There were very nice people on the boat, men going to Columbia and Panama, some a bit rough but all very nice to me and quite nice people coming here. I have womanised ever since leaving London – partly because they are the only educated and sensitive people here and partly because I feel very chaste now and know I am safe with them and would have hell if I noticed too much the lovely half caste boys who abound – women seem very anxious for friendship with men on the whole as they never trust each other and are quite ready not to flirt. I know that lady we saw on the platform fairly well but beyond looking like the Queen of Sheba she is not very interesting. There was a Russian girl called Davydoff who knew Koko* but did not like him and said he was not received only his sister – Jamaica is lovely but I have seen nothing of it, we live in a fashionable suburb which looks like the garden of Eden – greenness in every direction to green mountains on one side and the lagoons on the other. There is lovely sunshine not too hot and balmy sea breezes. I am writing on the verandah and beside me hover humming birds as large as bees. My boy is rather nice now and quite fond of me. He has two sisters, the elder like Eastwood, the younger very small, competent, attractive and amusing – we tango together, race our horses, make cakes and talk French but I shouldn't think she will ever impinge much but she lends a touch of intimacy to this languid hearty life. The father is quiet and kind, the mother I like best – she is very witty now I know her and very kind and intelligent – she quarrels with her husband and her daughters and gets sent cables to come back to England all the time and blank cheques, strings of pearls etc. – she rather replaces Sligger for me. I grow like Timothy and ride, play tennis, swim, run, but a day or two ago my horse went down on some tram lines and I am laid up with a strained ankle, water on the knee and several tiresome cuts and bruises. Everyone is very kind. I miss you a lot and whatever I think of inevitably leads to you and winters cold in Kirkby. To think we went to Seo, Europe is like a

*A Russian whom N.B. had met at Beaulieu.

dream here, everything is. You would like fireflies. Long letters follow soon. I am at the usual stage of being obsessed with the idea of you and I can hardly be said to miss you as thinking of you gives me such pleasure. Post going. Love to Jack, Freddie, Charles, William.

My love to your mother. Writing to-morrow but boat going now.

13 Dec 1925. Telegram.   *Jamaica.*

Blakiston,
Magdalene,

Lovely book many thanks and so sorry no Kirkby Christmas missing you badly Happy birthday much love send address.

30 Dec 1925.

Auburn,
Half Way Tree P.O.,
Jamaica.

We have been away for Christmas to the other end of the island, motoring through tropical gorges with bamboos a hundred feet high, over high mountain pastures and down to sugar estates and coconut plantations to a place called Montego Bay where we bathed four times a day in a coral lagoon among fishes weighing ten stone and others which had electric light in the evenings. It was very lovely but I missed you and Eliot's poems sounded like a crack of doom

    this is the dead land
    this is cactus land
    here the stone images –

I am glad you are going to be in London. I expect you will enjoy it. Go to the Russian Church near Victoria if you can. Jamaica is more lovely and more temperate than you would expect. It is so green that it is more like England than France is and the scenery is like carols on a Hawaian guitar.

There are no books at Half Way Tree; if you would be an angel you would send me a small Lear and write in it and also go to Zwemmer in Charing Cross Road where we went our last day and ask them to try and get me a signed Eliot in the limited edition and also to send me all the works of Rimbaud and Toulet they can get. I have brought a good many books with me. I have heart-rending dreams of you nearly every night. Last night I could have sworn I really did talk to you and woke with your voice in my ears. I sent your mother a Christmas cable but only put Woodhall Spa instead of Kirkby and it was returned 'not known'. I am writing after breakfast on the verandah surrounded by humming birds, honeysuckle and roses. Europe seems to be very tempestuous at present. I should like in a way to be among those storms; some of your letters sound like St. Agnes Eve. Another letter from you has just come while I am writing – they are a joy and make me feel very guilty for being so inarticulate, especially as you are seldom out of my mind. Do you think you could return Greek ethics to Professor R. M. Dawkins Exeter College Oxford as he wants it back – I had a letter from him, also from the Ram* whom I had congratulated. Dawkins said the modern Cretans called frost and rain κάιρος δία δύο weather for two for which they get a mark don't you think. I am not intimate with anyone here but I do not think I am considered a maniac or anything dreadful. Ask Koko if he knows Natacha Davydoff or Dorothy Brandon if you see him – you should have fun exploring London – go to Smith Square and Barton St. Westminster – there is a little street leading from Smith Square which has a very Spanish church which goes into Barton St and where there is a lovely view of the towers of Westminster over a wall. It is just near Millbank. China Town is not thrilling. If you go to Ti Tchong Lo 16, I think or 60, Pennyfields he will show you round. Li Chees are the best food there. I think Westminster Cathedral is still about the best thing in London, especially across Green Park. Do go and see my mother when she is back from Switzerland and give my love to any one you meet I know. The best food in London is at Boulestin's in Leicester Square. The Ivy runs it close. B. is a vile old man but very good on all things French, he knows me but probably doesn't remember my name. Claridge's is a nice place to take a book to for tea, the Café Royal is good for food and the café part amusing after dinner.

---

*A. B. Ramsay, Eton master who had been appointed to succeed A. C. Benson as Master of Magdalene.

[*Jan 1926*].

Noel Blakiston, Esq.,   Myrtle Bank Hotel,
Magdalene College,   Kingston,
Cambridge,   Jamaica, B.W.I.
England.

Dear Noel,

I am sorry to be doing so badly about writing but it is almost impossible to touch a pen or paper in this country '*c'est quelque chose de trop exprimé*'. It seems ages since I have written to you but I have done my best with a couple of cables and failed lamentably to write to anyone else. I have been laid up until about a week ago with a bad knee, ankle etc from a riding accident. I think I told you about it. My horse fell down on some tram lines at a canter and I hit the road all along my left side but broke no bones. My small boy is pretty trying, he is quite humorous and quite affectionate but that is about all I can say for him. He is incredibly selfish, greedy and conceited, old for his age in the most unpleasant way and young in the nastiest too – he is also a bridge and motor car maniac. I should think he will be a successful business man or possibly a lawyer. He rather symbolises *l'esprit moderne* and makes me feel a melancholy survival of the culture of the old world. He has two sisters both very selfish but nice as long as they are not considering themselves thwarted of anything, they fight most of the time with their mother whom I like best of the family so there is usually a battle going on. The mother is intelligent and amusing, considering her sex, and very fond of me – she was very nice while I was ill and is always helping me to get out for the evening etc. I would rather be with her than any of the others I think as there is no need to talk. She has a husband who goes to the office, is very tidy and fussy and to whom the rest of the family take their grievances. He is a yellow little man and the whole family are Jews though one must not say so. They are supposed to be the richest people in Jamaica but they don't live very excitingly as only the mother is extravagant and as they have a house in England near the Lock House and another in London.

The mother has some quite nice relations here who live in enormous 18th century houses full of silver and mahogany. I have seen very little of the island but it looks lovely – it is very mountainous and very very green. I don't find it at all too hot here, it is cool enough to sleep at night and it is nice being able to sit out or go for motor drives or to open air cinemas full of fireflies and coconut palms and never feel too hot or too cold. The days are either bright and sunny or green and laden with rain like it sometimes was on Upper Club or most of May this year. We work from 11–1 and read or sleep till about 4 from then onward one plays tennis or bathes or goes to a party and at night we dance or go to the cinema or out to dinner – we often bathe in the early morning too or ride or run. It is a fairly hearty life but doesn't impinge very much. One has to womanise in this country as all the men are utterly unromantic and talk filth or bridge or polo – half caste boys are nice but black people are rather difficult to stomach. I think the Central American ones would be more thrilling though there are some quite nice Chinese and coolies. Most of the fruits here are outlandish and insipid and one often gets the feeling that the Thames Valley is more tropical sometimes than this will ever be. Jamaican girls are nice on the whole; they are rather cool and competent and do not bitch as a rule. They are quite intelligent though ignorant and ill-read; except for a few gray bearded legislators they are the only people one can talk seriously to and they certainly are very lovely. I am fond of dancing as I always am whenever I start it again and have got quite good now besides being about the only man who can tango so that saves one the trouble of making conversation much. I haven't seen anyone here I like more than the rest or that I would want to see in England except to meet by accident when I was with you or Bobbie. As for the tropical climate etc. I have never felt so chaste in my life and I am perfectly content with dancing and drinking lime squashes and talking idly in cool rocking chairs. The island tends to make one sentimental and genial rather than passionate and I keep the sentiment for missing things. I miss Europe a good deal and England more than I expected – I feel quite a proprietary interest in Europe now and it seems deliciously complicated and toylike compared to the enormous and dull simplicity of the new world. Certainly the West Indies are the oldest part of it but the Britishness of Jamaica minimises that. I had my first earthquake the other day and rather enoyed it. I would like to see something of Central America before I go away. Costa Rica sounds the nicest country in it. I have a good many books with me and spend quite a lot of time in learning more French and Greek and Latin and Spanish as well as in appreciating masterpieces. I miss winter a good deal and I can't think of snow or frost or fires without them merging into you. I feel we are permitted reminiscence when the time letters take renders news so ephemeral, though things go pretty slowly here. I enjoy disappearing during family rows and then going over the details of our saga. Really this year has been fairly successful for us – we discovered how to destroy absence at Christmas and we had that week end at the Lock House at Easter and the walk to Gautby and Avignon and the Pont du Gard and Notre Dame. Then Lulworth which was my discovery of England and marks about my high watermark for sustained rapture and Winchester which was its very pleasant echo. That book is written by a pretty good fool but one feels that of everyone who has been to the places one has and it is full of facts and lovely photos and has a map and a nice cover and I go and read it once a day at least through thinking of Seo or Font Romeu. That evening at Gerona was good too; especially the line of houses along the river and the lights in the rain. Even the chalet had the walk by the slate pool and when ever I try to imagine you clearest it is framed in the window of the locked room surrounded by wraiths of mist and wrapped in that gaudy quilt like Heathcliff on his native heath. Our last meeting was best of all I think; I did not know static affection could be so intense till the journey down from Cambridge and our walk after lunch was very good though nothing to Childe Roland to the Dark Tower came – I know now I would rather be at Kirkby in the rain with you than anywhere else which I did not know before if you remember.

I enclose a wretched p.o. which I can't cash if you can have any better luck can you send me a cable with it? If you ask for a week end letter and send it on Friday or early Saturday you can send 20 words for 10/6 or 11/–. I also enclose a bad photo of me. Give Jack one if he would like it or anyone else. Do you know this

> Plus que le marbre dur me plait l'ardoise fine
> Plus mon Loyre Gaulois que le Tibre latin
> Plus mon petit Lyré que le mont Palatin
> Et plus que l'air marin la douceur angevine

It was written by Du Bellay (1560?) when he came back from Rome – the last line is fairly unbeatable and seems to sum up Bordeaux and Saintonge for me as well as much in you in England. Forgive the irresponsible tendency to sentimentality which this eternal summer produces. My small boy interests me a lot. He is fond of literature and has terrific personality but not all of it nice. He is very amusing and rags me very well. He set a Latin Prose this morning.

'Caesar was very intelligent and had an incredibly good figure with

marvellous eyes and superb hair. His tribunes were pretty idle but his books were definitely good, he was a lovely man', and I am not usually let off as lightly as that. He likes T. S. Eliot, the Odyssey in English, the Bible in Latin otherwise our tastes differ. I am really rather fond of him. It is hopeless to conceal anything from him. We both of us sulk a good deal and he is terribly hard to control. I must stop for the present.
    1926.
    A happy new year. I drank your health when it started. I haven't welcomed it very much and am having an attack of disillusion –

    between the conception
    and the creation
    between the emotion
    and the response
    falls the shadow
        life is very long.

I have met a nice officer who reads Proust but otherwise men here are pretty low and I am sinking into a champagne and cocktail existence and a predominantly feminine society where I am handicapped by a morbid horror of any physical contact except dancing and an equally morbid indifference to anyone the moment they betray the slightest interest in me. I try to find romance but get tired of someone as soon as they call me Cyril. I don't think I will ever be able to fall in love – for thine is the Kingdom.

Cyril

We should meet in May or April – I will write again, do please go on writing to me. I will cable for the other books. Send me Lear. I had a nice letter from Piers.

    In the lovely lofts of Bedlam
    in stubble soft and dainty
    brave bracelets strong
    sweet whips ding dong
    and a wholesome hunger plenty. is the good life really, but

    oisive jeunesse
    à tout asservie
    par delicatesse
    j'ai perdu ma vie –

My very best love to Jack and William.

Auburn,
Half Way Tree P.O.,
Jamaica.

Dear Noel,

I seem to have kept this letter for weeks and yet have nothing to add to it. Life is very long. It is cold and gray this morning and the wind produces the unfamiliar sound of falling leaves which gives me home sickness as surely as this weather would bring out someone else's rheumatism otherwise there has been nothing but sunshine and scenery so perfectly out of sympathy with sorrow or thought as to make the experience of anything worth writing down impossible. I dance most nights, play bridge most evenings, tennis most afternoons, work in the mornings and very often bathe which in this climate is liquid heaven. I womanise a good lot but they remain pretty foggy all the time and the ghastly obviousness of the whole proceeding rather appals me. I still feel very chaste but get fits of sentimentality in the evenings sometimes – this island consists of Jews, Jamaicans and Kiplingites (officials, soldiers etc) the Jamaicans are the nicest, the Jews the richest and the Kiplingites the most respectable – I met a girl who came to a fancy dress ball as a schoolboy (I went as an Arab) who reminded me a lot of you and whom I have seen a good deal of since for that reason. There are terrific family troubles in this household all day and all night which make my escapes from it a great relief – the two daughters fight their mother (they are always the attackers) and try to enlist their father on their side. They make a very fair Goneril and Regan when on the war path. I am usually considered an enemy as being in receipt of their mother's confidence and having been imported by their mother into the languid island and most battles rally round Charlie's behaviour. He makes a very fair Heathcliff and is devoted only to one sister who is usually rude to him except when it suits the game to make him the martyr and us the oppressors but as a rule he is the unbridled creature who has been ruined by his mother and presumably me. His chief hate is against the elder sister who is certainly selfish and conceited but hardly deserves the storm of malice which is rained on her while her mother looks on amused – she is 24 and the other day in front of a large lunch party insulted her mother and fell on her small brother and scratched his face and hands – the other sister I have seen leave the room in the middle of dinner when addressed by her mother and the husband has raged in front of me at finding his wife in my bedroom (also her son's) talking to me – 'In Jewry is God known' – Life is made bearable by the sunshine and the niceness of the mother who is humorous as well as witty and intelligent and always extremely nice to me and we laugh at everything together and I am saved by Charlie's saving sense of humour and the pathetic hope which moves all teachers that they are doing some good from utterly loathing and detesting him so that he and I and his mother are nearly always allies – we have just been asked on a yachting trip to Central America – but certainly won't be able to go – also I enjoy this pleasant social life and can escape very easily to the sporting club which is near here and where one can bathe, drink, talk, dance, at almost any time of day. I like teaching too and getting to know Vergil more by heart and learning new French words and the romance of Algebra and Geometry – if only I had someone less bone-idle, conceited, and prosaic to teach I should enjoy it very much. Anyhow one learns patience that way. I am writing in the calm after the storm as Charlie yesterday was rude to his sister, to his mother, was ticked off by his father and rude again to his mother, ran away and went without dinner, refused breakfast this morning, affected ear ache, refused to kiss his mother good morning or to address his sister at all, the usual family feud raging over enemy action and me being consulted about how one can get one's hair to turn white etc. I enjoy the jokes, secure in knowing I am going out to dine and dance to-night and in the possession of nice books to bury myself in. Really I am quite happy – this eternal sunshine and balmy breeze seems to make content the normal condition of the mind and reduces passion to sentimentality, loneliness to idle musing, the past to a dream the future to another and the present to a drowsy sleep. Charlie and his mother and I sail on the 5th of April and I shall probably be with them till the first of May – but two or three months is a long way to think ahead in this country – I am brown from head to foot, am rather stronger, but have lost weight. The sun is getting ready to set and the light is as golden as it can be before turning red. The niggers are singing in the kitchen, the mocking birds in the garden, and the smell of rose and jasmine comes in through the window, cactus land? Lotus land? I am alone in the house, shall I bathe or ring someone up or read? Sitting still is best in this island, where the smoke goes up from the house in the trees and Circe waits singing beside her loom.

Next day.

I have just had another very nice dream about you – all my soure-sweet days – I will lament and love – I too have enjoyed Shropshire Lad here – longing to see you but I find your reality unimpeded here – one must be Prospero or Caliban on this island so far I am Prospero except that I rarely think. Love and to Jack and William and the Ram.

C

24 Jan 1926. Telegram. Myrtlebank, Jamaica.

Blakiston, Magdalene.

Idling Lotusland Cactusland shades of Phlebas long letter sent much love for thine is the

2 Feb 1926. ˜ *Telegram.* Kingston.

Blakiston, Magdalene.

O for Kirkby damn the lotus dear you

Telegram. 3 Feb 1926. Kingston.

Blakiston, Magdalene.

Considered him days life is for time is consider in memoriam.

Feb 1926.

> Auburn,
> Half Way Tree P.O.,
> Jamaica.

Dear Noel,

Cables are an inadequate form of communication. Mine arrive two hours before I send them and must seem foolish and unreal while yours sound hostile and the advice about Phlebas who has over-whelmed me since Christmas Eve nearly drove me frantic –

O vilain pays, o juifs affreux
qui ronflent autour du malheureux.

March or April 1926.

Noel Blakiston, Esq.,
Kirkby on Bain.

Auburn,
Half Way Tree P.O.,
Jamaica.

Dear Noel,

Thank you for your letter. I have written to Jack who may tell you news of me – I wish I was with you. I miss you so much that saying so is irony – why write. The sun shines all day. I read all the time I can and exist the rest – Calypso's island without Calypso Circe's with only the swine – the country would be lovely if one ever saw it – I can't write letters to anyone and every one must think I have forgotten them – see Dr. Johnson on Bologna sausage, index to Boswell. See also Arthur Rimbaud, *Saison en enfer*, remarks on 'Bonheur' leading up to '*o saisons o châteaux*' – I avoid doing anything we have ever done like going for a walk or anything because it reminds me of being with you – the laugh freezes on the lips and impulses arise still born – I feel like Hylas held by the nymphs in the pond answering to the voice that wandered ever farther away – but perhaps you are Hylas and me Hercules – I cannot believe we will ever be together again, it would be so nice, and those books in the study, the green leaves in the orchard and descending unwillingly to meals. I sail on the 5th on the Carare and reach Avonmouth on the 18th I think of April, meet me there for God's sake if you can and we might stay a night at Bath or Downside straight away – or is it term time. Downside would be lovely – *amici fures temporis* – people live by what they write yet writing is such a dim form of existence – still it is better than reading, sleeping or eating I suppose and what I have seen of so called active lives, soldiers, sailors, officials and business men they waste more time than anyone – planters are a bit better – Sex is only defensible as a subject for inspiration don't you think – in itself it is unnecessary, I have learnt out here that physical beauty is worthless not only without intelligence to animate it (as opposed to high spirits) but without the intellectual domination of whoever admires it – oh these long winded words. Oxford, London, unreal cities, intellectual, sensibility, sense of values, sexual, homosexual, fantastic etc – what a jargon don't you think really – will you share a tower with me some time, a round and rather dilapidated one, we would have books and write them and play in a stream and ask the peasants intelligent questions: like Wordsworth – it is that or China. I feel the Sebastian like craving for vanishing by degrees out of the world – and for that southern China might be as nice as anywhere

> Between the Resurrection
> and the ascension
> between Eurydice
> and the swift Hebrus
> comes the passing
> *pressé de trouver le lieu et la formule*

Phlebas learnt the more under the water than Narcissus gazing at it? Arnaut, Phlebas, Orpheus, Narcissus, Tamunis, *quintette affreux qui partagent le Panthéon de ce nouveau Sévère* – when I come back I shall have no money and nothing to do – can one write without starving? no – but one can starve without writing – I should like to take a Cook's party round Europe, I shall appreciate it so well again – that is the active life – or else bury myself in my aunt's house near Pau and read and write and tolerate no one but you. But seeing you comes first, do come to Avonmouth and let's spend the day in Somerset. You could come from Morthoe – this is a silly and unhinged letter – don't quote it anyone – my best love to Jack and Charles and Freddie. Tell Freddie I hope he has been getting my film society tickets all right as one of them came out here. I will come to Cambridge if you can't meet me. April is the cruellest month – *un bel dì vedremo levarsi un fil di fumo sull'estremo confin del mare e poi la nave appare e poi appare la nave bianca . . . o quam te memorem Noel* I am soaked in French I regret to say – Rimbaud and Valery and also Voltaire, André Chénier, Racine and Co – I have written one or two French poems – nothing else, except some scraps and a lyric.

The vexing thing is that I have learnt so little here by experience that I had not already assumed from conviction. I have explored the mess, the office, the synagogue, the ball room and find there nothing to alter what I thought they would provide. I feel more indifferent and less hostile to their inmates – Girls are important in a country where no man has been educated enough to be individual because they at least are decorative and gentle. To love them on the other hand seems to me unthinkable they are so ungainly and so ordinary besides which the whole process of flirtation, the triteness of passion, the dreariness of marriage seem altogether disgusting. Also their influence on men is for the worse, they encourage 'manliness', vanity and worldly ambitions and they reduce all male beauty to a question of height and uniform – and they are so dull. Friendship with them is possible and advantageous in a place like this but anywhere else entirely unnecessary – I think dancing is permissible though. Male loves at least bear fruit in masterpieces like gravel in an oyster but all the time I have been here I have felt no consciousness of sex at all – only the beauty of ideas can give bodies any variety and long association must precede any embrace.

I think now, more than I did before, that art is the only medium where the individual by expressing himself is yet renouncing himself and though I have written very little here I feel literature absorbing my attention more and more and my neglect for everything else being more professional and less philosophical than before – I detest all existing schools, côteries etc and though there are a lot of people I want to meet I hope I shan't be in London or Paris or anywhere where the craftsmanship and nepotism of letters is over asserted. Lyric poetry I think is the best thing in literature and it consists of setting words to their own music – it is impossible to write anything longer till one has learnt never to write a bad line (which one can do by reading classics of any kind) – what are your views on a career? I think mine must be the nearest thing to literary independence if not actually literature itself – I pine for solid works of learning, Tacitus, Bayle and all 18th century compendiums. Do come and meet me even if we can only travel up in the train together. I shall never forget you because you have become the platonic idea of so much to me to which any new and unrelated phenomena are immediately referred (these sentimental friendships) it is that which makes you so hard to write to – love to Jack.

for he shall rise up at the voice of a bird, and
the daughters of music shall be brought low.

on such a morning grief would have stayed Adam's hand, remembering Eden, Orpheus would have moved more than ever in a dream among the Thracian wilderness and the Sleeping Beauty turned and sighed in her palace among the dripping trees; it wanted but the song of doves or the scent of woodsmoke that my heart should break and already it stirred strangely to the echo of things that had preceded the spirit's death; the faint and far off rumble of the César Franck Symphony and with it the memory of the Lock House woods and Proust among the fire tongs and mists at Minehead and the phrase that expressed in all its sorrow and finality the one fact of absence from

Noel and thinking of that I wondered if ever again we would sit in the study at Kirkby and talk and read or whether I had lost understanding and the chance of being understood and would only realise that loss even under the cruel intellectual thaw of a wet morning or ever the silver cord be loosed or the golden bowl be broken, the past claim its punishment and memory return into its own.

I think *Cloud Cuckoo Land's** a bit too simple and sensuous. After all the Greeks had abstract nouns and why drag in these squalid women? I am sure mine is better even what I have done (most of which now seems meaningless being about sex) except for the superior competency of her style. Still I like its uncritical lack of sentimentality.

P.S. Surely it was unnecessarily cruel of you to address an envelope in your hand with only a bill inside! Green woods of Kirkby, books on the study shelves, the end of spring, and you and me talking about ourselves! *Heureux qui comme Ulysse a fait son beau voyage.*

Thank you a lot for Lear. Thank God we shall meet in a month's time – O think Noel. Do come and meet the Carare. I would like to be with you when I see England again and enjoy the first benefits of understanding. I am more indifferent to my surroundings now than ever before I think but I rarely get a moment to myself – I have a lot to tell you. Do come to Avonmouth.

Best love to Jack. Tell him when I die Loulé will be written on my heart. I hope your reading party is a success. CARARE, Elders & FYFFES *remember*.

P.S. My grandmother is in Bath and would give us lunch if you could meet me. I would like you to meet her – she is well over 80. If you can't get to Avonmouth try and get to Bath – send me a wire to the boat (Carare) in that case. I will try and cable you when it arrives.

On the envelope:

ηλθε ηλθε παρα ποτάμον, ὦ φίλ
ἕταιρε, ὥς ἐνρησω και σε και
τον λίμενα

Cloud Cuckoo Land by Naomi Mitchison.

4 April 1925. Telegram. Kingston, Jamaica.

Noel Blakiston,
Kirkby on Bain.

Do please meet Carare Avonmouth 18th Sunday morning or join me Bath that day love

About 19 April 1926.

H. N. Blakiston Esq.   [London]

Dear Noel,

I am sorry about yesterday. I arranged to join my mother at Bath and thought you could come there or to the boat which I would like you to have seen as it is rather a nice one. I got your wire and wired to my mother saying I would go up to London and down to Bath by the next train and sent you a wire at Paddington telling you the special would be late and to wait for it if you could but when I arrived it hadn't been delivered. I suppose you had to go. It was rather depressing but I managed to collect Charles for dinner and we had a pleasant evening. I rang up Magdalene at dinner but they didn't seem to know much about you. I missed the only train last night and stayed in the Turkish baths where I did the night before we went to Calais together or wherever it was – I am going back to Bath this morning. 17 Vineyards. I cursed the special for being so late. We had a pleasant voyage though very rough. Rendall* late of Winchester was on board and is a very good man. England is unreal at present I can't make out if I have ever been there before or if I have ever left it. I think I have aged rather – I hoped you might have been able to get away the week end and we could have spent Sunday somewhere. I will come to Cambridge soon if you think it a good plan which I do – I wonder if Freddie would put me up – give him and Jack my best love and thank Jack for the book. I have a letter for him somewhere which I will send as soon as I find it.

Cyril

Horrible thought! perhaps you are meeting me to-day – but I said Sunday morning in the cable I think.

*Montague Rendall, headmaster of Winchester.

22 April 1926. Postcard.

H. N. Blakiston, Esq.,   The Lock House,
Magdalene College.   Deepcut.

I can come Saturday week if Freddie can put me up. I have sent him
a line about it. I am staying this week here with my mother. It is very
nice being here again. Give Jack my love and ask him to tell me about
Boni de C.* I vowed I would hear your voice before I got here. I
think that was the 4th – time I rang you up. What a pity you could
not hear mine!

Love

27 April 1926.

H. N. Blakiston, Esq.,   The Lock House,
Magdalene College,   Deepcut.
Cambridge.

Dear Noel,
   I will come on Saturday latish – I'll let you know what time later.
I have to go to Oxford first to see Sligger which I am not looking
forward to – Oxford I mean, not Sligger. I don't think I have ever
regretted a place less than Oxford; or rather felt more indifferent
to one. I am extremely happy here. I have a horse to ride which I
enjoy and plenty to read and all the solitude necessary even for a
Sebastian. I am longing to see you, (words, words, words). Give my
love to Jack and William. We dine on Sunday night I take it as Freddie
is away. I hope you don't mind me going to Oxford first.

   O for the unity which bias lends!
   O narrowness, how rich thy dividends!

I expect they are all at it already. I am awfully fat you know and my
face has grown. Give me simple fare by the way, one is not very apt
to notice what one eats when excited. Seeing you is only just beginning
to dawn on the real world of meaning, before it seemed to pass
understanding as much as seeing God or eternity the other night – more
words.

Cyril

*Boni de Castellane, aristocratic dandy.

I am enjoying this new lease of winter. Did you know the day my boat got in was the anniversary of our meeting in Avignon?

I will try and arrive for tea with you as the others may be at dinner – anyhow it does not much matter if we are technically alone or not. My mother sends her love. There are 2 gaudy barges in the Lock and 3 swans but more trees are being felled.

8 May 1926.

H. N. Blakiston, Esq.,   80 St. George's Sq.,
Magdalene College.   S.W.1.

Dear Noel,

I am sorry if you have been anxious about Jack. I was too. We just missed the London train on Wednesday. I hope all is well now. I enjoyed having him at home awfully. We would have wired to you on Wednesday, but were very short of money till I got some yesterday again. I hope Jack did not get into trouble. We drew a blank at Liverpool St. yesterday and he went on to K's Cross and was going to try the Hartogs' if that failed. He said he would let me know last night if he was still in town and I didn't hear so thought all was well. Can you give him the enclosed. It was very lovely at home and Jack made a very nice guest but I missed you a lot. I am sorry Jack was kept back from you. I was very depressed here last night after dinner and felt you must be too. Why did you like London? I think it is bloody and pine already for the Lock House trees and birds and for my brown bed and the noise of running water. The strike* is pretty dreary. I am a special constable and have got to go and guard something at 5.45 tomorrow morning. It seems a long way to the Devon cottage, the warm room by the wintry sea, and the guest of harmony. It takes me a few days to realise I have seen you. I suppose the corollary to you saying you never knew me so well is that I was never more myself which is cheering. I do not deny that one can be entirely different to what one has been before, but I do say that one cannot keep it up and so sublimations are justified.

Dere Noel I like you soe

I enclose 'on such a morning' which I seem to have carried off. We

*The General Strike.

123

must meet again soon. I am rather overwhelmed by Cambridge. Oxford I hold my own in, but with you and Jack I felt more at home than I have felt anywhere I think for some time. You have held me through all my permutations as if I was the old man of the sea and now it is for you to tell me which is the real me. William is one of the few people it is possible to disagree with without disliking. I hope we have got past change Noel, it is sad to think of so many dead me's that have known so many former you's. I think one can build up a fairly safe life on art provided only that one can create good art. *Plurima vanitas.* The trouble is that a bad poem seems, like a good poem, 'a little thing, but mine own' – still I think one must be pretty professional to succeed – I think writing is the only plant that could blossom from 'that Thracian feeling' which we both seem to get. We are obviously not men of action because though thoroughly capable of action we cannot keep it up – we probably cannot keep writing up either but we can never altogether get away from it – and when we do it is probably good for us. I wish Lear's Heath was in our bones – perhaps it is – only in England can mysticism go with sanity, e.g. Bunyan? Let us admit our fallibility, Milton probably thought his Latin poems better than Lycidas and I may be a better judge of you than yourself. Did not Gabriel Harvey nearly persuade Spenser to write the Faery Queen in hexameters and pentameters? This is a truly awful letter – let us be typical of the '30's (the 1930's? no, the 1630's). Anyhow I am not going far away from you again so think of me.

Cyril

Perhaps we could meet for a week end somewhere when the strike is over or we could stay at Rebénacq before you went to Biarritz. You would like it there.

Read the Constant Nymph again for guidance and write to me. I am depressed – about Bobbie for one thing. I am afraid our old friendship is of the past and the new one stands shivering on the frontier station in the drizzle of dawn and has lost its luggage.

> God attributes to place
> no sanctitie, if none be thither brought
> by men . . . is rather good conclusion to 'with all his verdure spoiled and trees adrift' the remark seems to bear some significance on indifference to geography though I don't see what. I am not

indifferent because I want to be out of London. I hope we can go back to Lock House soon. There is no coal there: but Mummie will go if she thinks I will have to cope with any wild routs here – she sends you her love.

10 May 1926.

H. N. Blakiston, Esq.,   [London]
Magdalene College.

Dear Noel,

Hasty scrawl. If you and Jack go to Avonmouth or anywhere let me know at once and I will try and join you. I cover that rear four. I have to get up at fantastic hours and watch deserted buildings for 4 hours and don't feel very excited. I had to keep the crowd moving at Marble Arch all yesterday which was better fun. I wish I was at home. I liked your poem awfully. It was surprising and is changing my views of blank verse. You caught the low and vibrant wistfulness of M. I will write again soon, write to me again now, 'way down in my heart...' I did like your poem. The cliff is real like the one where Lewis heard wings.

Am reading *The Forerunner** again. It's good. Love to Jack.

16 May 1926.

Noel Blakiston, Esq.,   The Lock House,
Magdalene College.   Deepcut,
                          Surrey.

χαῖρε Νοελ,

I couldn't quite make out if our two letters crossed – if so it spoke well for harmony that we both quoted the same two lines of Milton and the same paragraph of the *Constant Nymph*. Did you get my letter with one to Jack and 'on such a morning' enclosed all right? It probably weighed more than 8 ounces. I retired here as soon as the strike was over which grieved me as I had just been promoted to Scotland

*A novel by Dmitri Merezhkovsky.

125

Yard. I am glad the Holy Family was not disintegrated. Tell William though that omnipotence was no excuse for not finding something to do. I should think it was a sterile virtue though – I answered an advertisement in the *Times* for a secretary to 'a literary man' and came up against the most awful old satyr who seems anxious to have me. He looks like an old toad and knows all literatures. I think he's a satanist and shant go if I can possibly help it. A fruity unfrocked cleric of the nineties, anyhow I took 10 days to consider. I send you a couple of sonnets which is all the poetry I have written since I saw you and the debris collected round them – my notebook swells and I have filled 40 days since Cambridge, chiefly on the right use of Greek legends etc. I have been tackling blank verse again since your poem came. Here are the sonnets, one in a fairly minor key the first one did begin, 'Noel, I think' but I altered it to get a fuller first line

Confess, my friend, Lear's heath is in our bones
while the clear skies of Greece that once seemed ours
no more possess us than the year's first flowers
that wither in the hand – our hearts are stones
where the bright seed revives not, nor the tones
that charmed with longing through distracted hours
Tyrrhenian travellers – Not she whose powers
Narcissus slighted, whose white flower atones
for Echo spurned long since, can still inspire
ourselves in quest of the neglected byre
with dripping eaves, ill thatch't, and the uneven
approach by separate ways across the mire
through heath and murk and storm, until at even
we stretch cold hands to the uncertain fire
and meeting thus, will know we meet in heaven.

As when of old Tyrrhenian travellers
made sport of sirens, and awoke to hear
a strange sweet music on the windless sea
that banished cargoes, and accustomed eyes
to look for death, not Cumae –

in the sonnet, line 6

that lured poor sailors to regret the hours
that ever they left Cumae.

might be better, tell me.

126

or to forget the hours, or to the sirens bowers, and death instead of Cumae

one's ear gets tired before one's imagination.

> And the sad fate of Hylas whom the nymphs
> hid from his master till the Argo sailed
> bereft of man and boy, but not bereft
> of the sweet singing of the muses son,
> Orpheus, who little dreamt the end of love
> was hell twice visited, and Hebrus shore
> and solitude and the untimely loss
> of friendly face adorable.

It is only a matter of intensity that divides Wilde from Milton. 'The agonised attempts of Eliot to bind Leviathan with an hook or Wilde's facility to reconcile form with void' does that make any sense? I wrote a couple of lewd limericks about Hylas – I'll send them to the Father,* if at all. Give my love to the Holy Ghost.* It seems a very short time since he came here with his gift of Tongue.

> the gradual exercise of wisdom's Tooth
> will chaw your beauty and indent your youth!

I am going with my mother to collect some honey – do send me any more you write or have written. The second sonnet is still unpolished.

> *melius ne hic rusticus infame?*
> Oxford, the cloak room where I left my youthe
> for three long years, which when I would regaine
> had trouble with the ticket, and in soothe
> unclaim'd the foundling boy would still remaine
> A   article?
> The gradual exercise of wisdom's toothe
>   for
> had I not fled the cities of the plaine
> and found the muse a kinder God than Truth
> and learnt societie was mostly vaine
> that Art, good company, and learned Tomes
> affright poor youth as sex and cities doe
> and all the dismal academic crew

*N.B. cannot remember who these pseudonyms signify. The Father seems to have been William Le Fanu. See reference to Holy Family earlier in this letter.

dry docked in Lethe wharf – but he who roams
hears Orpheus singing in the Thracian wild
and love goes with him, like a rural child.

[and all the voluble, embittered crew?]

l.14. Youth instead of love? 10. as those lewd cities do with
all their

My mother sends her love. Write to me soon. I like Hyperion and the
bit where he dines is quite uniquely divine don't you think. I wish I
had your gift of off hand definition.

Cyril

Tell me more of this M and S with notes by W.R. – K etc. [?], is it
a new book? can you retrieve a book I left in William's room some
time as I may see you before him.

17 May 1926, Postcard.

H. N. Blakiston, Esq.,   The Lock House,
Magdalene College.   Deepcut.

Dear Noel,
    I am alone here at present. Think of me. Could you come here a
week end if I am still here or are you working hard? I am rather
intoxicated with the 18th century at present. I didn't know the *Deserted
Village* and *Traveller* were so good. Do you know Collins' poem on
Thomson's grave and 'Fair Fidele's grassy tomb' – Pope is rather
shattering too. I will write to-night or to-morrow. I wish you were
here as being almost the only person I know who appreciates the
18th ct. to the full. Greet the Holy Family if not fled to Egypt. I am
worried about your eyes.

C.V.C.

F.F.U. wants me to accept that old sorcerer.

18 May 1926.

Noel Blakiston, Esq.,   The Lock House,
Magdalene College.   Deepcut.

Dear Noel,
    Thank you for your letter which rewarded a walk up to Deepcut.
Trentishoe, Morwenstow and Culbone (nr. Porlock) look the most
deserted villages on N. Devon coast from my rather indifferent map.
I can't do anything more till I know what my career is going to be.
I am not going to the sorcerer as he is not rich enough. I may try
and get some job in Ireland. Charles wants me to take a cottage with
him in July but that would probably be in Scotland if it ever comes
off at all. I am alone here at present. It is rather a cold and windy night
and I sit by a log fire after dinner with Boswell and a few odd 18th
century tomes I unearthed upstairs. Let's make Boswell the basis of
any cryptic telegrams or cables we may have to undertake, with Eliot
for emergencies. Boswell has the advantage of practically everyone
one knows being in the index and as we both use the Headlam edition
we have only to give the number of page and column. It is amazing
how good Johnson's criticism on life and people is and how inspiredly
bad on poets. cf. Lycidas as well as Gray though the elegy does get a
good mark for 'a happy selection of images, but I don't like what
are called his great things' – still he quotes the same stanza as Tessa. I
think Gray is an interesting man but I still hold to my old classification

    Embittered academics
    Gray Callimachus Housman
    with scholarly polemics
    enlarged the mind of man

    but now that they are gone away
    we weep for bones in Africa
    and for the death of Richard West
    and Crethis who knew how to play.

Collins seems more intimate than Gray as a personality ['poor dear
Collins! would a letter give him any pleasure? I have a mind to write –
poor Collins for whom I am much concerned. I have a notion that
by very great temperance, or more properly abstinence, he might
recover'; and Boswell's note 'Collins was at this time at Oxford but

labouring under the most deplorable languor of body and dejection of mind –'] if we had lived in the 18th cent. we would only have to say we were hypochondriacs with the spleen and everyone would sympathise with us – they regarded all emotions as being natural and hence could consider them reasonably – I think the earthy mysticism of Isaiah and Eliot was about the only thing outside their ken – though Blake comes pretty near it. By the way I hold rather gloomy views about the sea, *onus deserti maris* as Isaiah aptly called it, πασα θαλάσσα θαλάσσα etc. I think ships are exciting but the sea inspires me with a sense of waste and a feeling of futility rather than humility (like the heavenly bodies). The sea has a tendency to go on and on – why this incessant rumble, this unharvested expanse where nothing grows and no one walks – *od' und leer das Meer* – I grant that I like ships very much and also the sea in summer and when it is perilous and stormy – but I don't think it is indispensable, like trees, and after all God could have obtained exactly the same effects with about a third of the expanse of water. I think our cottage would have to be within say 5 miles of it if not actually on the shore. There should be a combe going down to the sea close at hand or else the cottage should be among gigantic cliffs. The 3 villages I found all seem to be off the route of coastal charabancs though handy to towns and on the sea nearly. I am trying to write with a black cat on my lap. I spent last night in the mess with painful reminders of reading room – I now ride an enormous horse with a mouth of iron but very enjoyable – my cousin Graham de Burgh is a very nice William Egerton kind of soldier – vitality has been failing me fast the last few days. I send you some poems of Pain the last one being all I have written this week – poor Collins – you must be having a trying time working. I hope these letters don't distract you. The cuckoo sings in the boscage all day and the nightingales invade the garden all night. I think their forlorn and repeated low note is very moving though the rest of their song is chiefly apt numbers. A small boy fell into the canal yesterday and Nevil rescued him. I have discovered a lovely new walk of the true Constable and Collins scenery which makes a pleasant relief from moorland being all along oaks and beeches and meadow and high hedges and barns and ponds and village greens and seats of the quality to Pirbright church – *vox quoque moerim iam fugit ipsa* – *ille cantat, nos tacemus quando ver veniet meum?*

I suppose we've had it, our cottage must have smoaky rafters like the one in Comus. By the way I like Johnson's criticism of Mason's

Elfrida 'There are now and then some good imitations of Milton's bad manner' – that sounds like us! I think Flecker's development is more interesting than most Georgians, apart from Beazley's part in it he seems to have been very much the natural romantic determined to go through the classic (Parnassian) discipline and he seems to have fewer limitations than almost any modern – the Parrot is about as good 18th century as anyone has managed since Pope and the first verse of 'To a poet a thousand years hence' (I can't face evicting the cat to get it), seems to have the ring of the best pre-romantic lyrics

'In yonder grave a druid lies
where softly glides the stealing wave

seems close to the 'sweet archaic song'. It is a pity Flecker went in for the East. I think Keats' Ode to Melancholy is good don't you – next time you are feeling omniscient do you mind settling this little problem for me – does experience of life count for much in making literature – or is literary reality a quality based on ignorance of everything but literature? is literature life seen through a convention of life of its own? does Milton's mere acquaintance with R. King have any bearing on the sincerity of Lycidas and does the best work spring from danger and insecurity as Lewis maintained or from serene reflection? I must go to bed soon. I am bogged in 2 Narcissus poems, one blank verse (rather Wordsworth) the other lyric (it was the Schooner Hesperus) – but at present nearly all my forms of activity are at a standstill. Your letter cheered me. Do write to me; p.c.'s and hasty scrawls are ample – love to Jack – I may go away for the week end. I don't know. I wish we were going to the boy's camp together – it might revive us.

the maid of [? Parvies] whose unlettered eye
did first the God's quaint characters espy . . .

These are 2 lines for our epic –

Love –
Cyril

How shall our training end? It's a wise worm that knows its own turning! please have a mind to write! and don't take the querulous note of the last poem of pain too seriously. Let us arrange a debate for the holy family when it next meets. I suggest 'Was Cibber a blockhead?' as a good subject. As my mother is away I have given your love to the cat instead.

4 poems of pain
(thoughts of a dry brain, confessions of a windy nob etc.

I

To an East Anglian Poet

Adonis weeps and weeps in vain
   beneath his Syrian tan,
not his to cloud the limpid Bain
   with blood, a Lincoln man!

Too late Narcissus learns a place
   to cool his transports fond
he never could have loved his face
   had he looked in Gautby pond.

II

The anguish that the day dispels
   hangs heavy through the hours
when all the mouths of Dante's hells
   loom less profound than ours!

O money troubles why destroy
   the spring within the bone?
You took my heart when it sang for joy
   must you needs wring tears from a stone?

(why now wring tears from stone?)
The sea for 3 days off the Newfoundland bank coming home was like enormous oozy masses of lead coloured slate, the most depressing outlook I have ever seen with a dreary sky above it; but very pleasant after the tropics. One wanted some rum if one ever saw it through the porthole, it looked so cold. The sea is an effect, not a cause, don't you think.

III

From bondage into bondage
   See Penury enslave
the proud heart and the empty hand
   that spends but cannot save!

No liberty redeems the wage
  no service fraught with joy
when graceless youth or bigot age
  a borrowed light employ –

No friendly face adorable
  the steep descent can know
dark is the house where I must dwell
  and far the way to go!

IV

When blankness of the body born
  invades the weary mind
and every hope recedes forlorn
  and leaves a fear behind

When spirits and affections die
  and waves of dull distress
in oceans of satiety
  submerge the wilderness

O then with memories of you
  my last ideas embark –
not yours to stay the flood, 'tis true
  but you lend a hand with the ark.

[O then my memories of you – preserve the vital spark but theirs . . .]
but they . . .

May 1926.

Tuesday.   The Lock House,
                                          Deepcut,
                                            Surrey.

Dear Noel,
  I shipt you some poems by Mrs. Neville in Aldershot yesterday.
They begin to multiply at a vast rate. Here are some more.

Since friendship haunts Arcadian fields
  and Love is but a rural child
and every fruit the summer yields
  now sheds its blossom on the wild,

forsake the town and come with me
  to where the reedy Liris flows
no fairer woods did Daphnis see
  and Eden knew no lovelier rose:

That purely a literary exercise. The frugal poet gathers up the fragments that remain from each creation and makes a slighter sequel
hence the rural child again and the rest his expensive frame.

Stand close around ye artist set
with dear K to your shores conveyed
old masters sometimes will forget
the pictures that they never made.

———

Cardinal. 'And what is Connolly's profession now'

'My lord apprentice to a sorcerer
a fruity unfrocked cleric of the nineties
like an old toad that carries in its head
the jewel of literature, a puffy satyr,
who blends his Romish ritual with the filth
scrawled on Pompeian pavements – yet not lacking
the seedy courtesy of learned age
that finds itself respected.'

               'has he means?'
'A sorcerer is not an alchemist
he knows no easy road to opulence.
His stone is in his head, as I have mentioned.
The best work is ill paid – but he has means
though not enough to justify the end
a crude dependence on Apollyon'

———

But O to write inevitable prose!
that secret, Chiron, not a centaur knows!
'Absurd immortal, learn thy prose by heart
and any change will soon appear bad art –
avoid mortality, quotation, sex,
common as artifex and opifex

reject the precious, banish phantasy
and learn indifference to geography
admire my numbers, Pope was not so terse
who scorned th' excessive, and preferred good verse.'

———

Epitaph

Here lies a youth whose ill adventured years
once earned his own, and now a reader's tears.
He lived alone: whom nature formed to please
pleased only nature, knew no friends but trees.
Bondage enslaved him – he who made this song
lived long enough – 'twas not so very long.

I think that's about all – I hope you can come here and see the green-ness which entrances me at present. The nightingales are here but silent from cold and the branches seen through the drawing room window look like seaweed and coral through a diver's helmet. My mother wants to arrange for you to come but I don't know yet how long we shall be here. I think it would be sheer luxury for us to meet at present as a matter of fact, but none the worse for that. We would sit on opposite sides of the fire and read Blair's 'Grave' (1743)

[Invidious Grave! how dost thou rend in sunder
whom love has knit, and sympathy made one!
a tie more stubborn far than nature's bond.
Friendship! mysterious cement of the soul
Sweetener of life! and solder of society
I owe thee much – Thou hast deserved from me
Far, far, beyond what I can ever pay].

It has got very late writing to you. I will go on to-morrow. I am taking the Devon cottage rather seriously. I don't see why we shouldn't find somewhere for £10 or £15 a year, furnish it between us and use it when we liked. We could probably get someone to 'do for us' when we were there and be able to leave it without doing more than taking the key in our pocket – I would be willing to put my books and pictures in it and it would be a pleasant retreat – we needn't neces-sarily tell anyone where it was or that we had one at all.

My book has got into August. I think the great thing is to cultivate a professional attitude to poetry, take it as one's province, overhaul people and find them wanting.

20 May 1926.

Noel Blakiston, Esq.,　　　　　　　　The Lock House,
Magdalene College.　　　　　　　　　　Deepcut,
　　　　　　　　　　　　　　　　　　　　Surrey.

Dear Noel,

 I think an East Anglian poet would be welcome as long as not in dialect. I don't see why blank verse shouldn't be local – after all painters are pretty local and there seems a tendency to country spirit of late – Housman, a Sussex song book, the Lowery Road etc. – we might start the Bain school with Jack like Ellis, Currer and Acton Bell – Hen Bane, Wolf's Bane and Aphra Behn or something like that. I read Walter Raleigh's book on Milton, it's all right. M. is fairly easy game for patronising apologists, doubtless he was a poor mystic a century in advance of his time when it came to coping with Vaughan, Crashaw and Co. I read a lot of Keats yesterday: I must say I find it pretty hard to stomach. I liked the sonnet about Keen fitful gusts etc fair haired Milton's eloquent distress

　　and all his love for gentle Lycid drowned

Milton hardly knew King did he, as a matter of fact – still he made up handsomely for the omission – Gray seems to have been held up by lack of vitality a good lot – I think Milton's Sonnet on the nightingale is very moving. We have got 7 or 8 years to equal Lycidas which is something. I liked your lines, daylight and sin, is the best of those two. Rhyme is good I think only dangerous in the Pope couplet and impossible for any length in the heroic couplet. (cf. how Allegro and Penseroso though both compact of good remarks are hopelessly cloying to read) – and the alternate stanza of Gray's elegy is about the noblest metre in English. Compare Landor's epigrams. Blank verse has to be so terribly vital to avoid flatness unless it proceeds on a level of one fine line to 3 good ones or some such proportion. I think the fact emerges that even the slightest poem requires hard work if the dry bones are to live. I have written several more poems, about one a day, sometimes more – I'll send you a corpus when I can. I am struggling to write a short Narcissus lyric but held up at present by difficulties of form; should the transformation take place on or off the stage? And should be about as artificial as Benson's Phoenix or artless and Blake like? Dorpat* you should know is the celebrated university

*N.B. had a pamphlet by a professor at Dorpat, which maintained that Milton was an albino.

(which has undergone many vicissitudes) in Esthonia – I have been sent particulars of a vacancy for a lecturer in English at Riga where I would be in easy reach of Dorpat which is not far across the frontier. It sounds a good book. I may have to go to the sorcerer next week or the week after and try him for a month – he edited Wycherley for the Non-such and also Aphra Behn I think. That sort of man. In that case would you come here for a night or a week end and bring some work with you – my mother might or might not be here. I 'will write to you when I know for certain – Here is the end of my sorcerer'

> . . . crude dependence on Apollyon
> the latter promises, should he retire
> Hell and Eternity to be his pension
> a liberal offer, very, – God himself
> is not more liberal, more conservative
> of human effort than to let it burn
> into infinity, a vestal flame.

Card. 'but how is Connolly provided for'?

> My lord, death will release him from his debts
> for length of broadcloth longer than his credit
> and still unpaid for.

Card.

> 'tis just, 'tis rational
> Death comes at last to all who lend or owe
> treasure in heaven, 'tis best, Antonio.

Elizabethan blank verse is much easier than Milton's – Wordsworth's is easier still. It helps a lot to write long rhymed couplets if you get the first part of the tune of Poor Old Joe in your head. I do not think there is any confusion between Milton and Keats, the latter's poetry is so very fleshy and often flat, can you read Endymion? I have grown fond of the Deserted Village and the Traveller

> 'remote, unfriended, melancholy, slow'

is an astonishing first line. There is also an excellent analysis of Piers in the 4 lines

Contrasted faults through all his manners reign
though poor, luxurious; though submissive, vain:
though grave, yet trifling: zealous, yet untrue.
and even in penance, planning sins anew!

I dare say I don't come unscathed out of it. Cold has stopped the nightingales singing here – they frankly move me and are the unsuspecting victims of a poem as soon as they come back. A nightjar I think is more impressive though one is apt to mistake a frog for one – Can't we write an epic between us? it would get it over quicker. We must find a title. Theodoric, Genseric, Mezentius, Stilicho, Sertorius, that sort of thing perhaps or simply East Anglian? (in summertime on Tumby*) – I think imitation is all right as long as it is not a short cut but a genuine flame which leads first to adaptation and then to absorption after which the benefits begin to be felt. Otherwise eating a lion does not make one brave, not that there is any big game left on Parnassus. I think the main thing is to get the outlook of Milton or someone rather than to borrow the style, the unwinking humour, the large and civil view, the restrained intimacy, the discipline and the classic disdain, 'too much book' is perfect. I keep vitality going by long rides alone in the mornings or by considering greenness or reading the 18th century, Pope, Goldsmith, Collins, Gray – even Cowper.

Mummy sends her love. Will draw Dorpat for you. Write again.

Love to Jack. Will write to him.

1 June 1926.

H. N. Blakiston, Esq.,   Angel Hotel,
Magdalene College.   Midhurst,
                                     Sussex.

Dear Noel,

I got rather restive and borrowed Neville's bicycle after tea and came here for the night. 40 miles of good country. I am going to London to-morrow Naval and Military to my father. I read the *Upton Letters*† yesterday also those of Junius. Benson's style is pretty

*A hamlet in the parish of Kirkby on Bain.
†By A. C. Benson.

soapy but I think his literary criticism is rather good and it must have been rather a privilege to know him. I am tired and sleepy. Good night
Cyril

Sligger wants to publish my diary (now in November) via Buchan. These patrons. Love to Jack.

8 June 1926.

Noel Blakiston, Esq.,
Magdalene College.

Naval & Military Hotel,
Harrington Road,
South Kensington.

Dear Noel,
It will be nice seeing you on Monday. I shall be in London. Keep as much of the day as you can for me. Shall I ask my mother if she would put you up? I don't think we can go to the Lock House then. We might go to the Zoo. You and I and Jack might lunch somewhere together. I need recharging. I expect we both do. I came across a letter about our day in London when you met Sligger at Rumplemayers and we argued at Princes and went to Westminster Cathedral.

I also met Mrs Loxley who was nice and spoke wistfully of you and me at breakfast parties or tea at long leave. Good luck with your schools. This time last year our odyssey must have been about due. Johnson's lives of the poets are excellent reading. Dear Noel, adversity has remembered me and my father wants to ship me to the colonies unless I get a job in a fortnight. There is only Sligger between me and the gangway. I hope he may find me something. I liked him very much in London the day before yesterday. I am going to Downside with him on 26th. How long are you at Lancing, and where are you going afterwards? I couldn't do a Kirkby with you before you go to Biarritz? I don't want to go to the chalet.

Thank you for p.c. – moving.

I am going down to Gloucestershire to-morrow the Homestead Quenington Fairford will find me. I'll be back here on Saturday – o quam te memorem Noel – keep Monday for me.
Cyril

I am reconciled to poverty but not to bondage, could I come to Kirkby before you leave? My mother is out of London at present. Think of me and I will hope you a better fate in schools than mine.

'their acquaintance began early; the life of each was pictured on the other's mind, their conversation therefore was endearing for when they met, there was an immediate interchange of congenial notions.'

Johnson on Pope and
Martha Blount!

O nightingale that at the close of day
sings in the thickets, and in ancient land   every
sang to the heros of the muses' band
unseen as falling dew, and showed the way
to immortality – o canst thou say
if ever I their love shall understand
and coming now to try my prentice hand
with late and faltering song shall be as they?   them
O world, world, world – the sad tones rise forlorn
                strange sweet notes forlorn
from the dark alders by the faint heard stream
rise from the
and take no thought for me – such notes were borne
down a Greek hillside where the shepherds dream
the   upon
Some lonely 'Hill' God on his scrannel reed
a
calls to his mother, and the Earth gives heed.

11 June 1926.

Noel Blakiston, Esq.,   The Homestead,
Magdalene College.   Quenington,
                          Fairford.

Dear Noel,
    Thank you so much for your letter which has food for much thought I would like to dispute your order I think of human nature, nature, art – I think nature is rather inadequate without tradition really as in our quotation on the end of Eden, one must be able to attribute a sanctity. I wouldn't put people first either I don't think, with the exception of you I don't think they will survive the strain of being ends in themselves. Also you have left out oneself or rather the eidolon of same which one is apt to value. I mean the rather mystic

egotism of the Childe Roland to the dark tower came order which sometimes emerges out of a fever of renunciation of all external ties. I will go on reading your letter this is only the first brew from it. Granted about discipline but isn't the idea to discipline oneself to write rather than have it thrust upon one and one never regrets the loss of an examination answer or preserves a Sunday* question with the zest one takes with voluntary efforts – but I have hated examinations since my Brackenbury one which with the Rosebery just before gave me a phobia of all the insincerity and vulgarity required to get down to the level of one's examiners – but I think that is silly on my part and would not have arisen if one was not so coached in dodges etc at school. I am having a very nice time here considered as a relapse from care. I had to play in a jazz band the night I arrived for a charity in the village hall and forgot careers for the time. It is a nice 14th century house full of dogs and my cousins are very pleasant, one bucolic and cheerful and the other rather amusing – it is amazing how entirely ignorant the inhabitants of Bibury, Cirencester, Fairford and Quenington are of the charm of their surroundings – perhaps it is best for it gives them something of the supreme unconsciousness of stones and trees and therefore makes them more part of those places than if they appreciated them. Last year's hunting still provides most of the gossip. Lock House is no good I am afraid and my mother is away Monday night I think but wants us to come to tea on Tuesday with her. I am going up to London on Monday I dare say my younger cousin will be coming too in which case we shall probably go to the Savoy for tea, if you and Jack are up, come and join us there. I think you would like her, if you don't come till Tuesday let's lunch some-where – cheap don't you think – and spend the afternoon but come on Monday if you can and we can dine or anyhow meet in the after-noon. Can you send me a wire to-morrow or Sunday morning saying whether you and Jack will be up on Monday and if not where to meet on Tuesday and when. The little fountain in the Ritz is a good place to meet. Jack knows. It involves no capital, we might meet there Tuesday morning – if I know you aren't coming Monday I might stay in Oxford that day you see and at the same time if you are coming up I might not have my cousin with me and we could meet earlier probably. Do which you like. I think tea at the Savoy would be fun for the four of us if you and Jack can come Monday but you may have

*A 'Sunday question' was a written exercise on some set biblical subject that Eton boys had to do on Sundays.

nowhere to stay – Connolly Kemble Colne St. Aldwyn will be best for a wire. I will wire back to Cambridge if I change plans. Give my best love to Sligger and Jack.

Cyril

12 June 1926. Telegram. Cirencester.

Blakiston, Magdalene.

Cousin probably not coming meet Ritz lounge ten to one Love Cyril.

20 June 1926.

H. N. Blakiston, Esq.,   Balliol College,
Kirkby on Bain.   Oxford.

Dear Noel,
   It is very nice to think of you at Kirkby, auto-chthonic again, I picture you sitting on the low window side of our bedroom while the noise of pupils going to bed dies away – and it must be lovely there now. I like the quiet exaction of appreciation which places one knows well seem to expect. I hope the trees and the Bain are lovely. I spent a boring day and dined with my tutor at All Souls which was nice as most of the Fellows are polyglot lovers of literature rather than lawyers, historians, empire builders or weary tutors. I have been reading Pindar who is superb and mystifying and Theognis whom I want to study as being a very typical archaic Greek, I hope to get on with my book again soon

> τακόναι ἐντ᾽ἄν ἐίδῶ
> παῖδ ων νεογυίον ἐς ἥβαν

'I waste away whenever I see the fresh-limbed bloom of boys' is a good description of the general atmosphere of Bradfield,* I thought (Pindar on Theoxenus). I must stop soon or this will miss the post. It was marvellous seeing you, especially during the play when I had given you up and on that journey back.

*Greek play at Bradfield College.

142

Confined within these polished courts
    of academic stone
What wonder my intruding thoughts
    should permeate your own?

for you I tremble, you I burn
    till mind expectant, sees
your peace to-night when you return
    to move among your trees.

says the 18th century.

Much love
Cyril

Esplanade Hotel, Fowey, Cornwall, probably.

22 June 1926.

H. N. Blakiston, Esq.,   Naval & Military Hotel,
Kirkby on Bain.   Harrington Road,
                              South Kensington.

I wrote and told F.F.U. that he was honorary patron of the work.* I didn't say what it was about – but I thought it would cheer him. I pledged him to secrecy – what is this joke about 'the Romper' – is it you or Jack? and why? χαῖρε I can't get a cheque from anywhere at present. I looked at the Milton book which seemed rather prosy and disappointing, all theology. I will send you the pound when I can.

Give me a sketch of some drudgery for the first book – had we better put Merlin or someone in to have a little narrative or Lear – what were the chief Briton towns – I take it we invoke, at least you do, then describe this empty England, badge of Druid excellence and then put in stuff about Britons, Goidals and their habits till the Romans come? I have a history book somewhere in this hotel I think. I went to the Russian ballet last night I think modern musie is too like Brock. The work is my only consolation at present and thc more I see of Intellectual London the more right I think we are but I can't write much with parents at me. It must be nice at Kirkby. I saw Steven Runciman last night and am seeing Freddie to-day and Charles on Thursday – London is much too hot. Doubts, don't you think, by being acknowledged as such soon lose their sting. I have joined

*i.e. the epic that C.C. and N.B. were going to write together.

those two bits of blank verse I showed you and called the whole a distant prospect of Uganda. It will be nice when you come to London again. Boston was really very very adequate some how – almost perfect in fact.

Naval and Military. Love to Jack.

(*fragments of verse enclosed*)

> Phoenician traders finical to tread
> rough Cassiterides where never shines
> the sun of Tyre nor pagan prayers arise
> to Adonais or Melkanth the Great God
> worshipped in Sidon to Tartessus far
> and rock of Calpe where last 'naidios'
> speeds unreturning ears.
>
>   there the bad bishop
> prods the smooth choristers with gusty mirth
> to see himself a tyrant and confounds
> poor timid canons and with eagle eye
> bewilders their responses.

24 June 1926.

Noel Blakiston,   Naval & Military Hotel,
Kirkby on Bain.   Harrington Road,
                                                South Kensington.

Thank you for book. About work – my or our is rather a nuisance – 'this' will solve problem in some cases – 'my' coming in the first line looks queer as it will or should be the first thing Reader sees after the dual authorship – what about our, rather regally, on such occasions, and 'my' etc. where we are not speaking ex cathedra entirely – too much 'our' would sound romantic and 'my' gives us a chance to dissociate ourselves and, perhaps permits the chance of a compliment to each other before we unite to lower the curtain.

[*The rest of this letter is about the Epic. It does not seem possible that either C.C. or N.B. can have believed the project would get very far.*]

Your letter just come. Sound sense and will do bits as you suggest but must learn the story at Downside, writing again.

Noel Blakiston, Esq.,
Kirkby on Bain.

Naval and Military Hotel,
Harrington Road,
South Kensington.

I agree we must not write about the same things certainly and much prefer having set tasks only you must remember that my knowledge of English history is literally almost nil. I don't think I ever read the Saxons at all since I did them with Tuppy* but I will try and learn a little at Downside – obviously construction is important but the aim is on the whole to produce a kind of frieze don't you think in which every figure or scheme however slight stands out as the best of its kind – hence luxury is only so when it offends the construction by giving undue prominence to anything. In the end construction is but the skeleton which is required for the graceful body to have a good figure – as to being Miltonic it is all right don't you think except where we borrow rather than adapt – I mean the theory is that

1. Milton's blank verse is the only epic medium because it is more restrained than Elizabethan and more formal than Wordsworthian.
2. By seeing everything through Miltonic eyes we form our medium, the imposition of mind on nature (in this case M's mind on our own nature) that is at the root of good art – which cannot be naturalistic but requires to be nature represented in a formal way.
3. by both imitating Milton we keep our styles continuous

but (ah gentlemen!) we have no need to look with Milton eyes on what he looked at himself so no borrowing should be necessary. Time will probably shape our styles for us – they will fly the nest and for the time being Milton provides the discipline of style as history does the discipline of subject – we are not worried by free will.

I think in reading any epic it is the lyrical passages that one judges it by – the construction Reader is apt to take for granted unless it is faulty when he realises his epic to be but a collection of purple patches and likes –

11.30 P.M.
I am sending this now as it doesn't look like getting finished other-

*Headlam, an Eton master.

wise. I have been having a very hectic time with my cousin and am glad to be going to Downside. We went to a dinner party and dance at Claridges last night – then the Florida till 5 this morning with 2 cocktail parties at Ritz and Berkeley later and a wedding and dancing there and at the Savoy till dinner. I am supposed to be dancing at the Embassy now but have had the porter telephone that I am asleep. I will get on with work at Downside. I am coming back Tuesday but out to tea and dinner – ditto Wednesday but we might meet some time whenever suits you. Let me know.

Much love
Cyril

27 June 1926.

H. N. Blakiston, Esq.,   Downside Abbey,
46 Upper Grosvenor St.*   Stratton-on-the-Fosse,
W.1.   Nr. Bath.

Dear Noel,

How are you – I tried to send you a postcard in Bath but found no stamps there. I swam in the bath and came on here by a nice railway on a summer evening. Roger is here too. We went to Glastonbury last night and saw the Balliol players do the Hippolytus half way up the Tor – the sunset was good and I missed you – I doubt if the epic could have been written without that trip – not my share anyhow – it is pleasant here but fails to impress somehow – I think a school and a monastery don't altogether hit it off – and buildings are very new – I am fond of Sligger and Father David is nice.

I saw a very good Lewis sunset and am rather unstrung by it. I am writing this in Sligger's room for company – I have missed you a lot to-day and especially this evening – I mention this in the interests of telepathy – it is rather hard now to see a good sunset and not miss you – but we will meet very soon – I would give anything for us to have that cottage and to be starting there for July – I have been asking people about that coast and I hear there is a place called Glenthorne with some cottages just by Countisbury Cliffs and Culbone woods, just in Devon between Lynton and Porlock with Exmoor at the back, it sounds rather the spot but I don't see what more we can do at present unless we have rich jobs – I shall be back in London late

*The address of the Hartog family in which N.B. was tutor.

to-morrow night – let me know when I can see you and bring you back Blair's Woolf.* I am learning some English history. About movements, Tuesday I am rather full. Charles is going to be up in town only for that day but I could meet you in the morning or before tea if it suited you – I shall try and fix lunch with Charles – and am teaing and dining out – if you can ring me up easily ring me up Tuesday about ten – if it is hard for you send me a card to-morrow night. I should get it in the morning – I will meet you anywhere you like before or after lunch – we might meet in the park if it is fine – Sligger wants you to lunch with him on Wednesday – I saw and liked Freddie by the way the other day. Wednesday night is no good for me and Thursday I think I am going to the ballet with Freddie but am not sure – in some ways I wish we weren't in London together as proximity and inaccessibility are a disturbing pair but I dare say we shall survive and work requires it! I had a bloody lunch with Pringué† and a host of his tie-pinned cosmopolitan snobs – London is very hot too – If you like to ring me up after 10 to-morrow night I shall probably be in – 10 or half past – I would ring you up only it may be awkward for you being called suddenly. Kensington 5425 is my number. I would like to see you before we lunch on Wednesday. I am excited about your schools – we shall know soon. Charles sent a wire to me at Hartogs which they opened thinking it was from you in distress. I wrote Mrs. H. a note to say I was sorry for it being a nuisance as it must have looked proprietary a wire turning up for me there but C. thought I was lunching there that day. dear Noel – excuse sentiment!

Love
Cyril

with short letter from Sligger

'Cyril has no doubt told you about our peaceful Sunday here with Roger surrounded by Pax Benedictina. . . . I've heard some of the EPIC, very fine bits and apparently well sustained – but what an undertaking! Volumes and volumes! You are very courageous young men.'

*'Blair's Woolf' is a problem. Perhaps it refers to a book by Virginia Woolf that belonged to Eric Blair (b. 25 June 1903, d. 31 January 1950). KS. The writer, George Orwell.
†A friend of the Hartogs.

2 July 1926.

Noel Blakiston, Esq.,   The Berkeley Hotel,
46 Upper Grosvenor St.   Piccadilly, W.1.

Midnight

Dear Noel,

I am going to the chalet on Saturday – it will be a great help from the point of view of work but foul otherwise and it is only for economy till I go to stay with Logan on 19th (nineteenth) that I go. I am going to a party of Rylands at 11 to-morrow night or so – can you spare me to-morrow evening? ring me up in the morning – about ten – I have to go to the Lock House in the afternoon – could you come too? I may go with Charles if you can't come or we might all three go and I could see him before we go as it is only to settle about this cottage. (Sligger wants to give me a cottage) if to-morrow is quite hopeless for you I might try and go Saturday night or Sunday only ring me up. I am here with Freddie after the ballet. Sitwells were very nice to me last night. If we couldn't dine could you still spend evening with me or come Lock House? – I want to arrange what Saxon stuff I am to do at the chalet – I am glad you saw Sligger. Amor
                    Cyril

Would you like zoo tickets for a Sunday 2+1 childs?

July 1926.

Noel Blakiston, Esq.,   Chalet des Mélèzes,
46 Upper Grosvenor St.   St. Gervais les Bains,
                                         Haut Savoie.

Dear Noel,

How are you? I am rather happy here. I had a foul journey – the bracken at the Lock House was so lovely that I was angry all the way at leaving it so soon after my discovery and I didn't like France very much. The people here are very nice though a bit hostile at first except for Chris* but they seem to be coming round and I like them

*Chris Eastwood.

148

very much as they are restful and amiable and Jack McDougall* and John Sparrow,† a protégé of K's, are as intelligent as one could wish. Jack is going to Eton as a master so I am praising William to him as they seem to view it rather similarly. It has rained consistently, pleasant northern weather, and Sligger is charming. The chalet is amazingly unreal; I cannot believe that I or you or Bobbie have ever been here before – and house, landscape and people entirely fail to impinge in any way, it is hard to connect it with Wuthering Heights or the Constant Nymph or Lear's Heath and Othello. Everyone has gone to bed and I alone am lingering here – the timbers creak and the swollen Jaxartes booms outside. I dream regularly of you every night which is a consolation and makes going to sleep a pleasurable anticipation – last night we sailed down the Volga in search of caviare. Jeremy Taylor needs the hell of a lot of work which is a nuisance and Michael Field's garrulous correspondence seems to defy chronology. I hope I will be able to go to Cape Breton in August and we can sometimes meet and by the fire etc. I make no pretence to be anything but a wit here which works fairly well and makes for impersonality. I am writing an Elizabethan kind of opera for us to perform to Sligger à la Breakfast with the Borgia's with songs to go to bits of symphonies etc that we all know – In the first scene an Elizabethan tourist arrives at the chalet and apostrophises the Alps –

ye turgid crests of nature's rhetoric
bombastic Alps! on which I sourly gaze
terrestrial blisters! where a glacier falls
like matter from an ulcer – I can match
your boldness with bad language – yonder peak
is bare and scabrous as a carrion's tooth
bald as a don and as contemptible
while this green mountain that my footsteps tread,
this wen of soggy ground, this level lawn
breeds fit seclusion for the hermit old
and scatterbrained disciples who debosh
the mountain solitudes –
   Ho there within!

*John W. McDougall. Jack (b. 1903). Winchester, New College. For a short time master at Eton. Publisher, Chatto and Windus, Chapman & Hall.
†John Sparrow (b. 13 November 1906). Winchester, New College. Warden of All Souls.

F.F.U.:

    Ho there yourself, who takes me for an inn?
    'I come a pilgrim to FitzUrquhart's shrine'
    'FitzUrquhart has no pearls, and needs no swine'
    'Three hours I've spent, and twice as many mules'
    'Hermits are hermits to be rid of fools'
    'Why then take pupils such as Alan Ker*

    Sparrow, Macdougall, and Conolly are?'
    'Keep to blank verse, and leave my sylvan scene'
    'blow winter wind, thy tooth is not so keen.'
    'be blowed thyself, where yonder cavern yawns
    'go and yawn likewise, leave my dancing lawns'

then comes a prose denunciation by the pilgrim and

    'hear now my prophecy, the fit is on me
    even these very walls combustible
    will flame to ruin in an igneous hour
    till proud FitzUrquhart lost in far Cathay
    homes like a ladybird' –

F.F.U.:

    'O go to hell'
    'wretched FitzUrquhart, you have crossed Quennell.'

F.F.U.:

    'Turn on the chorus, bring me wine, I have
    immortal leanings – come sweet Charmian'

and the singing starts (not lewd) – the second scene is the burning of
the chalet and begins in Celtic style

    'It's a cold night I'm thinking'
    'Aye it's cruel cold'
    'It's unco frosty under the moon to-night
    I'm thinking we could do with a wee
    bit fire and himself gathering sticks
    against the day of judgement all this
    long morning.'

*Alan Ker (b. 11 November 1904). Rugby, New College. Fellow of Brasenose
1931–46. Fellow of Trinity, Cambridge 1953.

'It's a wonder the dominies get Plato's
Lysol and more wonder I'm slaving
on it, on such a night when the trees
are warping so you can't hear yourself
speak and there's girt frost in the tooth
mugs – do you hear from Tom Boase*
now?'
'Devil a word, since his death, devil
a word'
    a knocking outside.
           etc.

Here also is a Housman lyric recollected in tranquillity

Aldebaran the gypsies star
hangs high above the dark Azores
and jasmine scented from afar
the wind blows off their empty shores

the western ocean stretches wide
Fayal is faint against the sky
indifferent, and alone we ride
above the sea, my star and I.

I hope to hear from O. Sitwell about poems soon. Douglas Fairbanks and Mary Pickford were at that party, also Forster, Strachey, Margot and other celebrities none of whom I recognised. Freddie and Charles saw me off, 'no more to you now', to quote Henry VIII, except that I would we were together of an evening. Dreams are rather inadequate as one is not able to regulate one's conduct and mine are usually nightmares. I will write to you again soon. Bobbie seems to have relapsed again into primeval silence since I answered his last letter. It will probably be a shock to him to find out I am here – As a matter of fact I think I have come at the only time when I can really enjoy it as nothing but a few jokes is expected of me.

           Love from Cyril

I read and liked your nightingale simile again this evening. I am still stuck rather with work chiefly owing to the vast bulk of Jeremy Taylor which only induces comic reactions. Sligger sends love. It is

*T. S. R. Boase (b. 31 August 1898, d. 1974). Rugby, Magdalen. Fellow of Hertford. President of Magdalen 1947–68. FBA 1961.

a pity our last evening was so populous but I liked being with you and
Freddie.

17 July 1926.

M. H. N. Blakiston,
a Villa Zaldivar,   Aix les Bains.
Biarritz,
Basses Pyr.,
France.

Dear Noel,

Greeting to Biarritz – mind you go to Bayonne and if possible
Fuenterabia. Your nice letter came yesterday. I only know Warton's
Ode to Sleep which is excellent – I suppose you mean Joseph Warton,
not Thomas? (which Warton!) – well the chalet is over for me and
kept up its Karindehutte form to the end. I had to do charades last
night and there has been a lot of golf and singing and hockey and
'rich fooling' – but very united and unselfconscious and no envy or
intensity. I have paved William's way with Jack McDougall who is
going to Eton next term. You met him once and approved – I have
been dining with Mrs. D'Costa* here to-night – she may be going to
Biarritz. All being well with Logan I shall try and come to Cap
Breton in August – we could meet several times a week probably.
Patrick Balfour wants me to stay with him and I am supposed to be
travelling with Freddie in late September. My mother is at Dinard
where she met Bobbie. This is a hasty scrawl in a café before my train
goes – I liked your comments on 18th century and Warton a lot – I
heard from Patrick to-day praising you. Big Chilling Warsash Hants
is my address till August when I will let you know plans. Sligger wrote
for my book but publisher would not return it and said he was showing
it T. S. Eliot with a view to getting me work on his paper if he did
not publish book as it stands. Hopeful don't you think?

You would like Mrs. D'Costa who is very penetrating. I am glad
you liked Collins I think he is supreme – above Gray or Goldsmith
as you say – Sligger sent love. I will write again soon this is merely
statement of affection. I have missed you off and on in the cloisters

*Mrs D'Costa, the mother of Cyril's pupil.

at Bayonne. Thank Howard* for his message. Were Zoo tickets any use? If I have 2 jobs I shall be all right and cottage no empty dream.

Cyril

I went to Chamonix to have tea with Timothy yesterday, he sent love.

26 July 1926.

Monsieur Blakiston,
Biarritz.

Big Chilling,
Warsash,
Hants.

aux bons soins de M. Hartog

Dear Noel,

How are you? I wrote you a line from Aix and nearly, on an impulse, descended from the train at Folkestone that blue Sunday when you were there. I stayed Sunday night with Langermann† who praised you and came here on Monday evening and drank your health at dinner when I pictured you to have arrived. I wish you were here‡ – this is a small Tudor farm house made habitable by added windows, lawns, peach trees, and bathrooms and it stands a field away from the Solent and very close to the corner where it joins Southampton Water and the Hamble estuary. There is nothing marine about the country-side except that all the trees are frizzled by the prevailing wind and one can enjoy the music of the cirl bunting and the tranquillity of the cornfield, on the very edge of the salt waves. πάντ' ὥσδεν θέρεος μάλα μόνος and fruit and flowers excel. The prospect from this delightful house is entrancing – the low and wooded slopes of the New Forest appear across the yachts and liners of Southampton Water which are not so frequent as to destroy the estuary's rural charm. To the south the Solent stretches like a broad river, the woods of Osborne and the walls of Cowes are clearly visible and the horizon is bounded by the bare range of chalk hills in the interior of the island which lend a charming pretence of remoteness and space to the calm and soothing beauty of the view. The hills are hidden in wet weather while a clear day makes them appear higher and wilder than they really

*Howard Hartog, N.B's pupil.
†F. E. Langermann, New College, Oxford.
‡The country house of Logan Pearsall Smith.

are and evening transfigures them to a Lulworth mauve. Our days
are quiet and happy; Mr. Smith makes no appearance till lunch time
and I have the mornings to myself – he is the possessor of a small
sailing boat on the Hamble in which we sometimes venture forth
while wet days are easily beguiled in broadcasted concerts or the
hazards of chess. There are many pleasing books to be got through –
and a bracing tonic of work, while I am rejoiced to find Mr. Smith's
conversation a real blessing and his outlook open and intelligent
while a mutual interest in natural history and a very passable table
amply compensate for the lack of gaiety or the society of my coevals.
You would scarcely suspect that I could tolerate or be tolerated for
so long as the solitary guest of an absolute stranger! Naturally I have
read a great deal here and would like to commend to your notice
Gosse's Life of Gray in the English men of letters as an excellent
account of an admirable person though too nice and romantic I
cannot help thinking, for our philosophy and Mackail's estimate of
Milton in 'Streams of Parnassus' – the only worthy tribute which I
have read while he also adds the 16 lines of Comus 'which only
Milton could have written and only Milton struck out' – Monk's
life of Bentley has some merit as have the poems of Milman, Bowles,
Wilson and Cornwall. Milman on the whole would seem to shine
most as the historian while Bowles rather goes to illustrate how much
very meritorious work can suffer a total neglect perhaps alas from the
conscious archaism such as his imitation of Milton. Of modern work
I read with great delight Forster's *Celestial Omnibus*, a few short
stories which admirably illustrate the triumphs of pagan mythology
in a pastoral England and an unbelieving world and Mrs Woolf's
Monday or Tuesday which seems to express all the beauties of de-
composing English prose before it has dissolved into Gertrude Stein.
I confess however to finding in the Paradise Lost all that my inclinations desire – the serpent's speech in book nine when he first addresses
Eve is a compendium of animal ideals and sensible affection and it
seems a master stroke of the poet to present the serpent comparing the
scent of the blossom to the tree of knowledge

> to smell of sweetest fennel, or the teats
> of ewe or goat dropping with milk at even
> unsucked of lamb or kid that tend thir play.

for I think it is still a superstition that the snake milks these animals,
like the nightjar – to read aloud the Paradise Lost is the surest panacea

for the spleen could one but always bring oneself to it – alas I write nothing myself though the craving for a poem done sits on my heart like a cormorant. I am too torn between armchair and modernity to know how to express the scanty emotion which the gain of tolerance still leaves me. Gray is a fearful example, a fine scholar, friend, a letter writer, his only enemy inspiration, his only aversion his university! My plans and prospects are vague in the extreme. Mr Smith has made no mention of my future or my stipend though he seems disposed for my company and to appreciate the work I have already done for him and the praise of Sebastian which I have contributed to his forthcoming article on Pater – I still hope to journey from here to Aquitaine at the end of the month though alas I have no warrant as yet at all – so now farewell with my real affection – I imagine you at Biarritz, and think I understand you at Rye while my life is so similar and Mr. Smith so discursive – but often disheartening – about the intimate lives of our men of letters. O how could I know that what was going to be a long fond literary letter would turn out like this!

Were I to write to you as much as you are in my thoughts what a waste paper basket I should fill! Do you remember our wet walk at Southampton a year ago?

3 Aug 1926.

H. N. Blakiston, Esq.,   Warsash,
Biarritz.   Hants.

Dear Noel,
  I had written to you all this past week were I but able to bring myself to finish anything but I began to compose you an anthology of all that contented me most in the many books which are at Chilling and the weight of the extracts soon broke my pen. I will make short to tell you that I loved your letter and that Pringué truly sounds intolerable and Tours nice and that Acquitaine is certainly the most decently English part of the whole land of France. The eclogues, especially I think it is, the first, fourth, ninth, and tenth, are, with the second, of even greater moment than the Aeneid, and I know not in any language such rare and lovely songs – I would add that I think in Santayana we may have at last found a philosopher who will give us

unity without bias and consolidate our outlook on the world. I will try and send you a book of extracts from him when I can let the credit go. He is a materialist, that is to say he considers all ideas to be a part of matter though by far the most valuable part – thus he preserves Plato without the mysticism which offends and is respectful to though not believing in immortality or God. He writes intelligibly in an adorable style and gives sane and sweet judgement on nearly all the problems of this human life, while the man himself seems to be a complete Sebastian but more humane, and moved by a certain piety to the surroundings of his soul in childhood. He lives now in Rome with no ties, no letters, no books, not even his own, in perfect contemplation of nature and sympathy with humanity. Pearsall Smith considers him the greatest living writer and the happiest man and most clarifying intelligence he knows. I will send you the book. Eliot is 'much struck with my promise and anxious to meet me.' Logan wants me to live in Paris this winter and review French books for the Times. I don't feel very French at present but it might be fun. I would rather be in Cambridge which I had thought of doing. Kenneth Clark has been here this week end and has been very nice. I am enjoying sailing very much – it is simple and sensuous and soon I hope to be let out alone to pursue my own odysseys – bathing here is warm though the water is not translucent and I still fear madly for sharks. I shall probably go somewhere with Freddie in September. I dined with him in Southampton did I tell you on his way to Switzerland and drank your health and thought of the trams and the cinema and that day in the rain.

I like P.S. who is courteous, sympathetic, serious and amusing though vain, as authors are: lord Noel, what is this wish for knowledge of the world and this praise of shipwreck? and one can drown in a fiord as easily as in mid ocean, πάσα θαλάσσα θαλάσσα please continue to pilot yourself through beautiful! $X^τ$ may have been in love with everyone but I think in the case of the Pharisees it was rather γλυκύμι-κρος. I don't really know enough about him nor have I yet fitted in the denouncer and the Martyr to each other. I suppose one must wait a bit and then read the Gospels again. Maurois is something of a snare I think, especially by his facile construction of a scheme of things in all his biographies of the great – as K said 'if anyone will not take the trouble to read history, Maurois and Lytton Strachey are amusing enough.' I don't think M. is as slight as that but he obviously minimises difficulties till he has found a plot and trims old yew that in the churchyard stands into a peacock or a tub. I think his intentions are honourable only he is afraid to be dull – *ennui auguste*, as K says, must prelude any aesthetic emotion if it is not to cloy. The wind sings, it is afternoon, I am moved to an attic as irregular and low as that described in the cottage and one window frames woods and fields and the other in the corner where I write gives on the Solent and the hills of the island. Mrs. D'Costa is going to Biarritz with son – she wrote to ask how to find you – if you come across her you would probably like her – she is extremely intelligent (psychologically) and very sympathetic and amusing but sometimes has a silly worldly manner and talks too much – she is really nice at heart but can make awful mischief and her son is a complete little shit though speciously interested in literature and witty and humorous beyond his years. You might like them for a bit though but don't trust them far – the mother has been educated in Eliot and the *Constant Nymph*, Milton, *W. Heights* etc. and is fond of me though she might make quite incredible bad blood to you for no reason at all – she is rather that kind of woman but I have never regretted anything I told her – I have not read any very good poetry lately. K and Logan want me to write a biography of James Thomson and the Castle of Indolence 'and all our yesterdays have lighted fools the way to dusty death' seems rather hard to beat. I don't know yet when I leave here – I will try and come towards Biarritz if I don't actually get there. I enclose a few maxims from Santayana – I miss you often but always with joy – rather a consciousness of your presence in an idea, a way of life, or a view or a sunset than a sense of absence and loss, miss in fact is hardly the right word. Santayana, says Logan, has broken more hearts than any other man as he is companionable but not friendly and remains perfectly charming to anyone who goes to see him and entirely oblivious of him when he goes away. It has apparently nearly broken the heart of Bridges, Berenson and Bertrand Russell, and a millionaire who has built a palace for Santayana in his grounds and still waits at Florence in vain for him to come. S. is Spanish, brought up in America.

'Piety, in its nobler and Roman sense, may be said to mean man's reverent attachment to the sources of his being and the steadying of his life by that attachment' . . . 'so he is most profoundly pious who loses unreservedly a country, friends, and associations, which he knows very well to be not the most beautiful on earth and who being wholly content in his personal capacity with the natural conditions does not need to begrudge other things whatever speculative admiration they truly deserve' . . . 'Piety towards mankind must be ¾ pity – to worship mankind as it is would be to deprive it of what alone makes it akin to the divine, its aspirations – for this, human dust lives'

The supreme poet. 'It is true some genius should appear to reconstitute the shattered picture of the world. He should live in the continual presence of all experience, and respect it, he should at the same time understand nature – the ground of that experience, and he should also have a delicate sense for the ideal echoes of his own passions and for all the colours of his possible happiness' – He is excellent on X^{ty}. I will send you the book when I can and write again soon.

Cyril

Mrs Hartog is nice I think certainly, does Pringué know the world? He is considered a joke in Paris I have found out. He is very stupid you know only better educated than an Englishman of his intelligence would ever be.

Go to Bayonne, arcades, cloister.

3 Aug 1926.

Warsash,
Hants.

Dear Noel,

Thank you for your letter – I would probably have met you on my way back from the chalet as I was going to have spent Sunday at Boulogne and crossed on the next morning if I hadn't lost my luggage and had to go to Calais to fetch it. Have you read the Eclogues much? Do, if you have them with you, they rise to the heights of Lycidas and Collins and are not without humour or the dewy freshness of true pastoral. I agree about Aeneid VI. I read it in Jamaica – est iter in silvis (270) is exciting don't you think – here are some lines from the Eclogues

nos patriae finis et dulcia linquimus arva
hinc alta sub rupe canet frondator ad auras
nec gemere aëria cessabit turtur ab ulmo
(Fort Romeu)

———

Hic tamen hanc mecum poteras requiescere noctem
                         (ripe)
fronde super viridi: sunt nobis mitia poma
castaneaeque molles et (cheesc) pressi copia lactis;
Et jam summa procul villarum culmina fumant
maioresque cadunt altis de montibus umbrae.

'Even now the house tops yonder are smoking and
longer shadows fall from the mountain heights' (Loeb).
A good picture of simple life.

Formosum pastor Corydon ardebat Alexim
                    ——

quamvis ille niger, quamvis tu candidus esses
o formose puer, nimium ne crede colori
                    (See Boswell. Knight's trial)
                    ——

Pan curat ovis, oviumque magistros
                    ——

rusticus es, Corydon, nec munera curat Alexis
                    ——

'floribus Austrum
perditus.' I have let in the south wind to my
flowers – Milton's motto to his poems when they
were published (scirocco)
                    ——

'Daphnis ego in silvis, hinc usque ad sidera notus
formosi pecoris custos, formosior ipse'
                    ——

                    Saepe ego longos
cantando puerum memini me condere soles
nunc oblita mihi tot carmina
                    ——

cantantes ut eamus, ego hoc te fasce levabo. (burden)
                    ——

ambo florentes aetatibus – Arcades ambo
Et cantare pares, et respondere parati.
                    ——

                    nobis placeant ante omnia silvae
                    ——

and the end –

surgamus: solet esse gravis cantantibus umbra
iuniperi gravis umbra, nocent et frugibus umbrae
ite domum saturae, venit Hesperus, ite capellae –

———

See also 2nd Georgic 458 onwards and last 4 lines of Georgic 4. You
may know all these already but presuming you to be nearly bookless
I am trying to compile you an anthology of what there is here. Here
are some bits of Bowles.

Poor Warton! thou has stroked my stripling head and sometimes,
mingling kind reproof with praise my path hast best directed
through the maze of thorny life.

                    . . . but when life began
I never roamed, a visionary man
(for taught by thee, I learnt with sober eyes
to look on life's severe realities)
I never made (a dream distemper'd thing)
Poor fiction's realm my world; but to cold truth
subdued the vivid shapings of my youth –
Save when the drisly woods were murmuring
or some hard crosses had my spirit bow'd
Then I have left unseen the careless crowd
and sought the dark sea roaring, or the steep
that braved the storm; or in the forest deep
as all its grey leaves rustled, woo'd the tone
of the loved lyre, that in my springtime gone
wak'd me to transport.

                    are not 'drisly', and 'grey' well chosen?

Here is the ark during the flood (from 'the Spirit of Discovery
by Sea')

                So the Ark
rests upon Ararat, but nought around
its inmates can behold, save o'er th'expanse
of boundless waters, the sun's orient orb
stretches the hulls long shadow, or the moon
in silence, through the silver cinctured clouds

sailing, as she-herself was lost, and left
in natures loneliness.

———

Chinese religion (1114 B.C. Pre-Waley)

We load the sacrificial stands
　　of woods and earthen ware
the smell of burning southern wood
　　is heavy in the air.

It was our father's sacrifice
　　it may be they were eased.
We know no harm to come of it;
　　it may be God is pleased.

14 Aug 1926.

Noel Blakiston, Esq.,　　　　　　Warsash,
Biarritz.　　　　　　　　　　　　Hants.

Dear Noel,
　　Thank you so much for your nice letter. Santayana is being sent.
By the way do you know these lines from Chaucer's Troilus

　　Clean out of your mind
　　ye have me cast, and I ne can ne may
　　for all this worlde within my herte find
　　to unloven you a quarter of a day

They are good don't you think?
　　Thank you for the p.c. of Bayonne – and for the 'error of nature' –
Desmond MacCarthy*, the editor of the New Statesman has been
staying here – a very good man indeed – wise, humorous and kindly
with a complete inability to finish anything he sets out to do, and a

　　*Desmond MacCarthy (b. 1877, d. 1952). Eton, Trinity, Camb. Author and
literary and dramatic critic. Knighted 1952. His friendship and that of his wife
Molly and of his daughter Rachel were a great inspiration and comfort to Cyril
Connolly when he came to London, as these letters show.

pathetic belief that he is going to; the same gift of casual definition as you – we used to talk late every night – He asked me to write a review of Paul Morand for the N.S. which he took away yesterday and said was excellent; so I shall soon be in print, I will send it you. Logan is very adequate witty and sympathetic but rather bleak and scrupulous at the same time – very often a touch of William, especially in his writings and very much the Chinaman – friendship, reputation, comfort, scenery, good talk and disillusion with a touch of vanity seem his pleasures – he is the complete craftsman in writing and takes days over a sentence which in any case always contains 4 or 5 phrases stolen from the past. We went over to a niece of his near Haslemere two days ago – she was having a children's free week – i.e. 10 children lived in huts in the garden cooking their own food and keeping no rules at all except to report when they were ill – there was a swimming bath in the garden. She said they were all happy and sat up all night talking religion and bathed every night by the camp fire – it seemed ideal and I wished you and I had so passed the days of our youth but we went afterwards to see the children who were all at Fernhurst Circus. I talked to Desmond MacCarthy's children and they said nobody talked religion except once and nothing happened but quarrels and rudeness which passed for wit – the eldest boy was away in Midhurst all day because Elisabeth Robinson was there and the next one, the British boy's chess champion tried to order everyone about and Barbara hadn't washed yet because it was free week and the rest were very dull – as they had come there from staying with the Asquiths it probably would be but it was amusing to see how much keener the grown ups were about the pleasures of the scheme than the children themselves who hardly seemed to realise how happy they were. I am staying here till beginning of September and then going up to town for a day or so to see Eliot and one or two people and then joining Freddie in Vienna whence we go down the Danube. I am looking forward to the Danube a lot – fens. I suppose Gautby and our camp were the most pastoral things we have done. I mean we were hardly young men then – but I find that I associate you so much with earlier memories that till I examine the facts I forget that we are not at Lock House and Kirkby many times before we were – your first 4th of June for example I imagined you all the time I bicycled home which constitutes your first visit.

My mother met Bobbie in Canterbury. I wonder what he is doing there. I am 3 letters and two postcards to the good at present so not much seems to be gained by writing – Shall I come and live near Cambridge next term? Tell me your views? I would probably be in Paris if I don't. D.M. wants me to write a long travel book which he says Heinemann's will publish – he is a reader to them. There is also James Thomson which Logan and K want me to do – and Eliot may have something. Will you still be in College? Freddie thinks it a good plan for me to live near Cambridge but I am quite open – or I might live simply in France and write my book – and perhaps come to Kirkby for Christmas if you would be there – or have a cottage somewhere else – which depends rather on Sligger. I get £8 a week while I am working for Logan (till end of January) so I have already saved enough to travel comfortably with Freddie – I will send you the pound as soon as I get some cash in hand and end this now but it lies idle days waiting a longer completion. Fare thee well, child.

Cyril

23 August 1926. Postcard of Chichester Cathedral.

Noel Blakiston, Esq.,   Chichester.
Biarritz.

This is another cathedral. I have secrecy mania about my travels. I will send you addresses soon only do not divulge them and I can't communicate with Freddie at all till I meet him so am not sure what they will be – I will be here till 3rd September probably, trying to travel out with Jack. Haste. σύ δε χαῖρε

24 August 1926.

Noel Blakiston, Esq.,   Warsash,
Biarritz.   Hants.

Dear Noel,

I am sorry if I haven't been writing to you enough – if you knew how behindhand I have been with letters to other people you would forgive me – I sent you a postcard yesterday. I am sorry Biarritz is getting awful, practice Santayana on it, but that sounds cold comfort. Do you go back to Kirkby after it? or to William? It was Logan who sent you Santayana as it can only be got from the publishers and he says he likes to send it to anyone deserving but I told him I didn't know of anyone else who ought to have it as it was too good to be made public – when Logan wanted Santayana's help with the extracts, he had to send him copies of his own books which the sage had not thought necessary to possess.

I will read *The Egoist* when I can. The butler* sounds nice. We have been delayed with Logan's American relations whom he loathes and he and I stay upstairs playing chess most of the time – he has the most delicious fresh cynicism which he turns on them till they do not know which way to turn – thus (they are Quakers) 'Zoe will thee admit Carey is an awful liar' (cry of horror) Thou dost agree she is a bit inaccurate 'Yes' (with relief) – Grace, wilt thou admit she is an awful liar – (cry of horror) – yes, thou wilt, but will not let anyone else say so – Peggy, yes, thou wilt, if Uncle Logan is not in the room – but all this so boyishly from a benevolent looking old man that they gradually grow frank and sincere. I have written a story, I forget if I told you about it, it starts on the day of judgment and becomes a dialogue between Ecclesiastes, Aristippus and Po Chui which ends in consternation when they discover they have eternal life. Logan likes it and we think of sending it to America as I don't want to shock relations if it comes out in England and the pomps of *dies irae* are made somewhat mock of – also I would get more money for it in America. I think it would pass the censorship of you and Fitzgod.† I hope you aren't getting fat since thinness seems to be the chief sign of your godhead – do send me any photos of you that are taken at Biarritz as they are wonderfully reviving – Charles tells me Hartog calls down rupture on his guests – is he too bridling?‡ Are not the Bayonne bull fights cow fights in which there is great agility and no bloodshed? If so they must be fun to watch. I have suddenly been smitten with a longing for Ireland, the humid smells of greenness, bog and mountain and the headlands of Kerry streaming out into the west – if Freddy fails I shall certainly go there but there is no chance of that. We might perhaps try and go sometime? I want to write a short story called 'fen mad' – Bobbie has been motoring in Lincoln-

*In the family where I was tutoring.
†Jack Blakiston.
‡This legend must be corrected. Mr H. was a genial soul, who spoke no French. When a waiter or taxi driver annoyed him, his normal expletive to the uncomprehending foreigner would be 'I hope you have a rupture'. That's all.

shire and said he was much moved by the Bain – Sweet Bain run
softly till I end my song. Do not fear about my 'new introductions
and friends' they are not as many as all that – only Logan and Desmond
MacCarthy and you will meet them soon – I regard the Hartogs as
much more sinister – will Patrick too go into the family business?* I
think wisdom is indicated for us don't you think? I sent Sligger your
address which he lost the first time. I envy you sea side children,
they are at their best then – my only friend is an old goat tethered to
the road, we often sit together when Logan is still a-bed. Love and
cogitationes

Cyril

24 Aug 1926. Postcard.

Noel Blakiston, Esq.,   Warsash,
Biarritz.   Hants.

Mangroves and coral reefs. Do tell me if you believe in the immortality
of the soul, it seems pretty improbable and there is beauty in man's
privilege of mortality and in us being fellow travellers in the wilderness
'till our rest together is in the dust' but I would like to know what
you thought.

συ δε χαίρε
C

25 Aug 1926. Postcard.

Senor Don H. N. Blakiston,   Warsash,
Biarritz.   Hants.

Buenas nochez querido!

---

*Meaning presumably, would our brother Patrick in due course take over the
tutoring of Hartog boys?

25 Aug 1926. Postcard.

H. N. Blakiston, Esq.,   Warsash,
Biarritz.   Hants.

Here on the other hand more form than colour. An awful Norwegian
girl has arrived a friend of Logan's sister which drives me to upstairs
industry most of the day. Was it Lisieux or Caen you liked so – tell
me which to go to from Havre as I have a day to spare. χαῖρε Νοελ
φιλερημε

Cyril

26 Aug 1926, Postcard, of Hamble.

H. N. Blakiston, Esq.,   Warsash,
Biarritz.   Hants.

Et quamquam hoc flumen (id est Hambula) satis speciosum est, et
perveniunt multi pelegrini ad aquas suas, tamen meo judice rivulus
quidam qui Banus appelatur omnibus aliis praestat, et nec perveniunt
barbari nec naves, parvus et sinuosus enim est et ibi situs fuit templi
amicitiae nunc in ruinis.

Petrus Tumbeius* Annales

26 Aug 1926.

Noel Blakiston, Esq.,   Southampton.
Biarritz.

Today is a fine day and we are just off on a long sail thereby missing
a jumble sale in the garden to Logan's joy. I shall soon be a master
mariner – it is fun navigating creeks etc – have you learnt riding yet?
aren't foreigners awful. Why should one listen politely while they
murder our lovely language. Well it looks like Cambridge – where
do you go from Biarritz? Logan has given me Spinoza's Ethics with
Santayanian introduction, they look good.

Adios amigo

*Tumby (as already stated) is a hamlet of Kirkby on Bain.

H. N. Blakiston, Esq.,   Warsash,
Biarritz.   Hants.

The jumble sale is over, Logan and I were becalmed in Southampton Water. The first mist of approaching autumn has appeared since dinner – otherwise there is no news – it is not impossible to rise superior to an uncreative age is it? L. thinks one must adapt and be a critic – I refuse to be famous for a book on Wordsworth, although after all it was all Wordsworth was famous for. *καλη νηκτα*

28 August 1926.

Noel Blakiston, Esq.,   Warsash,
Biarritz.   Hants.

Dear Noel,

How are you by now? I am suffering from the fidgets which an approaching voyage produces. What do you think are the odds on Freddie for a travelling companion? I wish it was Fitzgod but there is a pleasant sense of reliability about Freddie as long as he has not sprung a mistress in Vienna which he is rather apt to do. Six weeks is a long time for me to be in one place and I begin to feel rather restless but have got on admirably with Logan all the time which is a comfort – Santayana and Spinoza ebb like the tide when one has to be polite to a Norwegian girl, ugly, voluble and sentimental. What a philosophy there is behind a word like *βάρβαρος*, why does God not strike dumb the murderers of our language?

I find Santayana ripens quietly in one's mind and suddenly outcrops in an almost beatific vision of the world – I think the argument against it is the small allowance made for madness, Lear's Heath, the salt marsh, and the situations arising from the irony or rage of a personal God though instead it seems to provide an Olympian serenity a great tenderness to mankind and all ideals which it has bravely and pitifully fashioned in the predicament in which it is found and a wide tolerance and a limited piety, with the grateful and modest detachment of an humane Sebastian, but sentimentality dies hard and to realise that 'man is relative and God impersonal' is a stiff mouthful don't you think when one has long dwelt in the fancies of τo $\phi\theta\acute{o}\nu\epsilon\rho o\nu$ and guiding stars – guardian angels – watching genii, fortunate encounters and sudden affinities not withheld from mystic unbelievers by Destiny. Santayana seems not to deny ghosts but leaves no room for 'a legendary white sea bird' to foretell misfortune to a celtic family and I suppose he is right but superstition is often content to remain in the house after reason has given it notice to quit. His materialism by putting ideas at the head of matter gives them an importance only second to their place in a Platonic system and he obviously contrasts 'materialism' with 'naturalism' i.e. the pagan renunciation of reason in favour of a strict modelling of life on nature rather than human nature – S. would have no patience for the Diogenes' who go naked and send the weakest to the wall with a smile because it was the life by which the cave man avoided the dangers of intelligence. The point also is if there is not in the happiness of this gentle and relentless ecstasy of philosophic calm a radiance that lacks the creative and aesthetic value of the lights and shades of an infirmer state – Shakespeare remains opposed to Goethe and Sophocles, Democritus and Aristippus, France and Montaigne – I grant the Sebastian Spinoza Santayana man who would be the first to appreciate the Agamemnon, Lear, Isaiah or the Waste Land but such an outlook would make it impossible to create in that way and the whole fire of their earthly mysticism would vanish from a serener world. Take away 'the burden of the valley of vision' Childe Roland to the Dark Tower came,'$o\nu\epsilon\iota\rho o\phi\acute{a}\nu\tau o\iota$ $\delta\epsilon$ $\pi\epsilon\iota\theta\acute{\eta}\mu o\nu\epsilon s$ the tree swinging and the *orribile torre* and you are left with 'nothing but well and fair' – but 'I don't think we care much about security' as Tessa said – tell me your view – I am perfectly willing to consider Heathcliff and the hollow men as fascinating perversions of the aspirations of mankind provided I could create anyone as good as them from my all embracing humanism but are not Wuthering Heights and The Duchess of Malfi worth a life of illusionless detachment from the supernatural or the insane? There is of course also the point about Seb. Spin. and San. whether their outlook was only really expressed in moods of mystical ecstasy (as Santayana lives in the whole time now) and provides no ethics for the combating of the ordinary dilemmas of life, envy, disappointment, or impatience or the undignified antics of desire and hence if such a philosophy is only valuable to the character that is so perfected by nature as to need, in reality, no philosophy at all. I am going to practice it for a day or so in France before I meet Freddie – and try and arrive at a purely detached observation and a soothing immersion in the universal flux. There is a danger in disregarding the unpleasant aspects of man as irrelevant to the philosopher concerned only with a tender piety to their ideals leading to the wholehearted and spurious optimism of the wilfully blind – once one has discovered that the candle is not cruel it is easy to forget that it still burns the moth. I must say that I found envy could be almost removed by a moment's SanSpinSeb – SpinSebSan at least would be the correct word. One is most grateful for a philosophy that softens Sebastian by allowing the loophole of 'piety' to include the love of home and friends and human kind while avoiding the sentimentality that usually goes with it – one sees why Lucretius thought Epicurus the saviour of mankind though I have a strong dislike of his watery and cautious utopia. *nox ruit, Aenea; sum fessus.*

from Achates.

30 August 1926. Postcard.

H. N. Blakiston, Esq.,   Warsash,
Biarritz.   Hants.

I drove a launch to-day, once more shades of Lulworth, and walked home by a lovely red and reedy sunset. Sentiment followed.

    How are you? Have you read the *epitaphium Damonis*, it is good, especially the middle. I have translated the first few lines into couplets but it is very hard. I go Friday and am passionately excited to be abroad again – I can hardly sit still and appetite fails.

'ἐρρῶτο
Cyril

31 August 1926.

Hugh Noel Blakiston, Esq.,   Warsash,
Biarritz.   Hants.

Dear Noel,

    I was glad to hear from you and that the treatment is any good. You saved mine at Lock House that winter. I gave Logan your thanks.

You must come and stay here next summer. We are going to have a yacht and go across to France. I will arrange it. You would like this very pastoral sea coast where the Island limits the horizon and the sea breaks beyond a field of yellow rye and the stately ships go on. Also this nice and ancient farm and the peaches and melons and Lulworth aires – I go somewhere with my mother for October and November but I will come and see you at Cambridge first – it seems criminal that we are not always together during these days of our vanity, still Boswell only saw Johnson 155 days wasn't it – but you don't look like Johnson. I am terribly excited about going abroad especially 2 days in Normandy where I can be alone with myself, think of you, practice Spinoza and drink in Caen and the French and the asphalt, bicycles, bare knees and spades and buckets of the sea side towns – could we be at Kirkby for Christmas? I would like that. I find myself more in love with wisdom day by day and have pleasant moods of ecstasy even on Sundays when at the thought of thousands of psalms and canticles sweetly ascending from all over the world I beam with divine condescension and a certain pride in mankind whose gratitude puts their creator more hopelessly in the wrong than before. I am developing a real feeling for humanity in the abstract though it is rather hard to apply it to the particular as I found during the tyranny of Logan's American visitors but still, what has a philosophic fondness of the race of man to do with one's personal inclinations as a social creature? Palestrina's Mass on the gramophone is good – can you understand Santayana's (Spinoza's) meaning of 'immortality' 'eternal life' etc by which he (they) make it possible to exempt eternity from any sense of duration of time so that our immortality seems to consist in identifying oneself with eternal things – though this identification must apparently cease when we die – either it is a statement with no real significance, like saying that since whatever we do, is done, say, is said and becomes an action that is absolutely true since it indubitably has happened and takes place in a sequence of events that continue to form the history of the world and which nothing that follows can un-say i.e. immediately becomes impersonal, unperceived and a metaphysical quibble or else – more probable, they are affirming a kind of Platonism (also recommended by Christ and Buddha) that by identifying ourselves with the eternal ideas (reality) we are real and immortal freed from the wheel and one with the flux – but what according to Santayana, are the eternal ideas since God is impersonal and man is relative? It seems mysticism arising from

170

materialism, strange progeny. See also his passage on the Christian doctrine of damnation and loss of soul etc. You say some of us will be immortal, can you elaborate into who will be and what you mean by immortality? Will you mess with me in the next world? – and we might have the mukes.* Stanley† shall be our mess fag and Jack and William will complete the 'Corcus'! Please devote your life to literature and don't go into cheese – I leave Paris for Vienna Sunday night and reach Havre Saturday morning – if you are really dying send a wire here and I could join you for Saturday night but I don't think it would be worth it unless we met half way (Poitiers, Tours or Nantes). Like Boston and even then it would be unsettling but if you wire I would come if necessary – wire here or S.W. hotel S'hampton Friday or to await boat at Havre but I don't expect you could get away.

I know no certain address yet – Astoria Hotel Budapest as good as any. I shall look into Ritz Hotel Paris on Sunday for a wire from Freddie, so write there if you can but nothing of importance. I feel sweet sleep descending.

χάιρε fellow sage
Cyril

Biarritz only begins to fill up September.

(*On envelope*)

Send photoes s'il y en a nec absorbeant vitam tartari
φεῦ γάιης ὅτον 'αφ ἡμετερης!
but drive far hence the
        of   and his
             the race
            of
           that

3 Sept 1926. Telegram.

| Blakiston, | Warsash, |
| Biarritz. | Hants. |

Can you spend Saturday night Bordeaux meet Chapon Fin 7.30. Cyril.

*Two adjoining rooms for boys in College at Eton, at the end of a passage round a corner.
†A boy at Kirkby on Bain.

September 1926.

Noel Blakiston, Esq.,
Biarritz.

Hotel Ritz,
Place Vendôme,
Paris.

Dear Noel,

How are you? I expect you were away and didn't get my wire. I found I could get to Bordeaux for to-night and back next afternoon to catch Vienna train in the evening so I thought that wouldn't be far for you to come and sent a prepaid wire on Thursday morning but got no answer nor could find one at the Southampton hotel or boats so I don't expect you got it and wired again from Havre. I thought Bordeaux, sunset, grapes, us etc. might have been good, especially if you were low and I would have liked to see Sicart again and arrive the same day I did last year, but it would have been an awful journey for me. I feel rather vacant here. I am waiting for Mrs. Berenson to come in. I think I shall probably leave Paris tonight and spend to-morrow night in Munich to see a good film. I am travelling leisurely and comfortably but suffer from aimlessness. I haven't heard from Freddie since he left in July but I suppose he will turn up all right on Tuesday. It is rather a compliment from each of us to trust so much in a spoken word. I shall be rather annoyed if he doesn't come, or more likely, has a mistress he can't leave, when I get there, as my *puer*'s mother wired to ask me to go and stay September at Biarritz but I had to refuse. I was sorry as I think I could have cheered you up and I rather like Biarritz but we might have got rather degraded together and I am not very much in favour of romances with pupil's mothers which seems to me rather drearily banal and Gallican. I think the mothers can usually look after themselves but cannot resist the desire to extract sympathy from youth and to find someone to listen to their life story – I don't think women of the world are so very unhappy or they wouldn't go on being women of the world nor on the other hand do I think they want to seduce tutors but I think they are a nuisance and ought to not be encouraged to skim the cream from the salt of the earth – who are apt to lose both dignity and detachment in the process – I suppose *Le Rouge et Le Noir* is the locus classicus of the situation with the mother at her nicest and the tutor at his worst. Love is a painful but not a dignified malady I think, like piles or forkers, one can't help it but is not proud of it all the same – it seems such a leak in the soul, that the just and sympathetic man should have all his judgments of one person obscured and biassed and his focus in one direction all blurred seems not a culpable but a pitiable (in some moods) or ridiculous (in others) but almost inevitable jape of nature. I am talking of passionate entanglements of course and not of diffused and implicit love which is I suppose the most admirable thing in the world — contrast Tessa's love for Lewis with Lewis' for Florence. I am ashamed of myself when I think of the false values I have given people by being carried away by their faces — and such faces too! When then the just man falls in love his friends should comfort him as best they can, and unite with him in deploring the unfortunate state into which through no fault of his own he has fallen — but when he does it again and again or when he comes to glory in his weakness or boast of his successes, when his malady is quartan, tertian, and irremediable in its vehemence they must abandon him to his creature, let him take it home and put it in his house and place a ring on its finger to distinguish it from his friends till the lapse of years bring him suppliant to their doors again. The one remedy to susceptibility seems to be the cultivation of the gift of completely putting out of one's life every one who is not present except of course the people who are indispensable and permanent realities, to forget as quickly as you take fire and above all to follow Spinsebsan who is here allied to the preacher 'better the sight of the eyes than the desire of the heart' better the vision than the reality, the spectacle than the feast

'he who bends to himself a joy
does the winged life destroy
but he who kisses a joy as it flies
lives in eternity's sunrise

but o the flesh is bruckle the fiend is slee! End of homily. Tell me your news to Astoria Hotel Buda Pest which I leave 8th so write soon — anything you have sent here or will send there will be forwarded.

I am sorry to leave Logan and the pleasant life of Chilling I will write so often — I haven't quite gathered why you were low — simply Russians and the ἀσχολια of mundane life? They seem cause enough.

bibo sanitatem tuam
adveniant epistolae tuae

sicut in acqua et in terra
*et libera nos a Farlow!**

Much love
from
Cyril

4 Sept 1926. Telegram.

Blakiston,   Havre.
Biarritz.

Pas trouvé response a télégramme allant Paris direct amitiés
Cyrile

9 Sept 1926.

Noel Blakiston, Esq.,   Hotel Astoria,
Biarritz.   Budapest.

Dear Noel,
   If your ears burn your health is being drunk much love from
yours in haste Cyril

Tokatlian's Hotel
Constantinople

Thank you very much for your letter. I would have answered it, only
it arrived in the middle of some unpropitious wanderings.
Freddie

[? *Sept*] *1926.*

Lloyd Triestino.   Piroscafo Merano,
                                                    Dardanelles.

Dear Noel,
   How are you? I hoped to get a letter at Budapest or Constantinople
– I hope you are not distressed about anything – I – alas this nib is

*Hugh St Denys King-Farlow (b. 14 June 1902). KS. King's. Princeton
Davison Schol. Shell (U.S.A.). MBE(Mil.). Mermaid Theatre Trustee. Master,
Needlemakers Co.

quite hopeless and belongs to the only pen on the ship. I will go on when I can get a pencil from somewhere. I dreamt we were at the Lock House last night and have been able to think of hardly anything else all day – we must meet as soon as I get back it seems years since I saw you, I wish we could have managed Bordeaux and then I would have started this voyage with your benediction. I will come to Cambridge if we cannot meet in London. It is raining hard and some time after dinner. I am in the smoking room and Freddie is near by reading Tolstoy in German, there are a few lights Chanak and Gallipoli which we have been watching till we got cold – o this nib, I will have to stop, σ'ἀγαπ ω καληνήκτα

3 Oct 1926. Postcard, of Corfou.

H. N. Blakiston, Esq.,   Venice.
Kirkby on Bain.

Dear Noel,
    Our communication seems fairly badly cut since ill starred telegrams – I will be in London Wednesday night – where will you be? I want to see you very much indeed and will come and meet you anywhere you like if you are out of town. I may find a letter from you at Venice to-morrow – we have had an admirable trip so far and are going back to Munich and Cologne probably. I hope you are not distressed – we must meet soon. We seem to see each other so little. Can I come to Kirkby for Xmas it will be your turn there won't it?
                    Yours ever
                    Cyril

11 Oct 1926.

Noel Blakiston, Esq.,   Grosvenor Hotel,
Kirkby on Bain.   London, S.W.1.

Dear Noel,
    You may have thought I was dead but you certainly predeceased me. I wrote to you from Chilling, Paris and Buda Pest and got no answer though I gave you my addresses there and at Constantinople in time – this apart from the wire you never replied to which I had

to bicycle 3 miles through the rain to send besides having to spend half the night in S'hampton trying to trace a reply before I could know which boat to go on – after this I resent accusations of being a corpse. I could not tell where I was going to be till I saw Freddie and found out how much money he had and I never heard from him between seeing him off in S'hampton and meeting him in Vienna 5 weeks later. I came out by Munich and met Freddie in Vienna whence we trained to Budapest and went by steamer down the Danube to Giurgiu in Rumania thence by train to Bucarest and Constanza where we stayed 3 or 4 days, the bathing is good there. We came back by boat to Constantinople where we stayed and on the Princes Islands and then by a Lloyd boat to Athens via Salonica; from there we went to Nauplia and sailed and talked and also to Mycenae and Epidaurus and back to Athens where we dined with Buschor and went by a Greek boat to Corfu and Brindisi thence by train to Venice where I got your first post card on the 4th and from there to Munich where we saw the vases and sculpture and next day to Cologne and back to Brussels – the best things were undoubtedly the Danube below the Iron Gates (Tchirak river) the steppes of the Dobrudja and the Black Sea and later the ruins of San Demetrius at Salonica. The Lion gate at Mycenae, and some of the Munich vases but every day had its marvels and Freddie and I got on admirably – I missed you a lot as a matter of fact and was worried by getting no news of you. I feel that our proximity in the early summer and Boston especially have been the best things in the year and I always consider blindness and the loss of your intimacy to be the only real ills. It is nice to be in England again and with the cliffs of Dover open and white beside the sparkling sea I seemed to be entering your domain; the only times I can attach a meaning to impersonal immortality is when you manifest yourself in the disguise of greenness, an autumn sunset, winter night or reedy tremor across the fens *O spiritus sancte!* I thought of FitzGod much too, I am looking forward awfully to seeing him and to hearing of his voyage – let me know at once to the N and M if this week end doesn't suit I am coming on Thursday because Freddie is going on Friday and I shan't see him otherwise. I could stay till Monday if you liked. I am going abroad with my mother soon, probably to Majorca or may be Corsica. In the visitor's book at Mycenae I found Florence Dodd! Cambridge without God the Father* will be sad indeed – alas that his tongue wags so and I have

*William Le Fanu.

just learnt that he has been wreaking havoc with my acquaintance with Dadie. I had a sad dream of you in Jamaica last night pining away among the logwood trees – I was very glad to see Logan again, I dined with him the last two nights and am lunching to-day. I am going to do some work for Desmond MacCarthy for a bit too. I saw K who was nice and Bobbie on Friday and went for a walk with Charles in the Park. Freddie and I went to the 5th symphony yesterday. Jake was there in the offing. I suppose you couldn't come up for a night and go to the *Constant Nymph*? My mother would put you up I expect but seats are very hard to get. I am still in that state from which inner happiness proceeds, detachment, independence, love of life, excitement with ideas – O for a warm and healing Apollo's radiance, a mind to kindle and explore and mellow everything it touches, serene and fitful penetration, philosophic and free yet always conscious of its first formed pieties to friends and land. Ideas do not flourish in the south much and it is good to get back to them and be able to read Spinoza again. I would like to tell you more of travels when I see you – I must dine with Freddie Thursday as he goes next day but we must meet before dinner.

Much love to Jack and remember me to parents.

Cyril

18 Oct 1926.

Noel Blakiston, Esq.,
Magdalene College.

Piccadilly Hotel,
London, W.1.

11.30 p.m.

I read the work in the train and liked it a lot – only the narrative bits in book III flag a little I think. I liked the portrait of the wise man, the cathedrals, the synod of Whitby and the monastic life. The *Constant Nymph* is just over and was shattering – the play is a very demeaned version of the book but Tessa is wholly adequate and no one else matters very much, Florence is rather too odious, Lewis too charming and Linda too vulgar, Antonia does not shine at all as she does in the book and Charles is too academic but Tessa was superb and the comedy of the Borgia scene and the party in the silver stye was very good indeed, one wept most of the time I found and Tessa dies in a tumult of sobs from the audience and in all the cruel purity of the unattainable. The music of her song with Lewis in the Borgia scene is very haunting. Jacob and Trigorin were all right. Roberto over done and Paulina rather good. I wish we met more – or 'things are done to one and one changes'. Is not sentiment our most peculiar quality and yet we try to spurn it. Dic mihi verba vera, precor, in futuro; quo modo aliter possumus veritatem diligere in mundo dei et in operibus nostris? crudelis veritas sed amabilis et quis dilexit eam liberatur. Scribam ad venetos ut prosequi facerent epistolas tuas. Multa passa fuerunt dum eram in partibus infidelium. Eheu quare non possumus casam habitare! est tibi frater sed mihi nemo et cum frondibus marcesco,

nec tecum possum vivere nec sine te
Cyril

20 Oct 1926.

Noel Blakiston, Esq.,
Magdalene College.

Naval & Military Hotel,
Harrington Road,
South Kensington.

Dear Noel,

How are you? Sentiment made the idea of going abroad so unbearable that I have arranged to go down to Minehead with my mother instead and cottage hunt – even if we can't meet we can at least correspond with more ease from there. I talked of you to Logan and he seemed fairly amenable to settling us in a cottage though he didn't actually suggest it but I dare say he will and he didn't know then that I was not going to Majorca and I only knew that I didn't want to go so far. I lunched and tead with him yesterday and dined alone with Desmond. Logan says Mackail is dour and precious, always on his guard and always talking to an imagined audience of adoring young ladies – Please don't adopt a career till I have tried with Logan and do keep the cottage in view. I suppose if I took one you could not come there at Easter? Or come anyhow and stay for a week next vac? I shall certainly marry if I don't see more of you though I haven't the faintest notion who – let me know the kind of cottage you would like to share and the rough locality which I take to be between say Bude and Minehead, on or near the sea but above it and within range of trees. Do write to me. I may come down to Cambridge again with Desmond. I go Oxford week-end and Devon Friday week – much love you.
Cyril

Noel Blakiston, Esq.,
Magdalene College.

I have spent two mornings with the pictures in this museum, this is a fairly good and unimpeachable sample – The best I think is a Watts which I have ordered us each a reproduction of. I have been given Mackail on Greek literature to review for the N.S. so I will do some praising. I have been leading the usual Logan-Desmond life since I got back. How fares the cat?

22 Oct 1926. Postcard of My Second Sermon.

Jack Blakiston, Esq.,
Magdalene College.

Dear Jack,

I am sending you this picture, irreverent as it is, from a real sense of the importance of art, which is almost, is it not, above morals in the sense that all great art points its own moral. I am sure you will agree, but if as a son of the church, you feel your conscience cannot permit you to keep this, I feel that perhaps it would be best to destroy it rather than to send it back by return as it might damage my reputation in this hotel were it sent back to me. I am sure you will do what you think right.

[?Oct] 1926.

Naval & Military Hotel,
Harrington Road,
South Kensington.

Dear Noel,

Thank you for your letter. I dare say living an ideal is better than writing of it but most careers make one as impossible as the other. My mother doesn't want to go to Minehead now after all and Logan doesn't want me to go abroad so I may live near London for a bit where I can get riding and get to London easily when lonely. Logan suggests Richmond as there is a hotel there where Santayana lived for years which provides sanctity anyhow we are going down to-day to look at it. I lunched with Alan* and his young woman yesterday and thought her rather nice. I had a nice week end at Oxford though it seemed very desultory after Cambridge. I gave Sligger your love, he was very nice about you. Bobbie is now a don at Magdalen. Piers seemed flourishing. I stayed with a don at the House and spent most of the time with Penderel Moon who continues the perfect anchorite, remote, intellectual, and bird like. I saw Beazley for a bit. There seemed still a good bit of gossip and sycophancy there, enough to make one quite glad to get back to London. I have been reading an old letter of yours this morning written from Kirkby the time Prabahka went to school. I am going to the Lock House this week end and probably for the rest of the week to ride and work and collect books. I told you I had Mackail on Greek Literature to review did I? He married a daughter of Burne-Jones. London is very lovely at present, especially the Park but I find, though not living a worldly life at all, that it is very hard to think connectedly of anything or anyone. The Lock House is certainly the best place I know to consider you. I think I shall go to Ireland soon if only for a week end. I missed it a lot on the bus to Norwich. I hope the cat is well. I am sorry this is such a bad letter. I suppose it is better than nothing at all. If you give a cat too much meat by the way it grows fierce and scratches. Compare oats and horses, lettuce and rabbits. I may come down again to Cambridge before the end of term. I wish you were coming to the Lock House. Some of Santayana's poems are rather good, I read them yesterday.

I rather feel walking in a mist these last ten days, people loom obscure and vague or larger than life size, but disappear before comprehended. And there seems need of the Dark Tower to focus them aright again, the same applies to ideas but it is hard to return to meditation in an ideal world when the real has so much to offer at present, intimacy, intelligence, grace and polish, 'it is not good for man to be alone' – *o societas, sola felicitas, o beata solitudo sola beatitudo!* My mother sends you her love.

Cyril.

*Alan Clutton-Brock (b. 8 October 1904). KS. King's. Artist. Art critic of *The Times*. Trustee National Gallery.

5 Nov 1926.

Noel Blakiston,   Naval & Military Hotel,
Magdalene College.   Harrington Road,
                                    South Kensington.

Dear Noel,
  Thank you for your excellent letter. I gave Rylands one to give
you on Sunday. I hope he did. I dreamt that Mr. Shenstone* showed us
over the Leasowes last night. He had a camel. Mummie and I went
down to the Lock House yesterday which was lovely amid autumnal
leaves. I fetched up the Pyrenees and too was reading yesterday of
Seo. I met Margaret Kennedy but could not fathom her much. I am
going down to Chilling on Monday to live there alone and try and
write my book. I can have the car and anyone to stay so I hope you
will come either when term ends or before. You must. I am looking
forward to it as my conscience about writing is very guilty. This is
in great haste. Do write to me at Chilling – I shall probably go
abroad December and January unless I go and hunt. I thought of
going to Font Romeu for the skiing – it would be better than Switzerland.
  No more now but much love. I will send the epic back before I go.
                          Cyril

12 Nov 1926. Postcard of Place House, Titchfield.

H. N. Blakiston, Esq.,
Magdalene College.

  This is where the only begetter of the sonnets lived.
                          χάιρε
                          C.

*Wm. Shenstone (1714–63) of Halesowen, poet and landscape gardener.

181

Noel Blakiston, Esq.,   Warsash,
Magdalene College.   Hants.

Dear Noel,

Thank you for your letter which greeted me arriving at this desolate house through the wind and rain. I occupy a large bedroom with an alcove and a fire and a small room downstairs. Alone with myself we wonder what we have in common. I agree Dickens is excellent but I have hardly had time to read any, I hope I will here. 'The World' I think is a real existence – the same bloody creature at Biarritz as at Kingston W.I. It is oddly like this time last year though Chilling seems blended with our journey to the Lock House and my departure for Avonmouth as I arrived here with a trunk and six suitcases. When are you coming to stay? Mind, you must and you would like this place very much. At present I am curiously excited by being by myself, like a mediaeval King introduced to his future queen and also desperately frightened of ghosts and rather regretful for the warm precincts of Molly's drawing room and Logan's chessboard. *A Nineteenth Century Childhood** (Heinemann) is a very good book and nicely got up. It is good to be in the country again and feel the 18th century closing in – and the 17th and 19th for that matter. I couldn't cope much with *Words and Idioms*.† Give my love to Jack and Freddie and tell him I will write very soon.

Cyril

O beata solitudo

I will write again soon and thank you a lot for your benediction.

---

*By Mary (Molly), wife of Desmond MacCarthy.
†By Logan Pearsall Smith.

Noel Blakiston, Esq.,   Warsash,
Magdalene College.   Hants.

Dear Noel,

Thank you so much for letter. I only know Johnson's Soame Jenyns – I didn't know he procreated. I will be here I expect when your term ends, whenever that is, can't you come for a week, nights are so unsatisfactory, provocative and unsatisfying – if you came for a week here and I could come to Kirkby for a week in January we might have something to go upon – we cannot live on this paper currency without augmenting our gold reserve. Try and arrange for a week if you can. I find solitude very exhilarating – I have seen no clock or newspaper since Monday but to-morrow I am going over to lunch with an Irish exile called Lord Killanin and the spell will be broken. I don't know what the earth smells like after rain as it hasn't stopped since I've been here but the gales and storms that batter at this house and the wild birds by the sea and glimpses of the island are very exciting – I go for runs most days and read and write and think. There is a nice cat here (though a bit Grand) also a gramophone and a car which we can go out in when you come – Netley is close and Chichester, Winchester and the New Forest not very far. I think the solitary is God, it is the chief privilege of the hermit. My book is hanging fire at present but I am writing more in the notebook vein – Logan approved so of my little blue one that he bought me an identical one for 1927 in the hope I would go on with the form – it is rather like the china eggs and river hens but has done its work.

I have been reading E. M. Forster, *Room with a View*, *Howard's End* and *Passage to India*. I think *Howard's End* is the best in the sense that it deals with the most serious, ethical and intellectual problem but there is a rural and Victorian glamour about *Room with a View* that is more pleasing and a width of characterisation about *Passage to India* that is more entertaining but neither the psychology of spinsters or the burdens of empire seem as important as the relation of the intellectual life to the administrative, Greek to Roman, Colleger to Oppidan, affection to efficiency. I think *Howard's End*, though the best, is the dullest. Dannreuther returned me some old letters which make good reading though hardly favourable to you –

they are confident and natural and there is a tang about them that seems lacking in everything I have written since leaving Eton. I would be afraid to be so flippant or so serious now – can there really be anything in Landor's 'modesty which gone for once is gone for ever' – did he mean innocence? παρθένια παρθένια πόι με λιτίασ ἐν οἴκῳ; Shall we compose a dictionary of the Victorian dialect? English weather is really worthy of a temple, its superb contempt of rule, its stimulating extremities and profound reversals make it almost a life interest in itself – nowhere else could a day like yesterday be sandwiched in between to-day and the day before, its buffetings bear no malice and its tranquillity holds no warning. Memories of tropic oppression, sinister calms and pathetic rains with earthquakes and hurricanes behind everyone's mind return to bear out this testimony to our weather which surely deserves an apostrophe in our work.

The apples in their orchard
   tumble from the tree
O will the ships go down, go down
   upon the windy sea?

and will the ships? how sleep the brave?
pomifer autumnus fruges effuderit et mox
   bruma recurrit iners
to where the heath with withering brake grown o'er
lends the light turf that warms the neighbouring poor!

Give Jack my love. If we meet only for week-ends our prose becomes separated from our poetry – hence the incompetence at Ely – and we have only met for week ends since Seo. Love.
                       Cyril

16 Nov 1926.

Noel Blakiston, Esq.,   Warsash,
Magdalene College.   Hants.

Dear Noel,
   Do you think when the mood is on you you could write down all you can remember of our early acquaintance, half by half, I am appalled to find that the past, which I thought I possessed so glibly, is really lost beyond all hope of animation. Try and recall any meetings

and conversations of your first six halves and anything we wrote each other, however insincere or however uncomplimentary, in the holidays too – I can only remember two encounters in your first half, at the first Coll. Amalgama, and at the final of the house matches – there must have been more – when did we first go to hall, to carols, to Soho? What actually did we quarrel about and did we meet at your first Lords? put down what we looked like, spare no one, and what ways we tried to meet as well as when we did – It is awful the way the halves merge into each other and the outlines dim – put down anything that distinguishes periods for you and what you can remember of Freddie, Terence,* Jake, Hughes† and everyone. It would be fun to compare our researches and if you would put down what you remember we might still shore some fragments against our ruins but perhaps you haven't forgotten as much as me through having written less of it down. I have been analysing the Past in my new diary for the last three hours, it is after midnight, and I feel rather exhausted – bicycling along the ferry shore with no lamps under a windy moon is good sport but I wish you were here – never mind how trivial or inconsequent your recollections are they can't be more absurd than mine – which long leave was it we dined at Paddington? I am trying to take a few pages of note book for each half and trying to add to them by degrees – we will be very glad to know what we were like then some day however deplorable we then seem now – my love to you. I will try and write most days. Freddie could help you to date things. I would like to get him to remember too but he might despise the pastime. Best love to Jack. I spent yesterday in society and was very glad to get out of it. I am going beagling to-morrow to see what it is like. I have a superb book of my great grandmother's called Cary's Itinerary, a sort of 18th century English Baedeker, we might go a tour staying only at the inns it recommends. I read *Trivia*‡ again this evening, it really is supreme.

*Terence Beddard (b. 30 October 1901, d. 21 August 1966). KS.
†B. P. Hughes. KS.
‡By Logan Pearsall Smith.

Noel Blakiston, Esq.,

Warsash, Hants.
(11, St. Leonard's Terrace,
Chelsea, S.W.3.)

Dear Noel,

How is life with you? I worship the Past – our Past – and like some great festival of the mediaeval church the services drag on: the lonely vigils of the memory, the great sacramental visions, the veneration of holy relics and the symbolic monotonies of ritual occupy these rainy days – as a mere matter of exegesis can you explain an allusion to 'plays' – in your first winter half? Was that *Twelfth Night* in College Hall or was that in the summer and in any case, did we see it together? I remember seeing something with you in College Hall but when and what escapes me – or was it Terence and I together and you next us? or were the plays some done by Oppidans – hence the plural. I seem to remember some intrigue about tickets but again can't remember what the plays were unless they were done by Goodhart's* ((?) Faustus) or Blacker's (but that was later) – anyhow did we ever go? No time for more as the post is just going.

I bicycled to Southampton yesterday but had no time to see what I wanted – apparently there are superb walls with every kind of gate and houses of every century down to the 12th scattered about the old town – we must go when you come here – and also see the tablet to Mr. Bennet Langton of Spilsby which I read was in the Parish church. I think we did not do it justice our afternoon there but then it was raining. Also, the Dolphin, according to my 18th century guide is the proper Hotel and where all the 'winter assemblies are held' – The way from here is very pleasant involving two journeys by ferry – one rural and the other urban.

No more now or this will miss the post. I have just read *Mansfield Park* which is admirable – so far I have always eschewed Jane Austen through dislike of her worshippers and of the Holiday Task atmosphere surrounding her. Give Jack and Freddie my love.

Cyril

---

*Goodhart's and Blacker's were boys' houses at Eton.

18 Nov 1926.

Noel Blakiston, Esq.,   Warsash, Hants.
Magdalene College.   (11, St. Leonard's Terrace,
                                                    Chelsea, S.W.3.)

Dear Noel,

Your letter just come. Do go on thinking and you may remember
more – or consult with Freddie. I never kept a diary at Eton unfortunately. Your letter from Bristol survives in its entirety as I wrote
it all out and sent it to Terence and he managed to keep the letter.
Yours is an astonishing one. I have also the record of a long argument
at the end of the half before and a good many of your opinions survive
in the letters to Denis the summer afterwards – but it is the early
period that puzzles me most – you wrote to me at Christmas and also
thanked Terence for the cigarettes – which you asked for, if you
remember, because you wanted them for your father. Your first letter
to me ended up 'wind, rain, sky, trees, think of me' – Do try and
remember more – a good way is to think of places and occasions
when we might have met and see if they suggest anything to you,
carols, secular singing, allowance, Lower tea room, college fives,
staying out, rears, the slab, chamber stairs, I think my name was
usually in your batch for shooting and we met that way in the Christmas Half, Cloisters, Sunday chapel, School concert, absence, didn't
you use to make me laugh in prayers, when was that? Consider
College as being a parallel to the Athens of Lysis with only formality
and festivals to permit intercourse and often not even that but proximity only. I would like to read *The Land** – Bring it when you come
here. Logan has often spoken of the authoress. It has been said that
all her technical terms come from a text book. I heard quite a lot about
her from the man who did the woodcut who was staying here in the
summer. I understand your feeling about death and Benson – 'youth
feels everywhere the presence of mortality but never the reality of
death' (C.V.C.) and that being the first time for you must bring it
home. I haven't felt it yet though I keep trying to and trying to
understand the actual moment of extinction, the body 'in articulo
mortis' – but fail. The value of death I thought was that it conferred
on one absolute possession of the vanished friend – and it seems very
hard to forget people when they are dead – Logan and Desmond for
instance seem to labour under the memory of their dead as if it was

*By Vita Sackville-West.

187

a tiresome illness and a perpetual vexation and this is rather encouraging as it supposes that willy nilly the dead are remembered and slightly mitigates the fear of self-convicting shallowness, of easy oblivion, and of 'a last regret, regret can die' – I don't think I shall die just at present but I think there is hardly any time of day when I should really mind dying – I feel I have lived such a lot already that there would be hardly any kind of experience that I had been deprived of, only quantity, and death, though by no means desirable, would not be unjust. I used to desire it passionately a few years ago and till quite lately (1923–or 4) – naturally it was the romantic sense of climax that demanded it, the fear of bathos and a vaguer apprehension of a squalid old age and a certain literary pessimism and sceptical despair – I remember the summer I quarrelled with you announcing that I would commit suicide the day I got an Oxford scholarship as a proof that it was done from no material depression – innocence again! I was worried though by the remark of Forster's I quoted to you – 'I wonder how far death does confer possession of the dead on one' – more than the agony of loss is the anguish of the obscurity of that loss and may not the 'memory of the dead' wipe out all traces of what they really were? Hence passionate and blundering reminiscence and frantic excavation of the mind with stab too deep or wide or shallow before the spade rings on stone. I believe the worst torment of separation is a kind of raging dumbness, a central loneliness that can hardly be expressed and dries up in a vexatious 'words, words, words' when one tries to give it form – Perhaps real grief is inarticulate – by the way have you read Sir Eustace Carr in *Trivia* – which gives some rather good glimpses of the power of death and how once one is attuned to consider it, one can never return to anything else – Incidentally is not our preoccupation with the other's death a tacit evasion of the worse evil of marriage?

I had a very pleasant and mellow letter from Logan this morning followed by two writing blocks. I miss him rather here. His bleakness, sympathy and exquisite humour have grown very necessary and there is a pleasant security in a friendship that is unlikely to end in misunderstanding or betrayal or unappeased desire. The pleasant thing about him and Desmond and Molly is that when they seem on the verge of platitude they always recover and go one better than the obvious remark. Desmond giving advice and ending with 'mind you, this is all the advice that I have never been able to follow, but it is the best' – and Logan giving the same advice afterwards and ending 'you see Desmond and I have all this vast vocabulary of exhortation, Desmond especially, that we have been storing up for years and years and never had an occasion to use, these great imperatives of admonition that we have had to listen to and never been able to pronounce ourselves' and Molly murmuring at intervals 'I'm sure he has too much advice and he can't go into lodgings, possibly, landladies always knock': 'Jobation' murmurs Logan, 'Job, jobation, Job's comforters, the patience of Job' – and then echoes of our own youth 'what has Dermot got to say Rachel'? 'He says that he has refused to join the corps because it is voluntary compulsion' – so long is the arm of coincidence that at this moment Desmond's voice rises up authoritatively through the scullery ceiling and the familiar rise and fall proclaims inaudibly the literary topic of the week to the cook and children. I do hope you can spend a week here, it would be a rehearsal of cottage life for one though we could do plenty of sightseeing if we liked – I could do with a glimpse of the island where I have never been and also of Chichester or Christchurch or Beaulieu Abbey and Romsey. Try and come for long. In view of our mutual ignorance of your first year wouldn't it be advisable to try and write down at odd times all we can remember of our intercourse since for now that my diary is lost all last year's proceeding, the Lock House (2) or Avignon, 2 Kirkby, and the Dorset, Seo, chalet sagas are all destroyed – the best way I think is to keep roughly chronological and within those limits put down everything relevant or not that one can remember – luckily I had a letter written from Gautby to Bobbie and another describing our day in London when Sligger tead at Rumplemayers – when *was* that Long Leave we travelled back together after Soho with Blair and Peter? It still harasses me. Did the strokes you drew like flag staffs mean to connect me and you because if so and they were horizontal wouldn't that mean that I was in upper Passage and not Lower – hence that it was your second or third half as I changed my room after that summer. The explanation is ingenious! I certainly remember your spending of your first Lords at Wimbledon – don't you remember how we went there together from Paddington on the grounds that you didn't know the way – and how we walked about while you were looking for some parent who didn't come till one or thereabouts? I confess I have only remembered it this moment and still a little afraid that I have mixed it up with next year when we certainly sat together in the stand and you explained contemptuously to me the qualifications of the rival batsmen. I can't remember my last Lords at all. I think I spent most of it away with Farlow – the year after we lunched at Princes do you remember just before I went abroad and the one after I was in Greece. When did we first meet in the National Gallery? or go there together? and when was the time I looked for you there and you looked for me in the British Museum? was that my last long leave? When did you stay with Maud? when did we breakfast at Peter's at the end of one half? – Try your letters home when you are next at Kirkby, they are sure to have them and often one finds the dry bones live. Dear Noel sir, may you be, may you become, *praesens*, er – I would translate 'present *cum adesis* – er – when you are with me *velut*, as, just as *ades*, you are with me, *cum absis* – when you are, shall I hazard? absent?' It might be put in a more Latin order when next we dine at Wymondham! When did 'the First Noel that the angel did say' affect us – your first or second winter? Much love from Cyril

Your reminiscences are scanty but exactly right such as they are. I mean only the important things there.

I shall go up to London one week end to stay with Logan and see the MacCarthy's. I might be able to fit it in with the end of your term if you let me know when it is and we could come down here together – only try and come for a week if you can – I have some things I have written I would like you to see or hear. Best love to Jack and Freddie.

perhaps

Hic jacet N. . . .
Absens Praesenti
Praesens in
absentia
(on a flat slab!)
C

[? 25] *Nov 1926.*

Noel Blakiston, Esq.,   Warsash,
Magdalene College.   Hants.

Dear Noel,
    Thank you. I will concur that Jack can do no wrong but I still maintain that he can make a mistake. Enough however, I don't hold

with the Sitwells you know. I think they are very tiresome but they were very nice to me in Spain and have been nice since. As a matter of fact I haven't read anything they have written in the last year or so; Edith is tedious, humourless, and combative, Osbert advertises, Sashie is the most remote but none are really our style. I am to meet Waley* on Saturday when I would rather like to know if he is like his poetry. I am staying the week end with Logan – I suppose you couldn't come up on Sunday or anything, no it would hardly be worth it. Thank you for your reminiscences, every little helps. I am still not sure yet of the death question – consider Heathcliff who gained very little from Cathy's decease – Proust in his last volume also analyses at some length what he calls posthumous jealousy: his mistress dies and he spends his time discovering that she had been unfaithful (with young women) and seems to find a vindictive pleasure in discovering it though equally an impotent rage since he can never confront her. Did you feel about me in Jamaica as you say you would about Jack in the South Seas, the possession of death already accruing – I felt nothing but fruitless longing occasionally becoming hysterical (I wasn't jealous I don't mean that) but the enormity of space seemed even more oppressive and to enforce the nightmare separation of Hercules and Hylas whose voice sounded so faint through the water that Hercules went to look further and further away. Also there is a kind of telepathy between friends which consists in a sort of general consciousness of their existence during the period while they are reciprocating it and this would break down with death – for instance I could never think of my grandmother when I was abroad though I had thought of her quite a lot just before and I found when I got back that she had lost her memory for that month and is only now getting better again – we know of cases of spiritual death which seem hopeless as far as existence after them is concerned – Jackie for instance must be alive somewhere now but can hardly be said from our point of view to live but I admit he proves the point in the sense that the fact of his spiritual death is enough to make his old self entirely one's own possession – yet it is not only one's own possession because he is spiritually dead – if the dead are immortal then they take their past with them? I can find no rational proof of immortality but it is just possible since I can conceive people, at least you, as a spirit, that they may be able to exist as such and capable of visitations. Is this all boring?

*Arthur Waley (b. 1881. d. 27 June 1966). King's. Translator of Chinese Literature. CBE 1952. CH 1956.

191

Vidi te in somnis fracta, mea vita, carina last night – and all the Hartogs and various complications including my *puer* who merged somehow into Prabahka – *vidi te in somnis fracta* is a good rhythm don't you think – I have been reading Horace, Propertius and all those pagan poets who had the art of using the thought of death to season an ode like ginger with melon or cloves in apple tart. Horace grows on one, infinitely delayed by being taught at school, till slowly the tang of his mannered truisms and the great barnacle covered odes one felt in all their freshness with the words that clank into place relentlessly like bronze doors in a Byzantine cathedral.

cum semel occideris et de te splendida Minos
    fecerit arbitria
non, Torquate, genus, non te facundia, non te
    restituet pietas;

One can see how hard he is really for youth to like, compared to Catullus or Vergil: his sourness and moderation, his earthy wisdom at first obscure the strange richness, the superb adequacy of all his work, his vocabulary seems a thick black soil that for centuries has born crops uncomplaining, his works are some walled in kitchen garden full of prize cabbages and lovely pears, and peaches climbing the wine dark stones just as Vergil's are more like the green lawn that has been turf from time immemorial – there is nothing of the hothouse about either and yet a certain opulence of age. By the way have you ever read *Emerald Uthwart* by Pater – another imaginary portrait – I did the other day and found it rather good, at least about school life and country houses though the style is rather more creamy than the average even. I read Benson's *Pater* and rather liked it but it brought on more reverie on death. Flavian dies in Marius his arms and Marius perishes in Pater's. Pater dies in the last chapter and the author who has from his allusions to Pater as a dead man made one think he was alive is really dead too – *et de te splendida Minos* – it baffles the imagination like the Indian rope trick. By the way do you know who wrote

Te spectem suprema mihi cum venerit hora
    te teneam moriens deficiente manu

Prop. Tib. or Ov.? I suspect Prop. though it is like Ov.

te loquor absentem, te vox mea nominat unam
    nulla venit sine te nox mihi, nulla dies –

I like Crabbe more and more – do you know his description of the fens, the saltmarsh and the gipsy encampment? I have no intention of marrying at present by the way though I rather envy the security of the marriage state, at least it is secure if finances are secure. Benson is always complaining of friends marrying in the diaries isn't he – The Chronicles of Wasted Time will be the title of my epoch making reminiscences I expect. What fun to preach a sermon with the sole object of making the congregation severally aware of their mortality! and see them bow their scandalised faces and plug their unwilling ears. I hope you can come and stay here. I must stop now for the evening meal. *Saepe te in somnis vidi* is probably what I was thinking of but still less do I know who wrote that. I shall be glad of a week in London.

This is a somewhat dreary letter I'm afraid – I am rather written out to-day owing to writing a sheaf of parodies to Logan – in my capacity as the new God I issued an ultra modern French manifesto to which he replied with a dignified prayer and I have now answered with a long mediaeval Latin rigmarole – out of which emerges my first commandment '*laborate homines ut ametis me tantum quantum ego me ipsum amo*' and the sudden revelation '*non prophetas volui habere sed pueros, non manna in deserto sed epulae in triclinio amoenae mihi sunt*' – then there is also a complicated correspondence as I wrote him a report from Miss Agatha Warsash, Principal, Chilling Home for Backward and Difficult Boys, asking what form of religious instruction I was to be given and followed by a 'secular report' from the spirit of 17th century, 18th, 19th and 21st century *manes* of the house all in their own styles and Logan answered with a letter to the Principal warning her against my morals and asking leave for me to come up for half term – I have replied with a letter very stiff saying that after what happened last night I may as certainly come up and as certainly not come back, a bad boy's letter from me, breezy and unregenerate and the report of the 'visitor' – a long parody of Walter Pater who visits Chilling and describes the scandal in full before returning to Brasenose not a little oppressed by the 'dripping eaves and puddled sceneries' he finds on arriving here. Let us become great Latinists together – it might be rather fun.

Χαίρε Cyril

Noel Blakiston, Esq.,   [London.]
Magdalene College.

Dear Noel,

   Hail. I am reading Crabbe, Horace, *The Prelude*, and *The Seasons*
simultaneously in search of spiritual (scenic) home. I hope in the end
to tell by the relief I turn from one to the other which I like the best.
The Prelude of course reads less professionally than any of the others
which is in its favour but Thomson is infinitely more lovable and
Crabbe seems to hold East Anglia in the hollow of his hand – but I
haven't got Wordsworth to Cambridge yet – I am trying to complete
my essay on Eden (I don't think you've seen it) and also an article on
Rimbaud but inspiration flags. Logan sent me a case of gramophone
records to-day which was exciting. Love. Cyril

The Prelude would help you a lot I think, it has the verbal modesty
you desire (and I) and also strikes the right note of intimacy and
unsentimental use of 'we', and us for him and S.T.C.

Nov 1926.

Noel Blakiston, Esq.,   [London.]
Magdalene College.

Dear Noel,

   Thank you for your letter. Don't get your hair cut. I agree on the
importance of music – I don't think it is as important as literature
because no amount of music will make us composers but it comes
next. I don't find myself much interested in the technicalities and
history of music or even in the lives of composers. I have the New
World Symphony here. I got it in mistake for a quartet and find it
very satisfying, strangely so for a popular and vaguely barbarous
piece. I don't like Strauss. Pictures I feel rather guilty about, at odd
moments they matter and I enjoy seeing them but I know, relatively,
much less about them than I did at Eton. Logan says Berenson, if he
could write, would be a modern Goethe, he has a universal grasp of
the world's literature and culture etc and knows practically every

European or Asiatic language but cannot write adequately and is therefore best in conversation. Waley said he thought K. had grown three times more didactic since he had gone there and my conversation was years more mature – I don't know if that is a compliment – he is a very beautiful man, like the perfect mediaeval ascetic but aloof and difficult. I spent Sunday evening with him and he came to dinner Saturday. I enjoyed my week end very much – I went to rather a dreary ballet and dreary night club, a dreary film society, and a dreary music hall but much intimacy was sandwiched in between. Molly and I have formed a die-hard secret society. I said you had better belong, it is non political and based on admiration of the last century and the better parts of the preceding one. You would like her she has the good points one used to admire in Mrs. Loxley, emancipation and a vein of divine madness – do read her book, A Nineteenth Century Childhood, it is excellent and good about Eton. Rachel and I had a midnight supper and discussed love: she thinks it is all right if one neither says anything or does anything about it and I tend to agree. Desmond was busy all the time, we have a chance of all going to Ireland in April, it has been mooted for months and looks like materialising, there is a good elfin brother at school. Desmond exposed Gertrude Stein rather well in the New Statesman, did you see it? last week? I like your quotations from Berenson. I did not know he was so understanding, do you mean you admire Luini and the post-Leonardos? I will try and collect my views on pictures, I think they are rusty though I enjoyed the Watts in the Victoria and Albert and the El Grecos in Munich. I think I have got most of the emotions people get from painting out of Greek sculpture and vases the last year or two. Don't minimise your genius or it may take offence – you can have genius without talent – anyhow I think you should go on writing. I did like the rest of your epic you know – my mother addressed the envelope for me – she had not read it. Culture I still think is bad though we must have a defensive quantity. Seo on the other hand is good. Don't get mixed up with Oxford, I know you would come to no harm but my Greek sense of pollution would give me no peace – a charitable thing to say of *alma mater*. I find Rimbaud's prose inspiring and am trying to analyse it on paper after six months without it. I am quite glad to return to solitude. I sorted your letters this evening, there are 150 or one a week for the last three years, of course a lot are postcards. I read through the first 36 (up to Lock House Christmas) this evening. I like the hard and crashing schoolboy of the Gautby period 'by St. Hugh do you mean "Yonge Hugh" – he hasn't much interest for me though he may have been a tart' (I didn't) – I have failed to recover any of your September ones from Venice, otherwise none seem lost, the earliest is Easter 22 (to Avignon!) previous to that there were three, possibly four, your first letter I nearly knew by heart, second is recorded to Beddard, third accompanied Lincoln imp, and there may have been another that Christmas or Easter – it is a pity I haven't them as it would lengthen the correspondence by two years though the Lincoln Imp almost counts as one – the pig I think I gave you before we quarrelled – try and remember which leave it was we travelled back together after dining in Paddington and going to Soho with Blair and Peter. It still baffles me. I gave you tobacco pouches on two occasions and possibly, from Switzerland, a donkey, but I think that was Timothy. By the way I suspect evasion of duty since you have said nothing about coming here longer than a night. Please come for a week after term or if (God knows why) you only can come for a night, come soon. Logan said I could have you as long as I liked any time I was here so if you like to try this in lieu of career it is going – I shan't go to Devonshire now as the MacCarthy's are going to the Asquiths for Christmas and not there till afterwards. I may very likely live with Logan in London the end of January to March which will be quite pleasant as I like Chelsea and Logan's house as well as getting on very well with him and having Desmond and Molly round the corner. I enjoy meeting new people but don't want new friends. I value detachment very highly at present and what Logan calls being 'the master of one's life' – I find a growing tendency to despise everyone rather irksome, you know the phase, surnames etc, the arrogance of the solitary. I shall go abroad at Christmas, I don't know where yet, I might join Bobbie if he still wants me to come otherwise Algeciras, Switzerland, South of France and Austria all seem possibilities – I would like a hedonistic loiter somewhere. Cecil Beaton wants to do the cover of my book. It is a good job he isn't paid in advance. This is a dull letter: I seem to have imbibed some of your *romana mordacitas* of the 1923 period. Please write often and try and come for a week, it will take you that to read your letters and they are well worth it. You might let me know when it would be. How about your 21ster is there anything I can get you? I suppose you wouldn't celebrate it with me in town, bringing Jack or any where else you would name? Could I come to Cambridge for it and bring you back? It would be too tempting to turn over the other page so am stopping here. Jack suggested I might come to Cambridge – I don't know if you are keeping it festively but I would come for the night if it would only be four or five. Adios amigo.

Cyril

Tell me what Oxford's like.

19 Dec 1926.

Noel Blakiston, Esq.,   Freshwater Bay Hotel,
Kirkby on Bain.   Freshwater,
                                     Isle of Wight.

To await arrival

Care Noel,
    accipe, precor, hanc epistolam in testimonio gaudii mei per te allati. Sicut 'acqua fresca' in deserto alloquia, colloquia immo, tua bibui, et nunc etiam, haud satiatus, 'δίρω' clamo. O Noel diligo te et ipsissimum tempus 'Noel' reboat

χάιρε

Cyril

eheu versificator flocci valeo!

[? Dec] 1926.

Dear Noel,
    '*Difficile est longum subito deponere amorem*' and working in the morning or pausing in the day, walking round the dining room eating ginger and sitting down to write again what shall I say ? There is no ill but absence, no ill but absence and really tears on the platform are better than the muddy thawing of the heart's frost to a less cordial sorrow. Inarticulacy settles down on me again and only the dinner gong saves my face – *saepe te in somnis vidi.*
    This I suppose is better than nothing. I will try and write to-morrow. Remember me on Christmas day and to your parents – I got this book when I left Eton.

197

25 Dec 1926.

Noel Blakiston, Esq.,   Chelsea
Kirkby on Bain.   . . . a day in the morning

Dear Noel,
   Thank you indeed for your two letters. I expect you will have got
a lurid fragment through Jack by now – I am still struggling to be
articulate but missing you defies words like the toothache, the thought
of this time last year is my only consolation for at least I am not
drugged with sunshine, parted by 4000 miles, nor tortured by the
thought of snow – Shakespeare on Jamaica, psalm tunes, and the
Belle au bois dormant.

   that in this desert inaccessible
   under the shade of melancholy boughs
   Lose and neglect the creeping hours of time
   – if ever you have looked on better days
   if ever been where bells have knolled to church –

I grant we survive absence better than anyone but when presence can
be so superlative and when we are both expecting early deaths it
seems such waste not to be together – I thought the best moment in
the C.N. was where she meets Lewis in the vestibule and exults in the
prospect of no more parting and I wondered if we could ever say
that too; it seemed the only remark we had not said that remained
worth saying – still on the whole το φθόνερον is kind to us only it
is so much harder to miss worthily in London, the ἀσχόλιαι tending
to reduce loneliness to a half conscious pain rather than a noble sorrow.
Still the involuntariness of missing is a pledge of its power and it is
right that you should fall like the shadow between the cup and the
lip. It would be lovely if we could really go abroad in the summer.
Has Jack told you of the magazine? I think it would be a good idea
if we amassed some poetry, stories, and dogma together and I had
4 or 5 copies typed for our own amusement so that we could refer
to our ex cathedra dictums on various subjects – I think we might
print the 50 best quotations, 10 from each language and also a short
encyclopaedia under letters of the alphabet – revealed truth, the last
word on Actuality, Action, Art, Actaeon, etc. and some of your
epic and epigrams but mostly things written more specially for the
paper, we could sift our contributions when I come to Kirkby – also

apophthegms, 'the wisdom of the Bain' etc anyhow it should keep us occupied. I too felt the Freshwater moon to be a high water mark and the sanctity conferred on it by Lulworth and even by School Yard to invest it with a significance almost of ritual, surely we are the slaves of our memories and trying ever to reproduce some heavenly idaeas, the types of which, the winter journey, the dark tower, the downland moon, even the dash through London, and the refreshment buffets afford us the feeble pleasure of an incomplete reminiscence – how many of our lives have we spent in the rumble of country buses or the shelter of gas lit stations! why do we search for sunshine when destiny requires of us tin roofs and long platforms. King's Cross, Peterbro, Oxford or Ely? If I was Orpheus you were Narcissus in your previous incarnation but whence came our meaningless regalia, our level crossings, or our milk cans?

I rashly said I would lunch with an American woman today and found she had asked 6 young men from Toc H – Anglican, military, bank clerks but it restored the ecstasy of absence instead of the dolor and reminded me of dinners with the head usher or Crace* when I was longing all the time as one only can at dinners to be talking to you (sentiment) – I have at last broken away and can go on writing – Logan liked his Christmas card and you have been praised by all the family: I agree that amateur pro intellectuals (Patrick Balfour e.g.) are good. I think I do mind what you are like a good deal because I am so coloured by it; I mean I realise you are much better than me in indifference to food wine and luxury and though not changing myself I like to feel you are without those weaknesses, which, if not actually squalid at present, hold such possibilities of advancing squalor; on the other hand your presence is such a positive virtue in itself that it makes me fairly uncritical of whether you are dull or grim; hence the frequent exclamations in the diary 'he is beneath this roof'! Absence when there is liberty to feel it, is but a rarified presence, a middle voice of the active verb – but presence, when once it sets in, is so infinitely lovelier, that it is almost a tragedy to put up with the lesser good. Your reality too consists so much in you being a person that it is almost an insult to find you in wind and rain or thought of snow – hence your indignant 'you'll be saying a salt marsh looks like me next'! The exile movement in the New World Symphony is still in my brain. I sent you one diary for quotations and the other was for sententiae, to shore fragments against our ruin and sow the land reclaimed from

*J. F. Crace, Master in College at Eton in Connolly's time.

the lethean wave. The Catullus I got in Cologne after leaving Eton –
O colonia quae cupis
ponte ludere longo!
a good tag in juvenal
(*rarus sermo illis et*) *magna libido tacendi.*

    I have another Cat. Tib. Prop. so references can be made. The phrase of the César Franck Symphony that I minded so at Minehead comes at the very end of the first half of the last record, I think now the symphony is a bit rough at times but still very good indeed and the Sleeping Beauty restores you the green summer. I only had one dinner with Jack but a good one – he seems to have had rather a bad time – nothing else has happened much – the MacCarthy's are away. I met Maurice there and we got on all right but Logan tells me he moved heaven and earth to stop them receiving me but was confuted – no friend like an old friend ! I find I have very little wish to see anyone or do anything very much and am content to write as much as I can and talk and play chess but no further than Wellington Square – we must certainly have a week end before term begins and I will come to Kirkby first. I feel the only way one can be truthful is to do nothing one would want to conceal, besides virtue now is almost a form of originality and while it is lovely to know that one is liked whatever one is, it is lovely also to impose a high standard on oneself enough to feel worthy of being liked as ultimately as that at all. I would like the Oxford Book of 18th century verse very much as a Yule tide gift when next you are getting some books – that and letters, the one I got to-day has saved my life in this orgy of Alys' philanthroper's Christmas. What a good poem – have I forgot my only love to love thee etc is that you read that night. I feel like Tessa 'all this time wondering what I have to give you' – soaring and impossible ethics, pride, reserve, and integrity seem the only things that are costly enough – reserve to other people, pride for myself, and integrity with you – I was glad to get Jamaica off my chest to you – as the diary only started in February. You must see that progress in oblivion was pretty slow and that unfinished letter I found you was begun the day I arrived and would have gone had I been left alone an hour longer at the same time as Bobbie's – I enclose the preface to our Athanasian creed.

Love from Cyril

loisible de posséder la verité dans une âme et un corps!

Forgive sentiment which is apt to obtrude in letters but I have ventured to retain it here from the analogy that it is always so acceptable in yours – faith begets works.

te veniente die, te decedente vocabo.

The object of this publication is to perpetuate the views of the editors for their own convenience: it is not a manifesto but a memorandum of their divinity and censure therefore is omitted as out of place in a work of reference.

Truth is revealed by grace, not experience, and, though life may contain more than the pages of this book, its surplus is irrelevant.

It is possible that the world may one day attain the perfection that has been realised on the banks of the Bain and the Meon: it is possible: but it is not important, and we are more concerned to record those minutes of our golden meetings that will in some wise preserve us from our not (ignoble? unworthy?) adversaries, from oblivion, our ghostly enemy, and from everlasting death, Time and Death.

Nothing can appear which has been published before although early work is accepted, most contributions are expected to have been written for the magazine.

[*Subjects for the magazine*]

Bain
Poetry
Stories
Last word on etc. (alphabet) and
Travel information England and abroad
indispensable quotations (50 from 10 in 5 languages)
Types of people
Manifestoes –
blasphemy
music
art K. Clark
    Bobbie Longden
epic
modern literature and thought
Self, Noel, Jack. –
    William – Eton revisited or Paradise Regained
    Molly M. Logan. Freddy.

3 arts. Intimacy, Literature, Travel.
   Art, Beauty, Culture, Debauchery, Environment, French, God,
   Homosexuality, Intimacy, Jesus, Knowledge, Love, Music, Nature,
   Orpheus, Pride, Quotations, Reality, Sloth, Travel, Us, Values,
   Wealth, Exile, youth, Zeal.

(*on envelope*)
Suggested name for paper
   The Athanasian.
amicitia ad Johannem.

29 Dec 1926.

Noel Blakiston, Esq.,   11, St. Leonard's Terrace,
Kirkby on Bain.   Chelsea, S.W.3.

Greeting, you – thank God these three consecutive Sundays are over,
I have a cold but not a bad one. I have written an account of one day
(the British Museum, lunch with Sligger, seeing you off, tea with
Molly) – it took 16 hours to write and is over 7000 words long! I
will send it you some time or it might do for *the Athanasian*. I am
also going on a bit with my Greek novel – I dreamt that we were at
Harrow and then last night that we were going in the train to Avonmouth through the lovely pine forests and cane breaks of Wiltshire
and Somerset and back to a tropical Kirkby. I dream a great deal of
Avonmouth. I think my tendency to dream of a lovelier England
must have been inspired by your epic. I am lunching at Boulestin's
again to-morrow with Logan and Maurice Baring and Ethel Sands
and will drink your health otherwise I haven't seen a soul. Can you
let me have Sligger's address some time as I can't remember it. This is
the sort of letter one writes with a cold. I will write again soon. Much
love and to Jack.

                              Cyril

O Cyril
since leaving Eton only 108 days in 1640 have been spent with Noel
that is only 6% of your time in the last 4½ years – and only 25 days
in this year as opposed to nearly 50 in 1925, 17 the year before and
14 the year before that.

life accelerates

92 Gray's Inn Buildings,
W.C.

Dear Sir,

By the will of the late Cyril Vernon Connolly Esq you have been made his literary executor with full power to dispose of all his manuscripts as you think fit. I enclose them.

Yrs very respectfully
Shadrach, Meshach,
Abednego and Friend Ltd

I also enclose his estate which was left to be divided between you and your brother after his debts had been paid.

30 Dec 1926.

Noel Blakinston Esq.,
Kirkby on Bain.

11, St. Leonard's Terrace,
Chelsea, S.W.3.

Dear Noel,

Thank you so much for your letter. I expect you have mine written on Christmas day now which answered your superb one. My cold is still tiresome. Molly is back now and we seem to be getting down to our book. Vaughan's trouble I think is that he can't keep up his level for a single poem even (except They are all gone into the World of Light) – I like though 'There is in God men say a deep and dazzling darkness' and

Grant I may not puddle lie
in a corrupt obscurity

is a good thought – as a mystic he is better than Herbert, as a poet worse don't you think. I would love to come that week end by the four o'clock then – and we must go somewhere too. I got a nice Collins yesterday. I will write tomorrow but am stupid with cold. Molly likes you.

Cyril

Love to Jack. Do both write hard for *The Athanasian*.

[*December 1926*].

Ritz Hotel,
Piccadilly,
London, W.1.

Dear Noel,

I got this this afternoon and came here for tea to read it in the sequestered haunts of our own hallowed enterprise. I am loth to part with it and you must bring it to the Desolate library. I will go on and read Cambridge and Residence in London in Logan's, they seem apposite. Let me know if you have it already.

Love from
Cyril

P.S. Fains being Coleridge!
Excuse the florid inscription.

This* is really an improvement on Piero who seems to have painted such ugly pictures when one looks again at them. Love to Jack to whom I shall write.

1 Jan 1927.

Noel Blakiston, Esq.,   11, St. Leonard's Terrace,
Kirkby on Bain.   Chelsea, S.W.3.

'Life accelerates' was meant intransitively, it gets quicker and quicker in the sense that one's mind grows richer and one's experience fuller – I agree that it retards anything else – I will come on Friday. The Marriage of Heaven and Hell is excellent I think, I really got my Balliol scholarship on that and Halifax. The proverbs of Hell are especially good don't you think and the Rimbaud-like vignettes (e.g. the pitiable and foolish young man scene) – I don't think I would accept them all now though, the proverbs I mean, and Vitality alas is useless without grace (or almost that bloodier word Taste) – if this is not so, America is God – 'exuberance is beauty' is rather hard to swallow don't you think, – then futility is not good in itself but it is a burden our generation has to bear, a useful humiliator, a check on pomposity – e.g. it renders Benson much more likeable – Milton's Satan unimpeachable – Bonheur is worse than futility, far – it exists

---

*Perhaps some picture postcard had been enclosed in this envelope.

for no reason till one mistakes fat for muscle, futility is perhaps sent to combat it. Catullus is a revelation of the awfulness of love. Tibullus was too sentimental-dainty. Propertius too self-pitying and conceited really to suffer but the other could take his own temperature in a delirium. '*Si qua recordanti*' is about the sincerest poem in literature don't you think, so much so that one does not raise an eyebrow at his naive '*si vitam puriter egi*' so obviously did he believe he had. My novel with Molly might be fun if it is finished, we are brother and sister in the 1780's. I have several things to tell you when we meet. χαῖρε

Cyril

1 Jan 1927.

Noel Blakiston, Esq.,   [Chelsea.]
Kirkby on Bain.

Dear Noel,

How are you? My cold is nearly gone. I forgot to say that there is an anthology of Childhood in Literature which might help you though I can't remember anything about it – I have just bought a picture in your name to which I am hastening to confess. Logan wanted to buy a flower picture at an exhibition by a friend of his to encourage them and could not do it in his own name as it would look like patronage and mine would be known to her so I bought in your name and gave Lock House as your address for catalogues of further exhibitions. This time next week! Love to Jack.

Cyril

V.E. It is paid for!
I am lunching with John Maud to-morrow. A happy new year. I hope we can raise our average in it of meetings to 50 again at least. Let that be our resolution – presence is a virtue!
These are paltry letters – I apologise.

4 Jan 1927.

Noel Blakiston, Esq.,
Kirkby on Bain.

11, St. Leonard's Terrace,
Chelsea, S.W.3.

Dear Noel,

Thank you for your letter and Art. You will have to teach me some gestures. I don't think one would miss anything written since Paradise Lost (or Samson rather) do you think really? I mean there is nothing inevitably new in kind since Milton. I said this the other day and scandalised Logan who found a paragraph in Bridges where he said that Keats had a warmth unknown to Milton who would never have thought of the epithet 'dusky' for the face of Asia – I referred Logan to Paradise Regained 'dusk faces under orient turbants lined' or some such phrase and confounded laureate and disciple, 'dusk' besides being a good deal warmer than dusky which does not suggest its derivation so vividly. I was reading in bed when the new year was announced. I still can't sleep till two, and I thought of you among bells and hooters, resolved to be more arrogant, reserved, and courteous and to see more of you. I envy you your before breakfasts, alas for the old age of my spirit, I lie late in bed to make the mornings shorter – the day begins with the dusk I feel – still London before breakfast is not very tempting.

I had a nice lunch with John Maud and we saw some good Van Goghs afterwards and then I had tea and dinner with Molly and chess with Desmond till the small hours. I read Benson on you while I was there, what tantalising dots. Molly grows more and more indispensable really as also does her log fire in this house of central heating, the children are away which makes it easier to see her and her swift sympathies are very welcome.

Tuesday

Thank you for your letter. Pat sounds interesting. 'My' London sunsets have been invisible the last few days, in any case I don't like them, sunsets in London only make one want to leave it I think. I dreamt you had some money and we went on a RMSP boat to South America which was to land us finally in Jamaica. It stopped at Pernambuco and Cuba, once on board we hated it and missed England and couldn't communicate with anyone to tell them where we'd gone and we had no passports so weren't allowed to go ashore and the sea was the colour of this paper* and crusty with white icing and everyone

*Bluish grey.

206

on the boat was bloody and we hid from each other and were given drinks in the bar. I got very depressed on Sunday evening and thought of surplices in school yard and gas mantles plopping in evening chapel and looking at you through my fingers in the sevenfold Amen. Last night Molly and I dined at the Ivy. Desmond is I think the wisest man in the world. I am sorry if *Stories from the Old Testament** caused embarrassments, I thought it might but Logan seemed to want to send it you so I said nothing. It is out of print you see and therefore an acceptable gift.

I heard from Jack last week. Perfection attracts pain seemingly as surely as beauty attracts perfection. *Omnia pervertit amor* is good. O frailty also. I am afraid of love and despise flirtation, yet I cannot stand on my own pride and fastidiousness and so give thanks for you; I would suffer torments if I did anything I had to conceal from you and you would think you were a testy and inquisitorial old Jahweh from the fear of the lord which is the beginning of my wisdom.

Cyril

It will be passing fair to be with you and FitzG again.

I am going down to see my grandmother on Thursday and must go out to get shaved now. The barber lives round the corner and charges 3d and reads Ulysses and Yeats' mystical prose.

16 Jan 1927.

Noel Blakiston, Esq.,   11, St. Leonard's Terrace.
Magdalene College.   Chelsea, S.W.3.

Dear Noel,

Silence and such stealth! and this is Sunday evening and as well I have a headache so it seems a fit mood to write to you. There was an intoxication in our farewell that supported me all yesterday and superlatives fail at the sweetness of my memories but the bleak streets and the blank day are gradually impinging and I no more stand 'as one that long hath taken a sweet and golden dream' (O Absolom, my head, my head!) it comes of these literary allusions and now my temples are reverberant but not cool – seriously I did not think

*By Logan, who gave a copy to N.B.

Perfection could better our week at Chilling but this escape and adventure defies all phrase.

I drank your health in several sorts of wine and also vodka at Maurice Baring's yesterday. He gave me a book of his about Eton and Astrakhan and has lovely rooms in Grays Inn. I missed you a lot there and have since without ceasing. I also have been distressed at what you had to go through last year, I wish I had realised before how bloody it must have been going home like that, that and your Rome journey and Pennyfields give me most food for thought I will be writing about Pennyfields I am thinking – I think really we are very alike and yet the quality of our minds do not fuse to parrot dullness as the processes of them are nearly always different if the conclusions are the same – then I feel too, considering how little we have been guests together we do well in company like Lewis and Tessa at tea. Of course we could talk for years without stopping really and ever since you have gone I have felt a stranger in this false world of exterior performance – strangers have never looked such phantoms and friends been so unable to impinge and I still feel dazed. People are only real in so far as they enable me to talk about you, the main flow of reality – we both really live a great deal in a world of our own imagination, really we could almost make our worlds coincide (as they did at epic time) 'with a little patience' – I find the idea of you travelling alone absorbs me as much as you probably – I suppose because there is in it such a lot of myself – then of course one has more to give to other people in proportion as one has explored more oneself so I suppose there is a selfish side to it. I think probably some of the most exciting things in the future will be the ways we behave in varying situations after we have attained perfect trust – I mean it would be nice meeting by accident in an inn in the Campagna one coming in and the other sitting reading – and as you say going by different routes to the same place. The aim seems to be that our dream lives be not conflicting – that our abstraction does not exclude each other as it excludes everyone else.

> – but I ne can ne may
> for all this worlde within mine hertes finde
> to unloven you a quarter of a day.

Then there is a goodwill born of proximitas, which though rather animal and remote from charitas is a very good purring sort of fondness and is the most tolerant of all forms of liking from its utterly unintellectual basis. All the way back from King's Cross I was thinking

> They, hand in hand, with wandering steps and slow
> through Eden took their solitarie way

which sums up the quality of Friday don't you think. I do hope we get Desolate – perhaps we could still do Rotterdam if you do not go down there again. Would you rescue Molly's book from Freddie and guard it some time. I will write to Jack soon. The Sunday post is just going – O Noel – How was Sligger by the way? I will write to-morrow if you don't mind this ambling – trembling with ten nine eight kind of thing – I got most of that novel done in time. I haven't seen Molly since you left – *Te spectem* Debussy Quartet *cum venerit hora* – comfort me with apples, stay me with flagons

– O Noel –

Cyril

17 Jan 1927.

Noel Blakiston, Esq.,
Magdalene College.

11, St. Leonard's Terrace.
Chelsea, S.W. 3.

Dear Noel,

Thank you very much for letter and the books, which are lovely. Of course one wants to be understood and wholly so but at the same time the harder one gets (rather than makes) oneself to be understood the more there is to give to the privileged whether Jack or me so the two states are compatible – I found the chief form of misery in Jamaica was in longing to be understood, hence the copla I sent you

> Green woods of Kirkby
> books on the study shelves
> nobody there but you and me
> talking about ourselves!

Will you thank Jack very much for the letter and the shoes and tell him a reply is brewing also that I haven't been able to get Desmond alone yet but hope to this week. Maurice Baring came round last night as I began on Pennyfields but I hope to get it written to-day. I heard from Molly who has a cold. She said you were delightful.

Business

The Athanasian had best be not typed, which dispels privacy, but

209

copied out by us on superb paper and when enough is done the one copy superbly bound I will send you and Jack some paper to write things on, be sure and leave a good margin – it seems easier than writing in a blank book as it gives more chance of last minute alterations etc. I would like to put in the introduction to my travel book (short) and the review of *Rien que la Terre* which does not seem likely to see the light anywhere else, also one or two poems, the day and Pennyfields if it is a success. Your 'Style', my introduction, Jack's general statement if he can manage it would come at the beginning then there are also the 50 quotations and the things you and Jack put in. Find as much as you can as space is no object – only merit. If you are selecting from epic I think it might be fun to put in your bit about pre-Roman England – the woods, and fens, and seas and catalogue of trees and I put my bit on trees too as an instance of minds marching alike – I am not in favour of us putting in any of our letters as the sequence may as well be kept entire for posterity and we don't want to see them twice. I think it would be rather good to have a few reviews, i.e. pages on any author we happen to have recorded, not living ones necessarily.

Later.

A strange coincidence, I got the cloak room man at the Ritz to tie up *The Prelude* and seeing twin slips with the same number for the next hat to be left I took one and dropped the other into the book which he had put in a bag. Then I thought you might think it was to mark a page so I decided I would take it out and put it in at 'Sweet Spenser' and the books he read at Cambridge. I undid the book again. It was already there. Logan is in a very bad temper over the New Criterion which makes him feel a back number and an effete old blockhead I suppose, I recommended him to go and read the *Deserted Village* which he never has done yet, Auburn by a strange coincidence. I opened the *Traveller* in the book shop to-day 'or by the lazy Scheldt or wandering Po' and it brought a whole whiff of our epic summer, the posts in the mud at Boston, and letters in the strike, and meeting in Town. It is good how well we do in summers which are not really our chosen season – we have really a summer tradition dating from our meals at Princes and talking at Lords – let us only meet enough and what may not befall? I will go to bed with the book of 18th century verse. You see I have no Jack and am at the mercy of my recollections as no one understands me here except partially though there seem a great many people who want to know me – it is so *vexatious* having to confide everything by letter and know that whoever one is going to meet at a given meal will not be an Athanasian – ('to preserve the past in writing, to dissect the present in talk, to discuss the future with silence is the mark of an Honest A') – 'An Athanasian is a young man with no visible means of intellectual support' Asquith. 'An Athanasian is a young man who thinks he knows everything – I have met several' Inge. 'A Melanesian is a young man something between a snake in the manger and a dog in the grass'. C.A.A.* 'An Athanasian is not quite good enough to get into the first Hockey Eleven'. D. Bevis† 'well καλοι καγαθοι who the hell are Athanasians anyway?' Jake‡ 'Quite simply, young men unable to get firsts'. C.M.B.§ '(I refused to join)'. 'Some bearable contemporaries' might be a good title for Jack – O God I grow facetious.

Goodnight Noel
Cyril

[? *18*] *Jan 1927.*

Noel Blakiston, Esq.,   [Chelsea.]
Magdalene College.

Dear Noel,

What a shit I am about that scarf – it is the mark of a William to make munificent protestations of friendship and refuse to perform anything less glamorous. Would this sort of paper do if I could get it uncreased and slightly larger so that if necessary things already copied out (e.g. Jack's essay) could be pasted on? or should I get them all typed? I expect you will have heard from me by now – I posted a letter on Sunday night and wrote twice yesterday but one I think missed the last post and won't go till this morning. I liked your 'Intimacy' awfully and after reading it *Formosum Corydon pastor ardebat Alexim* – incidentally I felt rather like that at the Bradfield Greek play. I would have liked 'Intimacy' if I had read it in the *London Mercury* even. Also Jesus. I was amazed by Jack's fluent masterful

---

*C. A. Alington, headmaster of Eton.
†D. Bevis, a don at King's.
‡John Carter.
§Maurice Bowra.

unforced French and learnt a lot from reading it – don't you think a good feature would be an anthology of the early twenties – i.e. quotations about the ages of 20, 21, 22, 23 – if you know of any other than these can you suggest them, above all if you have written (or Jack) anything bringing in the age you were (I have a poem on '20' somewhere, and four lines on 21')

Twenty

> J'avais vingt ans et je croyais encore
> à la puissance de la pensée
> > Valéry
> A vingt ans un trouble nouveau
> me suit sous nom d'amoureuses flammes
> j'aurais trouvé belles les flammes
> elles ne m'ont pas trouvé beau.
> > Verlaine
> > Gaspard Hauser
> Rimbaud. vingt ans (Illuminations. Jeunesse)
> > – not good enough
> > C.V.C. poem if presentable

Twenty one

> Johnson. Long expected one and twenty.
> C.V.C. Copla
> nunc oblita mihi tot carmina
> > – O swallow swallow
> per me si va
> > Abandoned one and twenty
> per me si va – and with no friends to follow
> per me si va tra la perduta gente.

Twenty two.

> Asclepiades. Mackail. 1.66.
> a lovely epigram – do show it Jack as it is his period.
> Housman – now I am two and twenty – and
> O tis true, tis true, etc.

Twenty three

> John Milton
> How soon hath time the suttle thief of youth

Late special

> Logan has just broached plans and suggests that we should go

abroad in February, first to Spain (I am to choose the places) and then to Italy to stay with Berensons, Clarks etc. and on to Rome. This means that I will probably be in Italy when you are and I absolutely *exact* (I seldom underline) but I really do beg, implore, command, beseech and take the dative, that you do come for a week, week end, or weak end of a week end, to Rome, Naples, Sicily, Ravenna (we meet at Ravenna you go by yourself from Garda!) Venice, Florence or Assisi, wherever you want to go to and for how long and that if you won't come with me that you go by yourself as my guest and that you announce this flatly before you go i.e. that you may stay away for a week and this I do beg of you because, because (courage he said and pointed to the land) because I amo, diligo, $\phi\iota\lambda\epsilon\omega$, love, honour, and obey you even down to $\phi\rho\iota\sigma\sigma\omega$ or $\phi\rho\iota\tau\tau\omega$ to thrill with passionate joy. O Noel do, in a week at the end of your visit we could see Florence and Rome or you could and possibly the temple of Paestum or the marécage by the Sicilian Sea. DO, Do, princeps, do! I throw in as a mere trifle that Desolate is still to let and that I am going to see the man (who lives in Chelsea) to-morrow. Waves of nearness, waves of, waves of

Nearness

Of course I will come to Cambridge or you to Desolate before I go. 'Intimacy' is so good that it is confined for several days to pocket. I drink to Jack to-morrow noon. Good God the child's been reading Rabelais, W. Pater. Sir I smell enthusiasm, Johnson. Comfort me with apples, stay me with flagons.

Yours ever
Holy Church

I will write for scarf to-morrow.

The Athanasian

Athanasius contra mundum,
discipuli supra'
[Merlin]

printed in East Anglia
1927

Jack and Noel.

213

P.S.

Logan says that a new *dictionnaire philosophique* would be an excellent form and would make money if published – shall we not concentrate on this – *les nouveaux encyclopédistes* – we could have jokes.

Alps. See tripes (ten)

Brides. We don't know much about brides.

Brides les Bains (Hte. Sav.) see Brides.

Day. Days vary in length and value – we append an example (7000 words follow)

Disease. Love, life, and literature are perhaps diseases.

Δίς ἔς τον αὖτον πόταμον οὖκ ἄν ἐμβαίης see Actuality.

Eton. Many are called but few are chosen. 'O woe to him whose will is weak under the blossom that hangs on the beak, O woe to him whose will is strong he shall rise up at the sound of a gong'.

Understanding. No peace passeth understanding.

Might it not be better to abandon *Athanasian* and go straight for the encyclopaedia? Let's try and get it done by the summer and travel on proceeds! A shilling encyclopaedia! think of the scope for penetration, humour and the discovery of our own ideas –!

Much love from Cyril

19 Jan 1927.

Noel Blakiston, Esq., 11, St. Leonard's Terrace.
Magdalene College. Chelsea, S.W.3.

Dear Noel,

How are you? ἔγω δε σε μαόμαν and soon in any company but yours I shall be ill at ease. Desolate alas is rather difficult as Phelas Gibb (I keep wanting to call him Phlebas) wants £40 for his bloody studio though the rent is only £12 and it has 3 bedrooms, kitchen and sitting room and pantry and seems in every other way good though and for primitiveness. I will write to Miss Halliday.

I am tired and have been trying to find a school for my cousin whose mother Lady Chetwynd has just died and whose father is dead too. Gabbitas* is drear even when one comes in loco parentis as did my mother and I. Then I had tea with the Clarks and missed you. Let us do *the Athanasian* anyhow and go on with the Encyclopaedia as well.

*Gabbitas and Thring, educational agency.

No more now – I answered boy D'Costa's letter yesterday and got
a wire to-day 'I will be with you 10.15 to-morrow Benji' which was
unexpected but I will have to support it. I wish I was a callous heart
breaker – or just callous still I suppose I am fairly.

Much love.

Cyril

20 Jan 1927.

<table>
<tr><td>H. N. Blakiston, Esq.,</td><td>(dated for posterity)</td></tr>
<tr><td>Magdalene College.</td><td>(they can guess the place)</td></tr>
</table>

Dear Noel,

Thank you for your letter – you say I am 'writing well' as if letters
to you were an academic exercise. I am glad you thought of Bradfield –
my feelings there were first of anxiety looking everywhere trying to
see you and after I had caught your eye the rest of the play I was spell
bound with impatience and could hardly keep my seat. The cat when
the milk is on its way from the table to the floor was a Job beside me
though when we met there was nothing to say but $\mathring{\eta}\lambda\theta\epsilon s$ – I think the
pagan setting and the green trees and the promise of rain and the
brown legs and reedy piping of the flute players wove the whole
meeting into a complete Lysis – *O venus o deesse rendez-moi le temps
de l'antique jeunesse* seemed appropriate and

$\epsilon\mathring{\iota}\theta\epsilon\ \lambda\acute{\upsilon}\rho\alpha\ \gamma\epsilon\nu\acute{\alpha}\eta\nu\ ^{\prime}\epsilon\lambda\epsilon\phi\acute{\alpha}\nu\tau\iota\nu\eta$
$\kappa\acute{\alpha}\iota\ \mu\epsilon\ \kappa\acute{\alpha}\lambda o\iota\ \pi\acute{\alpha}\iota\delta\epsilon s\ \phi o\rho\acute{o}\iota\epsilon\nu$
$\Delta\iota o\nu\acute{\upsilon}\sigma\iota o\nu\ ^{\prime}\epsilon s\ \chi\acute{o}\rho o\nu$

which I wrote in my diary after – do you remember the birds and
the thin spiral of incense from the altar. About Italy Logan has decided
that my impulses are all to the good from the creative moods that
follow them – at least when you have a hand – II he quoted your
remark about my letters being the product of my idleness in Molly's
drawing room as 'a charming thing to have said' and the fact that
Desmond has been praising me has robbed it of any application III He
told me after Exmoor that he would never consider any money that
I spend on you (and Jack) to be a form of extravagance, that he loved
to see it, and that to have reached our stage of $\kappa o\acute{\iota}\nu\alpha\ \tau\alpha\ \tau\acute{\omega}\nu\ \phi\acute{\iota}\lambda\omega\nu$
was one of the rarest things in the world IV The money you and I

215

spend in Italy will only be part of my wages or come out of what I saved by staying at Chilling last year. It is not as if he was *giving* me money for the occasion – if I hadn't gone to Chilling we could not go to Rome that is all. V He has far too high an opinion of you to think you are a sponge (the waster and the sponger by Hogarth. 127). I love writing about finance to you, the same obscure pleasure as having a cheque with your name on the back and then there is a good twelve o'clock in the morning friendship about it – as you say – 'I like and love' [I seem to be losing all restraint in letters. I am sorry] Well after all this, I think you should feel no objection in coming, the only thing is where you would like to go. I would love to go to Rome with you but you seem so keen on seeing it alone – perhaps we could go together and you could sight see alone though I am just as sure the Sistine chapel is the centre of the world as you are – How would it be if we arranged a tour so that you saw quite a lot of places alone on the way. I think the way from Garda to Rome would be by Verona, Mantua, Bologna and Florence or by Padua – all good places – well supposing you went to Verona, Mantua and Bologna and Ravenna if you had time alone and we met in Florence and went on to Rome stopping in Florence on our way back perhaps? We might go to Perugia on the way to Rome (I have never been to Perugia) or Assisi – I would have money for a week I should think. That is to say a pound a day each and three pounds each railway fares – well suppose I had £25 I could give you five to spend how you liked in coming to join me so that you could go to Ravenna if you liked on the way and only keep some new impression for me will you as your delight so quickens mine. Damn, this has missed the post, and remember I am working for Logan and Desmond all the time and how I choose to spend my earnings is nothing to do with him – though as it happens he approves – I shall be saving as much as I can all these next months so that we can do something in June and after – i.e. we might unite at Chilling for a bit and then go abroad or vice versa or scour England – what a superb week we will have! Verona and Mantua I have never been to except for an hour in Verona and another in Bologna so they would be your property if you saw them on the way and if we went to Rome via Perugia and Assisi they would be new places to me – say you took 10 days or rather nights and spend two on the way, one Perugia, four Rome, one Assisi, two Florence, or one more before you met me if you like and one less in Florence (though with two you could meet the Berensons) (Does this bore you?). Well if you came second from Garda to Florence it would only cost you a £1 which would leave you three for sight seeing on the way and one for fare back (our six would be Florence–Rome and back + cabs and cars etc.) – the three pounds would easily do you three days before you met me and we could always take more money out of the June fund. Whether ten days is too big a slice of the vac is the only problem – the shortest we could manage would be two on way – 1 Perugia – three Rome – 1 Assisi, 1 Florence or 8 days – or one on way and 4 Rome or two Florence – anyhow it seems fairly feasible don't you think which we little dreamt when we talked of it in the snow. When you are rich you must take me, bald and toothless perhaps and muttering prognostications of my early death. I lunched with John Maud to-day. I don't think one could stand him for long – We went to the Flemish pictures again where I missed you as also at tea with Logan where were a lot of people and the Clarks. I met David Garnett in his shop and he got very excited about the encyclopaedia and is going to contribute some articles to it – I gave him 3 months and Carte Blanche, ditto K – They will of course have nothing to do with *the Athanasian* but will help to fatten the encyclopaedia which it will surely need. Benji D'Costa descended on me this morning looking as Desmond remarked 'afflicted' that is to say with strange splints supporting his figure in all directions. He has had meningitis and paralysis and his parents are in Biarritz prosecuting an American gigolo (friend of the mother's) who stole their car – all very like a cinema. Benji had been trying to use my name to open illicit accounts with London shops and confided that the blow on the head which had occasioned his six months rest and the prohibition to use his eyes had been a pure invention as he had concocted it the day after the match in order to 'stay out' the week end – I felt mildly interested to hear that my oral agonies had all been unnecessary and pointed out that the good God above us had punished his falsehood with a genuine affliction, or rather saved his face for him and that he would do well to keep his secret from his family who might not see the point of the joke. He replied that he was not on speaking terms with his family so I let it drop. I dare say it is a lie as well though it is amusing to think of his case being written up in the *Lancet* as obscure and tortuous when there was nothing the matter with him – He has had to leave Marlborough since his illness and seems fond of me and rather apologetic for his forward ways but he left me with a nasty taste in my mouth and I was glad to put him back in the limbo out of which he so suddenly came. K. is very much about the place but I confess to nursing a secret heresy (which I only dare confess to you) that he is a crashing bore – it may only be envy but Waley suggested it too; his wife, I do not think, will do. When in company with K I miss you and Jack to fever heat so staying with him will be a good preparation to getting in to your train (we won't get out at Florence till we are on our way home – it would spoil the escape. I like K by himself but the Pict in me rises to his Scot every time. I think one might like David Garnett rather a lot – he is such an amateur – when I come to Cambridge before I go to Spain we might go out there. This might still go if I took it to Sloane Square. I have written to Cave! I have written to Cave! I have written to Cave about your scarf!!!

I feel I will always be able to write to you better since Porlock though the connection somehow is obscure – I think a sense of legitimacy has crept in but the explanation may crystallise. I never can finish a letter to you without wanting to put something in to it afterwards but this time I have remembered it before – Logan has given me his first edition *Prelude* so we can use the volume for our terser communications – as 9.31 for instance (I will look that up)

'and all the nicely guarded shows of art' (is that Flemish pictures or a forecast of Florence?)

Good night.
Cyril

I am so glad Jack is writing: I think he does it so well. I have had remorse about Flatford – I didn't realise what a compliment you were paying me in asking me to go there I wish I had realised you lived there. I will send you some writing to-morrow.

Warning some of this letter is on both sides of the page and some is not.

22 Jan 1927.

Noel Blakiston, Esq.,   [Chelsea.]
Magdalene College.

Dear Noel,
How are you – Sunday will be a relief when you don't get a letter from me I expect. A violin is being played next door – I have been

to a tiresome tea-party and then on to the Savoy to see a Frenchman who is starting a revue he wanted Noel [erased] (don't miss this slip, posterity) Logan to do something for – He was a very lovely young man wrapped up in furs and elegance and ease but seemed sad and reticent and I have felt worried about him ever since – his name was Levy Grünwald as most French people appear to be nowadays. My spirits are rather low with Desmond, Molly and Maurice Baring all away. I will send you back 'This style' when I have copied it out to-morrow morning. I hope you like the Encyclopaedia idea as a sequel to *the Athanasian* – were those two diaries of any use to you? It has snowed here all day but the snow has lost its sting since Exmoor and I view dispassionately the descending flakes – or did as it is all slush now – I talked of our Rome journey (or wherever you would like) to Logan – and he was all in favour so the last scruple should be removed. I feel so melancholy this evening that I think I will stop if you don't mind and try and write (it is the violin) a poem. I have had very nice dreams of us being up to Crace together in C.1* lately, one night we shared a desk, another Alington came in and shouted 'which of you hasn't got a book?' It was me.

Cyril

Give Jack my love. I am sending him a book.

[*?24*] *Jan 1927.*   [Chelsea.]

Noel Blakiston, Esq.,
Magdalene College.

Dear Noel,
    Thank you for your card. I am sorry you are run down – I can't come to Cambridge at once but if I come on Friday 4th of February would that do and we might go to Dedham and Flatford for a night and let me make amends for my surliness or to Lynn and Blakeney if you have lately been to Flatford – would you ask Freddy if that would suit him or at least I will write which would be simpler. Can you carry on till then or has my image faded – I love your letters. *Te veniente die, te decedente canisco* 'I keep on singing', not found in classical

---

*i.e. working in the same class at Eton, under the master Mr Crace.

Latin – Martineau's dictionary – we could stay in Cambridge all the time if you would rather but we can talk better out of it – II. Your travels. I hope you don't think I was limiting your time to 3 days on your own. If you can take more from Garda have them and let me know how much gold you will need only I stipulate for a week for us to see Perugia, Florence and Rome – we might go out to Ninfa one day and see the city and the Pontine marshes. It looked such a good place in Picturesque Italy – Paestum calls but time is fleeting – that quotation by the way was

ambo florentes aetatibus, Arcades ambo
et cantare pares, et respondere parati

I would rather have written the Eclogues than almost any book in the world and when we die would sell my soul to go to an Arcadian heaven. This sounds like Vol. II of my table talk, sorry. Anyhow we can talk over the whole scheme at Cambridge – do you think Jack would accept an 'ἐρανον so that he could take a day or two off from Garda while we are away? I would like him to see Venice or anywhere he would like while he is in Italy but it would spoil your exploring if he came with you I think unless you would really prefer it. I am sorry this all sounds so business like. I don't think I can manage to go to Cologne with him so perhaps this would do instead – anyhow you must go where you like and for as long and we will have a divine week afterwards. I have been having tea with Molly at Claridges – she is not going abroad till Tuesday – Logan tells me that Maurice wrote to Molly and apologised for what he had said about me and took it all back – I don't know who has got at him – it can only be from policy or he would have written to me – but perhaps he does not know I know – it doesn't seem very important. I am sorry Sidney* is not well. I have had psalm tunes badly these last few days and especially to-day, what a lot of strange things we find in common, the domination of psalm tunes we never could have imagined. I hope you don't feel you have nothing in common with me and that it is all a myth – I have known London lowness take that turn – John Maud pointed to the Oxford Book of 18th Century verse and said it was a thankless task and a worthy thing to have done which made me realise our superb isolation – I don't say 18th century verse is first rate but what matters more it is somewhere where we can be alone – I am re-reading the Gray, Walpole, West, and Ashton letters – would you let me give

*Our cat at Magdalene.

them you and mind reading them, they are superbly relevant and exciting and the best thing for lowness. Gray and Walpole complain of Cambridge, to West who complains of Oxford, Ashton echoes. They are full of appreciation of Eton, of each other, and of the classics, nothing else seems to exist, Gray is witty and fond, Walpole elegant and West who died young rather lonely and biting but all serious and charming – They make one long to get up our letters (yours and mine) in the same way. Well, we will. West I think would have been a great poet – here are some stanzas of his Ode to St. Mary Magdalen.

> Saint of this learned awful grove
> While slow along thy walks I rove
> The pleasing scene which all that see
>   admire, is lost to me.
>
> Lost and enwrapt in thought profound
> Absent I tread Etonian ground
> Then starting from the dear mistake
>   as disenchanted wake
>
> Oh! how I long to be with those
> Whom first my boyish heart had chose,
> Together through the friendly shade
>   to stray, as once I stray'd!
>
> Their presence would the scene endear,
> like paradise would all appear
> more sweet around the flowers would blow
>   more soft the waters flow –

Don't you think that is as good as Collins, and when he was only 18 – and hardly has the 'flow' died away than Gray begins 'It rains, tis Sunday, this is the country; three circumstances so dull in conjunction with my nature are like to give birth to an admirable production.' Then West's views on Oxford

> Meantime how heavily my days now roll
> the morning lecture, and the evening bowl!
> The cobweb school! the tutor's flimzy tale!
> The feast of folly! and the flow of ale!
> Who would not laugh if such strange things there be
> For me I hate the odious scene and dream of thee.

fits in as well as Gray's 'for all the employment of my hours may best be explained by negatives' does Cambridge and Walpole's 'Let us extend the Roman Empire and cultivate two barbarous towns o'errun with rusticity and mathematics' rubs it in. Then the frankness of the 18th century is good when they were not afraid to begin their letters 'O dearest *dimidium animae meae*' (Gray to Walpole) or to end them 'fare thee well, child' (Walpole to Gray) – besides understatement, I suppose there is the method of humorous overstatement (Tessa's diary) which is probably the better for conveying fondness as is the other for disapproval. Then it might be William writing 'Tydeus rose and set at Eton: he is only known here to be a scholar of King's. Orosmades and Almanzor are just the same; that is, I am almost the only person they are acquainted with, and consequently the only person acquainted with their excellencies, Plato improves every day, so does my friendship with him. These three divide my whole time though I believe you will guess there is no quadruple alliance; that was a happiness which I only enjoyed when you was at Eton.' (Walpole). I am afraid all these extracts must seem very dull – but tell me if you would like to have the book as I would like to give it you (I have a copy too) and it would cheer you up if low but I would not like to dump books on you that you are not likely to read – an antient custome – You talk well enough I'm thinking and will of course talk better but I think that springs from maturing and becoming oneself in all company. I don't think it is serious – but silence is in the end fatal to intimacy because unless it is rare it ceases to be a bond – Silence crowns an emotion but does not beget it. A new saying of St. Athanasius has been discovered –

'*Urbs subrepet et fatigat rus, erra*! (the town corrupts, the country bores, travel!) I liked your Larbaud quotation. I think he is the least pretentious of the French moderns, and possibly the least original, but gentle and generous and good on travel and scholarly. The 'quadruple alliance' letters saved my life in Jamaica, or were among the books that did. How many hands have lately polluted the Duke of York – I dreamt of English tropics again last night. Crace held a mass moonlight meeting on the grassy slopes and called on me to chant a passage of Vergil – I wanted to sing it to a psalm tune but was afraid of shocking him so stood silent – someone next to me passed 'a e e e b b a' up on a bit of paper, it was evidently a tune to sing it to but I was unable to read it and went quite red with Crace waiting and all these shining moonlit faces gazing up at me – then I saw yours and we bolted and hid by the ablution benches, for I must to the greenwood go, alone – a banished man.

If I am vital, so are you and the relief of sitting down to write to you after dinner is more than words can say – but I prose.

good night.
Cyril

'in Cambridge there is nothing so troublesome, as that one hath nothing to trouble one everything is so tediously regular, so samish, that I expire for want of a little variety.' Gray.

Contrast also your day for work with my dearest Celadon

Yesterday morning being the morning I set apart for lying abed till one o'clock. . . . (Gray) but West is the nicest. Corydon.

great Alexis and his noble frère.

I am dogged especially by 'people do err in their heart, for they have not known my ways'. Love to Freddie.

Damn, I have left 'This Style' in my bedroom. I will send it to-morrow. The post will go while I copy it out,

Caves report nothing known of your scarf.

25 Jan 1927.   [Chelsea.]

Noel Blakiston, Esq.,
Magdalene College.

Lo here am I writing to you again but, Jesus, you have given my heart such a tilt that everything else has fell out of it! Well, all the world seems crossed in love and I hang alone like the apple on the topmost bough, *O ego ne possem tales sentire dolores!* This is a wet windy day as ever you saw and yet to walk out in it is most exciting and even in the London streets the air reminds me of the woods of Ireland and stirs my heart to travel – it must be sad weather for Cambridge that promises so much that it does not fulfil, it offered me £5000 a year as I sang in my bath this morning and I was almost writing to you to suggest we three took a house in Westminster and gave our lives to St. Athanasius who was never partial to strangers. I sleep prodigious badly and feel surprising ill at the sight of breakfast, time drags till I come to Cambridge and I refuse invitations with spleen, since I never go out, but I know I'll be bored and yet it needs all the courage in the world to decline it. This letter I meant to compose like T. Gray but I've outshot him by a clear decade and nearly caught up with Congreve. Well, if it is too long in the mark it cannot be too short in the matter, a Mrs. MacCarthy is coming to lunch and I am alone to entertain her, then there's your brother that must be writ to, and a plague of a thing on style that I've still to copy out and a dinner to give to Rylands whom penury, neglect, and the colic have reduced to a sorry state so they say, so with no inclination I must bid thee fare well and will write again on the morrow though I fain would cry 'O crudelis Alexis nihil mea carmina curas (this not because you say so but because they read so dull your servant. Cyril

Your nice letter just come and I am sitting down to Faguet,* most of the encyclopaedia will be long, the length of activity or vocabulary – only a few need be epigrams just to liven it up – please put all your thought under headings like Intimacy or Canfranc† that is all that is required. I would like to see your Canfranc thing when done though I have vague touchiness about my unwanted telegram – anyhow it is as well that should wear off. I will order the Gray to-day, it won't be here till to-morrow, then I will write in it and send, I am seeing Molly off to-morrow and breakfasting with the Clarks first. She had to put off going – she came here to lunch with me to-day – the most interesting way to Garda is by Flushing, Cologne, Frankfort, Munich, Innsbruck, Brenner, and Verona; it is also the dearest even if you went third, the next most interesting (and dearest) is by Basle and the St. Gothard, the cheapest and worst by the Mt. Cenis. You haven't destroyed letters since I left Eton much have you? The book might begin like this.

Easter 21.	Cyril to Terence (about you)
	" " "
	Noel to Cyril (quoted)
Summer 21.	William's diary. section I.
	Hopwood's vale.
	Cyril. frag, of poem.

*Author of a book on Plato.
†A Pyrenean frontier place, where some men had heaved some sleepers down a slope that had just missed N.B.

Summer vac. 21.	Cyril to Denis (about you)
	" " Jackie.
Christmas half.	William's diary. Sect. II.
" vac.	Cyril to Denis.
Easter half.	–
Easter vac.	Noel to Cyril
Summer half.	William's diary. Sec. III.
	Cyril's poems.
Summer vac.	Cyril to Noel
	Noel to Cyril
	etc. to the present day

+ also Cyril's poems and the two letters to Bobbie that are about you – we could write footnotes to the letters and put in accounts of the unspecified times, like my last Easter half – after I leave it might be better to put in my letters to and from William up to about two years ago and then to put in Jack's to me and yours and Jack's to each other if they are not unkind at my shortcomings – the thing would be to get one copy of all our letters typed and annotated and keep it as a private printing – then we needn't leave things out – there are two possible treasure troves – William may have a lot of very old letters of mine (only those written before I left Eton are really important) and Charles may as well –

I am so glad you approve of all these letters I was afraid they might be a trial – it grows dark and the time is at hand to go forth and order Gray – O gorgeous fourth of February! Well we won't go away for the night but see to it we are alone and can talk, we waste our precious youth when we are with other people together and also you may feel lonely or I that you are tied with a thousand other ties. I would like to give Jack 1000 lire to spend as he likes while we go to Rome, then you would not feel selfish at leaving him or unkind at having to break it – that you are going to Rome – besides he would like it too – if he would rather stay in Garda you could both use it to go home by Munich if you liked only do tell me if he would mind such a selfish gift. Your letter has comforted me much, dear you.

Molly is going to Nice and Vence with her sister, we have great arguments about women though she agrees really that they aren't very nice. I said they were just unnecessary – though really I have no use for them I think at all –

Noel Blakinston, Esq.,   [Chelsea.]
Magdalene College,
Cambridge.

Dear Noel,

I feel like ringing you up but the necessity of answering from a crowded lodge makes me feel that it might only be an encumbrance ἔγω δε σε μαόμαι do go on writing to me however low you feel, I love your letters – this weather they supply the sole inducement for getting up just as the pleasure of your company seems the only reason for going to sleep, at which by the way I am succeeding very ill – Crimine quo merui juvenis peacidissime divum?

O that March was turning to April and our meeting at hand in the sunshine of the Umbrian spring! I would like to go to Urbino with you but time seems so limiting. There are so many Italy's, the shady pastoral country of Horace and Vergil and Poussin and Claude, the mystical, mediaeval, pre-Raphaelite Italy and the gorgeous opulent world of Popes and Venetians, and best of all, I think the sunny gem like shores of Magna Graecia and the temples by the Sicilian Sea – but how to see them all? especially as they are nearly all mutually exclusive – what fun if we had been Romans of the time of Vergil and, sick with culture, gone to spend our summer in exploring England which would then be the forest, fen, and druid kingdom of our epic, imagine returning and being laughed at and thought mad and raising our glasses across a crowded dinner table to murmur *Anderida* or *Meonwari*! *Vectis*, I mean. I think *Anderida* is really Pevensey but I have no means of finding out. Let us make it the Athanasian for the Isle of Wight anyhow.

Pause, while I go out and buy a pen. I too am pretty low and dull, that is I don't like any company but the best and the best seems out of London. I hardly see a soul here while I should think your lowness proceeds from having to see so many. I loathe people who tell their stories more than once and so grow absent as soon as Logan begins in company. Life is too short to say the same thing twice, don't you think, unless it is 'I like you' – I like to make a joke once and then leave it. I can never make it so well again while Logan likes to polish his stories like a row of brass pots and is not ashamed to tell them twice to the same person – of course most people forget such a lot certainly that it is probably new to them.

An overwhelming consciousness of dullness has just come over me – these letters are dull, dull as hell – dull as heaven, you probably skip them, soon they will all come back tied up in blue ribbon – Dear C.V.C. After what has happened I am sending back your letters. I think if you ever manage to read them you will see that I am right.

N. Blakiston

Dear Connolly,

My brother asks me to say that he wishes you all success in your career, that he will make no further attempt to recover his scarf, his 'style' or the pound he lent you at Boston. *You are simply too dull*, and everyone you come into contact with is dulled too – I shall not write any more or this letter will begin to look like one of yours –

John Blakiston

P.S. a piece of advice, *don't* quote, don't recommend books, and remember that the quality of your wit and your affection is rather too shabby for our world.

Dear Cyril. Yes do come to Cambridge on the 4th. I am so sorry I shall be away. Freddie Harmer.

Dear Connolly

A word in season: if you are coming to Cambridge keep clear of Magdalene – *cantabit vacuus coram latrone viator*

ABR (A. B. Ramsay, the Master)

Dear Cyril Connolly,

Yes, of course I can put you up and you must dine with me on Saturday. I have asked Dick Steele*

Ever thine
Ormerod Wayne†

*R. C. Steele. Dick (b. 21 June 1905). KS. King's. BBC Education Dept. OBE.

†R. S. O. Wayne (b. 27 August 1904, d 5th. January 1959). KS. Trinity, Camb. Colonial Service.

Dear Connolly   The Cloisters
    If I can ever be of any use to you tip me a line; no, I am afraid I
shan't be in London for some time.
                         Wm Le Fanu

Sorry Friday impossible suggest come next year don't write apologise Wayne
                              Grosvenor Hotel, Victoria

Dear Freddie,
    Yes, you can breathe again – I saw him off.
                         Alan

I feel Milton's 'The Mind is its own Place' is a remark fraught with
metaphysical meaning but I can't do more as yet than write it down
on bits of paper. Do go on with the Athanasian, won't you, and
remember it is more important than the encyclopaedia to which we
will have to admit other authors.
    O monogamy hard as mahogany, o blessed chastity (rare at the
varsity) as St. Athanasius sang at the Aryan dinner 323

    [St. Athanasius
    said nothing fallacious,
    the statements of Arius
    were more precarious]

    The Egoist

    [St. Athanasius
    said goodness gracious
    there'll soon be a cult
    of quicunque vult!]

dear Noel, I think we might be able to stay at Rebénacq in the summer
which would be nice don't you think, though best if we were there
when the grapes were ripe. Jack's French essay has been a joy. Make
him go on writing.
                         fare thee well
                         Cyril

When they said 'Athanasius', stay in and do Statius, he answered
'No fear', I'm off to Nicaea.

final version

Said the elderly Saint Athanasius

the public is always fallacious
they've made quite a cult
of Quicumque Vult
but ignored my selections from Statius.

Gossip might be added to the ten tripes, I will write to Jack to-morrow.

Next Friday week!

26 Jan 1927.

Noel Blakiston, Esq.,
Magdalene College. [Chelsea.]

Dear Noel,

Thank you for your nice letter which I got in bed this morning – I am glad mine are not as drear as I feared. The night you couldn't sleep was about my worst too and I thought much of you.

This Debussy weather is very disturbing, like the Unquiet Grave.

'The wind blows up to day my love,
    with a few small drops of rain
I never had but one true love
    and she in the grave is lain'

I think your Canfranc writing will be good for sure – I have had the Gray sent off also a rag book with it, it will be nice to think of you opening the Gray – the guide books were from my mother – I thought they might excite you – if you still feel low. I am so tired with translating that I have nothing left to say – O Friday week – O Friday week, would say my thoughts, if they could speak! at least if they did not sink back at once into a despairing attack on *veneris muneribus potens* – O plague it has settled down on me again like a blight and I must give up and retire to my bath to cope – a curse on all literary conscience – what's wrong with 'rich with love endowed' – I liked your Plato a lot and found it more stimulating I expect, than I should find Faguet, now with Jack's Racine, your Faguet and my Morand we have 3 very good French reviews to our credit in the Athanasian – perhaps you would try doing some anthology into English verse if you felt strong, especially sec. 1.66. the Asclepiads for the 'twenties' anthology. (Yes. Sleeplessness could be well done)

> Love is not love
> that alters when it alteration finds

is a good effort for Shakespeare don't you think – I wish I could arrive at it. Of course we hardly like each other at all as yet, but we may, with years, we may. I have masses to say to you, do see that we are alone – how nice about the squash court they are so awful when they sweat – is it not Pope who says

> Dear college squash court, strewn with withered leaves
> where broken glass descends from splintered eaves
> where flannelled youths in friendly strife perspire
> and lay their coats beneath the tattered wire
> what though thy walls exude a livid stain
> more green than Willis, and more dark than Wayne,
> – for there we played κάι ἐγω δε σε μαόμαν

(Unlike most Pope not only unpublished but unwritten till this moment). There are several poems I wrote when I left Eton that you have never seen, I dare say one day they might interest you. One quite good *vale* ending

> O Beatrice and the Duke of Cleves
> with whom I dwell alone
> do you too long for those fair eves
> the moon shining through the leaves
> on the wine dark stone?

You ought to read the second eclogue if you would learn more of Alexis – the slant at which I write betrays an unbearable optimism – *O crudelis adhuc et veneris muneribus potens* – so it goes! I am on the track of another job for FitzGod but may know more when I see him, it is not in the catalogue. Yes a nest of singing birds, a most compact, most free and independent school, I am glad to have written a poem again, though I dare say it is but an epigram – How are your eyes by the way, I would like a bulletin – in return I can tell you that I go to the dentist on Monday – to live the rest of my life with you in a one roomed house in desert inaccessible and to write a letter to you across the table every day is my modest view of heaven – ('what does Cyril say, Noel?' *'O, touiours le même sujet!'*)

27 *Jan 1927.*

Noel Blakiston, Esq.,   [Chelsea.]
Magdalene College,
Cambridge.

Dear you,
   My temper is foul. (More sleep!) and Chesterton is trying to be funny over the wireless – so fail not thou who thee implores, for thou art heavenly he a 'perfect scream'. More sleep ! I would like to hear more of your anthology of insomnia. A deluge of dullness (laughter) which will drown the whole world (laughter) . . . cocktails . . . Charleston . . . vulgar . . . stupid . . . monotonous . . . magnificently dull . . . (cheers) . . . laughter (laughter) . . . futility says Chesterton, I am holding to you like the dentist's chair, the arms of it I mean. Chesterton I suppose is the dentist. Well he has been turned off. Vergil is really awfully good, I read the 9th Aeneid (Nisus and Eury-alus) this morning and liked it a lot. This might be your pines of Canfranc. I thought of them.
   (I took a *sors* by the way just now and got *'ille asper et improbus ira saevit in absentis'* which suits my mood –

   Pinea silva mihi, multos dilecta per annos,
   Lucus in arce fuit summa, quo sacra ferebant
   nigranti picea trabibusque obscurus acernis.

   'dim with dusky fir and trunks of maple.'

Then the wood in which Nisus and Euryalus get lost is good

   Silva fuit late dumis atque ilice nigra
   horrida, quam densi complebant undique gentes
   rara per occultos lucebat semita calles. . . .

the last line is magic don't you think 'here and there glimmered the path through the hidden glades' – I would not foist the crib on you if I didn't have to use it myself. Then the rich audacity of Euryalus his death which would be unbearable if done this way by Keats

> pulchrosque per artus
> it cruor inque umeros cervix conlapsa recumbit
> purpureus veluti cum flos succisus aratro
> languescit moriens, lassove papavera collo
> demisere caput, pluvia cum forte gravantur.

was ever mandragora so well grated? I wish I could sleep, I wish I was an angel child, I wish we could go to Sicily. I wish, I wish – in the summer let's do some intensive reading – you could do Vergil and try and read it aloud which after all it was meant for – we might make a June idyll out of Chilling with strawberries, sailing and the classics, and perhaps go abroad later. I might have some money – we would be there alone. I think I will go to bed and read the *Egoist*. I am longing to see you and will probably need it by Friday, I mean be low and angry and then feel it all dissolve with meeting. Couldn't we dine alone a night or two? *J'aurai gelt* as the French say. (I would not have made a joke like that but when angry or low one is not 'master of oneself' and various wolves see Moeris and prowl to guide his hand.) Molly was touched by Pat's 'I think I'll walk by myself, it's duller' which she has been using in a letter. She and Desmond and Maurice Baring have a strange idiomatic language of their own into which I am being initiated. Don't you think a feature of *the Athanasian* might be a bibliography of Orpheus, Hylas, Narcissus, and the Drowned Man – it is such a fag copying out long quotations but a list of what they were would be admirable, with a short account of what they stood for, and perhaps the best example of each given in full – thus Lycaon (Iliad 18) is the first drowned man, there are sundry in the anthology, then comes Palinurus, who fulfils the main condition of being drowned in a calm sea – of modern ones Phlebas, Heredia's *Corail*, Rimbaud's *Bateau ivre* (2 lines) Ophelia, *La Jeune Tarentaine*, the wave's intenser day etc. Well this is a poor letter from a poor spirit, only a week now!

Fare well
Cura ut valeas
Cyril

How much better Boswell is when one gets to know something of Mason, Mitford, and the slobbering apologists of the eighteenth century's lesser fry. Mason especially must have been unbearable. Ashton's letters are amazingly dull and pompous don't you think and when he tries to be funny or to define the sublime he is unbearable. The other three were very Athanasian I think and finely unput upon abroad – one can trace Gray trying to make Walpole like the Alps and Walpole to make West with equal degrees of failure – West I think was really adorable, one feels that Gray grew darker and darker with the years and Walpole perhaps more worldly and more of a dabbler in literary fashions while West avoids the smugness of one and the frivolity of the other. But I like Horace Walpole very much and he is very different I think from L. Strachey's picture and probably one of the best friends that has ever been. Gray's Latin poems are lovely don't you think, *mater rosarum* especially, but as far as letters go I think ours are probably as good as theirs and soon will be as confident. West's '*Thatched Cottage*' is nice and Marvellian.

For *the Athanasian* – will you correct and say if line five is best the way I have altered it or as it stood. I am haunted by this poem and its terrible hostility – imagine if William suddenly turned something like that out in the E.C.C.* when crossed sufficiently – I can't do the first line so as to render properly the force of Potens. I had said 'O cruel to love, though rich with love endowed' but Logan said it must be 'richly' – would you pass 'rich' in that context rich or richly, of which, or with which, these are the narrow bounds into which translators' force reality.

Hor. Odes IV. 10

O crudelis adhuc, et veneris muneribus potens,
inspirata tuae cum veniet bruma superbiae,
Et quae nunc humeris involitant, deciderint comae
Nunc et qui color est puniceae flore prior rosae
Mutatus, Ligurine, in faciem verterit hispidam;
Dices heu! quoties te in speculo videris alterum,
Quae mens est hodie, cur eadem non puero fuit?
Vel cur his animis incolumes non redeunt genae?

Cruel youth to love, though with lover's wealth endowed
when the unlooked for winter of thy pride
falls with the locks that now thy shoulder hide
and all the rose with which thy cheeks are proud

*Eton College Chronicle.

233

droops, Ligurinus, into dimness paling
then wilt thou cry, oft by thy glass reminded,
O that, a boy, had I been this way minded!
or with this mind, youth fled not unavailing!

Your block will do for Athanasian fair copies then they needn't all
be re-copied out.

Good-night!
Cyril

28 Jan 1927.

Noel Blakiston, Esq.,   [Chelsea.]
Magdalene College.

Dear Noel,
Thank you for your letter about cement. I stood with you and
was amazed by the dark satanic mills and my eggs grew cold. My
temper is a little sweeter to-day for which relief much thanks, it blows
quite a gale as I write and Logan is reading my Hard Sayings from the
notebook which has blossomed into an enormous stack of white sheets
like Japanese flowers in water, things look better in type than one
would expect, you know, and I have divided them into long things,
poetry, short long things and short things. There will be a lot for the
encyclopaedia there I think, it is all curiously saturated with you and
the Lock House in the early summer – we have done what Bobbie
and I could never do – forged an Eden for ourselves to be alone – and
there are seasons in our paradise like Altamura's for it is never station-
ary and each day a new animal presents itself docilely and waits to
be told its name. One beast I find hard to like as I should I am afraid is
Meredith: I feel that the *Egoist* is a fine idea, and true and *de te fabula* –
but '*quel ton, quel effroyable ton*' the appalling style, the middle class
snobbery, the jokes that aren't jokes, the cleverness that is not clever,
and the clumsy tiring badinage of the 'He has a leg' type made the
first chapters hard work but now I am getting in to it I am beginning
to like it better and the pathos and tragedy of egoism seems vital and
needs badly to have been written about. I am glad you are going to
Basle, get out and see the Rhine if you have time there and if at
Milan don't miss St. Ambrogio which is a good basilica. I pine for

Friday. David Garnett asked me to go over there on Friday as he is away the week end but I don't think I shall as it is too much of a business. Thou wilt come and meet me perchance? I liked your picture of me writing among my scraps of paper in the last hour of day – do you mean the day of life as our latitudes are not so different that while you lay tossing, I should be working against the set of sun. Every item in my note book has been done on a separate piece of paper, the grandest sheet *que la blancheur défend* has nothing but 'It is amazing what a lot one can stand' written at the top. I love these windy nights when Logan has gone to bed and panes rattle and trains shunt and I write to you. When my early death overtakes me I shall haunt this terrace and be seen to walk at dead of night with a white letter to the Sloane Street post office, all nearer mails being gone; well there are more ignoble ways of appearing. William perhaps will run spectrally to early school or Maurice sit flushed upon his purple sofa. In the seats at the end of my coaching guide is mentioned Cinnamon Grove, Merlyn's Bridge, near Milford Haven, the abode of Captain Roach, don't you think it is an ideal address and Captain Roach, sinewy and unsocial, with his strange habits of foreign parts, his uncouth mutterings on the other side of the hedge, his telescope, his musty tomes, his herbarium, his little daughter Barbadoes whom he lets run so wild and his short way with the villagers a most sinister occupant. He is indifferent to the fair sex and yet sometimes bewilders the old spinsters of the village by displaying a most enchanting gallantry and assiduous manner but as he always chooses the ugliest for the purpose, and as however affable he is in the street, he will never set foot in their house, no one knows what to make of it. Then the Grove itself is not much in the run of common houses, the wealth of shrubberies that descend the short cliff to the sea make all the grounds a wilderness and the strange cedar firs creak in the wind like an inn sign or rub their boughs like disembodied spirits. The house you must know is long and low and yet with a most uncommon tower at one end of it and crowned with a mouldy dovecot long untenanted. The captain spends all his time in the tower or the study and goes only in to the village to buy necessities or fetch strange parcels from the carrier – sometimes he sees Barbadoes playing and tries to talk to her little friends but the clean shaven lanthorn face, the black eyes, and the horny teeth which seem so big that his words wriggle out through them and fall in the air with a jerk so frighten them that they always run away 'Que tal, Barbadoes' he always says and stalks off to the grove, his old braided coat and rakish hat being more welcome to her playmates than his parchment skin and coffin face, most horrible of all when wreathed in kindly smiles – 'There goes old Roach' the bustling doctor exclaims but the Captain can't tolerate the profession and stalks by on the other side. I would be most glad if you would tell me what you have heard about him and if you know aught of the Rector of Merlin's Bridge, a fine scholar so they say but a most unorthodox divine or of his simple curate that heard a voice one night on the Milford Road bellow right in his ear 'Oiga' so that he near fell off his cob with terror and told the Reverend Mr Alabaster that he would have to leave the neighbourhood – and would have, if it had not meant leaving Dr. Jones' sprightly daughter who wonders why her father speaks to Captain Roach at all, since he's never answered that busy man except once when he said 'If you was with me at Caracas, Hermogenes, you'd have treated yourself for starvation on the Maracaibo Cay.' Pray tell me all you know of the Alabaster household and the stout young curate John Bain and ask your brother if he knows aught of the man from Corcubion that arrived on a visit to the captain and startled the poor fellow on the road. No more to you now for the hour is late, but I wish this time next week were near. Tell me of these odd characters over the week end. The wind howls and I have almost frightened myself. Good night.

Cyril

Tune Jesu pro me perforatus

Hymnus.

C.	Care Noel, Noel care quam jucundum est amare!
N.	O Cyrille, fas est fari non amarum est amari.
ambo.	O Cyrille ⎱ Care Noel ⎰ mi sodalis. nunquam fuit comes talis!
C.	Tu si constans, constans ero
N.	Sis inconstans, non abero
C.	Tibi non cadenti cedam
N.	mentienti tibi credam

ambo.	O Cyrille ⎱ mi sodalis Care Noel ⎰ nunquam fuit comes talis!
N.	Te persequar in deserta Certus, quamvis lux incerta.
C.	Te cum solus vis manere Solum sino permanere.'
ambo.	O Cyrille ⎱ mi sodalis Care Noel ⎰ nunquam fuit comes talis!
C.	Nox cum venerit suprema oscula dabis postrema, ore mellis, atro crine. O te spectem mea fine! Vale dicam, mi sodalis. numquam comes fuit talis!
N.	Te natantibus ocellis flebo meo ore mellis, sine te non possum stare heu, nec semper lacrimare! alius erit sodalis.
C.	Puto non, sum immortalis.

attributed to St. Cyril
of Cyrene

30 Jan 1927.

Noel Blakiston, Esq.,   [Chelsea.]
Magdalene College.

Dear Noel,

Poor Sir Willoughby!* faith, child, he is terrible like and I get so many pinpricks from each chapter that my heart bleeds; yet I am fond of him, which I suppose but continues the similarity; and, please, I hope Clara doesn't get away with that old stick Whitford – or he have to marry the wan Laetitia. I have got to where Clara is trying to break it off and gone for a walk with Laetitia after the scene in the

*In *The Egoist* by George Meredith

breakfast room. Was it sent for my affliction? Pride . . . the world . . . extinct. . . . I catch many echoes and am reminded uncomfortably of the chalet – but in Spain I was worried because you seemed to agree with everything I said for a quiet life, while Sir Willoughby would have minded more if you differed – O say that you have some sympathy for him, beset by all these treacly women!

If at the chalet Piers seemed Whitford to my Willoughby, to Piers at Minehead I was the Whitford to Maurice's Patterne, so the roles are only relative and since you and Piers have ended by cleaving (or being cloven), to your Willoughby's in the end may it not indicate that with all their faults, they love the best? It may be your turn to be one next, the Kingdom of Patterne is within us! but if only he hadn't been such a bore he would have been an admirable man, what are Willoughby and Clara but Lewis without the charm and Tessa without the constancy? I don't mean you would have given me the book as a lesson but I feel that it must have been so real to you because dear Willoughby was so intolerably like me οὗτος ὁ μηδέν – but I think I am a bit better now than the chalet say, but not much and when you see it coming out say 'isn't that rather Sir Willoughby?' and I will understand – and, please Noel, my second name is Vernon! 'The gulf of a caress hove in view like an enormous billow hollowing under the curled ridge' seems to me an admirable sentence, as also 'Her terrible isolation of secrecy in a world amiable in unsuspectingness, frightened her' 'She listened gravely, conceiving the infinity as a narrow dwelling where a voice droned and ceased not. However, she listened. She became an attentive listener.' These seem the best things in it so far and the last a terrible phrase of art. I feel for you and I expect you feel for me as I sit here picking out my stings. 'A narrow dwelling where a voice droned and ceased not' pictured a railway carriage to me at once. But what a good book! Delius 'in a summer garden' is being wafted across the room by the wireless. I am alone, it is four in the afternoon and a Sunday. I have thought so much of you to-day and yesterday as several times to hear your voice, but you must speak louder! I am glad you liked Ligurinus (it was not meant to be personal)! – I have altered it a little and the first line is now

'Cruel youth, though long with love's whole wealth endowed'
dullness for dimness in the fifth line, and
'or, minded thus, youth fled not unavailing.'

The last which has the double meaning of guarded thus, youth flees just the same, as it has the Latin sense of his mind changing too late. I imagined Ligurinus and Horace meeting, 'just a moment, Ligurinus, I want to read you something' 'well I hope it's short' 'Yes, quite short' 'about me?' 'it might be taken to be about you.' 'O Christ, *toujours le même sujet*' 'O very well' (rolls it up) 'Well I might as well hear it, go on.' Horace reads. Ligurinus shifts uneasily from foot to foot and looks at the ground. He looks rather flushed and sullen, he is wearing full change under an overcoat and a top hat. When Horace finishes he looks pensive, 'yes, there's something in that but I must go to absence' Horace grins 'I thought you'd see my point – perhaps you'll come for a walk with me on Sunday?' 'Thanks all the same, but I think I'll ask Brassey.' – Horace 'you –' Ligurinus goes to absence.

Logan says Whitford was taken from Leslie Stephen, father to Virginia Woolf and Adrian, husband to Logan's niece. The style too improves a bit after the beginning and is often really subtle. O Friday, dear Noel, will meeting me at the station be allowed when it is your day of work? I really feel so perplexed about it I don't know where to turn, I am sure your brother would never forgive me, and please God I should never forgive *myself* if I thought I was to interfere with your *work*, I realise how important these two terms are going to be to you and all that depends upon them as I am sure John does too and I could never bear to have it said, and you know people do say these things 'he knew quite well that they only worked on one day of the week and, if you please, he chose that day to come down on. Perhaps I had better not come at all. I picture Thursday night as something like this – the scene is your sitting room – Jack and Noel working in feverish silence. Occasionally they groan. Jack. 'Are you ready Noel, if so I'll hear you.' Noel. 'Yes, carry on' – Jack – 'well, let me see – Gray, Walpole, West and who?'

N.	'Acton'
J.	'Ashton'
N.	'Ashton'
J.	'What did they do.'
N.	'Write?'
J.	'Yes – what did they write?'
N.	'Letters'
J.	'Poor souls.'

N.   'Well it doesn't say they had to read them'
J.   'What do you like best'
N.   'Ashton's poem'
J.   (looking at a letter of mine) 'No, West's poem'
N.   'West's poem'
J.   'Which does Cyril think he's like?'
N.   'Walpole?'
J.   'Gray'
N.   'Ashton.'
J.   'I'll look it up'
N.   'I say I think that'll do'
J.   'We'd better cut the pages.'
N.   'You think of everything'

Jack cuts pages.

N.   'Who wrote the Prelude'
J.   'It says on the cover'
N.   'I'm asking you'
J.   'Collins? No? Tibullus? No? Ford Madox Ford!'
N.   'No.'
J.   'Give it up'
N.   'Here it is, read it.' Jack reads it.

Ten minutes later. Noel 'Who wrote Li Po, Jack'

Jack.   'I never heard of it.'
N.   'Well I don't expect he'll ask you that, have you learnt
          your part?'
Jack.   'Yes. I think so.'
Noel.   'Well we'll rehearse.'
Jack.   'I think you're right Noel.'
Noel.   'I think so, middling'
Jack.   'but I don't agree about Martianus Capella –'
Noel.   'you prefer Racan?'
Jack.   'prefer is hardly the word, there is nothing in Racan that
          is not in Pontus du Thyard'
Noel   'Nothing in Capella that is not in Fortunatus, in Theo-
          datus, in Commodianus of Gaza'
Jack   'I disagree – I say, with Ponsard, "*je m'obloque*" '
Noel   (to Sidney) 'what do you think Cyril?'
Jack.   'I'll be Cyril. Well, sort of, thanks Jack, they're Russian
          aren't they, well it's so long since I read them, thanks I'll
          have another, that I sort of mean to well – er – can I have

another cigarette?' Noel 'and then I ask questions?'
Jack. 'Yes I think we'll tie him up.' Noel. 'Yes, tie him
up first and then talk him over, it's all right about the
gramophone?' Jack – 'Yes, quite, I've arranged to play
the wedding march as Ravel, the Hallelujah chorus as a
solo by Casals and the overture to Egmont as the Debussy
Quartet.' N. 'Well he's sure to be taken in by one and
then we can stop his mouth – Hullo Freddie – what's
the matter?'

Freddie.	'God, it's bloody.' N. 'what's happened?' 'I gave the Eighteenth Century Childhood away at a dance.'
Jack.	'Gave it away badly?'
Freddie.	'My good fellow, it's a book – Cyril's book.'
Jack.	sympathetically. 'Ah!'
Noel	'You think he'll ask for it?'
Freddie.	'Sure to.'
Noel.	'I'll put the Benvenuto Cellini out where he can see it.'
Jack.	'Isn't that rather a red rag?'
Noel.	'No, it's a red herring – he always thinks I stole it.'
Freddie.	'Thank you, you're very noble – O yes and William is going to be in Jack's bedroom and to come out for his lunch when you take Cyril to play squash, can you get him out by two o'clock?'
Noel.	'I'll do my best – but what about Piers?'
Freddie.	'He's coming to tea disguised as a freshman – I think that's all.'
Jack.	'Well, we must be turning in, we've got the morning to learn up those latitudes Noel – good night Freddie –'
Freddie	'Good night Jack – the stuffed jake has fallen to pieces, I was thinking of putting it in his bed – it's gone in the middle.'
Jack.	'I'll leave the N.R.F. out. De Musset indeed'! Noel 'Ingente"! J. 'Good night Noel' 'Good night Jack, good night, Sidney, Cyril's coming to-morrow.'
Sidney.	'waow – waaooow – waaoooooooo'

This is not a very funny letter, the children's service coming through
on the wireless spoils the touch – but it is better than silence so I send
it. The moment when Clara discovers the word is egoist is very good
don't you think?

Cyril

Noel Blakiston,   1, Hanover Square,
Magdalene College.   London, W.1.

Dentist's waiting room

Te spectem suprema mihi cum venerit hora
    Te teneam moriens deficiente manu

'O lovely race of Athanasians crowding all
    Sail to their distant harbour, the adoration of posterity'

I wrote to you from here 5 years ago
They were his last words.

31 Jan 1927.

H. N. Blakiston, Esq.,   [Chelsea.]
Magdalene College.

Dear Noel,
   This but a scrawl for the post is going and I have been out to
dinner where I missed you – I liked your Canfranc which was simple,
sensuous and revealing, especially your return alone which, like
Pennyfields, seemed like a letter from myself – I hope that doesn't
sound bloody – I will write better to-morrow – your strange friend
likes you strangely.

   φιλέεσκε γαρ ἄιν ως
   ὦ γένος ἀνθρώπων Αθανάσιον ἄφρονες αἴει

can you supply a pentameter?
O Friday. Viernes, Venerdi.
Freitag, vendredi, et dies Veneris currite cito!

I will let you know about the morning coach, it depends on the
dentist and Maurice Baring. Procure us many meals alone, for I have
gold. Think of me in the torture chamber where I have five teeth to be
stopped, and think of you. I liked your long nice letter.
                                                    Cyril

1 Feb 1927.

Noel Blakiston, Esq.,   [Chelsea.]
Magdalene College,
Cambridge.

Dear Noel,
    Thank you for your letter. I didn't mean it was a thrust but I thought
it must all be about me but Logan tells me that everyone thinks the
Egoist to be about them. I had a Turkish bath with Sligger again
non sudore vel dolore this afternoon. My jaw has ached all day from the
dentist's where I shall be every morning till I come to Cambridge
and I feel tired and low. Here is a poem written at the dentist's.

'Sea gulls over Hanover Square
Climbing the airy hills
I stare at them from the dentist's chair
The sun stares at his drills

O that a bird I might ascend
and scorn the world beneath
They do not have a same-house friend
    but they have no teeth!

is not '*quaerens me sedisti lassus*' a lovely languorous line. Canfranc
would be a good word for a charade.
    I am suffering from loneliness induced by toothache, I have three
more to be done. Your tale of your convulsion of loneliness makes me
lonelier still for it was presumably indifferent to me while mine always
points one way and is worst in company. How brave you were to
borrow money from the young man on the Geneva train – I could
perhaps come in the afternoon to Cambridge and we could tea and
dine alone – suppose we went out to Ely on Sunday and dined there –
we might go to evening service, at this moment I could do with a
penitential psalm – *o dolor, o dentes, cur me torquetis inermem?*
    I have written a Latin hymn for you, it is fond and pastoral and
goes to *Jesu pro me perforatus* but I would rather give it you when I
see you as it may be hard to translate, though it has a certain grace. It
emerged from hours of insomnia – I was very fond of Yeats and like
him still and liked your quotation very much indeed. You have not
sinned. [? ?] 'et libera me de poenis inferni et de profundo lacu, ne
me absorbeat Tartarus, ne cadam in obscenum!' Tucker would sing

that stanza. Bed calls. Farewell nostro señor de los desemparadores. Do write to me before Friday. ἤν δγιαίνομεν ὤρα enters the brain as the last lines leave it.

Cyril

How true about Poetry! I dreamt this night of Maracaibo.

3 Feb 1927.

Noel Blakiston, Esq.,   [Chelsea.]
Magdalene College.

Care tu

I will try and reach Cambridge at 3.58, leaving London 2.34. *Tempus fugit* is not ingenious nor true. We might have tea together – I have gaudy plans for Italy which fain I would discuss. I will bring 'style' and Pennyfields, and gold. Dentist irks. Vergil I read and wintry Horace and Martial, the first ουγα* man. He liked the Pontine Marshes. He was born and died at Calatayud. It is Arab for Job's Castle. Your p.c. cheered me a lot. Compliments, fondness, sympathy, they are so comely and reviving – I had a moment's sheer ecstasy reading Horace in bed at night over the glow and excitement of the Soracte Ode, its windy, wet, November thrill, the logs, the Hide and Seek, the curious 18th century or Victorian air of open fires and solid hospitality and the line '*nec veteres agitantur orni* corrected to *ulmi*' conveyed a spasm of you and Chilling (perhaps it is *ulmi* not *orni*) and Exmoor snow. Last night it was Vergil who moved me

> hic gelidi fontes, hic mollia prata, Lycori,
> hic nemus. . . .

and this about you

> Gallus, cuius amor tantum mihi crescit in horas
> Quantum vere

the idea of fondness increasing from hour to hour is fine and bold. Have you read Horace his fifth satire which is very good and robust of his journey to Brindisi and full of the sense of travel – really the

---

*One of Cyril's key words in Spanish signifying 'hoy, listen to me.'

world of pastoral seems the best of all ideal civilisations, think of the baldness and vulgarity of heaven compared to the downs of Sicily and the Arcadian valleys and the snatches of song '*Pan custodit oves, oviumque magistros*' or '*Αἴτρα μάτερ 'εμα*' which one might hear at any moment murmured confidentially and adoringly from some ugly, grinning, toothy young shepherd in his uncouth Doric – Have you read *Go She Must?* David Garnett's new book that is out a week. It looks very good indeed and begins with snow and a nice clergyman, not unlike the Rev. Mr. Alabaster. It seems to be about Hilton. I liked the Dorset of *The Sailor's Return*, so unselfconscious and unsympathetic but without the Hardiesque gloom. I buy pesetas! This time tomorrow I shall be nearly there! There is a front page on Pater by Logan in this week's Literary Supplement. I have been lunching with my mother and am writing from there. The flowers should stand up straight in the bottom of the water as if growing. '*dulces moriens reminiscitur Argos*' is good of a dying soldier – I imagine leaving Paris on the Sud Express, reaching Bordeaux night and a voice crying Irun! and the snows of the Guadarrama and Old Castile 'realm nobly poor and proudly desolate' as Santayana calls it. The next thrills entering Andalusia through the Sierra Morena, the sudden vision of greenness after the brown, and the soft air, the evening, the first white houses and the streams pouring down to the Guadalquiver. Baeya! Venta de Cardenas! Hombre! Amigo! Oiga! Psssst! Usted va a Cordoba? 'A Granada' nada nada, sienta se! a las nueve y media a Granada. . . . de coche-camas y de grandes espresos europeños 'Tres morillas tan garridas

   en Jaen

Axa, y Fatima, y Marien!

usted no fuma? gratias! Ah ingleses! . . . cuentas – muy caro

I hoped you heard the Ravel Quartet, that dayspring of anguish – did you recognise the 'O Noel Bleeder' theme of the 2nd movement? quatuor et viginti horas vale

Cyril

Notice

In view of the visit of Prince Honk to the college Friday next has been granted as a half holiday in his honour instead of a day of work. Friday's business will be transferred to Thursday afternoon. Prince Honk would esteem it an especial courtesy if he were met at the station.

The guard of honour will parade at 6 a.m. with blacked faces and remain at its post till sunset. Shoulder pads and plucked eyebrows.

Roach. adjt.

There follows some writing in an oriental script
signed HONK P.

8 Feb 1927.

Noel Blakiston, Esq.,   11, St. Leonard's Terrace,
Magdalene College.   Chelsea, S.W.3.

Dear Noel,

My mother would be delighted to put you up and you must let her know when you will be coming a week or so before. It will be very close to Victoria for you but it would be best to avoid having to carry heavy luggage up all those stairs. I had lunch and tea alone with Maurice and we discussed books and Latin and Russia. He is very fond of Ninfa and has written poems about it. He may be in Rome when we are. I miss you and feel sad. I am afraid my tongue kept me from saying anything of much interest.

This is out of a whirl of packing which has to be done to-night, and to-morrow perhaps there will be a letter from you. I think Desolation is fond of us for she often joins us when she sees us together and though she says nothing we feel that she is listening. What you said of feeling tired stirred me. The bond of fatigue and isolation is almost as close as that of shared ecstasy don't you think and *quaerens me sedisti lassus* seems somehow to the point. It was thinking that if we are tired together it is really just as valuable as being thrilled that made me think it would be worth while really to try for Tripoli where we would at the worst be lost together – if we fail to be inspired – the difficulties are time and whether foreigners are allowed there now but I think with luck we could go from Naples to Siracuse, Malta, and Tripoli in about 3 days and after 2 nights there go back to Siracuse and across to Palermo. So let us try for that. Please do not omit to wet your eyes my friend, and my friend's brother. By the way tell Jack that Maurice Baring having gone all the way through Chénier to find four lines he could not remember in a poem he had forgot it turned out to be the Jeune Locrienne. O Tripoli, O Siracuse: there is one good sonnet in Herédia about Sicily it comes late on and is about a coin. *L'Etna nourrit toujours* I think it begins. By the way an omen for us

Sive per Syrtes iter aestuosas
Sive facturus per inhospitalem
Caucasum, vel quae loca fabulosus
    Lambit Hydaspes.

Dear Noel, what ever is inside that Vergil I shall love it for its cover. Find things out about Sicily and Tripoli and think of Lycidas life at Chilling in June and think of me

prensantem nequiquam umbras et
    multa volentem
dicere –

                    Cyril

I hope you enjoy the quartet.

Barbaras Syrtis ubi Maura semper aestuat unda!

8 Feb 1927.

Noel Blakiston, Esq.,   [London.]
Magdalene College.

Dear Noel,
    These are translations from the Greek anthology. I am sorry I have not the originals by me. I did them in my bath.

The silent, the slow voiced, the sweet toned
    Noel of Kirkby
Lies here under this stone, wondering,
    near to the sea

Mackail's version differs slightly

The silent, the slow maturing, the sweet voiced
    Noel of Kirkby
Lies here near to the sea wondering: under
    this stone.

II

He whom the Thames and the Cam, and the Bain
    gave life to, Myiscus
lies on this lonely shore, nor revisits
    Anderby

III

Here by the windless sea, by the white walled
    city of Oea
Lies Noel born by the fens to be the
    prey of Libya.

IV

Thou fadest, friendly winter, thou
fadest, and thy winds mourn for
thee, and we, thy chantrey priests,
mourn, and by Porlock and Yarmouth
we swear, by Exmoor and the Island,
that we will not forget thee in thy
exile but go to meet thee when the
year relents, and thou, O winter,
wilt return.

The first three would seem epitaphs on a sailor, perhaps exercises written on such a theme rather than actual inscriptions. Oea was the ancient name of Tripoli but 'Anderby' and 'the Bain', I have been unable to trace. Myiscus however is probably a different person to the Noel mentioned in the other epigrams. One certainly is written by Simonides.

Thank you for letter. This sent from the Golden Arrow in Victoria. Love.

10 Feb 1927. Postcard of the lady of Elche in the Louvre.

Noel Blakiston,   Paris
Magdalene College.

   She is not changed.

C.

10 Feb 1927.

Noel Blakiston, Esq.,
Magdalene College.

Café Riche,
10 Place Clichy,
Paris.

Dear Noel,

I am writing this at night having been to two cinemas, in one there was Jannings and standing room only, in the other boxes and nothing worth seeing so I having failed at both have not had a very grand evening and am having coffee in here at eleven. It is cold but Paris is strangely foreign and exciting and very gaudy and Vaudeville. One might be very happy living in Paris I should think. The *Flèche d'Or* is a magnificent train, sleek and white and shining like a python that has shed its skin. One day in it go will we. Filthy coffee. I hope my epitaphs did not cast a gloom on Libya. I used to think of dying there. I look forward to the Sud Express and Bordeaux and Madrid but don't feel much in the mood for cabaret life. I don't know that I really want winter to end just yet. We get on so well in it. It is pleasant so far travelling with Logan, but he talks too much. The band begins to play. Cold pastoral should be good in June – we might try sleeping out at Chilling or even in the New Forest. Logan does not come down till mid July probably so we might have even longer together and perhaps Desmond or Molly would come for a week end. Desmond you would like. He and Maurice (Baring) are supposed to be the two rarest spirits in London so it is pleasant that they should be the only people I know there. Maurice thinks there is no difference between Collegers and Oppidans, or Oxford and Cambridge. He is Athanasianly uninfluenced by other people's opinions and is not ashamed to praise rather ordinary things or to dislike a great many more ordinary things still. He seems the complete amateur, with a horror of competitions and set pieces of any kind. When he wants to look something up in an argument he rings up a bookseller to send round all the books about it by special messenger, he goes all the way through a poet to find one quotation trusting to his good luck that he will come across it early and has no copies of his own books or ability to revise anything he has written. His voice is very limpid and his caprice infectious and he is superbly unimpressed by achievement for a person who has spent so much time among people of action or literary men of action.

249

Next morning.

I will end this and write again soon, it is cold and light and sunny. I have been getting sleepers and lunching well and going to the Louvre – Has your Herédia and Theocritus come? H. gets the wild forest life of Greek mythology, the jungle side supremely.

Cyril

Love to Jack

diary. June 15. Chilling.

6 a.m.–8 a.m. read B. the first act of Anarcharsis. B. I thought was impressed.

8 a.m.–8.10 a.m. breakfast, radishes and rusks.

9 a.m.–11 a.m. read aloud 2000 lines of Drayton's Polyolbion while B. declaimed the rest of Hoccleve. We shall soon have covered English literature up to the Elizabethan decadence.

11 a.m.–11.2 a.m. Break. B. said his saying lesson (the 4th Georgic)

11.2 a.m.–12 noon. the needs of nature. Read the Inferno there. B. copied out my letters (war period).

12.0 noon–1.0. Set B. his papers. B. learnt his trains.

1.0. lunch, rusks washed down with radishes.

1.15–3.15. hoeing. B. hoed 5 more swede rows and half a wurzel than me. This must not happen again.

3.15–6.15. B. doing his paper. I shaved.

6.15–7.15. writing to B. There are times when I feel the slave of habit.

7.15–7.30 dinner bread and cress.

7.30–11.30. read B. Anarcharsis again to see if it sounded different by artificial light. B. thinks not. bed.

11 Feb 1927.

Noel Blakiston, Esq.,   Au Chapon Fin,
Magdalene College.   Bordeaux.

Dear Noel,

It seems impossible to realise that you haven't been here. I suppose it is true. We have just arrived. The new Sud Express is very beautiful but with all the armchairs and kitchens one misses the thrilling rackety journey to the wagon restaurant – the joy of sitting down among its savoury smells and lingering after one is due to leave for one's squalid

250

third or bourgeois second – also there are no corridors to go out and stand in. We went and saw a writer called Du Bos yesterday who functions in the N.R.F. He seemed rather sad and donnish and had lovely books and a room looking over the Seine on the island behind Notre Dame. Paris was gray and arctic. I had a thrill on coming to Bordeaux again, the green Poussin woods and golden sunshine of Entre Deux Mers and the lovely rivers and the solidarity of this town with its respectable houses and cobbled quais. Then there will be a good dinner this evening and wine to drink your health in. I find when I am very tired or very excited you automatically take command and enter in to these extremes of feeling almost professionally, with a latch key and a special peg for your hat. I will take this out to a café and go on with it there. I met the Spanish wine waiter tell Jack who recognised me at once and whose first remark was 'you have come from Egypt?' it turned out I once told him I wanted to go there. Athanasians seem to prefer Spain to Italy and cats to dogs. Logan said you were Vergilian which I think whatever it means and whether it is true or not is a compliment. I tend to fear that being so well understood by you may make me careless of the trouble you take to do it and hence egotistic – so I thank you officially for the balm, absent or present, you invariably shed. Asked why he was so silent and abstracted in all company the sage C'on lee replied, what need is there to speak? I sit in the sun.* (*He meant he was thinking of his friend) – C'On Lee was one of the fine examples of faithful friendship – on one occasion he and his friend No-El spent six months in a hut without speaking and on the last day Con-L'ee turning round said 'Hullo, where did you spring from?' As a matter of fact is not the Chinese civilisation perfect when one of the sages was so renowned for his chastity 'that he could take a lady to sit on his knee without anyone imputing the slightest impropriety'. It is quite cool here but not cold like Paris. I find it very hard to realise I am travelling as a rich man and find I have a strong inclination to discourage Logan from buying cigarette boxes, or taking rooms with baths. I suppose it will wear off. I am too tired to write a good letter but I assume you would rather hear often and sketchily than once a week at length which would lessen the sense of movement though deepen the object moved. Logan is enjoying himself and is terrified out of recognition by the brutal efficiency with which I arrange his travels. When I said we got to Angoulême at quarter past three meaning to have said quarter past two he looked at his watch in the station but did not dare to contradict me! You could hardly be more here if you were here, so you can or at least I can say that you are here ('You hear that Jack, he says I am here') ('Where?') 'in Bordeaux. Rather cool don't you think' 'Yes – I've got my prep.' 'O, sorry, Eurip?' 'Yes – rather knotty, by the way, where's Bordeaux?'

We go to Montaigne's château to-morrow and on by Sud Express at 6 to Avila, Escorial and Madrid. Will you get your passport endorsed for *TRIPOLI* when you get it done for Germany and Austria and Holland (and Greece and Turkey!) – in case.

Cyril

It is hard to write letters travelling as the imagination has usually over eaten by the end of the day. Love to Freddie.

Ho there! buenas noches!

11 Feb 1927. Postcard of Montaigne's château.

Noel Blakiston, Esq.,   Bordeaux.
Magdalene College.

Dear Noel,

We motored here to-day, it was green and crisp and sunny and nice dogs sported under the yellow walls of the château which is rather Du Bellay with view and vines and Poussin sunshine. Montaigne decorated this tower with an anthology of sayings of contented scepticism – he is not, I think, a young man's man. He had a strange friend. I drank to Prince's* in Yquem at 300 francs the bottle to-day and have been sitting in the park in the sun. Why Noel, we will ride on camels! Avila to-morrow and tawny and scudding highlands of Castile.

Love to Jack.

12 Feb 1927. Postcard of Irun.

Blakistons Esq.,
Magdalene College.

   *Prince's restaurant in Piccadilly where C.C. and N.B. had once drunk Yquem when school-boys.

SPAIN!

Il fait nuit noire à Irun on voit les lumières de Fontarabie – combien des fois nous sommes arrivés ici! la gare en est encore saturée – con hermano o otro hermano o la lengua castillana.

13 Feb 1927.

N. J. Blakiston, Esq.,   Madrid Palace Hotel.
Magdalene College.

ATHANASIAN. I am ATH. Noel Anas (S!) (Ha Ha) Jack. Ian (or Jus) love to both from ATH (el pobrecito loco) For the Athanasian.

Towards a catalogue
of the holy places.
There is room for additions
They are divided into 3 classes

Class I.   Spiritual homes, where one has lived a life time in a moment, or, for a moment, wished to live a life time.

II.   good places with no essential sight, or alpha sights but not spiritually habitable or places that present an image which experience has not yet ratified, hence they remain un-canonised, like saints, till they have been proved to have worked a miracle.

III.   Places too large to be wholly good but solid and exciting cities where one would not complain of an enforced exile. Sanctity is assumed for every place that follows

Italy	*Greece*
Taranto	Delphi
Syracuse	Nauplia
*Tripoli	Santorin
*Mantua	Mycenae
*Ninfa	Mytilene
Ravenna	Salonica
Rome	Athens
*Urbino	
Venice	
Brindisi	

Italy (cont.)
Cagliari
Florence
Palermo

Central Europe
Cologne (Germany)
Constanza (Roumania)
*Astrakhan (Russia)
Adakaleh (Yugo Slavia)
Bruges (Belgium)
Basle (Switzerland)
Middelburg (Holland)
Munich (Bavaria)
Novorossisk (Russia)
Salzburg (Austria)
Constantinople (Turkey)
Rustchuk (Bulgaria)
Vienna (Austria)

France
Class I.
Avignon (Vaucluse)
The Pont du Gard (Gard)
Bayonne (B. Pyr.)
Font Romeu (Pyr. Or.)
The Chapon Fin Bordeaux (Gironde)
Class II.
Albi (Tarn)
*Cette (Herault)
*Orthez (B.P.)
Pau (B.P.)
Perpignan (Pyr. Or.)
Class III.
Nîmes (Gard)
Marseilles (Bouches du Rhone)
Toulon (Var)

Spain and *Portugal*
La Coruña (Galicia)
Elche (Alicante)

Other places
Cartagena de Indias (Columbia)
Malta (Brit.)
Damascus (Syria)
New York (USA)
Peking (China)

La Seo de Urgel (Cataluña)
Almeria (Andalucia)
Gerona (Cataluña)
Granada (Andalucia)
Mojacar (Andalucia)
Tetuan (Marruecos)
Tuy (Galicia)
Vianna (Portugal)
Barcelona
Cadiz
O Porto

> pending visit. Toledo. Motril.
> Salamanca. Huelva. Trujillo
> Braganza etc.

I have done 13 of each, twenty should be the limit.
Love from Cyril

an asterisk denotes a place admitted only on a priori intuition.*

13 Feb 1927.

Señor Don Noel Blakiston,   Madrid Palace Hotel.
Magdalene College.

Dear Noel,

Thank you so much for your letter, send me some more. They make half the joy of arriving at places so do send some to the Hotel de Madrid Seville and the Reina Cristina Algeciras. I am writing to you after dinner smoking a large cigar. This is a very grand hotel, all light and carpets and a melodious tango band. A Jack Hotel – as opposed to a Jake hotel with its large selection of English books or a Gabby† Hotel with its glass cases of diamonds and pyjamas and love among the lift boys. A Cyril hotel should have a Moor who makes coffee, a Sligger Hotel is always jolly and the 3rd on the list in Baedeker then there is the Roach hotel with its stables and steaks and strangers arriving at midnight. Of the Cyril-Noel hotels I will not speak for they are shining and inaccessible peaks that the average millionaire is

---

*Apart from France, it is unfortunately not clear from this letter what class C.V.C. intended to designate to which places.

†The reference is to Gaby Pringué.

content to look at with a wild surmise – did you know (which I did not) that the place we had tea at in Paris is the dearest hotel in Europe and the hardest to get a room in – I have been thinking of the hotel in Seo where we overslept our dinner and you read Wuthering Heights. The more I think of Tripoli, the more I think we must go there, the more I think of where we must go the more I think of Tripoli – it was mooted that I should go there before we arranged the Seo trip do you remember and I can think of nothing nicer than to hold Africa and the desert and a real oasis in your company with a few Greek temples to soften our return – could you try and find out about boats, which go chiefly from Syracuse, also sometimes from Naples, I think once a week from S. If you could find out if it is possible to go and spend 2 or 3 days in Tarabulus (el Gharb) and get back to Syracuse you could arrange your exeat better. The line is the Società Italia, the fares not excessive. I think we may have over fifty pounds for our jaunt so we should be able to manage it, if there is any left we could spend an Athanasian day in Munich on the way back with Jack. I can't say how lovely it is to be in Spain again – I sat and ecstasied in the wagon restaurant after Irun, to think that it surrounded me as thick as the darkness we (you, me, Jack) so much assume that it is the best country that one forgets how hard it is to explain why the sleeper reminded me of ours to Toulouse and I woke to see the sun rise over the snows of Guadarrama and the tableland as broad and bracing as the Spanish carriages. Avila was impressive, gaunt and desolate 'of barren acres simple minded King' – the snow lay in wisps under its Romanesque towers and an icy wind blew through its high crusader gateways 'realm nobly poor and proudly desolate' where Santayana and Santa Teresa first saw the light – the drive was exciting, over the usual tawny waste with shepherds shivering in the winter sun and muffled herdsmen staring from among the rocks, the cape carts, or the flocks beside the frozen pools – the sun shone all the way and the snow and forests of the Guadarrama rise in front like a wall, we climbed a very good pass with Font Romeu country all round and descended to the bleak Escorial, a mixture of Princetown gaol and the Brompton Oratory. I was not disappointed for I had not expected more and the last vestiges of Logan's independence (he had insisted on seeing it) vanished like Chilling celery – the El Greco however was magnificent and I bought a reproduction of it for you. I also have our railway tickets and will send you mine for Pat's museum – (only in Spain could one escape with two unpunched Cooks tickets from Bordeaux to Irun, Irun to Medina, Medina to Avila, and a supplementary one!) There were no photoes worth buying alas – the approach to Madrid was lovely with no suburbs only a distant view of it across the plain and a climb through woods and public gardens to the heart of the town. O wild and bubbly tangos and their long forsaken Sidney Shusha wails! We stay here till Tuesday when we go to Toledo and thence by the Mancha and the Cervantes country – (fancy living like Don Quixote at Argamasilla!) to the Sierra Morena and the south. Ronnie has a record called the Danse Macabre (Saint Saens) which somehow seems to give the atmosphere of the tableland of the Castiles. I expect my high water mark of feeling to be the ride from Granada to Motril and Malaga – I shall do it alone, by bus – and spend a night at Motril among the cocoanuts and sugar cane (*el mes era de Mayo quando hace la calor!*) I hope the Theocritus arrived – do read him before we go as it is impossible to read anything in the South I think, imaginary worlds pale before the reality. As to Blake I think he is an indispensable. I worshipped the Marriage at Eton and have worshipped almost everything of his since but stuck in the prophetic books. I think he has the rare Eliot-Isaiah quality of earthy mysticism as opposed to the ethereal apocalyptic kind, songs of experience are the best I think and he has the perfect desultory lyric gift like Chinese poems and the Coplas. Rimbaud is the French Blake – *oisive jeunesse* is like a song of experience and *la Saison* like Heaven and Hell. Then Blake is superbly English and rural without being artificial and blends the wisdom of the serpent with the innocence and spontaneity of childhood, in fact he is a good man, subtly childish and brightly cruel. Spain one loves for what it is and takes the wrinkled sulky little millionaires with the forlorn peasants or the ruddy perspiring parish priests. In time I will like you in this way and am surely nearer to it than I was and in this way you probably like me with my drear pedantry and morning beard. Roach I feel was something of a gaunt caballero and at home in the straw strewn venta or the noisy parador. He was often heard mumbling strange lists of names, Covarrúbias, Guadalajara, Beniajan, Jimenes de Libar – most lonely mountains, the Libar, I feel rather sick from mixing cigar and lemonade so I don't think this letter will last out the page – it is amazing how often one feels sick, especially travelling. I was sick at Messina station when last in Sicily don't let's go there. I think Tripoli and Astrakhan are the only places that have inspired images as vivid as places I haven't seen in Spain so it will be a real pilgrimage to go there. I don't much mind if we do quarrel all the time, it will come to the same afterwards and presence – you know the Athanasian saw. I too can't say how I wish you were with me but if you read between the lines you will see I have been saying nothing else, and you appear almost continually sometimes as a vast green overcoat and a red scarf and sometimes as a soothing glow. Thank you very much for the photo by the way *quamvis ille niger, quamvis tu candidus esses*. Send me any more that you find – the band is waxing gayer and the harsh babel of Castilian voices rages around me. I think I shall soon be beginning to understand you, but by then, I expect, you will have changed! What about a tower at Motril? by the sea and in an African huerta of steaming fruit trees with a view down the hill to the blue fields of cane which smell sweet at night and back to the snows of the Sierra Nevada from whence cool breezes blow – would it be too luscious or would the wildness (40 miles from a railway station) and the absence of the academic blessing make it durable? I feel a villa in Italy would be death – if you like Italy better than Spain will you tell me – it will be a terrible scene.

N.   There's something I want to say
C.   Go on, you know I like whatever you say.
N.   I mean it's awful.
C.   I think I can stand it (complacently).
N.   I like, I at least I think I like, no really I do like – O God! (buries his face in the mosquito netting).
C.   'Some woman?' (acidly).
N.   'Worse – much, much WORSE!'
C.   One of the tripes? not, not, going to Chartres?
N.   I like Italy better than Spain.
C.   Well of course, well for someone who's hardly been to Spain, in fact 600 000 people would say you hadn't been to Spain, no 400000 Basques as well, when a million people would say you hadn't been to Spain, well, I daresay you must feel you want to unsettle me at times but – either I don't believe you or I do and you are joking, which is it please – I mean I hope I, I know. I like you for yourself, but my poor Blakiston, Noel I mean, look here I must go. O no, O yes doubtless, O yes I shall always be glad to help you, feel the same I mean – why you have chewed right through the mosquito netting, it's not really much use now is it – change beds? poor soul you can have both – no, I'm not

258

offended, only amused, just rather amused, O I know I deserve it – quite, I'm unbearable there are more tactful ways of saying – (exit) so – you have given me hints – Avonmouth – Bordeaux – Yarmouth – Yah, Yah, Yarmouth.

N.   'Which Yarmouth?'
Cyril.   'Which Poussin?'
Noel.   'Pooh, Pooh, Poussin.'
Cyril.   'You've lied enough.'
Noel.   'I've stood enough.'
Cyril.   Ha. O Ha. O Ha Ha Ha! (runs maniac)
Noel.   He looks like Harry.
Cyril.   'Ha? Ha!; O Ha Ha Ha!'

Please write often – love to Jack – O April April
                         Cyril

15 Feb 1927. Postcard of Toledo.

Noel Blakiston, Esq.,
Magdalene College,
Cambridge,
Inglaterra.

We have been here all day which is rather wet but the town very fine and the gorge of the Tajo lovely and some of the cloisters and Moorish walls – I don't think it goes into the holy places though and it is too trippery to be as exciting as Seo or Trujillo looks. I have a superb guide book the Murray's Spain of 1845 done by Richard Ford in superb English and fine romantic efficiency – it is a book to read at Cambridge even more than in Spain. O Tripoli.

Feb 1927.

Noel Blakiston, Esq.,   Granja Nacional,
Magdalene College.   Granada.

Dear Noel,
    This washy ink proclaims Abroad. Thank you so much for your letters, I sent an Armada to you between Paris and Toledo. I hope some arrived. Tell me the result of the career conference which is worrying me – I am afraid the feast of St. Pepys is ill propitious to any romantic conclusion. There has been a lovely sunset which I have

watched over the superb snows of the Sierra Nevada and later among the peasant carts and trains of mules winding across the bridge of the Genil. I am drinking some incredible kind of tea, infusion of garbage, which they have given me in mistake for something else – I will wait till after dinner where there is a better pen and try and translate coplas till then.

We had a lovely journey here from Madrid first over the desolate Mancha which was white and sunny, we saw Argamarilla in the distance and then came the Sierra Morena green and aromatic and deserted mountains stretching away in the sun, then a good gorge and Andalusia represented by a beggar boy singing a trailing song beside the carriage and a thousand miles of green corn rising along the Guadalquivir like English tropics and transfigured downs till they vanished in a golden Claude like haze, most soothing and so wide. Then more mountains and the dark and finally here with a full moon, a splitting headache, a letter from you, and bed to the noise of rushing streams. This is really one of the best places in the world, the air is crisp and bright and though it is still winter it is such gaudy winter and so warm to sit in the sun. The moorish park of the Alhambra is all oaks and elms and ivy and you would think it England till you see the white houses, slot windows, caves, prickly pears, and precipices of the Albaicin or the green vega of Granada still as a lake below or the snows and glaciers of the Sierra Nevada behind or the Alhambra perched above like an apricot. Inside it is a miracle of warmth and grace and the myrtles smell in the sun and the gold fish swim in the tanks and the doves coo. We walked down the cypress avenue to the Generalife of which you have the post card this afternoon but after the Alhambra the best place is Granada itself where every street has some unknown palace or grim prison and all seem different temperatures, white and narrow and ending in green sky or broad and brown and arcaded with the white snow mountains at the end. Assuredly we will come here on our grand tour. It is odd being here again and remembering places where I missed you and where I wrote to you or sent frantic wires. Psalm tunes recur at sunset but it is hot and southern and I can do nothing to lessen your odium, for it is not even too hot but deliciously fresh and good walking weather as at Font Romeu. I think a lot of our voyage but so far no image is clear but a warm deck smelling of tar and us under an awning and over the jade Syrtis awaiting palms. I am much moved by the Spanish coplas which I have been finding and which seem to rival Greek epigrams

and Catullus or Waley for passion, subtlety and desultory song – I
sent you one, here are more.

> Suspiras que de mi salgan
> Y otros que de ti saldran
> Si en el camino se encuentran
> Qué de cosas se dirán!

Salgan, saldran, sortirent

> El candil se esta apagando
> La alcuya no tiene aceite . . .
> No te digo que te vayas
> Ni te digo que te quedes.

> The lamp has got no oil in it
> the stove is pining away
> I do not ask you to go, to go,
> I do not tell you to stay.

> Para rey nació Davi,
> Para sabio Salomón
> Para yorar Jeremias
> Y para quererte, yo.

> yorar=llorar to weep

and this for paganism

> Esta noche vendra uste
> Y entrara por er postigo;
> mi madre estara durmiendo . . .
> entiende usté io qué digo?

> La perdiz en el arroyo
> Los mirlos en el zarzal
> Mi corazon con el tuyo
> Y el tuyo no se con cual.

> The partridge takes to the stream side
> the sage the blackbirds choose
> and my heart goes with your heart
> and yours with whose? with whose?

> Mas quisiera contigo
> Vivir en guerra
> Que estar en paz con otra
> que me quisiera.

Rather would I love with you
to live at war
than at peace with someone who
would love me more.

No serás tú el primer hombre
ni yo la primer mujer
que se quisiran y se olviden
y se vuelvan a querer.

You will not be the first of men
nor I of maids will remain
who loved each other, forgot each other
and came back to love again.

This useful for examinations

Le pueden quitar al rey
Su corona y sus estados
Pero no pueden quitarle
La gloria de haber reinado

and these for hate and desolation

Tu calle ya no es tu calle
que es una calle cualquiera
Camino de cualquier parte

Your street already is not your street
it is just some street or other
leading in some other way

El corazon tengo triste
y el almo tenga confusa
Algo me va a suceder . . .
Triste corazoń, que anuncias?

Te lleven al cementerio
Te entierren junto a un padrón
y yo escriba este letrero
'No tenia corazon'

Se acabará mi querer
se acabará mi llorar
se acabará mi tormento
y todo se acabará

Of course they all go to very long music and draw out on the final vowel so that the rhymes look very queer but as they are mostly in Andalusian the last consonants aren't sounded and Viene rhymes all right with 'iremos' which both sound eh-eh-eh-eh- and va with mas. My translations are not meant to be good only to make the Spanish clearer.

> Del jardín salen las rosas
> de la marina, los peces;
> De mi corazon, traiciones,
> para ti, que las mereces –

is a good Catullus

> Yo le he preguntado a un sabio
> Como se olvida un amor
> Yel Sabio me ha contentado
> 'Ay, si lo sapiera, yo!'

> No tengo quien por mi llore
> Sino la triste campana:
> Si yo me muero esta noche
> me entierran por la manaña.

> Por aquer camino yano (llano)
> arsé los ojos por berte (verte)
> Los tuyos no me miraron.

> Mas vale callar que mal hablar.

Tomorrow is going to be a good day, we motor from here in the early morning to Motril over the end of the Sierra Nevada and through the Alpugarras, Durcal, Lanjaron, Orgiva, and then along the coast to Velez Malaga where Logan goes on to Malaga and I go back in the car by the straight way as far as Alhama where I shall spend the night and go back to Malaga for the next day by Velez or Loja. We have a superb car and it should be marvellous scenery, snow part of the way and views of the Mediterranean and descending into the sugar canes and tropics of Motril and then going along a deserted corniche of mountains to Velez. From Malaga we go to Cordova and thence motor to Seville by Ecijar and Carmona and after four days there (Hotel de Madrid) to Cadiz by boat if possible and thence to Algeciras. We may take a boat by Valencia and Barcelona to Italy from there. This is a dull drear letter, forgive it. I live for Tripoli and the Greek temples, if you have to be a schoolmaster we can at least have most of your holidays together, don't you think, but I am troubled and distressed about this awful career question – and Jack too – schoolmasters go sour don't they – tell me the worst – I take it even the worst can't be final and we may be able to get something better before you go down. Give Jack my love, a letter pends, it is late and I must pack. One day we will go to all these places which will be dim till then. You are here in spirit so you can't envy me after that. It's not fair! Foster sounds nice. I think of you with fogs and atlases. Love from Cyril.

Could not us three stay a night in Munich, I could provide – there is much to see there and we could then go to it by the mountain railway from Innsbruck over the Tyrol – O Tarabulus seemingly fabulous, O Tripolitaine far from the Bain.

Feb 1927.

Noel Blakiston, Esq.,   Hotel Regina,
Magdalene College.   Cordoba.

Dear Noel,
    I will write you a long letter from Seville as I have a lot to say, this is only a scrawl. I have been having seizures of loneliness in the night and at the set of sun and one has descended now. There are moments when the whole burden of absence seems to descend and the most enjoyable prospect, the most secure and salutary surroundings, the most apparent defences, and the most enviable future seem but the hollow mockery of circumstance to one whose happiness, integrity and creative ability is solely dependent on an alas who knows how occupied human form! Time drags, drags, drags, and distance sobs on the stairs, a pale spectre of what it was this time last year, it is true – but how long o Lord how long till the train to Sicily – these lonely seizures we would feel together I dare say just the same however directed to each other they may appear, but shared they are defeated and at the worst cast but a melancholy radiance, a subdued harmony on two poor wandering souls. I will write to-morrow. I enclose the nearest portion of Spain to my hand and whisper a magic word of which you will hear more – Almuñecar
Love to Jack
Yours Cyril

train just going (7 p.m.) to Seville.

26 Feb 1927. 7 postcards in an envelope, and a scrap of paper.

Señor Don Noel Blakiston,   Seville.
Magdalene College.

a

How about canoeing down the Tagus? or the Minho? or spending
a few weeks like this? O for a letter from you at Algeciras – here it
still rains and my cold is worse – we go to-morrow to Cadiz and then
hire a car. I see all fares to Sicily are half price from inside Italy so
all is well. χάιρε

a+1

I shall find the chalet rather hard to fit in as I can only go the beginning
of July or in September as I promised Logan I would be staying at
Chilling while he was there for sailing etc and if we went in September
we would be wasting precious time – I am not wildly keen about the
chalet, unless we had plenty of time – perhaps it will arrange itself,
anyhow Sunningdale* seems a good scheme. I have bought a record
called 'La calle mayor de Jaca' sung by Fleta, tell Jack.

a+2

This is the middle postcard, at least there isn't a middle postcard
yet – the point is these postcards look rather odd without a stamp and
postmark and almost disappointing but then how much odder they
would look all arriving at once. Give Jack my love, I would like a
message from him or a letter if it is not too much.

a+3

This really is the

MIDDLE
postcard –

I feel rather deeply about Shanghai, and torn between half baked
imperialism and a feeling the Chinese or indeed any Xenophobes are

*N.B. was making up his mind to take a temporary job as an assistant master at
Sunningdale preparatory school, where his own schooling had begun.

usually right. Tell me what you think of the affair, it disturbs me rather, one is really so British.

N

There are times when I feel I shall take nothing to Tripoli but a notebook and a pencil to record your speech and ponder over it in angustia or tranquillity as if it was the rubbings of the sacred inscription of a vanished race or strange plants dried between the blotter or comic bulbs informally breaking ground and emerging like the Japanese water flowers or eggs to be blown or prognostications of Cassandra three witches, Delphic sybils and Dodonian trees – but all this implies that they are obscure which they aren't if only I listened to them more instead of frothing myself 'moving within the limitations of my own mentality', they are merely wise, and Vergil, Blake like – dear you, you realise though it won't matter if you never utter?

N—1

What a good saying is the Greek proverb which protests against 'telling me my own dream'. What can one answer to that sort of thing that is not bitter or untrue – as if I said to you that winter, you know, is really an acceptable season of the year, or that a poet you younger men ignore and who deserves a place outside the dictates of your ruthless fashions is a certain John Milton of whom you doubtless have not heard. (These are semi-imaginary grievances, no one, luckily, has said anything like that – but they will, Oscar, they will). Your conduct to the explorer of Seo is really classical in its restraint and celestial rectitude. *adveniat regnum tuum.*

N—2

Is it a myth or does not everyone without exception react entirely differently to us to the simplest things, and is it a myth or is not this reaction in us, though similar, entirely the coaeval, coeternal, a consanguineous evolution of ourselves and not derived from one to the other in priority of birth or inspiration –? I mean why do half our stock of unpresentable truisms have to be explained as if they were paradoxes from the mount? 'No' is surely the only answer to 'are you literary' – O when when when shall I drink of the fountain? at least I know when but what what what shall I drink in between?

(Scrap of paper)

Could you bring some of your records to Chilling when you come in June it would be nice to play them there. Debussy especially. I liked Ronnie's Brahms quintet. I dreamt Ronnie and Jake were captains of the school and made me 2nd keeper of College Squash. A high dignitary apparently but I spent all the time getting Maurice Whittome* to take my photo in places where I saw you were standing at the back, absence etc. so in that way I got two of you glimpsed – very good they were.

20 Feb 1927.

Noel Blakiston, Esq.,
Magdalene College,
Cambridge,
Inglaterra.

Grand Hotel Madrid,
Seville.

Dear Noel,

I have just found your flotilla the pinnace like a fluttered bird being the one to the Chapon Fin which has caught me up unimpaired by time in its gentle sting. I don't quite see what you mean by a protected friendship do you mean that I protect you, assuming the paternal (=pontifical, Cecil,† Florence, sentimental and unreal) or that the friendship itself is protected from the slings and arrows? Assuming (ii) on re-reading, I like the idea of the sanctity of the outer courts but would maintain that as far as the friendships I have known go, we do moderately well in company considering how well we know each other. I mean one is impatient in company and really we meet so little that we have very little practice at that art, but we aren't interfering as many people are (compare the discussion on correcting husbands at lunch with Logan) – then our friendship (*que Dios la guardia!*) was formed in circumstances of romance rather than of association, e.g. as one makes friends with people in one's own election or whom one sits next to in school and hence intimacy of night and solitude was for years far in advance of that duller but necessary

*Maurice Whittome (b. 15 December 1902, d. 15 July 1974). KS. Corpus Christi, Camb. Entered H.M. Custom and Excise 1932. CB 1955. Knighted 1961.
†In *Room with a View* by E. M. Forster.

intercourse of breakfast and lunch. It is the aim of this society to encourage the relations of its two members by throwing them together at the drearier times of day when dullness is almost a duty, I mean apart from behaviour in company we would probably be so disappointed to find each other dull and bookish that it would amount to a grievance in itself in fact I would say we lacked practice rather than the gaiety you speak of – are we gay people? The word on paper looks odd – digression – (perhaps this all is a digression, I am writing rosy with brandy and dead tired from the train) – I had clean forgot συκάμινον and whether you laughed or not, one forgets such a lot and my silly remark about the Vergil was a piece of nervous shyness for which I could have bitten out my tongue a moment after, I suddenly felt at that moment that I must say something and that it must be or rather that I wanted to say it to you about something that concerned us – if I had said 'you will write, won't you' it would have done me just as well – I don't mind about the συκάμινον as I realise from your taste in drawing that you like me for qualities not wholly apparent to the eye, οὗτος ὁ λῖτος! And Ronnie always rankles with Cambridge inferiority complexes and the memories of election fights – (which he need not, especially) – I did write you a long letter from Chilling about the flaws in our relations but I never sent it as it seemed unnecessary on second thoughts, it is somewhere there – I think I attributed the failings to a lack of absolute trust which centres round the obscurity that surrounds our crises owing to our cowardice in discussing them and a certain tendency to craftiness in you and blarney or saying what would most delight the ear – in me – but honestly I do as a rule mean what I say and when I effervesce in praise it is not the sudden rediscovery of your charm after the oblivion of absence but a mere culmination to that unpleasant state and if I say that I have had no dalliance by the way it would not be a pleasing falsehood but the truth. I think I am only just beginning to understand you and your view of me as well and both are infinitely reassuring but at present so tantalising that one grows resentful of company and the interruptions of daily life like Lewis reading Tessa's diary. One fault seems that I, ineradically apparently, still go for the best or nothing, or at least detest the consolation prize, and the same motive that makes me send you no more postcards because I can find none good enough of the places (when any are really better than verbal accounts I suppose) makes me feel time wasted when we are together but not alone – I enjoyed talking to you about Vergil when Freddie and Jack were playing the gramophone, but you I felt, found it ill-bred and impolite, yet it was natural and by yielding to the temptation, it enabled us to get over the constraint of company by a *tête à tête*. But I do mean a thing for ever if I say it once, I mean I do not extemporise under the cold of the moon nor gratify a momentary desire to say fine things if I say I cannot live without you. This is so rambling, really I had better go to bed. I think we did not have out the golden calf question sufficiently incidentally, it did not seem quite satisfactory if you only can dispense with one pursuant to Jehovah's regular supply of manna and perhaps behind our schemes to be so much together there is an element of fear. Still I feel that perfect trust is the key note of perfect intimacy in company and that with us, our trust is not equal to our understanding. Chalets, Avonmouth and my Jamaican silence being perhaps to blame. Good-night Noel.

II

I have been having a tiresome cold, chestwise, and it has rained, every day. Vitality is rather low, and I continue to feel nothing will happen till Sicily and time has just somehow to be got through, still this impatience would be quite unbearable in England though extreme enough here. There are some nice streets in this town, we go to Cadiz on Saturday and then Algeciras where we shall be nearly ten days so write – I feel the first half of this letter is rather bloody, one gets so bleak the moment one tries to anatomise on paper and ink makes things look blacker still. Vergilian is quite right, I have been thinking of your sayings to-day and particularly your remark that one does not get old, but one gets very tired. What a good word descansarse, to untire oneself is, in Spanish, I look forward to Sicily as that but have fears it may be the opposite for you – digression, for a proper irregular verb, irresponsible in tenses and impossible in meanings, give me 'caber, to be able to be contained'. The ride from Granada was magnificent mountains, snow, gipsies, almond blossom and a fine view of the yellow canes spread out beside the sleepy harbour as we came through a tunnel and looked down on Motril. The Sierra de Contraviesa, between the S. Nevada and the sea are very fine and wooded. Motril to Salobreñas was through the cane breaks and after some hills we came to Almuñecar for lunch. I had heard of a little house for sale there from the concierge and we took the owner along. Your advice is needed badly. The house is very small, 3 rooms and a tiny kitchen but has also a garage, a vine to sit under and an outside staircase up to the flat roof, it is clean and homely and has the most perfect view being on a low hillock behind Almuñecar itself and having outlook in front to the sea, about 400 yards away, the town of A. rising on a hill in the middle, Moorish and castle crowned, but clean, while at the back on each side are high mountains, very jagged and bare. All around the house below it stretches the vega of Almuñecar which is practically all sugar cane and scattered palms. There are many streams and two great tanks at the back of the house which incidentally has electric light. Behind is a rather higher hill with 3 stone pines on the top and a path going up into the mountains. A breeze blows always. The garden is tiny, it would all fit on to a tennis court but more could be got underneath and there are some bamboos it would be nice to have. The garden is in two semicircular terraces and a bit as well by the front gate. We counted over 20 kinds of fruit the chief being bananas, custard apples, and lemons but also guava, apricot, pear, fig, vine, orange, tangerine, locquot, quince, strawberries etc. There are many flowers and carnations and stocks and roses were blooming – it is looked after by an old man and his wife who are both superb and the people of Almuñecar seemed quite beautiful, children especially, and utterly unspoilt and very welcoming, there are cottages round the villa and a little chapel. It is 50 miles from the railway station. I can't tell you but I want your advice about doing anything about it, it is for sale but the man wants rather a lot, £700 though I dare say he would take less, meanwhile he offered to let it to me free for the winter to see how I liked it before I settled anything (he is a Spanish artist) – Logan offered to give it me but he would hold it over me if I did not live there so I said I would rather try it first – the point is would you like staying there, supposing say you were a schoolmaster and would Jack? it opens up the whole question of the south, I think it would be lovely in winter and sunsets and evenings always magnificent and the peasants would be virgin soil. We could go into the mountains on a mule. But if Porlocks and things are better it would be better to leave it. We might go and look at it in September. Would you feel tied there? would books become unreal? would loneliness be too acute? There is a fountain in Almuñecar with 2 enormous ilexes over it and children filling pitchers through tubes of sugar cane in the shade – also quails in cages outside houses and everything calculated in reales and measures of land which are supposed to be obsolete – but it is Greek and welcoming, not wild and dirty like Motril or hot and

270

dusty like Malaga. There are fine mountains beyond it and buses to Malaga, Granada and Almeria. It seems ideal but I fear loneliness and Phlebas feelings – would a Desolate be better? It depends largely on what you would like – here is a plan.

The 'old people' live by the garage. Their wages, our food and taxes practically nil. The cane is green or greeny yellow and about breast high. Water good.

(a drawing)

We went to a bullfight at Malaga but left after one *corrida* – it seemed rather a fatuous occupation, the men looked so stupid and undignified beside the beast though I can conceive enjoying it very much if one knew a lot about it, I thought the horses part was the dullest but was not upset much as their protruding entrails etc looked so unreal that one did not feel it while the bull was much worse being so obviously alive at one moment and dead the next with all its features disintegrated somehow and blood coming out of its mouth like a tap. It has worried me since rather, and the sense of coming doom over the whole proceedings – Cordova was lovely again and we heard boys voices in the choir in the depths of the forests of columns like birds singing in the sleeping beauty's palace in the woods – all was dark and tree stems. I hope you don't think my impatience is a polite gesture to avoid appearing over exuberant in contrast to Cambridge but truly I am as hard put to it to shift for time as you would be – *difficile est subito longum deponere amorem* and think of sights and Murillos and whatever one thinks of abroad – but I long to hear your voice and enter your charm like a train does a railway terminus. Give Freddie my love and write. Your letters are a joy. Let us leave the discussion of the beginning pages of this till we meet. I regret sending it really but am too hurried (post going) to extract the apology for my remark about Vergil.

Coplas

It rains all day in Seville
the patios are full of rain
and sitting by the window sill
'ἐγ̀ω δε σε μαόμαν

The young are silent in the streets
and silent are the old
and silent is the oiga-man
he does not like the cold

If it were not for the fountain
you would think you could hear the stove
Singing to Sligger on his holy mountain
and to Roach at Cinnamon Grove.

hace frio, hace frio
y mucha lluvia
'usted es ingles? Ingles, io,
he visto America.'

en el norte es invierno
el tiempo sempre es malo
y muy malo el gobierno
pero a Sevilla, no.

Almuñécar, Almuñécar,
dreaming among the canes,
with no English, no Americans,
and no window panes.

Could one read Blake at Almuñecar?

[? 1 *March*] *1927.*

Noel Blakiston, Esq.,   Hotel Reina Cristina,
Magdalene College.   Algeciras,
                                                          Spain.

Dear Noel,

Delenda est Carthago. Here is a schedule the result of a sleepless
night which I submit instead. The point is whether it would prove
too tiring for you.

Thursday April 7. Noel arrives at Verona and takes a first class
return ticket to Palermo at half price, there being reduced fares
from any town in Italy apparently. He leaves Verona at 10.30
and reaches Florence at 17.45 via Bologna. Here Cyril joins him
and they reach Rome at half past eleven muy cansados. Sleep
at Rome.

Friday morning 8th. Seeing Rome.

Leave 1 o'clock, lunch on train and dine on the Sicilian boat.

Saturday 9th. Palermo 8 a.m. see cathedral and cloisters in morning,
Monreale afternoon, sunset in the evening.

Sunday 10th. Museums in the morning. Leave Palermo 13.0 reaching Alcamo 15.39. motor up to Segesta and back to Alcamo by 19.0 thence train to Castelveltrano or Selinunte (20.6, 20.44, sleep if possible at Selinunte)

Monday 11th. See Selinunte in morning and go by bus from Castelvetrano to Girgenti. Sleep at Girgenti.

Tuesday 12th. at Girgenti.

Wednesday 13th. Girgenti to Syracuse.

Thursday 14th. at Syracuse.

Friday 15th. morning at Syracuse. leave 15.30 for Taormina 18.40. motor up to theatre for sunset and dine at the nicest hotel. Leave at 21.23 on swift train. Sleepers will be taken if possible.

Saturday 16th. Naples 10.0. (Glimpse of Paestum for the wary). Rome 14.30. afternoon in Rome.

I. leave Rome 17.10. sleep between Orte and Foligno? Spoleto Sunday 17th. go to Urbino (Easter Day) and sleep there. leave by bus or car for Pesaro or Rimini to catch 9.30 train to Bologna (lunch), Verona (6 p.m.). and Jack and Brenner. Munich 6.50 19th – 8.25.

or II. Or stay at Rome (16th) and Florence (17th) or go on (15.40) 16th to Florence (midnight) and save a night to be spent in Sicily.

I think the latter would be too tiring however and Easter might be nice in Urbino. The services of a competent pedant, showman, and fault finder have been engaged and in order to cheapen the expenses of the party they have been united in one person. Advice is given free of charge, the following regulations are enjoined by the company.

The $\left\{\begin{array}{l}\text{pedant}\\\text{showman}\\\text{faultfinder}\end{array}\right\}$ is always RIGHT. Any infringement of this rule will be met by the strictest applications of the penal code (Trials for Travellers. Sect. I).

We seem to see most of Sicily that way only let me know if it is too much of a rush for you. We have only one night in the train and no early starts which are a bore, we have a morning for the Sistine chapel and an afternoon for the forum and the two nights on the way back are very elastic and can be adapted to seeing almost anywhere. It would be fun if we could take sleepers from Taormina. Cadiz was lovely, a city not built with hands and the drive to this Anglo-Saxon nirvana quite wonderful with pale blue sea and Atlantic breakers on white sand and beetling cliffs of Africa and fields of Asphodel and cork woods full of wild narcissus and the aire, luz y gracia of Andalusia over the green bean scented downs or glittering marshes with white Vejer and wild Tarifa to explore and the Reñon de Gibraltar poised over the sea like a cloud to crown the sweet Elysian drive. The English are nice and simple with their universal sameness, their charities, Anglican churches, ignorance and cleanly faces, I feel like Herodotus among these naive homesick empire builders, and Gibraltar seems already the goal of coming to Spain, I am looking forward to seeing the East side which is steeper and going to Tetuan again. How different patriotism becomes when it is the creed of a minority and carried on by the waters of Babylon instead of the playing fields of Waterloo. Shall we write a book about Wellington, nobody has, and he is an admirable man don't you think, e.g. when accosted 'excuse me, sir, I believe you are Mr. Jones' he said 'if you believe that, you'll believe anything' which is a good impromptu. I was glad to get your letter last night. I think Sunningdale is rather a good idea, it will be nice for you to go somewhere where you were yourself and where Pat is and where Dacre* is in command and not like being cast on a strange world, also small boys are so much nicer than Etonians don't you think and you would enjoy teaching them, then private schools stamp their politics more feebly on their staff than do the big ones and so would produce less bitterness and squabbles and also less of a type than say, Eton. I should think the average private school-master is a bit of a bore but without strong views on education or running a house or games or the Corps, then you will have holidays which we will spend won't we? and will be near London and the Lock House and have time to travel and write and always be able to give it up if you want to and something else arrives. I don't see what better job you could get straight away and it would mean we could go abroad in September before your term – We could probably go abroad nearly every holidays and always meet couldn't we for part of them? My view is that you go for the last month of the summer term and see how you like it but I think it would be the nicest thing you could do for this next year anyhow and it would make a lot of difference to you knowing Dacre instead of being thrust on a strange bullying man or with a scheming wife – but try it first, only stay at Chilling as much of June as you can and we could fit a glimpse

*N.B.'s uncle who was headmaster of the school.

of West Country in probably – but I was glad to hear of this and it cheered my aching head for it has ached a lot lately and I have got bored with eating, one day in the middle of a thought, my skull will come through my skin! What is to be done for Jack now, he is really far more of a problem but as Logan says he is probably 'a good mixer' which is more than we are (you probably dissociate yourself from this all the same) – I grant going to Sunningdale is hardly an exciting career which you said you might like – but it needn't be a career and would be a nice way of waiting for something exciting to turn up, or we might find it in the vacs – only you will try and meet won't you that we may train for our adventure. More Englishmen look like Don Quixote, *el caballero de la triste figura,* than do any other race, a good point. O Sicily, *jam mens praetrepidans aret vagari!* I hope I won't tire you out. Can you send me your Garda address again, I seem to have lost it. It is raining again to-day. Yesterday was a miracle as it was sunny and we motored. If you are settled at Sunningdale we could see about taking a cottage somewhere in England, London, or abroad. Do write here often. I think we leave on the 9th on an Italian Lloyd boat to Naples and Genoa. Give Freddie my best love, I mean to write to him. It does not look as if anyone in this hotel is likely to stretch my fidelity but the general impression of cleanliness and gentility produced by the English is really admirable don't you think compared to the flashy foreigner or the churring of locust broods of wandering Americans. Much love and congratulations on Sunningdale (what are your views on it?)

Cyril

I am still trying to stir up Logan to write to Virginia Woolf about Jack.

3 March 1927. Postcard, Gibraltar.

Noel Blakiston, Esq.,
Magdalene College.

Dear Noel,
   Hic est Petrus. This is the East side that one does not see, while the other postcard is the side opposite Algeciras. The English smells are very strange, the shops are good, man rather vile.

Cyril

This is the rock – all smiling, shapely and serene when you make its acquaintance.

3 March 1927. Postcard, Gibraltar.

Noel Blakiston,
Magdalene College.

'Here and here has England helped me'. I had a letter from Father David. Will you come and see the eclipse with me in June. This seems quite a moving place.

Cyril

leave on 9th for Naples (Excelsior)

4 March. Gibraltar.

Noel Blakiston, Esq.,   Hotel Reina Cristian,
Magdalene College,   Algeciras,
                                                  Spain.

Dear Noel,
  Insufferable post watching, agonising letter waiting, executions of time, sobs of impatience, and the unbearable pressure of absence has become so strong that I can stay here no longer and am going to Fez: I do not reproach you for having driven me to this step!! I have only chosen it because it means spending five days in perpetual motion except a short break at Fez itself and as to Fez itself I will make the best of it and try and think that I went there for pleasure, then there may be letters when I get back here on Tuesday – I find covering ground rather an opiate and staying here unendurable. I go to Tangier to-morrow and by bus to Rabat the next day and Fez the next and then back Rabat the next and Tangier the next – I am excited and will write and tell you about it – it was Marrakesh and Figuig I think that I said I would not go to without you so my conscience is free – but

how to wait another month? Address S.S. Conte Rosso, c/o Lloyd
Sabaudo & Co., Naples, Italy for March 11th, O that you were
coming to-morrow – still have given me the will to go.

Cyril

Presence=understanding=security=talk=listening=ecstasy=Por-
lock.
Absence=Mors

This is the sort of letter I *would* have written you from Jamaica or
rather the futile page of yesterday is –

(*in the envelope with the foregoing*)

Hotel Reina Cristina,
Algeciras,
Spain.

Dear Noel,
   I am pining away and sunk in loneliness and have been these many
days, O Sicily! *Quid valet omne decus, desit si cura sodalis?* Sun and sea
and palms seem like an echo of Jamaica and bring with the same
loneliness the same inadequacy of words.

THE MIND IS ITS OWN PLACE 'The insufferable sufficiency of
breath'
how   the   are
and how remote the kind

Drawing of the 'Road to Kashgar'

4 March 1927. Postcard, 'fêtes du Mouloud'.

Noel Blakiston Esq.,   British P.O. Tangier.
Magdalene College.

Dear Noel,
   This is a good place and quite unspoilt. The simplicity and excitement of the East is overwhelming and makes me regret Tripoli but

perhaps we will make up for it somewhere else, I don't think anywhere one sees so many entirely different and arresting faces or such wise and venerable infants and such wise and infantile old – the story tellers still seem the chief amusement and hold vast audiences with tales that last several days. The Spanish consul was fetched from his Café,

4 March 1927. Postcard, vue generale.

Noel Blakiston, Esq.,   British P.O. Tangier.
Magdalene College.

II

to give me a visa for Fez and I waited for him among the freesias and arum lilies. I get to Fez to-morrow night via Rabat. 12 hours motoring in a vast charabanc. I am feeling much better and restored by the East and by travelling again. The 5.40 at Florence compels my imagination at present – let me know your Garda address and write to Excelsior Hotel Naples for me.

4 March 1927. Postcard of petit porteur.

Noel Blakiston, Esq.,   British P.O. Tangier.
Magdalene College.

III

I think Granada and Cadiz are the best towns in Southern Spain. Perhaps we could come here in September or even go to Marrakesh then but it would be terrible hot. Anglophobia is rather strong – they are so lank and gaunt and drear – I apologise for rather a savage letter from Algeciras. It is lovely weather now.

March 1927. Postcard, panorama Fes-el-Bali.

Senor Don Noel Blakiston,   Fez.
Magdalene College.

I

Dear Noel,

aqui mucha lluvia mucha! Viemos a Fez otra vez. Mas vale tomar el vapor de Burdeos a Casablanca y despues andar a Marrakech y en caravan a Figuig sobre el Atlas porque las carreteras del Morte de Murruecos son muy fastidiosas y el paisaje lo mismo sss q ls Cyrilo

March 1972. Postcard, un souk de la Médina.

Noel Blakiston, Esq.,   Fez.
Magdalene College.

II

this is a good place and alarmingly unspoilt there are three towns, French, Moorish and Jewish and the Moorish has 18 quarters and 100000 inhabitants, nothing on 4 wheels is allowed in but richly caparisoned chieftains gallop up the narrow streets the gates are locked at night and all the houses have vast bronze doors and cedar carved portals it is a gloomy and rather sinister place except for the Souks where small boys wind silk round their big toes from one side to the other.

March 1927. Postcard, Zaouïa Moulay-Idris.

M. Noel Blakiston,   Fez.
Magdalene College.

III

This morning it is raining hard and blowing, this hotel is an old palace in a corner of the old town and is locked up at night like a fortress while dismal trumpets are blown outside proclaiming the necessity of prayer. It is Ramadan at present and nobody eats till the evening when there is music and wailing from dark houses and running water. I regret the Spanish yoke which sits much easier on the Arabs than the dreary French colonial system and the cheerful friendly inhabitants of Tangier are preferable, unless one knows Arabic, to these sinister and indifferent bundles of rags. Abenamar, moro de la Moreria.

7 March 1927.

Senor Don Noel Blakiston,   Café Central,
Magdalene College.   Tangier.

Dear Noel,

I write in the Petit Socco, a square about as big as chamber on allowance night to contain Jews, Arabs, Berbers, Spaniards, French, English and Americans – it is dusk and I am sitting out on the pavement having my boots cleaned, in a moment the cannon will be fired for the Arabs to break their fast – They do not eat from 3.30 in the morning to half past six nor smoke nor drink all Ramadan and do all their ordinary work. It is rather a lesson in fasting as they never talk about it and don't seem to be any the worse for it besides doing it whether they are rich men or Americanised touts – there is a romance don't you think about the rich Jews and Moslems whose houses are of mud outside and gold within; who dress and feed like paupers and are held in respect like the patriarchs and the sons of the patriarchs, there are good Arabs here who play roulette and baccarat all the evening quite impassively. They have thin faces, large eyes and moustaches that turn down like Bellini's Mahommed II. At Tetuan live many Jews with the keys of their old houses in Cordova and Granada, from when they left with the Moors – the Jewish girls are very lovely in the biblical way and in Fez wear gorgeous mediaeval dresses of green velvet and gold braid like pictures on bible markers. Arab women look more like oxen than you would think it possible for human beings, the good point about Spanish I think is their homely wit, the 'aire y gracia' that sits so well and earthily on their matronly shoulders. The worst types round here without exception seem to be young English officers who glare, English women of the sour, drawling, militant, gray haired type (there are few Florences) American men and French Bourgeoisie who don't penetrate N. of Rabat luckily – there you may see the papa, red and round and black and bloated gobbling like a turkey cock, there is madame mean and managing, there is le petit in his velvet shorts, his beret, and his exhibitionism, and there is the dreary boulevard, the grand magasins du Louvre, the officialism and sordidity of their native land – a bitter letter but I have been anti French for some time and am always surprised to confirm it, I feel like a good patriot of the 1820's – then English really are intolerable abroad. The canon has just gone amid cheers and soon the children carrying bowls of stew home will fill the street. About nationalities I think the French are rather awful, the Italians, at least the Fascists (cynical, theatrical, bête) worse and America, at least U.S.A. the private view of the ruin of the world – at least of all the things one likes in the world but if one accepts this absolutely, e.g. that it has got to be and will be ruined (standardised) and that America is not necessarily the cause but only the most advanced case of material civilisation wedded to vulgarity, there remain consolations, such as finding places that aren't spoilt and not being surprised by their destruction into the attitude of the grumbling, sentimental, oldie worldie type – on the other hand Spaniards one likes without explanations, Germans are clean and decent and reasonable and artistic even in factories, Austrians are gay and northern, Russians probably interesting, Arabs charming, Greeks sanctified and Bulgarians are nice too because they are not Roumanians. The Portuguese we allow because they have carried Dagoism to its highest point and because they have good costumes, the trouble is what to make of the English, hypocrites, bores, fools, glarers and yet the most just and wholesome and honourable people in the world – one must distinguish between England and the English, between the English abroad and the English at home, between the English who have made liberty practicable and the public school bigot 'service' class – then there are more exceptions to the type in England than anywhere else in the world don't you think – it is the stronghold of individualism which is the only quality that Americans cannot buy (distinction comes with the third generation) – I think Americans are the cure for Anglophobia – a dry letter this but I must dogmate on this subject – of course French language is good and Italians are not always a nation of Babington Smiths popping paper bags. Greenness is vital isn't it –

Cyril

11 March 1927, Napoli.

| Noel Blakiston, Esq., | The Conte Rosso, |
| Kirkby on Bain. | Lloyd Sabaudo. |

Dear Noel,
    The Sierra Nevada are disappearing. This boat is large and luxurious and full of Americans and unutterably dull.

sierra de Granaa
montes de Aragon
campos de mi patria
para siempre Adios!

Thank you for your postcard which I found when I got back to Algeciras and which was reviving. I like the grace and the composition and also the strange title – I look forward to letters in Rome though dread bad news – curtailments of Chilling or abandonments of Sicily – I don't know why but waiting for letters somewhere is as alarming as it is reassuring. Almuñecar is somewhere in the haze at present, if only there were some Spaniards on this boat and one just could listen to: oiga!, mira te! and; hombre! for two days more – Anglophobia is very strong and also anti Americanitis –; Abenamar, Abenamar, moro de la moreria, el dia que tu naciste, grandes señales habia! Now boredom numbs the writer's hand and the pen falls from his listless fingers, *bruma recurrit iners*. I can only read Spanish irregular verbs and keep down nothing else, though they are no more palatable than dog biscuits, still there is a fine flavour about a good irregular verb, a rakish distinction, a nicety of ear, a mannered and vigorous genre of mastery, as one watches a good rider on a prancing horse or the passes of the matador one savours the civilisation which has courageously and rightly produced tener, tengo, tiene, tendria, tuvo, pongo, querré, quiero, quisiera, io me marcharé, oler, huele, desosar (to remove one's bones –; deshuere usted! remove your bones!) and attained the nicety of

no son todos los que estan
ni estan todos los que son!

I can imagine a grammarian taking a spicy piece of syntax away to chew like a dog retiring to a corner with a bone – the attraction of it I suppose is fourfold. A. objective, the logical necessities of language which compel certain words to take certain forms and II the taste and elegance of their pronunciation, where the irregularity is due to that (mangeons etc) and B. sense of mastery over a knotty subject and II the privacy of knowing about such things which are subjective pleasures less dependent on the nature of the actual object of research. Larbaud's thing on Portuguese was the right way I thought to write about language but sentimentally done as most French writing is. The English triumph seems to be in having separate words for to love and to like which *aimer* and *querer* have to double in France and Spain, this should refute our alleged coldness as a race though not loving and liking but glaring and growling seem the chief characteristics of the English abroad, still they are quieter than Americans and the men have not voices like the rattle of a walking stick along a tin paling. Alpujarras is one of the roundest Spanish words for pronunciation don't you think and if I was a musician I would write three short pieces, one bright and smacking, one drear and haunting, and one green and arboreal and call them Jerez de los Caballeros, Argamasilla, and Bembimbre – as it is, the last Spanish words addressed to me were 'dos reales señor caballero' but like the boy who sold Jack and me papers at Vigo the sound of the words is sweeter than their import. Cosas de Espana. This testy dull letter at any rate the image of my mind.

Love
Cyril

11 March 1927.

Noel Blakiston, Esq.,   Napoli,
Kirkby on Bain.   on the Conte Rosso.

Dear Noel,
    This letter is the letter of the most bored person on the most boring boat on the most boring day of its most boring voyage. I was never much of a dab at expressing my feelings and I'm not, thank God, the sort of fellow who's always talking about himself, analysing and all that, but when I'm bored, I'm Bored, and I say so.

Yours
Cyril Connolly

it may be because I'm boring myself.
P.S. I thought it a good joke 'on bored ship'.
Soon we shall see Sardinia.

Plate I.
Map of the patient's mind. lat 40°. time 10.30 p.m. Mar. 10th. 2

    Ora pro nobis!

Look at all this blank paper!

P.P.S. Food is nearly as nasty as drink?

11 March 1927.

Noel Blakiston, Esq.,   Excelsior,
at 80 St. Georges Square,*   Napoli.
London, S.W.1.

    Escucha, amigo
    quando volveré
    Estara contigo!

    I hope you have a nice evening with my mother and love to Jack.
I go on to Rome this evening. Bobbie I think is meeting me. Really
almost everyone is a bore – but Americans are surely the most peccant
part.

Cyril

We will drive along by the sea before the boat goes.

16 March 1927.

N.B. Esq.,   Grand Hotel de Russie,
c/o Rev Fothergill Robertson,   Rome.
Villa Rampolla,
Garda,
Verona.

Dear Noel,
    Thank you so much for your 3 letters which I got here (one from
Austria). I am glad you like my scheme – but may I change it? I went
to the boat place here yesterday and found that the Tripoli service
is much more feasible, there is an express boat in 23 hours each way
and a reduction of 50% in fares. Could you manage this?

leave Verona 6th	(sleep Rome)
" Rome 7th	(" boat)
" boat 8th	" Palermo
" [go to Segesta] 9th	" Palermo
" Palermo 10th	" Siracuse
" Siracuse 11th at 5 p.m.	" boat

*The address of Cyril's mother.

,,	boat 12th at 4 p.m.	,,	Tripoli
,,	13th	,,	Tripoli
,,	Tripoli 14th at 12	,,	boat
,,	boat 15th at 11	,,	Siracuse
,,	Siracuse 16th at 3		
	(Taormina)	,,	train
,,	train 17th at 11 p.m.	,,	Florence
,,	Florence 18th at 10.50 a.m.	,,	Munich Verona train

This means getting Tripoli instead of Girgenti and we would spend 2 nights Palermo, 2 Siracuse, 2 Tripoli, 2 boat, 1 Naples boat, 1 Naples train, 1 Florence, and 1 Rome. Segesta and Taormina as before – I think it would be worth it and one may not have the chance of seeing Tripoli again and it would be fun going where I had not been together and laying hold on Africa. I have been looking at photoes of Tripoli which looks very good with Turkish mosques, Roman arches, and palms etc. I really do think it would be worth doing and make also our furthest south in the Mediterranean – the boat is amazingly cheap about £3.10. 1st class return with all meals and we would have a lot of time for Sicily getting another night in Palermo and the best part of 3 days in Siracuse – Girgenti is infinitely less moving than Segesta (which has a theatre as well) and I do think worth missing for Tripoli – which is I believe almost unique (for whiteness and oasis spring) – I do hope you will approve, I think it makes a bit of difference being able to go and come back so easily and without impairing the sequence at the Villa Rampolla. I know no one who has been to Tripoli so for our acquaintance we would be true explorers. Let me know your views hastily as I must see about cabins etc if we go. I have had a nice time in Rome and am delighted to be with Bobbie but we have made no attempt to sightsee and only talk and eat and play Spanish gramophone records – I am keeping the Sistine for us – and on our way back the Appian way. We go to Florence to-morrow to stay with K. I miss Spain a lot and am lucky to have met a family of Argentines on the train from Naples so that I can still listen to the tongue as they are in the hotel though their pronunciation is odd. We have just been to see (Bobbie and me) Henry IV on the film which is very good and disturbing. I am dead tired and will have to pack most of the night – I have one or two photoes and things for you which I will send along to Garda soon. I hope the magazine was a success. I am in a poorish state at present with a tendency to be wild and bloody, secrecy mania, rudeness etc – also a vein of materialism (cocktails, torpor, dance) requiring to be bled hastily before Sicily but Bobbie and K I hope will accomplish it and I am, by degrees, thawing to books again. It was odd getting your letter about the Waltz Dream as I had been thinking to-day of spending a week in Vienna after I leave you and had decided to do it and not try and see anywhere else except Salzburg. Bobbie wants me to go to Athens or meet him at Constanza but I don't think I can run to it so I will probably be home beginning of May. 'Soon Sicily will be within the bounds of probability' (Lord Balfour, Rectorial address, Chilling University). I am writing a film scenario and also a Handbook on the Balkans to help Bobbie in Greece. I wonder how he and I and the K's will get on – we were not a good trio. Is Jack angry with me? He never seems to exist in your letters, and he might easily be – I feel in an odd way angry with him, probably he is working on second thoughts. What fun our dinner on the train will be – and our tea, no I will be too late for tea – if the worst came to the worst you might prefer me to go to Tripoli and you to do Girgenti meanwhile, and this would give you your solitary travels so might be good for you but I don't honestly think it would be time wasted if we went nor will the E and the W clash too much as we see our Greek things first mostly and not as a sequel. We might have time in Florence to see a picture or two. Good night.

Cyril

I hope you have a good journey out – tell me about it my address is at Chiostro di San Martino/Settignano/Firenze. I feel as if we are under the same roof at last – I have been looking at 'Picturesque England' in a shop. We must get it.

18 March 1927. Postcard.

H. N. Blakiston, Esq.,   Arezzo.
Garda.

Greeting

Cyril
Bobbie

Noel Blakiston, Esq.,   Chiostro di San Martino,
Garda,   Settignano,
    Firenze.

Dear Noel,

Thank you for your letter. About Florence I think it would be a good plan certainly. Things are rather difficult because Maurice Bowra comes here on April 1st and as I have apparently become his *idée fixe* now it is not well that we should meet, nor have I any desire to. This means that I shall leave Florence on the 1st and go probably to Bologna, anyhow I will come back to Florence on the 5th and meet you there, even if I do not come actually on the same train. I will take a room for us at a hotel (Minerva, being Sligger's) and we will come back there for the night of Easter Sunday. We might go to Rome by an earlier train the next day so as to get there for dinner instead of at midnight. Only owing to Maurice we would be pretty incognito at Florence if you would not mind otherwise K could have put us up and you could have spoke with Berenson. I haven't taken much to him yet, he talks the whole time and downs everybody else, and though he has enormous and universal knowledge and is excessively stimulating, half his remarks are preposterously conceited and the other half entirely insincere, it is like hearing an academic Lloyd George, a verbal Proteus, though he has when present an endearing charm. It is very annoying the way everyone in Settignano seems absorbed in the great man and the guests of the Berensons are perpetually coming down here to air their grievances and go through all the refutations that they could not make – nothing is ever allowed to upset him, conversations at meals are deftly turned, contradiction is extinct, and the visitors return to scoff after they have come to pray. Mrs B. is the nicest person there, large and broad and homely in a Chaucerian way and clever too but I give up reckoning how many times Berenson goes into Desmond or I Tatti to Wellington Square. If you take a ticket to Florence I will manage all the rest till we get back to Verona. I will send you gelt for the Florence ticket if you like. I think I can get a 30% reduction from Verona here. We are just off to see the Galleries. Do write often. K is very nice indeed, and I like Jane otherwise I haven't met anyone to move me here and enjoy most throwing assegais and writing Bobbie his Balkan handbook which has some fine purple patches on loneliness and satiety. Love to

Jack. A man with a name like Fothergill Robinson must surely be a pompous old bore.

Love and to Jack
Cyril

Ask F. RoBinSON if he knows K (for he does)

20 March 1927.

Espresso

Noel Blakiston, Esq.,   Chiostro di San Martino,
Garda.   Settignano,
                                               Firenze.

Dear Noel,
    Thanks so much for your letter. I am glad you liked Venice. I agree that St. Marks (inside) is terrific – did you by any chance ask for my letters there? I sent you a grumbling letter and the black book (which destroy if you like) – it is not so embarrassing as it looks, and there are one or two jokes in it. Plans are slightly different. I am going to stay with the Berensons on Friday and will be there (I Tatti – Settignano), till I come down to meet you on Tuesday and we will stay the night in Florence (Minerva Hotel). – Wednesday K will motor us up here for lunch and down again afterwards according to which train we take to Rome. Maurice and John Sparrow will be got out of the way. I have finished my guide book. My longest continuous work and good I think though very hurried. I felt like Gibbon after it this morning and rushed out to throw assegais. Berenson seems to like me though I disagreed with nearly everything he said and corrected him about the birthplace of Juvenal. This time next week –

Much love
Cyril

21 March 1927.

Espresso

Noel Blakiston, Esq.,*   Chiostro di San Martino,
at Villa Rampolla,   Settignano,
Garda,   Firenze.

Dear Noel,

How are you, and how do you find Italy, it is a joy to feel we are under the same roof again or comparatively so but bad for me as the Italian expedition begins to seethe and simmer again and will inevitably boil over if I cannot find some way to control my mental fidgets – I think I probably have got more imagination than you and when it dwells habitually on the future it is capable of getting out of control – hoicking me desperately out of my surroundings into a frantic how long o lord how long of uncontrollable impatience – so write to me as much as you can for the restitution of easy communications is the most reassuring thing to my restless mind and breaks one slowly into meeting instead of making you drop punctually from the blue – I hope the new Tripoli scheme appeals to you for I am Arab and oasis mad and plan riding on a camel for the first time and walking out in the evening along the waveless sea and sitting in Arab cafés listening to strange instruments and buying things in bazaars – and then the sea voyage should be good and coming back to Syracuse by sea and seeing somewhere new together – if you append your royal signature to the Tripoli scheme it will become law and we can begin to get tickets for there is a sort of extra passport thing we have to get I think or possibly 2 each to let us go half price on the railways. O Sicily. A good book about it is *The Rulers of the South* by Marion Crawford which Fothergill may have – not worth buying I shouldn't think – Bobbie and I came here on Wednesday and Bobbie went away to-day – I got on perfectly with him and shall miss him here but K is rather easier with Jane added though a bit dogmatic and garrulous before set of sun. It is a passably nice house with a passably nice view and a good chef and I like the life with its daily drive to some church or gallery or neighbouring town and the Berenson menage looming

*This letter having travelled around Italy was at length delivered at Villa Rampolla on 29 July 1927, and was thence forwarded to Kirkby by Fothergill Robinson.

over like the Big House to the agent's cottage – Logan seems at his best there. We all dined night before last and saw Berenson in his native haunts – He was tiresome at dinner and trounced me vigorously for liking Lawrence's book on Arabia and the Waste Land, he was in the wrong and so grossly unfair as to provoke K and Logan to violent defences of Eliot whom they hate and Mrs. B. to hasty and unavailing changes of subject but he improved afterwards and was interesting and stimulating about 'our geometric civilisation' and kindred subjects. He is obviously a purely feminine mind and with a whole May swarm in his bonnet but capable of fine lucid and inspiring talk when he can be made to realise that his audience deserve it. Mrs. Berenson very large and kindly and the atmosphere of Hartog luxury over all. Logan very sprightly and rebellious in contrast. I may go on and stay with them the week before you join me so you can tell Fothergill Robinson that you are going to the Berensons if it is of any use to you, I think you said you would have to – K appears to know as much about pictures as B.B. almost and sight seeing with him is really a pleasure as one has not got to wonder whether he is wrong – I miss you a lot especially at dinners, and after dinners, especially the one at 1 Tatti where it felt like the interminable and tiresomely clever kind of evening one spent with Alington over again – do please write to me or I shall get guest-loneliness among all this sophisticated culture – About Sicily I am rather in favour of a hard and fast programme if you accept Tripoli because the hotels are so crowded that we will have to get rooms weeks ahead and so it is better to stick to it and then can book them in time and also our sleepers and cabins on the Tripoli boat. We need only take a light suitcase each and our brown suits to wear for dinner, I shall leave luggage here – you could too or else Jack could take it to Verona – our Florence–Verona train has through carriages to Munich so picking up Jack would be easy. I may have to get out at Innsbruck and go thence to Vienna if there is no room on my passport for a German visa – it is well that you get your visas etc before we go to Sicily as we shall have no time hardly anywhere for them. The food here is good and I have a nice room with a view and books and wood fires – it is as good a place as any to wait in and write Bobbie a 'Handbook to the Balkans' in the style of Richard Ford. Do lets write often now we are so close and tell me all you think of Garda – *O care tu*, I am sure Sunningdale is best while Pat is there to look after you.* Love to Jack.

*N.B.'s brother Pat was now a pupil at Sunningdale school.

Sicily consumes me like fire from heaven – I don't think it will be too hot – and we won't have much walking – we will stock Pat's museum from Tripoli don't you think –

Much love

Yours excitedly

Cyril

26 March 1927.

Noel Blakiston,   Firenze.
at Villa Rampolla, Garda.

Dear Noel,

I have got all our tickets to Sicily and Tripoli and things are beginning to look exciting – I shan't hear till to-morrow about our sleepers from Syracuse but they are amazingly inexpensive as indeed everything seems to be. Can you tell me if you are settled for the Verona–Munich journey as if so I will be getting my visa. I think it would be good fun if you and Jack still feel up to it, and you can get transit visas on the train at a pinch, only my passport being so full makes mine awkward. I am looking forward to Verona and it is a great relief to have got my guide book done and sent away as the hate of all things of one's own creation is beginning to come on. I am getting pretty fed up with Florence gossip day and night, *on dirait Jamaique*, and this absurd belief in stories, raconteuring, i.e. repeating with gusto the same tale two or three times a day. I feel bored and look it and resent casting a damper on people's garrulity – if only one's face could be arranged to think of something else without looking superior. I go to I Tatti on Friday. Summer is icumen in! I shall soon feel about our departure on the Rome train like leaving Oxford for Lulworth or London for Porlock Weir – more riddance than parting and adventures ahead.

1 April 1927. Telegram. Firenze.

Written four times Tuesday perfect please wire acknowledgement I Tatti Settignano

Cyril

4 April 1927.

H. N. Blakiston, Esq.,   I Tatti,
c/o W. Fothergill Robinson, Esq.,   Ponte a Mensola,
Villa Rampolla,   Sotto Settignano.
Garda,
Verona.

Dear Noel,

I have written to you four times since I came to Settignano (apart from Arezzo p.c.) so I would suggest that there is something rotten in the state of Denmark. I also wired on Friday. I am staying with the Berensons. Maurice Bowra and John Sparrow are at K's. Tuesday is perfect. I will meet your train and have arranged that you sleep here as I thought you would like to visit the great man. Wednesday morning we go down and sight see and then come up to lunch with K. I am leaving some luggage in Florence, and only taking a suitcase to Tripoli. We will want our brown suits for wear in the evenings. Only book as far as Florence, I think there are cheap tickets here from Verona. We will want our passports Wednesday morning. Hotel Villa Politi. Siracuse 10th and 15th, Minerva Hotel Florence 17th best addresses.

Love
Cyril

It was grand of you to bear up so well about writing in spite of my apparent silence.

April 1927.
H. N. Blakinston,   Tatti,
Garda,   Settignano.

Dear Noel,

I have written to you four times from Settignano as well as the postcard from Arezzo. I would suggest that there was something rotten in the state of Denmark. Meanwhile thank you very much indeed for writing to me so often and behaving as if nothing had happened. I was rather puzzled too. I sent you a wire yesterday but I expect I would have heard from you if you had received it. You are to sleep here on Tuesday and I will meet the train – it may make sight-

seeing rather difficult as we are to lunch with the Clarks but we can
go down to Florence in the morning and again in the afternoon and
it will be nice being seen off to Rome. I thought you would like to
meet Berenson and see his pictures, besides we save a hotel. I have a
suite of sitting room, bed and luxurious bathroom here and feel like
Michael Arlen. I suppose you haven't evening dress by any chance? I
have paved the way for you not having any – if you have a lot of
luggage we can leave some at the Florence hotel, that is what I am
doing as we will be there a night on the way back. Maurice Bowra
and John Sparrow are staying with K. We will want our best suits
for evenings, and clothes for the train and the oasis. I am just taking
a suitcase. I nearly sent you tickets and things, what a good job I
didn't. Don't book further than Florence by the way. I think the
weather will be on our side. Addresses. Hotel de France Palermo 8th,
9th. Villa Politi Siracuse 10th and 15th, Minerva Hotel Florence 17th.
I hope you still favour going by Brenner and that we can reenact the
Munich train. Alarm and sense of futility in writing to you make this
letter dull. However in spite of my silence you still are coming on
Tuesday, which seems the important thing.

                                    Cyril

[? *April*] *1927. Postcard of interior of Siracuse cathedral. Never posted.*

Likely places for Cyril lost

Spain
  Granada,
    Washington Irving Hotel
France
  Chapon Fin
    Bordeaux
Balkans
  Palace Hotel
    Constanza, Roumania
Central Europe
  Continental Hotel
    Munich
England
  c/o H. N. Blakiston, Cambridge.

21 April 1927.

H. N. Blakiston, Esq.,   Hotel Astoria,
Magdalene College.   Wien.

Dear Noel,

I am afraid you must have had a bloody night. I had a large and
lugubrious dinner and stayed in the Mitropa till Regensburg and then
found 3rd so full and painful that I changed in to first till the Austrian
frontier and then was too tired to leave it – after I had been marched
through miles of corridors to get my 2 visas – which only my lonely
glory in the empty first class carriage made obtainable at all I think –
then I stayed on it till Vienna so I start with an enormous deficit –
my feet ached so – did yours – however I had a good night and dreamt
you were an angel – you were barely recognisable and flew about
'looking after' me in a more than mortal way, very bright and straight
and wearing the fixed unreal smile of royalty. Still it was stirring at
least the moment I recognised you was. I have been low to-day and
loneliness is gnawing. *quid valet omne decus, desit si cura sodalis?* I
looked at pictures in the morning and was very moved by Brueghel,
chiefly as a satirist, he makes a ghastly presentation of Renaissance
Nordic bourgeoisie, puppet figures against a dull cold sky, mirthless
enjoyment, snivelling children, grovelling men and nagging women,
all the loves of all the Harry's and gluttonous beery professional
entertainments on faces blank and cold – he draws human beings like
little fat bugs and they look like Japanese paintings but does northern
landscape with superb insight and sympathy, especially some cattle
going along a road on an autumn evening. I will try and get you a
post card of it – His realism with people, 'surrealisme' with places,
is like Crabbe with his dowdy villains and inspiring views – Vienna
seems a nice town and much less domineering than Munich – the
people seem frank and idle and the parks and streets are good – but I
pine, I don't [know] what I shall do – rush back to England in a day
or so probably and then wish I had stayed abroad. I am in for a bad
backwash after Sicily like an elderly man who has suddenly lost his
job. I have forgotten what I have been living for with the future
become the past and Chilling not yet vivid enough to take its place –
you are right that I don't look beyond the near future – this is chiefly
from profound lack of faith whence the idolisation of security (e.g.
school and childhood when you could not stray beyond a given date)

but I find it so hard to believe that one will be alive even in 3 years that I must be living every month as if the next one was my last – this makes me also bad at castle building as I don't like imagining what I feel I cannot possibly perform which seems intellectual drug taking – then one's golden age seems to be for me and you I think in a way in the past and to make one apprehensive of what the years have in store – that would explain the reality of Eden and Platonism and Wordsworth as opposed to Shelley (the world's great age begins anew) and the optimists – it is not that though one enjoys Sicily more than we enjoyed anything at school we feel that the romance of Sicily is a studied situation, a sanctuary taken from the encroaching world, while at school it didn't matter what one did, it was romantic because one was a boy – e.g. does not the feeling of unworthiness *grow* on one while before one took beauty of surroundings as one's due – this is not underestimating Sicily but half the thrill of Girgenti came in its echo of Eton and Ourselves when young. This sense of living in a sequel tends to be the canker gnawing at the heart of undergraduacy and to make one feel so old at times – we do not rise to salute the dawn but we remember the twilight, about the time of the buying of buttonholes – part of the melancholy of beauty then is that it is retrospective – point – the essence of female flattery lies in their treatment of 'men' as 'boys' thus enabling them to continue and feel romantic without trying to be so. 'Such a sweet boy' can be over 30 and wear summit collars, a yellow first finger and a signet ring. But then I had time to notice in my vision of Eton that it was nothing without one's friends, no sanctity exactly in Milton's meaning and nothing but hostile and desiccating stillness in the dark shades and dancing dust shafts of New Buildings silent and suppressed beneath the fixed eye of the invigilating sun and think of 4 o'clock school in flannels or worse still of sitting in the hot desk with one's coat off and the bleached unlovely Eton shirt and the probability of ink on one's white tie – the frame is nothing without the picture and the picture a great deal without the frame for even at Eton one was always bitterly envying the attic boyhoods of Lysis and Alcibiades and the fields that cool Ilissus laves. This rambles – being looked after is only the practical side of being understood – one is the action, the other the state but it is a good feeling and surrounds one like a glass case I found or rather, like the steam in upper showers on a cold day. Abraham's bosom or 'for underneath are the everlasting hands' – if it were not for you Noel I would have to choose between religion

and polygamy – it was odd you know – in the waiting room yesterday – it can't be yesterday I told you I understood you and for the
moment saw the whole of your mind and like a green aquarium,
static in itself but inhabited by ideas only not only did I see the
thoughts dart like fish but I felt I knew the things on the bottom
better than you even, the imperceptible stir of the grains of sand, the
twitch of a feeler, the shooting eye of a whelk, the hermit crabs
pining – I saw the bubbles that would never come to the top and
heard the limpets relax their tension, the translucent greenness lay
around – my mind I fear is different, it festers and rains frogs and the
ten plagues of Egypt rotate like a sky sign in Piccadilly – I think our
greatest practical discovery on this trip has been of the importance
of the East which does indeed seem like a dream to salute or at least
a subject worthy of life study and incessant travelling – it can be loved
for itself don't you think and we also become Ourselves through
loving it – (Ourselves shall always have a capital like God). I shall
only tell people we went to Sicily unless questioned, so jealous do I
feel of Taggiura and the market – which-is-not-to-be-named. What
was good I think was that travelling in luxury we yet managed to
live austerely – at any rate in spirit – for we were never bloated,
satiated, or over-weening as rich people when young often are. I
think the places were largely responsible for this, Castelvetrano for
instance seems as if we went there on a walking tour – but I think all
the same we have concurred with our sage and serious poet Spenser,
and behaved like the true flag wagging Christian – I am skilfully
writing this letter from $7\frac{1}{2}$–9 p.m. so as to save by having no dinner –
the more I think of our Eden conversations the more coherent and
valuable they seem. I do believe we have really reached a system and
can begin to be great poets in the Santayanic sense – I mean I think
we had noticed all these things before but only in one island did we
really estimate their importance which was a discovery in itself – let
us keep it secret till Chilling and then see how we can make it – They
hand in hand – tolls in the memory as I write this and I am afraid to
go on with the theme for fear of being taunted by the Magnificat
tune – About Faith don't you think, Pascal's remark in *The Spirit
of Man* – I was trying to say at the station by the way that shaving
was a case where you had not grown like me (for you never get
shaved) but had come to understand my need for it and always asked
me if I had a good shave (which is lovely) – but I had become exactly
like you on the island and hardly shaved at all – one is the female

gift of insight as opposed to approximation e.g. the wife understanding about her husband's pipe etc – the other the character changing and getting more like in non-competitive things (in many ways getting like someone is a nuisance – e.g. if you stand lost in reverie and I stand too you say 'let's go' – (this is not a grievance though it sounds like one) – also approximation is not the same as adaptability for the latter consists in imitating someone as a result of presence, is often anything for-a-quiet-life . . . and also holds in it the seeds of inevitable reaction – approximation however is a slow growth and goes on in absence while presence only verifies it – thus one was adapted to Tuppy* by his presence but one grows more like Sligger in his absence and from this there is little reaction while Tuppy is immediately succeeded by C.A.A. or Henry Marten.† Absence is really the important thing, or rather importance in absence, for the present compete with no one, but the absent compete with present, and with God – as in Innsbruck one sees mountains at the end of every street so in Absence every train of thought will end in you – thus even appetites follow suit and a hunger makes me miss you just as repletion makes me rejoice in you – evening brings reminiscence just as night breeds anticipation –

I have written enough I feel and have saved the price of a dinner! Thank you for coming to Sicily and for contributing to the most sustained ecstasy of my life and its most perfect $'αυτάρχεια$ – o words, words, words – but thanks all the same – you know though glib I am not self-delusive and I don't tell everyone with perfect sincerity that I shall never be able to travel with anyone else again. (Of course I shall travel with them probably but I mean that there will be a reservation in every moment and a condescension in every enthusiasm) – for I on honey dew have fed and drunk the milk of paradise. Don't gush.

I send you the stamps – it seems a pity to halve them and my father will be satisfied with the snails. How was Cologne? You must be just about at Cambridge. O Noel!

Love from Cyril

---

*Headlam, an Eton Master.
†Henry Marten, an Eton master, later Vice-Provost and Provost.

27 April 1927.

H. N. Blakiston, Esq.,   80 St. Georges Sq.
Magdalene College.

Dear Noel,

Beneath this roof once more! i.e. England. I have just got back this morning, everywhere I went was dust and ashes; I stayed in Vienna 2 days longer and liked its cafés and restaurant and population and met some of the artists and saw a good circus and went to Prague a day which seemed a good place, gloomy and defenestrated. Freddie has been there – I came on to Dresden and saw the pictures and thence to Rotterdam where I went to the Hague to see the Vermeers which had been my goal since Florence. The daughter (she is an Arab) was well worth it, almost the best picture I have ever seen and a worthy bride for your Sistine head – buying a reproduction of it broke me however and I came second (= 3rd) from Rotterdam to Gravesend with a Conrad crew of 14 niggers who drank and fought upon the rough North Sea – I arrived here feeling like an orphan and lunch was my first meal for 24 hours, still I wasn't sea sick. I don't give Holland many marks. Thank you for your letter to Vienna, I'm afraid I have only written to you once and am sorry but I felt so drear and desultory that I wanted to wait till I would get a quick answer. I shall stay at the Naval and Military Hotel so write to me there – I will write you a decent letter soon. I am going to tea with Molly now and my mother is here. I spent dinner hour last night wishing I had come back with you and Jack and planning out what we would have done. Sacrificed my gelt and all gone first and dined at Boulestin before you left for Cambridge – I shall be a bit penniless the next few days but sure of food and a bed anyhow – Mummy sends you her best love.

Cyril

You were right about Shakespeare and Milton.

29 April 1927. Grub Street!

Noel Blakiston, Esq.,   Grosvenor Hotel,
Magdalene College.   London, S.W.1.

Dear Noel,

Love and joy come to you – this a terribly nasty scrawl to say I can't write for a bit as I am working day and night for Desmond – we start it one morning and dine at half past ten writing reviews of books without reading them and rhymes to go with pictures we haven't seen – I am making over five pounds a day which is all to the good and just getting luggage out of the cloak room here before an all night sitting. I am staying for the crisis at Wellington Square but write to the Naval and Military – I have to go back now to settle Joyce and Stein – this is a good life and Desmond has offered me £20 a night when he comes back to do with him the whole of the literary New Statesman! Molly is lovely too.

Best love and to Jack and Freddie. I dreamt you were dead and rose again.

Cyril

5 May 1927.

Noel Blakiston, Esq.,   Naval & Military Hotel,
Magdalene College,   Harrington Road,
Cambridge.   South Kensington.

Dear Noel,

How are you? I have just got your letter to Vienna. Did you get one from me there and also a line from my mother's? I am feeling pretty limp after working with Desmond till five this morning and then doing errands. I envy you your backs and evenings – it was almost this day that we went to Grantchester. (Paradise Regained) – Yes books are for reference 'Take anything from these shelves that you covet, but I forget, you don't care for books, it is one of the odd things about you' Desmond to Cyril, yesterday evening. Still one book is sometimes useful. Do write to me as much as you can for we must needs communicate when moving in such different worlds – I sympathise with the examination and won't pester you with books and 'must reads' only in blankness or exuberance, greenness or urban summer heat, dull sickness or crude callous health remember me. I talked to Desmond about you at some length yesterday. What other news? Desmond says Stoke's book is ridiculously bad but I have not seen it. Never mind the whip being lost, we have still the idea of the pink egg and the reality of the pink slippers. I am giving Dermot* the Pan(?) pipes. He has done a very good portrait of Desmond at work in oils. I enjoyed my 'hard times' in Grub Street and the pleasing and remunerative working off of efficiency and charlatanism. Best is the curious and unreal feeling of not belonging to the planet that mutual absorption in a task produces in its off spells, I mean the feeling of autonomy, that going out into a cabaret to get one's dinner at 10.30 p.m. fuddled with Joyce and Stein and coming back about half past twelve to go on with them – well it is over now and Desmond goes abroad on Wednesday – Would you sometime elucidate the digs question – I mean when you spoke of having rooms in London have you really arranged to have them with someone else or was it that you were appalled at the idea of sharing them with me? I would like to know as I might try and get a permanent thing in London if I thought that you, if you came to London, would live with me. I think we would get on well in digs (Chilling was quite a test) and we would enjoy exploring London – the only crab is that London tends to debase one's standards rather and we would get our thrills from ritz-like things – but I think it would be good and I would like your views on it. I am in a very unsatisfactory state at present, I feel rather off the right track somehow and yet don't see what to do. I am suffering badly from loneliness and at all times am painfully aware of you, at least of the fact that you alone can understand loneliness and consequently diminish it by sharing it – I find almost the most valuable reminiscence of Sicily is that we both had absurd panics in the sleeper, of death and collision – I believe that much of our loneliness comes from a lack of faith in material things, we are not taken in by the specious homeliness of luxury nor lulled by such dull opiates of fear – I can understand for instance feeling that every illness I get is incurable, even a lump on the side of the head seems so concrete as to be never likely to subside and it is this disbelief, this awareness of the dimness of this visible world, that makes so many of the supposed cures of loneliness worthless and at the same time gives one a feeling of age that makes the blithe chatty Pearsall Smiths seem like babes – we

*Dermot, son of Desmond McCarthy.

together can only share our loneliness, we cannot remove it but then of course we get as well the sense of unity, e.g. of being the only people alive in the universe which is the very opposite of loneliness and the original bliss of our first parents can have been nothing more. To acknowledge loneliness is half the battle is it not? Anyhow I am depressed and drifting and cheered up only by Wellington Square. I had a good evening there last night with Rachel and Dermot as well as Desmond at his sagest. I did a thing on a Russian called Rozanov for him and also finished an article on cats of his which made me miss you, I got another five pounds for that so that I have had the pleasant sensation of earning £20 in a week, 8 from Logan, 2 from the N. Statesman, and 10 for all night sittings with Desmond, not bad for a waster (it gives me a feeling of capacity, otherwise no thrill) but I found Fleet Street rather exciting and may do it again after September – it is rather a nuisance having to stop after such a taste, but Desmond goes abroad to-day and I know no other editor. I have an article on Sterne to do as well that will bring another fiver if I succeed in finishing it. Please egg me on – otherwise I find London desperately artificial and am destroyed for lack of greenness, while the vitality to go into the country is ebbing fast.

I loathe this hotel and am never in it unless I can help which means that I spend too much money – my mother is out of London and the man in Parliament has to be all this session in his constituency, not that he will keep it, so with Desmond gone I have no *raison d'être* and besides get bored so quickly in other people's society. I ran into Langers last night who was depressed, he has moved to Chelsea, and Leigh Ashton this morning who has been in Greece with Bobbie. I went to two cinemas by myself. Metropolis and the Student of Prague and met Brian Howard there and went a round of night clubs with him, dreary work, and went to rather a good detective play called Broadway with Quennell on Saturday – to-morrow I have to go with Rachel to a dance for a Foundling Hospital that Alys Russell has packed us off to, and next day I was asked (not by Alys) to go to a party to meet the Blackbirds – whom now I have lost all interest in. My sex troubles are like Sydney and yet nobody attracts me and even if they did I would soon get bored with courting, do write often or as often as work will let you, I find your letters balm – I don't see myself enjoying anything till Chilling and yet I shall go on in search of artificial pleasure, giving meals to people I don't like, talking and hating myself afterwards, being bored, being listless, or roaming the streets in the dark. Molly is the only person who understands anything, Logan has to have everything cut and dried till one wishes one had never said it, I can't bring myself to write to him and his mail is growing querulous – I am alarmed at the patrician depths of my cynicism – I mean the low view I take of human nature and take so instinctively that I have forgotten it is low – envy, stupidity, ingratitude, and meanness seem to be the only basic qualities of the human race – Molly seems the only other person in London with any pride – what a bloody letter this is. I'm so sorry. I think I am only complete when with you, and find you the natural conclusion of all my trains of thought that run from the particular, like the square of sky at the end of a street. I am so glad you liked Lawrence's book – I meant to give it you as a memento which was why I asked you if you'd read it but funds were too short when I got home – I was reminded of Butcher and Lang as well but it seems as a book, don't you think, all about Tripoli? I have read nothing here – yes Granada is the best place in Spain really, only the Parthenon compares with the Alhambra and it is besides a most stimulating northern town and yet with a Southern appearance. One could work quite hard at Granada and the life of the spirit is not dead. It is also very high and cool. Who do you know that has been there? Granada and Cadiz are the best towns in the south of Spain, not Seville, Jerez, Cordoba or Malaga. We really write to each other such a lot largely because we don't trust each other to remember otherwise – at least I think it comes in a lot – while with Charles, say, it is the reverse that makes one not write at all. O a cheery correspondent I must be to have! The pencil part of this letter was written dining alone in a Chinese restaurant. When it is posted I shall wish I had not sent it. So I expect, will you – I believe nobody can have a good time and be happy. Having to read a book by a Russian is very deleterious, especially one of the good old 'Happiness is humiliation' kind – Langers spoke with affection of you. I am going now to see Waley. I feel I must be seeing someone. Foreigners are all ridiculous, they are stupid, silly, sentimental, ugly, humourless, malicious and generally inferior – so many English on the other hand are unbearable – the academy for instance is ghastly. It is amazing how small London becomes when you think it includes someone you don't want to see – till you make it an article of international law between us that we invariably carry out the material duties of friendship with efficiency and humour, e.g. that we return books through the post if asked and can be relied on to go and do anything unpleasant like that – I think we have room for improvement in that line and it would not interfere with your work like any long ethical controversy would while the better we are at it the less we resemble William's bland ineffectuality or the dank sympathy of Bloomsbury that implies no obligation. Well, Noel, this is a bloody letter.

Cyril

[? 12] *May 1927.*

Noel Blakiston, Esq.,   [London.]
Magdalene College.

Dear Noel,

The letter dated Saturday wasn't posted till Tuesday if that explains anything. I should have thought sexual loneliness was the least important of any kind, and not the only form of it – also it is obvious that loneliness springs from a lack of faith in material things, but this 'dimness of the visible world' is surely a better thing than 'believing in them hard and respecting them' – The blockhead is never afraid; of course we are probably meaning different kinds of material things. My 'material things' if you believe in careers – clubs, letters after your name, respect from the hall porter, latchkeys, season tickets, invitations, knowing on which side your bread's buttered etc. you probably never know loneliness or fear while the sanctity of material things is never soiled, but still loneliness is preferable to that and loneliness is surely just as much a lack of belief in God and the reality of his love for the human race as it is a lack of belief in the efficacy of civilisation – and you don't really think material things should be believed in hard and respected unless it is a new treaty with the world, or you wouldn't feel that the roofs of sleepers fell in – on the other hand if you mean by material things trees, buildings, cats and bread you are quite right but you are believing in their unmaterial qualities, the greenness of trees, the wisdom of buildings, the integrity of cats, and the innocence of bread. Symbols in fact. Hence why should not Eden be a symbol that all can understand for to take it as more would be to plunge into Christianity with a bellyflopper – one must be metaphysical about it – i.e. take the facts absolutely literally because in that way they will produce a more coherent meaning, Eden is no more

to us than Orpheus or Narcissus except that it has a fuller significance –
I mean we do not 'believe in Eden' any more than we 'believe in
Narcissus' only we need it to explain a great many things and Narcissus
explains only one (love's egotism) – Then surely the brain-imagination
compound (mind) is far the most personal part of personality so that
personality waxes and wanes with the volume and intensity of pure
mind's efficacy like the changing cylinders of urban gas works – which
though metal diminish with the air inside them – hence purely physical
ecstasy, the strawberry slipping down the throat, the moment when
the music stops, the good half volley, for all their temporary vitality
are never memorable because the mind is never called in to perpetuate
them, the body shoots the moment and the mind stuffs it, and without
mind the body's pleasures are irrelevant so that all valuable ecstasy
is in a sense platonic, it is the gratification through the senses of a
spiritual want, and because it is this it carries equally the germ of
unrequited sorrow – thus a squeeze of the hand can be a meaningless
form or a walk in heaven and it is the mind which decides what it
will be, and works up the five fingers to their pitch of itching expectation, tingling enjoyment and quiet peace, for no two hands can be
in themselves so beautiful and so dull as to make so much difference
between a shake of them, a hand is nice because it is a nice man's hand
and what more purely mental process could you have than that?
Think how much of the intensity of Sicily was due to the idea of Eton,
i.e. what the walk to the temples of Girgenti gained by reminding us
of the field path to Ward's Mead or the roughs in the boat by being like
camp. Eton was our Eden and gave us grace, greenness and security,
the security to rebel, the greenness to worship, and the grace to love,
and only through the mind do we retrieve these things, for it alone
can string the beads that experience gives us (give them me, give them
me, no!) and make the bodies' pleasures holy with a sense of insatiety
instead of disgusting by reason of their easy fulfilment *'par l'esprit on
va à dieu'*. Lord, what a truculent controversialist you have let loose!
Are not the five forms of major loneliness, fear by daylight, waking
alone, anguish, exile and death, and of these only waking alone is
physical and that hardly sexual in the strict sense of the word. (The
five minor ones, being disagreed with, being a beloved, being a guest,
being asked to explain and being no longer alone or being discussed).
The tutor, the guest, and the beloved, three lonely men (+ the bore
and the solitary traveller, makes five), the usher, the philanthropist,
and the lover, three graceless men, the man who despises popular

success, the man who is not afraid of death, the man who gives money
to beggars, three frightened men.

> The bell that I dared not ring?
> the hands that I could not take?
> the step on the stair, the eyes I avoided?
> I send these flowers, for their sake
>> (Pringué's song)

> la noche del agua recia
> me ta partes con tu capa
> en la puerta de la iglesia

(the night of the strong rain you sheltered me with your cloak in the
door of the church)

> a las doce de la noche
> niña, mel levaron preso,
> y para mayar dolor
> me ataron con tu pañuelo.

(at twelve o'clock at night, they made me prisoner, child, and for my
greatest sorrow, they tied me with your scarf)

> Alli no hay nada qué ver
> por me una barca que hubo
> tendio la vela, y se fué

(here there is nothing to see, because a ship that there was, has set
sail and gone).

I dined with Waley on Friday, rather harrowing, and had a long
talk with him the day before under a willow in Gordon Square – He
is nice indeed but censorious – I thought the 'Blackbirds'* in real
life were quite awful. I spend most of the time at Wellington Square
and find Molly indispensable, and Rachel very soothing, we spent
yesterday morning by the round pond admiring the tin loofah trees,
the bracken chairs, the real water, the newly painted ducks, and the
old men sailing their little yachts. I am wretchedly dissatisfied and
hating self and London, it is far too hot here, much hotter than Tripoli,
I can't endure being by myself for a moment and then hate myself for
wasting time with dismal acquaintances whom I despise – I want
either to be buried in the country or to be ridding myself of surplus

*A troupe of American coloured entertainers.

efficiency and truculence and without Desmond it seems difficult as Logan's affairs require only patience and polishing – you say nothing about lodgings in London (he's peevish this morning, that's what's it – I'd make all foreigners parse 'that's what's it') – will you pronounce some time – I think I shall definitely set up house here in the autumn and spend as much as possible of summer buried in the green. Let our Eden book be rather like the Marriage of Heaven and Hell.

Thursday.

These dreary letters never get finished I dreamt we were in pupil room together – Minns* helped us with our verses – London is bloody, unreal artificial. Logan is back and Molly gone. I saw Sligger yesterday. He wants you to be a monk. Do answer about living in London as it is more urgent than it seems. I am going to Oxford for the week end. I don't really know why except to see Sligger. Logan is rather awful, Molly and I and Rachel and Hope Mirrles played analogies about the Pearsall Smith family, Logan was guessed by 'what fruit is he or she like?' 'a rather woolly pear' – I have to write an article on Sterne for the New Statesman and find him unreadable which is troubling me. I read bits of *Go She Must* and *To the Lighthouse* and they awoke a rural longing that is cankering all my days – you will come to Chilling as soon as possibly you can – but I will see you at Cambridge before. We must go to Falmouth and Father David. O greenness. Molly is a curse going to Margate to finish a book there when she alone can soothe with questions about our time at Eton. Do send me a line before I go to Oxford or write to c/o Sligger, better still. Greenness is in their hearts while they live, and after that they go to the dead. Logan droning on about the reel quoility in Sterne. Do forgive these angry letters, nobody else gets any at all and I am still paying heavily for Sicily, but I refuse to repudiate emotional debts or to make my peace with the world by 'taking things as they are' (dupe of the 2nd best) – How's William? I liked your nightingale and nettles and have thought of them.

Love from
Cyril

Books *Are* awful
'The book, the foreigner, the literary man' (Fred II. de Tribus Impostoribus tom. XIII).

*C. E. Minns (b. 2 August 1904, d. 12 March 1962). KS. King's. F.O. journalist, schoolmaster.

Anyhow only you could melt, soothe, understand, remove this bleakness – SPLEEN – so it will have to go on.

20 May 1927. Postcard from Euston Station.

H. N. Blakiston, Esq.,
Magdalene College.

With all best wishes for your Tripos
C.V.C. Patrick*

24 May 1927.

H. N. Blakiston, Esq.,   [London.]
Magdalene College.

Dear Noel,
    I am not sure if I can come to Cambridge that week as I am probably going to Scotland the week end Freddie is away and may stay up over it with Patrick or Charles, otherwise I could come Tuesday to Friday perhaps if that would suit Freddie – I suppose if you go down on the 11th you could come to Chilling early in the next week couldn't you? I might put Scotland off altogether and go up in July, perhaps that would be better, it would mean more money at Chilling too so that we could go west for a little. I will let Freddie know this week. I thought your Tripos started to-day, anyhow whenever it does I wish you well.
                                        Cyril

I continue low.

*Hon. Patrick Balfour.

25 May 1927.

H. N. Blakiston, Esq.,   [London.]
Magdalene College.

Dear Noel,

I find Logan and his sister vacate Chilling on the 10th so 11th will do admirably – I will come to Cambridge that week and we can go down as you suggest. Do, if you can, collect some gramophone records. Debussy quartet in particular if possible. I haven't read Moby Dick though I know I ought to – I read rather a good bad novel called *Dusty Answer** by Lehmann's sister that you might like. I could come on the Wednesday before you go down. I went to the Chelsea Flower Show to-day and the orchids were good otherwise London is intolerable, and you would find a longer letter from me as dull as before. Wish Jack well from me in his schools and let me know how you are getting on in them.

Love
Cyril

P.S. I was seeing Patrick off when we sent that line, the Scottish express looks better than any foreign train, especially the sleepers.

26 May 1927.

H. N. Blakiston, Esq.,   Ranelagh Club,
Magdalene College.   Barnes, S.W.13.

Dear Noel,

I can come Wednesday – that's fixed. Father David writes to know when we would go. I think we had better settle when we meet – I'll let him know that it would be the end of June sometime. It would be better to stay at Chilling and then wind up with a journey there. I am here with my mother, there are good trees.

Love
Cyril

Dusty Answer by Rosamond Lehmann, sister of John Lehmann.

June 1927. Postcard.

Noel Blakiston, Esq.,
Magdalene College.

Martin Cote,
Oare,
Wilts.

Dear Noel,

I am staying here with Molly and Rachel. We are near Savernake
forest and there are some very good hills as I expect you remember.
Yes, I am just beginning to have a nice time.

Cyril

I will come by a train that gets in I think at 7.14. We might walk to
Downside.

[? *June*] *1927.*

Noel Blakiston, Esq.,
at Mr. Harmer's Rooms
in King's College,
Cambridge.
in the county of Cambridge

King's College,
Cambridge.

Midnight

Dear you,

What a bloody thing to say – of course I get boils on my tongue
when I say things like that – please do forgive – after our walk
yesterday it would be absurd to say I knew you less well than at
Porlock and dinner to-night was nice too – but I was feeling low
this evening and having to stop looking at travels made it worse and
I feel that time is wasted here that is not with you and time with you
wasted when we are not alone – and it seems so long till April. I am
wild and bloody, and now remorse punishes me and you must think
me ungrateful and it is nine hours till we will meet again. I am sorry
I am sorry I am sorry, and nine hours till we meet again.

Here lies Cyril Connolly
    under this stone
He died when he was twenty three
    He could not let well alone.

No, but I was bloody, and though I am suffering for it, why should
you?

309

1 July 1927. Postcard.

H. N. Blakiston, Esq.,   Southampton.
Sunningdale School,
Sunningdale,
Berks.

Dear Noel,

Thank you for your letter. How are you liking Sunningdale? I had a line from William who said he'd seen you. Bobbie has been here and Peter for the week end. I had a very good time with Freddie who restored my credit on the river. I am plunged in Greek and bored by going abroad and the chalet – I will write from France, a better letter.

Love from
Cyril

[? July] 1927.

H. N. Blakiston, Esq.,   Chalet des Mélèzes,
Sunningdale.   St. Gervais les Bains,
                                                 Haute Savoie.

Dear Noel,

How is Sunningdale? I disliked Normandy intensely and this is a foul chalet. I am going away as soon as I can, to-day week I hope. I shall stay in town a couple of days and then go down to Chilling. I shan't really be happy till I have got something to do in London. I read *Jude* to-day and liked it a lot, have read nothing else memorable, found *The Land* disappointing, Hardy's poetry rather cheap. I spent 4 days at the sea side by myself and rather enjoyed it though it rained all the time. What are your plans? I suppose you are going to Ireland. I am not looking forward to Chilling – I am not much looking forward to anything. If I were to expand upon the people here it would probably annoy you. I assure you I am not in love. I am glad I don't look like [. . . . . .]. I am sorry I am not like Lord Melbourne. Maurois' *Disraeli* I think you would like and also Morand's *Bouddha vivant*. We must be sure to meet again *quand du stérile hiver a resplendi l'ennui*. Write to me here.

Love from
Cyril

It is after dinner – I have just been into the chapel which is full of bats. Love to Pat. I feel very Heathcliffe.

Cyril

Sligger sends love

Where is Jack?

2 August 1927.

H. N. Blakiston, Esq.,   Warsash,
Kirkby on Bain.   Hants.

Bank Holiday

Dear Noel,
What has been happening to you? Did you like Sunningdale or not? I wrote there from the chalet. I have been here two days – it is restful though full of awful women, I spend most of the time up here (top storey). I have taken a tiny house with Patrick in a place called Yeoman's Row (opposite Brompton Square), it is in rather a slum and really hardly more than a studio but beautifully furnished. I have a nice sitting room of my own and there is a large living room, two minute staircases, two bedrooms, a bath and a kitchen. Patrick found it. I hope you will come and stay there as there is a divan in the sitting room and you can sleep in my room. The same with Jack. Patrick took it from the 1st Sept. and I am afraid I shall have to move in then so that makes Spain or anywhere rather out of the question. I am going to give London a proper try and shall be doing fairly regular work for the New Statesman. Patrick will be out most of the time. I shall have a cat. I continue in a state of unrest if not actually seething. The London cat is here now and takes marvellously to the country, I have been watching him with Shusha, I am turned very much in upon myself and am keeping a voluminous journal in the red morocco book. The Debussy quartet is here and I play it on wet days but it is not summer music and I fear to dim its wild flavour of Minehead. When are you going to Ireland? Where is Jack? I feel a terrific sensation of growing old 'coming at last to these farthest Syrian hills Attis or Adon' – but I enjoy the feeling which has a certain vigour.

Indifference is rather rife, and sister spleen. Do tell me all your news. Father David sends you his love.

Yours ever

Cyril

It will not be far from London to Sunningdale and less far still from Sunningdale to London. I shall be more comfortable than I was but rather poor. O how I pine for autumn it is a season worthy of us.

Aug 1927.

H. N. Blakiston, Esq.,   Warsash,
Kirkby on Bain.   Hants.

Dear Noel,

Thank you for your letter. I have been in bed with tonsilitis which is rather tiresome. I am better now. Perhaps you could stay a night at Yeoman's Row on your way abroad or failing that on your way to Sunningdale. Anyhow I shall be there all September. I too am writing a novel, strange we should both have thought of it. I have had to put you in, otherwise there is no painfully real character. I find working out a good plot the hardest part and then keeping to it when you start to write as everyone in it tries to run away with you. Tell me what yours is about. My hero is a wild unhappy witty boy, sent down from Oxford, and running away from a boat at Gibraltar. He is bound for the Colonies. He murders someone and is finally killed. It is called Green Ending. The book opens in Gabbitas and Thring. I doubt if I shall ever finish it or get all the parts to hang together. Do tell me as much of yours as you can without making it stale. I am using the Lock House before Jamaica and Porlock probably as copy. I hope you don't mind. It is humiliating to have to borrow real characters and impossible to invent them. It is really a grotesque phantasy of my own lean years in which everything is distorted and everyone is produced. A strong touch of Haworth but when I start to write I at once become vain, affected, and facetious. I think a novel should have a good plot, but it is very difficult to find one. I knew you'd stay with Piers. My novel is the tragedy of irresolution, of the flaw of indifference and loneliness bitching up everything else. The hero has every good quality but only intermittently. He tries in vain to spray the native hue of indecision with the pale cast of acts.

Cyril

It is very hard to transcribe ordinary talk. I tried at the chalet, one can begin as a diary and then move it into fiction. Then ordinary talk is such ghastly tripe once voice and gesture are removed. A novel is a fine repository for spleen.

10 Oct 1927.

Noel Blakiston, Esq.,   26a Yeoman's Row, S.W.3.
Sunningdale.

Dear Noel,
    Thank you so much for the tickets. Are you coming up too? I have heard nothing from Jack. I am awfully sorry for not writing but I have been terribly busy, having had to do an article every week instead of every fortnight 4 weeks running as well as some short reviews as well. I owe you a long letter and will try and send you one. I am very happy and in love with life and London and the autumn and Yeoman's Row. I get on with Patrick very well. We have had quite a lot of people here, Logan and Desmond and Maurice Baring and I find being in one's own house pure ecstasy. I have been riding with Rachel in Richmond Park to-day and am dining to-night with the Berensons. K and Jane are here too. I see Freddie a good deal. I had a very nice week in Paris but spent all the time in a Spanish cabaret where they played flamenco. I met Hartog at Victoria. He looked younger. How are you liking Sunningdale? Bobbie came here for a night but I hardly saw him. It is odd Eastwood doing so well in the Civil Service and Piers failing. This is a dull letter but I have to do an article by to-morrow morning. The last one took me 2 hours! Do you mean to come up for the Chaliapin? The streets here are lovely and improved by fog. Logan is nice. I am independent, happy, interested in acquaintances, and consequently barren of any ideas.

My love to you
Cyril

It was very nice of you to send us tickets. I looked in vain for you at the Promenade Concert.

313

11 Oct 1927.

Noel Blakiston, Esq.,   26A Yeoman's Row, S.W.3.
Sunningdale.

Dear Noel,

Just got your card. Freddie can't come Thursday, I couldn't get at him over the week end and he had a party fixed up with his sister for Thursday and told me he couldn't manage Tuesday by mistake. He can't possibly come – He might be able to join us for *supper* afterwards. Are you staying the night? If so, where? I could put you up if you liked. William isn't in London so I can't give him your other seat – are all our seats together, if they aren't I could bring Rachel or someone, anyhow she could talk to Jack. I don't know any other men that would do. Patrick can't come. We might all have supper here. Wednesday I am afraid is hopeless, we have a lunch party here and I am having tea with Logan and dining out – no, I could put off Logan and you shall come to tea here, come in any time as soon as you can after four. Freddie appends his address. Would you be in London Wednesday for *certain* – send me a p.c. when you get this to say and I will arrange with Logan. I think it would be fun on Thursday to have supper here – and I look forward to seeing you at the concert, and on Wednesday I hope – if you'd rather I won't bring anyone to the other seat –

Love from Cyril

8 Dec 1927.

H. N. Blakiston, Esq.,   26a Yeoman's Row, S.W.3.
Sunningdale.

Dear Noel,

I hoped I could come down with my mother to see you, but I couldn't wangle it. I am sorry about that Wednesday, I thought you were coming to tea *anyhow*, I only meant that I had a woman coming (the mother of the Hammersleys) and that we could talk better if you came beforehand. I didn't mean to put you off, and I didn't know you'd be round so early and went to Cecil Beaton's private view. My mother said you didn't look well or happy, I suppose it is hateful to

314

have that said about one but I am sorry and sympathise if it happens to be true. I jog along rather drearily and the life of the spirit grows more and more dim. I have signed a contract with the Nonsuch who are bringing my guide out in the spring. I am also doing an essay on Travel for Heinemann's and a pamphlet on Friendship (satirical) for Duckworths. I shall give the N.S. up in a month or two. I am very fed with journalism and literary people. I like my house very much and get on quite perfectly with Patrick. Piers came to a couple of meals here but obviously disapproved of us and we found him donnish and very Oxford still. I wish he wasn't going to Florence, I must say. I go out to the Berensons in February probably and may go to the Balkans again with Freddie in April. Freddie dines here once a week and is delightful. I didn't like William, whom he brought round once, and he certainly didn't like me. I write diary (long) chiefly and nothing else. I like London except for tea parties and gang life in Bloomsbury or with the Sitwells. I like Rosamond Lehmann. I see the MacCarthys and Logan as much as usual and do not really go out very much. Patrick is very gay and social. I am looking for a Siamese kitten. I have a sore throat. I thought Basil Bartlett was very nice, he is probably going to take this from us – Patrick had a letter from Pringué asking for news of you and Jack. I should think Piers will be an admirable tutor. I live deplorably in the present, but unambitiously. David Garnett has been very nice about the book and is having it published in America as well. I really have lost all interest in it – I should like to make a lot of money from a novel and a play, drop writing, go to S. America, come back, marry, live in Ireland or the W. of England keeping diaries and going occasionally to London or Spain. I should marry a low brow probably. I am really too anti social to get the best out of living in London. We rang Piers up at Naas but found he was in London! You probably think I am changed and intolerable but I am much the same. Let me know when you will be next in town, and what your plans are about the Civil Service. I go to Chilling for Christmas. When will you be passing through? Have you come up often? I am sorry for not writing. I owe everybody letters.

With love from
Cyril

[Sunningdale]   26a Yeoman's Row, S.W.3.

Dear Noel,

I shall probably go down to Chilling about the 19th–27th – we must meet if you are going to be in Town before then – if you came up after 19th would you like to stay a night or so here, you could have my bedroom. It might help you to have a *pied-à-terre* as my mother will be away and Patrick I know would like to see you, or Jack might rather have it if you stay with the Hartogs. Anyhow the room will be there. No news except that I still have a sore throat and feel generally poorly. I am motoring to Southend with Freddie on Saturday.

Love
Cyril

[*early 1928.*]

[Sunningdale]   26a Yeoman's Row, S.W.3.

Dear Noel,

I got some sort of message of goodwill from you from Freddie via William. I did think it was pretty rude of you not even to come and see me or let me know you were coming to London after I had written to ask you to stay. It was so rude that I rather liked it, with that deep seated vanity which makes one enjoy enjoying a story against oneself. But it didn't leave me anything else to do. As a matter of fact I have missed you a good deal and often thought of the boat to Tripoli and wished we had never come back. But I think it is important to make the most of those rare spells when one is interested in oneself and I thought it was probably best for you to develop a career sense etc. etc. I thought that as I have been feeling very old lately, you would rather wait and catch up. I mean we all, we Athanasians, have certain worldly appetites, which we can only control by gratifying, I mean desire for efficiency, responsibility, normality, success; I don't think they're bad impulses unless they're thwarted when they take hold with such vehemence that they wreck people later (compare the snobbery of unworldly people who become worldly in their old age). I thought you probably felt all this and that we had better work off our unpleasant sides separately. Of course I know that our quarrel was

316

technically begun by you but I don't think that makes any difference, it was liable anyhow because ourselves when together was so much the best of ourselves that it soon would have ceased to be our real selves at all – although the most real thing about us. It is both easy and dignified to live romantically, but while one is doing it a host of unromantic appetites are accumulating to be fed. I am still feeding them. You see I don't feel prepared to be romantic till I have got a settled foundation in reality. I don't want to run away till I have made a home to run away from. At the same time I haven't ceased to feel romantically about you – so that while I could enjoy a good dinner with Bobbie or Jack or Freddie and listen to their love affairs, I should only be miserable if I heard about yours. I'm not prepared to be a good friend nor adequately spiritual to be a lover. I do feel more protective and paternal about you than before, but so, I expect, does Pilkington. Then I doubt if I am a very good influence. I don't mean I'm a bad one but I simply have no sense of mission or vocation except for appreciating life – I don't like writing or literature, writing seems to me only a form of preserving the moment or clarifying friendship, a success of any kind I think is only desirable as a manner of avoiding the bitterness of failure. I think the trouble is that even if you have a vocation for, say, teaching – you can't spend your youth among small boys unless you feel that it is by choice and that you have other ways of spending it (e.g. a social life in the holidays or something). If you want a job in London you will find it pretty difficult to get, and if you get one you must either be able to live in London like a foreigner, poor, solitary, and neglected, or have an income and a position that will enable you to live as you feel you have a right to and which you will soon overspend as soon as the appetite for society is quickened by the indulgence of it. Of course I have a soif for luxury which you are lucky not to share, so you may find it different – only if you are thinking of coming to London, remember that you will have either to enjoy obscurity, or to suffer many of those painful feelings which affect the poor man living with the rich, acquiring hardly the inclinations which he cannot indulge. I have really had a very nice winter, I have fed well, slept well and made a lot of new friends – actually I know as few people as ever, I mean if Patrick goes out to dinner, I have only Freddie to ask in, but one doesn't make new friends of one's own age after going down – even though one loses most of one's old ones. This is a dreary lecture in that pedantic manner which you know so well.

317

Noel Blakiston, Esq.,   11, St. Leonard's Terrace,
Sunningdale.   Chelsea, S.W.3.

Dear Noel,

As Mahomet won't come etc., perhaps you would put me up this
week end. I am going to Florence by the end of next and doubt if I
shall be able to manage Spain at all. I am staying here till I go abroad.
I should have to read novels nearly all the time if I came, if you wouldn't
mind that.

Love
Cyril

10 May 1928.

Noel Blakiston, Esq.,   I Tatti,
Sunningdale.   Settignano.

Dear Noel,

Thank you so much for your postcards. I am writing this in the
Café where we met last year. I liked the gates of Cadiz and the Cerdagne and envied you deeply being in them again. I feel Cerdagne
and Roussillon should be the cradle of all travel, I mean I would rather
be there, say in the Wagon Restaurant between Carcassonne and Cette
than anywhere else in Europe if I had a vision of travelling when at
home or in another continent. It seems the essence of France (Mediterranean) and Spain – or rather the expectation of Spain. I have had a
dreary month here, I enjoyed Paris a lot, there is some very good
low life there, particularly a place called the Bal Colonial where you
get the full blast of *le charme nègre*. I find B.B. a bore and the life,
so formal, blank and cheerless in spite of its luxury, at i Tatti very
wearing. There must be something radically wrong with an existence
which compels you to spend so much time talking to dull people
whom you will never meet again. Nicky is far the nicest. There have
been a lot of celebrities knocking round but the more one sees of
celebrities the more one realises how much they need it. The same
true of the rich. I mean the really rich, long past spending anything. I
would much rather have been in Spain, but I hadn't saved any money,

now I think I can make a dash there in June. I met a man called Roger Hinks at the B.M. who had heard of you through Wormald.* I didn't like him. The nicest people here are the Keppels. She was King Edward's mistress, superb material English comfort, and bluff Edwardian life, real people like the Londonderrys and the Winston Churchills staying there and no fuss made about them – otherwise Florence riddled with American bankers, snobbery, cocktails and culture. My phobia of art and Italy has become so ingrained that I haven't been inside a museum or outside the garden except to go out to dinner. I leave here on Wednesday and go to Venice for a couple of days, then Innsbruck and Berlin: I want to see the Brenner by daylight. I am looking forward to meeting the Nicolsons, but not particularly to motoring through Germany. I get to Paris by the end of May and shall probably stay there a bit sampling the Latin quarter. Then a dash south in June and home to Chilling. I want to go either to Cette, Montpelier, and Barcelona, or to Corunna and the N. of Portugal again – did you and Jack go there after all? Did you see Evora? I know you think I am lazy about Spain, but actually it is more a consuming passion than ever. I am completely bored by anywhere else. I have chucked the New Statesman till July and failed, *quia amore langueo*, to do anything for Desmond's new paper, *Life and Letters*. I feel very old and ailing, with no interest or belief in anything that's going to happen, I want nothing but obscurity and to be left alone to go back to the places I liked going to. Perfect freedom and no ties, but I am skewered by the thought of Racy and haven't really any freedom at all.

> et si je redeviens
> le voyageur ancien
> jamais l'auberge verte
> ne peut bien être ouverte.

Bob Trevelyan saw Cecilia Fisher† in London, it appears she is v. fond of me, and if I had a regular job (e.g. was sealed of the tribe of eligible breadwinners) she would take me up again but she is afraid of 'nothing but unhappiness' etc. etc. if R. and I met at present. I may plunge for the grindstone, I don't know, anyhow I want to have a last fling for the summer. We must meet when I come back to England. I have

*Francis Wormald (b. 1 June, 1904, d. 11 Jan, 1972). Oppidan at Eton. Magdalene, Camb. Professor of Palaeography at London University. CBE 1969.

†Cecilia Fisher, wife of Admiral Sir William Fisher, and mother of Racy Fisher.

read nothing of interest except *Ulysses* which I found quite absorbing and do recommend you if you can get hold of it – fascinating technical experiments, no culture, and a great deal of real beauty – with bad conscience – all we like sheep – at the back of everything – the Agentite of Inwit he calls it. I saw Piers here once or twice. I wish we had never left Tripoli. I think Girgenti was a real high water mark – whatever followed must be a decline – that walk through the fields where we met Gillies,* that sunset, and the man singing to the mandoline on the boat on that hot evening. Do write to me – tell me exactly where you went in Spain and what you thought of it. I will write to Jack, please give my love to him. Hotel du Rond Point, Champs Elysées, Paris will find me the end of this month. Hotel Gronbek Prag up to the 20th. Fare well and prosper, much love from

Cyril

Your p.c.'s saved my life the days they came.

3 June 1928. Potsdam.

Noel Blakiston, Esq.,   c/o British Embassy,
Overseas Club,   Berlin, N.W.23.
Park Place,
St. James St.

Dear Noel,

I am so sorry to fail again. I have been asked to go and stay with some people on the Riviera and shan't go back to Chilling. But will go on to Spain with Bobbie when he leaves the chalet, from there. It is very pleasant here, only Bobbie, me, Harold† and Raymond Mortimer living a luxurious reading party life at Potsdam, on a lake. We have a boat and bathe, when bored we go into Berlin to a cabaret crawl. We went to Hamburg for a week end and on to Lubeck and the Baltic. The Baltic was good, very like Lincolnshire, a little fishing town (Wismar) with steamboats going out to cafés on islands on a wide estuary by green fields. No tourists. Northern sunset, fantastic houses. How is your exam?‡ It must be awful working at it in London. It was

*M. M. Gillies (b. 27 April 1901). KS. King's.
†Hon. Harold Nicolson.
‡For the Civil Service.

v. good seeing Jack at Chilling, we had an awful journey on the liner among ghastly Americans, *impingualitum locusta*. I am thrilled by the thought of Spain we hope to go San Sebastian–Corunna–Vigo Braga and Oporto–Braganza–Zamora. Salamanca. (Batuecos, Hurdes) Alcantara, Plasencia, Merida, Badajoz, Evora, Lisbon–Huelva Seville–Cadiz–Gib. (coast). Malaga (coast) Motril Granada–Almeria and home by Barcelona.

I am so sorry to put you off about Chilling – but it saves me such a lot not to have to come all the way back. I shall be back the end of September.

Much love
Cyril

July 1928.

Noel Blakiston, Esq.,   Warsash,
Sunningdale.   Hants.

Dear Noel,

Thank you so much for your letter about your Spain trip. It sounded v. good indeed – better than mine. We motored through romantic Germany, thought it frightful, and down the more satisfactory Rhine. It rained all the time and I was ill from some bad champagne. Berlin was great fun however. I stayed alone in Montparnasse studying artists, bad artists but all free – and came here when my money ran out. Logan and his sister are here but they will put you up if you can manage to get here for any week end. Do try and come here if you can. I shall be here all the summer, not in town at all. I stayed with the Nicolsons at Long Barn on my way back, we went over Knole. I have had a heated literary correspondence with Vita ever since. I am becoming a tough, an anglophobe, and reverting to intolerance and intellectual pride. I am leaving Patrick and going to take up unfurnished rooms somewhere the other (Bloomsbury) end of London with Gladwyn Jebb, that is if he doesn't marry. I am writing a lot just now. When is your exam? Where are you going to be? How do you feel about it? I have thought of you a lot since I have been here. You would like Vita Nicolson, she is your style. I suppose you will go to the Hartog dance. Will that be fun? I haven't any news for you as I haven't seen for ages anyone we know. Logan seems older and quieter than usual. I don't think much of *Life and Letters*, a barleywater magazine. I am less depressed than I was and have gone back to friendship, egotism and wenching. I think flabbiness, which forms the pulp of the modern world, is the natural outcome of tolerance, kindness, and lazy geniality – all the virtues in which I spent the winter and so I have gone back to pure hating again – the difference between Bloom and Stephen Dedalus. I have gone back to the New Statesman too. I am so glad you liked Cadiz – it is the town where I should like to live. Have you read or thought anything good lately? Or said it? I haven't – except *Ulysses*. How are Freddie and William? and Kirkby? I have a vile cold and ought to be in bed with it – we will have a good time this winter exploring London. I should like to live in Southwark. Don't live in one of those Cambridge rabbit warrens if you can help it.* Anyhow we ought to be able to meet a good lot – if you will put up with my years – I don't know how old I really am at present – I feel paternal to Gladwyn, who is 28 or 29. Do write to me here, I promise to answer.

Much love
from Cyril

You must come here one week end. In or after your term ends – you can cram here through it all if you like – only I must see you.

Summer 1928. Postcard.

Noel Blakiston, Esq.,   Warsash,
88, Gloucester Terrace.   Hants.

Dear Noel,

I am so sorry but we have found a liner on Monday morning to Hamburg from S'Hampton and we are going on it, so shan't be in London after all. Jack sends his love. He is here the week end in this atmosphere of bathing, sailing, packing, travelling and eating more fruit. It was good to see you but in August we will have more talk. I will keep book for you. I was going to have brought it up.

Much love from Cyril

*When, after passing into the Civil Service (Public Record Office), N.B. came to London, he joined Freddie Harmer and William Le Fanu and other Cambridge friends at 72 Kensington Gardens Square in the autumn of 1928.

Summer 1929.

Noel Blakiston,   Warsash,
72, Kensington Gardens Sq.,   Hants.
London, W.2.

Dear Noel,
　　Jack is here. I am doing you a guide to Spain as a wedding present, at least to Granada and sus abrededores. If it's not ready you'll have to put the honeymoon off. Perhaps you could come down here for a night some time when you aren't booked up. Jean has had appendicitis and is convalescing up in the mountains. I think otherwise the affair will prosper. Remember that only you and Freddie and soon Jack, will know the Spanish and Corsican side of it. It may not come at all to London in September but go straight from here to Paris. I am writing and vegetating pleasantly. Autumn is my spring and won't be long in coming. I am offered my page in the *Statesman* but Sharp* says I can't take it if I am not going to live in London, balls why should I live in London to turn out a weekly dope on life in general. *Je me'n fous* to it. Besides Jean has refused to be a debutante and is spending the whole winter in Paris. I feel a pleasant expectancy, a sense that exciting things will eventually happen. I detest all adaptations and surrenders to any fixed habit of living, and look forward to getting free of England and discovering new beauties in America, to being more free, *disponible*, rebellious and untethered to careerist drains on one's vitality. My novel progresses.

Cyril

Congratulations on the announcement.†

1929.

Noel Blakiston, Esq.,   Dinard.
72, Kensington Gardens Sq.,
London, W.2.

Dear Noel,
　　Thanks so much for your letter. Hope you got two from me, – do let me see your novel some time, it sounds fascinating – if you did

*Evelyn Sharp, of the *New Statesman*.
†(*Of N.B.'s engagement.*)

send the M.S.S. let me know as I never had it. This sounds aggravated but it's not, only it is terrible if one does lose papers. Perhaps I could come and read it sometime. Yes, separation is awful – I find it almost impossible to cope with, but then I have had 4 months of it and America is so far away. A Berenson-Strachey army descended on Chilling and I had suddenly to make room. Logan was distressed but couldn't obtain room for me and is now facing the monstrous regiment. Alys Russell* is very anxious for you and Giana to come to St. Leonard's Terrace, and wanted me to ask you both to Chilling for the week end but, now, there is no week to have an end for. She is very pleased about it I think (so were Nicky and Mrs. B.) She told me the Russells as a rule always made a row whenever any of them married so you are very lucky to have been so naturally accepted. Flora Russell apparently was engaged to George Duckworth and prevented from marrying him by the family 'because no gentleman would propose in a railway carriage' – result he married one of the Herberts and 'high hatted' them and she hasn't, has she, married at all. I agree with what you say about Giana, I should think she is a mine of unexpected qualities, a *belle au bois dormant*, so detached and yet so alive. I think your impulsiveness will be good for her, and you can't be impulsive without confidence and she will give you that. It is impossible I think to continue to exact from life the standards one has acquired from literature single-handed – the world as opposed to Eton or Cambridge has such an undertow towards obscurity, blankness and Scotland standing where it did, that without a better half one is bound to succumb – and most people do when they've got one. I don't think otherwise our affairs have much in common – only I would like you to understand the nature of mine as much as I do yours. Freddie told me you were very angry at being supposed to be in Spain with me. Of course I couldn't know you were getting engaged at the time but I would like you to understand it was meant more as a compliment than as a last straw. Freddie has taken my name in vain with his parents in some similar alibi, I've also spent several imaginary evenings with Stally in the days when she was forbidden to see Peter, it's on the whole a mark of friendship to rely on someone for jobs like that, and it was only Jean's mother who was told. I know you disapprove of my incontinences but for me they had a certain value, after all I am a writer. I should like to be a good novelist and for me, naturally highbrow and rather incurious the 'body urge' just gave

*Formerly wife of Bertrand Russell.

the impetus enough to acquire a knowledge of entirely different characters and conditions of life – it was also of course a reaction to Racy and respectability – but that is over now – at least the Racy part is though I still feel a rooted dislike to respectability and conventionality in the English middle class sense. Besides the desire for repose and quietness while endemic in you, always there, is only epidemic in me and brought on by too much travelling. I dread the idea of settling down, though bored by now with being alone. Also I have plumped against England. I loathe London except for a few interesting people, I am tired of the country except possibly in autumn and early winter – Porlock or Freshwater remain superb – but I do feel it is a dying civilisation – decadent, but in such a damned dull way – going stuffy and comatose instead of collapsing beautifully like France. I know the symptoms are much less evident than one imagines they are. Kirkby is still perfectly Kirkby, but I feel really that the English country house, like English music, painting, seasides, bright young people, or delicious people not so young are all somehow sidetracked, irresistibly unvisited by the life-giving tide. I don't know what will take its place. I suppose America will – but I want to clear out of it, not to be hurt any more by beauty spots being ruined, nice houses having to be sold, I want – again as a writer, to belong to my period, (which all we like in England doesn't), to be on the winning side. What I like about Jean for instance is her purely American side, complete freedom from sense of guilt about anything; it is rejuvenating for one in a pagan way. Of course I wouldn't like it if she was not detached from it herself, able to regard aqua-planing across the St. Lawrence into Canada behind a speedboat as being only one form of amusement and reading among the canes at Almuñecar as another, but it gives me a feeling of release from the bogies of the old world, of our civilisation, and doesn't exclude occasional tranquillity as well. Marrying an American is really rather exciting and dangerous. Even one who is anti-American herself. I think America is the death continent right enough, a great youthful boisterous robot without any distinction of thought or idea of a soul – but oldy-worldy England is such a dreary opposite, not distinguished, fibrous, intelligent but a great sleepy pear. The Anglo-American problem I am sure is the most *real* motive in modern life, it invades society and art as well as politics, commerce, empire building, navies and the amateur golf championship. I shall be in the thick of it and happy there. This I suppose all sounds very vague but I want to explain how glad I am not to be living in England and not to be any more susceptible to 'nice English girls'. I'm trying to show, on a 'one man's meat' basis that I am really very lucky. You see though I fall in love easily I fall out with equal facility, I'm not easily marriageable by any means, having tried living with Jean and living without her I am on completely safe ground about my feelings – this wouldn't be necessary with you, but is vital to me, who can't afford to marry someone about whom I still feel illusions – or vice-versa – I find Jean almost entirely compatible (except that she has no head for place-names!) and having already quarrelled frequently (usually on patriotic questions) I know that we can easily make it up – like Giana she is masculine in mind and feminine in feeling, but there I suppose their resemblance – though that is a big one – stops. Of course 18 is almost tiresomely young but also while it lasts refreshing and she is very mature and intelligent for that age. She will be extremely rich in time, which would be amusing. Her family are very nice as far as I can gather, but ordinary rich quiet Americans, without her touch of Heathcliffe-Kathy. As to plans, prospects etc. she is coming over at the end of September with an aunt I think and will spend the winter in Paris, so shall I if I can wangle permission from the *New Statesman*. Jean will go on painting, probably, and we will become decorous again. Meanwhile, in far off Maryland etc., her mother will go and visit her grandmother (father's mother) a rich old lady and arrange for her to give Jean an allowance as well, on which we can probably get married in the spring. I loathe the reality of engagement and marriage and dread the talk and fuss that will be made about it – but being married in America won't be so bad. Then we might go to Mexico, I don't know. We'll probably live in Paris mostly and plan in the summer to go on a yacht to the Greek islands – will you be free? Would you like me to come to your wedding – I could come over for it as I want sometime to go to London with Jean, who'll stay with my mother. If not, we must meet as you go through Paris, on your honeymoon, if you can spare the break in your solitude with Giana – my guide for you has got as far as Granada now. We'll dine together and then have coffee in the Mosque if you and G. are willing. Remember not to let the Spanish part of my affair go beyond Freddie and Giana. You must be blissfully happy, I'm not. This is an awful hotel, place full of Times-crackling Englishmen, only came here (Dinard) because close S'hampton and no desire to go anywhere at all. I am paralysed by separation, it's really unendurable and one gets panicky at that distance away.

326

You were superb to send those postcards, you have been superb all along. Do send Jean a wedding card if you can manage it, but I think no suspicions have been roused. One hasn't much time for friendship I know in your happy state but I hope we will see a lot of each other when both spliced. Do write again when you have time. Tell me more of Giana and give her my love.

Chilling seems my only available address at present. Tell Freddie am writing to him.
Read Lawrence's poems *Pansies* they would interest you.

Nov 1929.

Noel Blakiston, Esq.,   Taverne Scandinave,
Public Record Office,   Paris,
Chancery Lane,   29 et 31, Rue Davin.
Londres, W.C.

Dear Noel,
    Thanks so much for your sweet letter. I loved seeing you and Giana and we missed you both very much after you had left. I'm glad you liked Jean. We both felt that you thought she was tartish before, but there seemed nothing to be done about it except to let meeting undeceive you. She's quite the most untartish person that I've met. It was as if I'd thought that Giana'd 'caught' you. However, the misunderstanding is over now. Jean thinks Giana beautiful, like a Holbein drawing, and said you and she were the first of my friends she's met who'd ever admitted they were enjoying themselves. I thought we had a perfect evening and I hope we'll have plenty more. I get very impatient with the ignorance of women, they're all so badly educated, and when I have to impart information I hate myself for doing it – I feel I ought to be with my intellectual equals instead of winning these easy triumphs. That makes me bitter and I make some acid remarks about American culture standards, at which Jean says 'well if you hate me so not to know things I'll go and look 'em up in the dictionary if you'd rather' – which of course I wouldn't – does this vicious circle ever occur with you? Of course the trouble is that I'm emotionally homosexual still – I see red at the idea of any infringement of my liberty by *la femme*, of any theories of gallantry that I

327

will have to apply. In fact I have extremely bad manners. All American men are tipsy with chivalry all their lives while I usually can't remember not to light my own cigarette first, not that Jean is at all exacting and feminine, but that I feel ungracious when I catch myself out. Every Englishman, don't you think, is really contemptuous of women – the sanctity of the smoking room is always at the back of his mind, in Catholic countries, Ireland or Italy, it is much more extreme but I think we have the fear of being run by them as well as the feeling that they are obviously inferior. Nicky told me that England was the only country in which at dinners etc. it is always the woman who makes conversation to the man next to her rather than vice versa – in America the women rule the roost – the men fool them of course, but they boss the men, there is no primogeniture for instance and all money is divided between the children, hence one son of the house surrounded by adoring sisters is never known. Also 'coming out' in America is such a 'hommage' to the daughter in question that they sometimes go mad. Every girl tries to have 40 boys to supper on Sunday night, or 20 men to 'cut in' on every dance in an evening. This is not mere worship of nubility for, once married, the young husband slaves away to give his wife all his money – which she spends on clothes and culture, a wife is a man's shop window, and even if he fools her by keeping a mistress it only means another woman is getting clothes and culture instead. Jean hasn't any of these ideas, but she has been so used to the American atmosphere that all the same she finds my capacities for thoughtlessness as perpetually startling – though really I'm not nearly as thoughtless as the average Englishman who expects his wife to stay at home and housekeep, and, as a treat, to come out and walk behind his gun. This is really more at the back of our Anglo-American disputes I think than anything. I don't think either you or I are really intellectual snobs, but we are so used to geography and other forms of accurate information that we probably seem monsters of pedagogy to women – especially as it takes them some time to find out how efficient we are. I got 'flu just after you left and have been in bed practically ever since. We are terrified lest Jean's rich relations have been caught in the Wall Street crash, we haven't heard the result of her mother's visit to them yet. We are very excited about the yacht and spend much time planning how to make it comfortable. I really think Jean liked Giana more than she's liked any woman she's met through me before, and I was delighted by her charm. I've never seen her so happy and lively before; it felt like meeting a new friend whom one knew one was going to like rather than seeing an acquaintance suddenly brought closer to one.

We have been very occupied lately with the animal world. I bought two white mice in order to stage a gladiatorial show with the ferrets some time ago, they killed one dramatically but the other escaped and lived in the room ever since, it chewed all the papers out of a note book and made a nest with them in a drawer. It used to tick round and round the room counter clockwise. Well it must have been a female for it had a litter, we suppose, and ate them all but one, which escaped and began to tick round and round the room on it's own. It was a tiny gray mouse so small I thought it was a spider, and used to be able to crawl out under the door. One day I found the white mouse in the middle of the room with it's only child in it's teeth. It bounced up and down on top of the little creature making the most extraordinary noises, a demon of bullying ill-will and then disappeared leaving the gray mouse with a broken back. We were furious and finally caught the white mouse in a long stove pipe that I'd bought to give the ferrets a tunnel to run through. We put a ferret in at each end, there were shrieks of an agonising mouse, in the best style of Greek nemesis, and then the ferrets pulled it practically in two. Bianca grew quite untameable after this, and bit my ear. So we changed her for an Angora kitten that was too wild to come out from under the bed for two days but is now settling down. Meanwhile I bought Jean a kinkajou, not a proper one but a kind of lemur creature from Madagascar, with thick brown fur, monkey's body and hands, and a long pointed face with large brown eyes. It was so timid that one could not pick it up but so affectionate that it clung to one's neck and spent all it's time trying to put it's highly specialised tongue, 3 inches long, down one's ear. Looking for ants I gather. It grunted all the time and we christened it Bom Jesus, but had to call it 'the Mugger Mugger' from the noises of welcome it made. The mugger would jump on to one's shoulder from any part of the room or the street, flying through the air over people's heads with a face of godly longing for it's home. In restaurants it would snatch the spoon from one's hand and grow peevish and everywhere it would make the most awful messes, it seemed just a machine for shitting and peeing, and had a genius for sitting where it shat. We bought an oil cloth sheet to keep it on, but when it's time was come, it would go and rear underneath it. Finally we took it back and exchanged it for a pigmy Brazilian marmoset, so small that it could sit in an after dinner coffee cup. It was socially adequate, singing

329

like a bird and appearing from one's sleeve to snatch spoons like the Mugger, but last night Jean took it home and it died of some obscure disease in the night. We both feel guilty and aren't going to get anything instead. Luckily the same night a large white cat appeared in my room, taught the black kitten to make messes in a box of sand, and having succeeded where we failed, has departed again. I hope all this doesn't bore you, but at present we are more interested in animals than in people. I have had ochlophobia lately. I think the French are a detestable nation, dishonest, dirty, sentimental and banal. The most tartish people on earth. Have you read about the Rigaudin murder? They arrested an Armenian called Armazov on suspicion and used thumbscrews for hours to get him to confess. Apparently they have a torture chamber (called '*la chambre des aveux spontanés*') for suspected witnesses, make them come up for examination naked and wind tyre tubes round their head and then inflate them. It's very silly to get interested in these cases of injustice for nothing makes one madder and nothing is so unprofitable for we can't ever do anything about it. I hope to God Jean and I will be rich simply to avoid contact with these millions of disgusting human beings. I wish we were all at Porlock weir. I suppose you are in your dark office now and Giana in her dark house. We are in this dark café. Jean is reading Valery Larbaud's Barnabooth and has found '*Oui tu ne t'élèveras jamais jusqu'à la compréhension du style parvenu*' this is where we will always rise superior to B.B. Jean is very efficient and mends my socks. Yes she is 18, but 19 this month I think. She is in a way exactly her age but very much older than English equivalent in most others. She suits me perfectly because she is affectionate rather than passionate, fond of good food, good books, good films, good talk, good places but essentially domestic and equable – she has a natural taste for the first rate rather than any restless intellectual pretensions, she never tries to be clever but her preferences are usually bright. I like her jokes as well.

I really can't say how much I liked seeing you both, and how pleased I was we made such a good quartette. I really think the yacht can come off now, for it makes all the difference that Jean can have a woman she likes on it, as it is really wretched for her to have all her girl friends in America and be thrust on our highly sophisticated world. She sends you both her love. I think our quartette must form often because it bucks everybody up – you and I can work off our masculine intellectual pugnaciousness, our taste for locations, and Jean and

Giana can agree on the horrors of marrying schoolmasters, or simply men.

Much love and to Giana from Cyril

I liked the poem a deal.

We are off to dine at the Manor House Private Hotel near the Gare du Nord since Jean is yearning for a Nordic atmosphere.

Christmas 1929.

Noel Blakiston,	Sledmere,
16, Beaufort Gdns.,	Malton,
London, S.W.5.	Yorkshire.
forwarded to	
Fonthill House,	
Tisbury,	
Wilts.	

Everywhere the feast of the Babe.

Dear Noel,

Thanks so much for your superb letter. Err, Ur, Urtz etc. are all in the Cerdagne. On a wet Sunday afternoon in Paris I thought of the Pyrenees and got Mara's* mother to let her and Jean go south for winter sports for a long week end. We arrived at Font Romeu and found the hotel shut and no snow but stayed at a smaller one. We bought 2 ferrets (Paco and The English Rose) and a Siamese kitten. It was very cold and sunny, superb air and views. Mara stayed indoors and read most of the time, Jean and I walked to Les Boullouse (where we went, together) – it took us 5 hours to walk there and the path was lost in the snow so we had to climb all those ridges round the little mountain lakes we saw as best we could. When we arrived the inn was closed but we got a meal from the man who looks after the reservoir. We had to walk another 10 miles afterwards by the road. Another day we walked from Font Romeu down to Llivia, where I sent p.c. and then on to Puigcerda, where we had lunch (and were given *Château Latour* 19 in mistake for French *Vin Ordinaire*). Puigcerda was very bright and Spanish. We bought a ticket in the Christmas lottery (1st prize 15 million pesetas) and walked back to

*Mara, Jean's sister.

331

Bourg Madame. Then it snowed but not enough to ski, only enough to make walking impossible – so we came down to Perpignan. The ferrets liked Font Romeu, they dug in the forest and chased each other down the long passages in the hotel, they used to flatten themselves out through the crack under the door and crawl in by another in to Jean and Mara's bedroom where the kitten was, when they couldn't reach the kitten they climbed on to the bed and got under the covers and went to sleep. One morning they made 6 climbs on to the bed and descended each time with a pat of butter. I came in just in time to see the English Rose crawling under the wardrobe with the butter knife. They do love tangerines and claw them for hours. We give them baths now fairly often. The kitten meowed so much that we gave it away. We both wanted to kill it. We went from Perpignan to Port Vendres and Collioure and then into Spain again as far as Rosas, Figueras, and Cadaques. Cadaques is a most lovely place with a fine ruined monastery at hand. We came back by day as far as Limoges.

Where is the tower of Barbarossa? Paris is bloody, we have got to hate it. Jean hates people as much as I do and we detest the French in particular – we want to erect a museum of human stupidity with exhibits from all countries. Money is vital to avoid one's fellow men. Jean has gone down to my mother in the South of France, I shall join them soon after New Year. It is a good thing they get on so well. We spend most of our time killing off Jean's relations and discussing where to live, Jean plans houses and gardens – her mother's house in Baltimore has more bathrooms than bedrooms and more cars than there are people, 6 cars for a family of 5 including Jean who doesn't drive. The butler of course has a car of his own, as well as his own house and a cottage at the seaside. Our idea is to travel as much as possible and then find a house if possible near the sea or one of the estuaries between Plymouth and Torquay – the Yealm, the Dart, Kingsbridge etc. – there are five and I believe the country is quite unspoilt and not spectacular like Cornwall or Dartmoor. Jean makes sweet drawings – Museum of Human Stupidity – *Musée de la bêtise humaine* – the Façade – the Salle de Bureaucrats etc. the Menagerie, the House; she wants to build a modern Corbusier house with a flat roof which can be used as a pelota court and various other innovations. We chose S. Devon because we must be able to get abroad at a moment's notice and Plymouth is the furthest place from London with fast boats to the Continent except Queenstown. We also discuss the yacht a lot, I do hope we will be able to manage it, I really think it's quite possible. Jean also wants you and Giana to come to America with us in a year or two, her idea is that we go from New York to their house in the Adirondacks (near the 1000 islands) and then motor from there to Chicago, there we put the car on a Mississippi steamer (they connect with Chicago) and go down to New Orleans, then we motor across New Mexico and Arizona to California, up to San Francisco or Vancouver and then take a boat back by the Panama Canal and the West Indies. She says that apart from the fares she can get us put up everywhere in America so it wouldn't really cost so much. We don't intend to see much of America when we get married, we want to keep all our money for the yacht so won't probably go out to California or anything but try and get Jean's grandmother to open up her house on Cape Cod for a short honeymoon. It's at a place called Hyannisport. Jean is afraid if I'm more than 6 weeks in America I shall begin to abuse it and lose my temper etc. enough to upset her family. We still haven't any definite news yet. Nobody notices the passage of time in Baltimore but we feel something ought really to be done. We should have news by the New Year. Jean refuses to marry me unless she has £2000 a year 'as otherwise she might have an inferiority complex' – her mother approves of me but feels she can't let us be engaged till she's seen me – so I shall go to America as a friend of Jean's on a visit and blossom there into a fiancé and then a husband. We both hate the fuss of getting married and would much rather get married here and not go to America at all if we could help it. All the same I think I shall like America for a short spell. We have the *Guide Bleu* to England and solemnly read through the Hotels, Poste, Bains, Restaurants, etc. at Spalding or Okehampton. We are very happy really, I love Jean dearly and we are both genuinely unusual people – we want to make films on the yacht and have worked out two, we want to film Peter's poem 'Leviathan' – mostly on the Anapus at Syracuse and we want to do a film of you called 'the Wrath of Apollo' – my idea is to use the film as a medium for writing lyrics – for intertwining beautiful landscapes, images, incidents etc. and show-ing them with appropriate music – I am bored stiff with writing at present and would like a temporary change of medium – everybody writes the most awful cock, either pretentious cock, solid cock, or childish cock and for the moment I'm through with it. I thought *Farewell to Arms* a very dull book – artificial and sentimental – the dialogue boring, the descriptions William Morrisy and disingenuous the heroine a shit. 'Why do you hate the rain?'

333

'Because I see me dead in it' etc. etc. But I did like Robert Graves' *Goodbye to all that* a lot; I think you would too. Gow seems fond of his bit of gossip – he told Bobbie too that he had seen me with 'a most awful woman' in Spain. I should think he's a pretty good judge. It's curious how amazingly sensitive one is about the people one marries. I understand now why young husbands tend to lose all their old friends; I used to think it was because the wives were snobbish and jealous but I think it's really because the husbands are so quick to fancy imaginary slights. I haven't quarrelled with Peter but I've never had a long letter from him, only a postcard just the other day. I'm going to write to him soon about it. It's all a mistake I think but my fault for not writing mostly. I like his book a lot but I think his style is too latinical and rather woolly. Jean says *High Wind in Jamaica*, the *Memoirs of a Fox-Hunting Man* and *Le Bal du Comte d'Orgel* are the only good modern books – she wants to know if Giana can play chess, I taught Jean and she would like to be able to play with Giana on the boat. Jean admires Giana enormously and is quite reconsidering her contempt for English women which she gained at her finishing schools. I look forward to having a brother and sister-in-law of 16 and 17 and we occasionally exempt them from our holocausts and day dream slaughters. They send me nice messages.

I am having a very pleasant quiet Christmas here – there is no one else besides the family* but Eric Hatry, brother of the unfortunate Clarence – is coming to-day. This is a vast house with two ballrooms, two dining rooms, a hall as big as Saint Pancras, a chapel, four other sitting rooms, a Turkish room and an armoury. In the park stands the Parish church with a few mounds round it where the village stood before it was removed and put up somewhere else where it didn't interfere with the view. The Eats are Swell. I am fond of this family, they are all interesting people. We act charades, make films and hope for hunting. You mustn't call me a Bohemian – Richard Greene is a Bohemian – they are made of much sterner stuff than I. I am quite different, I am a *Hybrid*, a person who lives alternately by a standard of Intellect and at that time associates only with people who don't bore him (an intellectual in fact) – Then the Imagination steps in and I live by that for a bit, a bohemian life I admit, but not the life of a Bohemian, then the homesickness which is engendered by my intellectual and imaginative love of freedom going too far for my emotional and social cowardice. How narrow (for me) is the line which divides

*The Sykes family.

334

an adventure from an ordeal and escape from exile? I am governed by an alternate appetite for adventure and security. I must have somewhere to run away from and somewhere to come back to; I like the gossiping scheming clique life of London as much as I hate it, I enjoy the untartish dullness of country life as much as it bores me, I love and detest foreign countries. It is excessive love of one's country as much as hate of it that makes one live abroad.

I am too much of a snob to be a bohemian and much too fond, not only of security, but of a sense of respect and social power. I can't bear to be disapproved of by waiters, porters, hotel managers, hunting men, barbers, bank clerks, though I wouldn't mind writing anything that would annoy them – I can't bear to be unpopular though I enjoy being hated. My trouble is, as I told you in Paris, that as a child I admired my die-hard relations and they disapproved of me – instead of the genuine bohemian's hatred of respectable people I feel contempt and a longing to be accepted by them – like those mediaeval emperors who fought and yearned to make peace with the church. Jean, having been brought up as a rich girl always has no sense of insecurity, of the precariousness of one's status, one's next meal etc. like I have but as she was treated as un-American, odd, highbrow, cold, 'snooty', at all her girl schools she is a more wholehearted rebel than I – but that doesn't mean that she is a Bohemian either, only that she refused to live in a country she didn't like among people who bored her. Mara felt the same and now one is going to marry me and the other, less fortunate, a French Duke. I am a Fred II, a Roger Bacon, a creature of a transition period, not a full blown renaissance type at all. I expect I shall appear considerably more and considerably less conventional after marriage in proportion as I grow oblivious of conventionality. Poverty has always prevented me from being myself though I dare say I should rise above it. I only like people of fairly high or fairly low degree because they are the only ones who have escaped standardisation by democracy – intellectuals excluded of course – I don't know how long I'll be in London. Very little I think – but I'll certainly contrive to see you.

No time
Much love to Giana
Cyril

Am writing to Patrick

Early 1930.

Noel Blakiston, Esq.,   Hotel Ritz,
16 Beaufort Gardens,   Paris.

Dear Noel,

We were going to America to-morrow – but I can't get a visa here
and have to go to London for it – Jean and I will be in London on
Tuesday–Wednesday. She's staying with my mother. Couldn't we
all go out and dance dine etc, make it a farewell party – we'll have some
gold. Tuesday night that would be. I'll ask Patrick to join us if
possible. Our wedding is fixed for April. We've written to father and
grandmother but not heard yet. Mother will give Jean £1000 a year
anyhow and I have TWO HUNDRED! ditto from *Life and Letters*.
I'll ring you up Tuesday morning – we might dine quietly at Beaufort
gardens and go out for supper? It Patrick can't come would Freddie
like to?

Best love to Giana. Cyril.

2 April 1930.

Noel Blakiston, Esq.,   Baltimore Club.
16 Beaufort Gardens.

Dear Noel,

Sorry for not writing – this is a bloody continent you would hate
it – scenery always manqué and inhabitants all bores or drunken bores.
We count the days till we leave it. We are being married on Saturday.
Timothy is being best man and Anthony Russell an usher. They are
both coming for the night before, when we're having a party, and
staying over till Sunday when Jean's sister is taking them to Washington. We are being married in the evening and having a champagne
supper and a dance afterwards. We leave for New York at midnight
and sail on the 9th on the Mauretania. We'll probably be in London
quite a while – apart from our passages and New York expenses we
shall land with £300 in honeymoon cheques, so hope to have a good
time on it, when we've spent all our honeymoon money we're going
to take a villa at Cap Breton in the Landes, 12 miles n. of Bayonne, for
the summer. You and Giana must come and stay there. The American
is a contemptible civilisation – still it helps one to understand Trap-

pists – and I enjoy the atmosphere of wealth and respectability and telling lies to interviewers. You would like Jean's house however which is in beechwoods looking down to a lake and we are less bored in it than outside it – but bored all the same. The young generation is quite awful – pack of drunken shits. It is a world of money, jazz, motor cars and speakeasy's – books non-existent (though the old go in for rows of bindings) conversation unheard of. I don't mind America being such hell but I hate the impetus it gives one to everything erudite and donnish for that I think is a hell too. Well, don't let's talk about it. I came to America tourist Third with a cheque for ten pounds and I leave plus five hundred, a wife, a mandarin coat, a set of diamond studs, a state room and bath, and a decent box for the ferret. That's what everybody comes to America to do and I don't think I've managed badly for a beginner. We both have sworn never to come back here however. I suppose I shall be seeing you almost as soon as you are getting this so I won't say any more. Give our love to Giana and Freddy and Jack. We'll probably stay at Jules hotel but we may get off the boat at Plymouth and come up slowly to London. The great thing is that for a week or so I shall be rich enough to enjoy England, as I have always maintained that, granted enough money not to be depressed by it, it is the nicest place to live. American girls are really awful bores too, their façades are more impressive than English ones, but that is all. I am quite a success here and grown adept at concealing all my feelings. It is American good taste that is so deadly, not American vulgarity.

Much love from Cyril

Mr. and Mrs. Daniel List Warner request
the pleasure of your company at the
marriage of Mrs. Warner's daughter
Frances Jean Bakewell
to
Mr. Cyril Vernon Connolly
on Saturday evening, the fifth of April
nineteen hundred and thirty at half after
six o'clock.
Stone House
Woodbrook
Baltimore, Maryland.

337

Noel Blakiston, Esq.,   c/o Cooks, Lisbon.
6, Markham Sq.,
Chelsea,
London, S.W.3.

Dear Noel,
   Forsan et haec – we are touring the Med. on an American cargo
boat going eventually to Lisbon. Very comfortable indeed as there
are no other passengers. We went everywhere there was to go in
Greece and are very glad to get away from it. We may take a villa
for the summer at Mont Estoril if we like it. I hope [?] gave you our
parcel of clothes safely. It is very hot and sunny our boat goes to
Naples then down the Spanish coast and up the river to Seville. I hope
the *Salax taberna* still shows you some life. Much love to Giana. Have
you a son? Love Jean and Cyril.

Jean is very much better, quite recovered.

6 June 1933.

Noel Blakiston, Esq.,   Princes Hotel,
6 Markham Sq.   Hove.

Dear Noel,
   I wonder if you would awfully mind posting that parcel of clothes
to us here. I could put it negligently in a postscript, but it is better to
get it over. It has my tropical suit inside, and I am certainly going to
need it. Please add the postage to the £5 I borrowed from you at
Smoky Joe's.
   We got back from Lisbon yesterday, we came back with the
Girouards and left Brian Howard at Montserrate. We were all of us
jailed for knocking down a commissionaire in a bar and only got out
through getting Marcus Cheke to arrange bribes for us. The North
of Portugal was v. lovely as usual but we didn't care for Lisbon and
the South awfully. I think Madeira is really the place to have a house
at, in spite of the cruises, it is cheap, you can grow tropical fruits, bathe
all the year round and choose your altitude up to 3000 feet, the meat
and the butter are excellent and there is a mail direct in 3 days from

England every Friday. One gets to need a regular newspaper service very much, besides there is a funicular to go up in and a toboggan to go down, so one needn't take any exercise like Switzerland. England seems inconceivably ugly, only a change from yellow brick and slate to red brick and slate to tell when one goes from a town to the country. And everybody looks so certifiable.

Thank you so much for your postcard. I'm so glad you liked my article. It was very nice of you to tell me. We have two more lemurs, young and dirty and clinging, and screaming all the time. Betjers would get engaged to them. Will you both come down and dine with us one day? Just step into the City Limited, at London Bridge at 5 o'clock and come and join us, or come to lunch and bathe. We are going to try and find a furnished house near the Downs for the summer, later we hope to go to Stockholm and down through Germany.

Much love to Giana from Jean and me.

Cyril

23 June 1935. Postcard. Photograph of the Heathfield Hotel, Sussex, a modest Victorian building.

Noel Blakiston, Esq.,
6 Markham Sq.

O yes – we accept with pleasure. I wonder if you stuffy old civil servants realise just what young emancipated British architects are *doing* – I know nothing interests you unless Anne Boleyn met H. VIII in it – but we *provincials* ha ha! who know something of Corbusier and Mendelsohn are busy just now on a rather big thing. And this little effort of yours truly on the other side is only a hint of it.

C.C.

HORIZON
Edited by Cyril Connolly
6 Selwyn House, 2 Lansdowne Terrace, W.C.1.

Terminus 4898

4 Nov 1944

Dear Mr Blakiston,

I have read your two stories with increasing enthusiasm, the last a beautiful piece of writing. Do you know that I edit a magazine? And that it prints short stories too? I was at school with an H. N. Blakiston, a very excellent wicket keeper, who I believe went on to Cambridge but let his cricket drop. A pity as it often serves as a stepping stone to a pleasant career. I wonder if you are any relation?

Yours very sincerely
Cyril Connolly

We too are always interested in discomfited clergymen (see story in September number).

22 August 1962.
[6 Markham Square,   White's.
London.]

Dear Noel,

As I have now reached the age when the Fisher King sets his house in order, I wonder if you can help me. I have a strong urge to leave some memorial – though I cannot decide on the form – of the most formative years of my life from about 1925–30, and I am sorting out all my documentation on the subject. Like most people who 'never throw anything away' I suppose I have still got about 60% of the material. I have just put a vast quantity of letters from you (and Jack) into a heap and propose to sort them chronologically over the weekend. As you have an archivist turn of mind and are, I suspect, a victim like me to the *eheu fugaces*, I wonder if you have preserved by chance any of my letters to you or occasional MSS notebooks etc, also any letters from Bobbie, Sligger, Jean etc., or do you think Jack has? If this be the case, could I get them typed or photostated or/and would you like to do the same with yours when I have arranged them? I would not of course publish anything without you seeing it. I really want to describe our intellectual climate in the late 20's and the impact on my life of Jean, Paris and America. I don't want to go beyond my marriage really. It is the general radiance (although we were fearful bores I am afraid, prigs certainly) that I would recapture, especially the qualities of the dead – R.P.L. Sligger, so unduly neglected and unappreciated. Even if you have burnt everything in disgust, you still have a memory, hein! It is not true as I wrote in my last travel piece that I did not remember other visits to Sicily, it was necessary to say so to avoid reminiscing. I am happy with my wife and daughter, hence the chance to live at last decently in the past, as one should.

Love to Giana.

Yours ever
Cyril

20 Sept 1962.

[6 Markham Square,
London.]

Bushey Lodge,
Firle, Lewes,
Sussex.

Dear Noel,

Thank you so much for your letter. I had no idea such an enormous corpus existed! I don't think I have nearly so many letters from you, owing to never having had a house for any time, but there are a respectable amount, together with analyses of the friendship, graphs, unfinished letters and précis and reminiscences on bits of paper of long leave at Peter Loxley's etc. I thought a lot about the book in Ischia, during siesta. Decided to have it only as far as getting married, April 1930, but perhaps a little further through May – but essentially it ends with choice of mate in 1929, like you (one was really already married by then). I think it should start around 24/25, perhaps with being 21. 1925 seems to me the moment when signs of adulthood appear also in the handwriting. One has to overcome a deep and very genuine horror of oneself. The first thing is to collect the data, then to arrange it into years and then months, then to go through it eliminating everything that is boring, then to see what pattern unfolds and adopt the form most suitable to it. It will require very sound judgment. Any photos are of the greatest possible interest. I seem only to have chalet ones.

Over the Hump
The erotobiography of a cryptopath
(one million copies sold before publication)
over 1500 pages! only 63/–!

I am afraid women enter one's life like the Barbarian Invasions, a whole culture is destroyed. If I can ever achieve anything out of this, I should like to dedicate it to you. If you see Jack perhaps you would

341

see if he has preserved anything. I greatly enjoyed our lunch and you must come down for a night later in October. We are going to Madrid on Sunday for a quick trip to Santiago, Braga, etc where I went with Jack. Much love.

Cyril

1 Nov 1962.

[6 Markham Square,
London.]
Bushey Lodge,
Firle.

Dear Noel,

I see from the addressing of your envelope that you are now back from Italy. I had a late September early October visit to Galicia, back to all the places mentioned in one of the letters. I found the first batch when I got back; I had been hoping for a fragrant whiff of the aroma of youth, a few gleams of vintage tokay – instead a deluge of bath-tub gin and bottle-stench instead of bouquet! I am still reeling from the shock. Of course the letters are interesting – indeed they recall incidents that I had totally forgotten like the trip with Jean and her girl-friend to Font Romeu, but the vulgarity, cruelty, paranoia, obsession with money etc, how quite quite dreadful. I see that I shall have to stop 'Over the Hump' at my wedding at the very latest and that by the time one had taken to women

'the hour for lies and her'

one was already ruined. Perhaps 1926 and 1927 was the better period.

This is just to thank you enormously and to say that I face the batch which arrived this morning with great trepidation. 'Jack has material' now means something sinister. It will become a poor man's Nuremberg. Jean's sister is writing her account of the wedding (a 'Prohibition' one) – that should put the lid on it.

Could you come down one night?

Much love from
Cyril

9 Feb 1963.

[6 Markham Square,   Forest Mere Hydro,
London.]   Liphook,
Hants.

Dear Noel,

Thank you so much for the last batch and charming letter. I read them with great interest and regretted the loss of a tiny diary of mine I once had with exact details of Sicilian trip. . . . I would like to lend you my red diary referred to in the letters. It explains why the correspondence flags after Sicily. . . . The Sicilian expedition ends the age of romantic friendship because it was so perfect that it could not go forward unless we lived together like Kyrle Leng and Bob Gathorne Hardy or Ricketts and Shannon, and we weren't homosexual. . . .

Yours ever
Cyril

INDEX

345